Advance Praise for

What's at Stake in the K–12 Standards Wars

"In discussions of K–12 standards and assessments, we hear a great deal from the education establishment, but very little from academic scholars, especially in mathematics and the sciences. It is impossible to understand exactly what the educational issues are and what we should be trying to do in standards-based reform if we do not also hear from the experts in the academic disciplines our students must study. This collections of essays by nationally known scholars and scientists constitutes the first substantial effort to correct this situation; every essay is food for thought for educational policy makers."

Eugene Hickok, Secretary of Education,
Commonwealth of Pennsylvania

"This is the most deeply researched and powerfully reasoned book yet written on K–12 educational standards in math, science, history, and language arts. It is a superb work. I am dazzled by the learning and patriotism of the teachers, scientists, and scholars who have probed so deeply into current state and national standards, carefully assessing both their quality and the 'research' used to justify them. This is must reading for anyone in a position to affect educational policy."

E.D. Hirsch, Jr., Linden Kent Memorial Professor of English,
University Professor of Education and Humanities,
University of Virginia

"Standards-based school reform frequently inhabits a world right out of *Alice in Wonderland*—one in which standards aren't really standards and reform contributes absolutely nothing to the improvement of schools. Sandra Stotsky has assembled a set of papers to cut through the false claims and distortions. This is an indispensable volume."

Tom Loveless, Brookings Institution

"*Standards Wars* is a valuable guide to the big battles about academic standards that erupted in the 1990s. The contributors analyze the bitter debates that accompanied efforts to set standards at the national and state levels and shed light and reason on important issues that should concern parents, teachers, and policy makers."

Diane Ravitch, Senior Fellow, Brookings Institution;
Research Professor, New York University

"In the stormy seas of K–12 academic standards, this splendid collection provides needed navigational assistance. It responds to a bizarre shortcoming of many state and national standard-setting efforts: the absence of serious scholars deeply grounded in the subjects for which standards are being set. Dr. Stotsky has recruited many of the ablest thinkers in the core academic fields and they have addressed themselves lucidly and passionately to the key issues in their fields. All who believe that sound content is the wellspring of good standards will benefit from immersion in these pages."

Chester E. Finn, Jr., President, Thomas B. Fordham Foundation;
former Assistant U.S. Secretary of Education

What's at Stake in the K—12 Standards Wars

PETER LANG
New York • Washington, D.C./Baltimore • Boston • Bern
Frankfurt am Main • Berlin • Brussels • Vienna • Oxford

What's at Stake in the K–12 Standards Wars

A Primer for Educational Policy Makers

Edited by
Sandra Stotsky

PETER LANG
New York • Washington, D.C./Baltimore • Boston • Bern
Frankfurt am Main • Berlin • Brussels • Vienna • Oxford

Library of Congress Cataloging-in-Publication Data

What's at stake in the K–12 standards wars: a primer
for educational policy makers / [edited by] Sandra Stotsky.
p. cm.
Includes bibliographical references.
1. Education—Standards—United States. 2. Curriculum
change—United States. I. Stotsky, Sandra.
LB3060.83.W53   379.1'58'0973—dc21   99-14687
ISBN 0-8204-4490-1

Die Deutsche Bibliothek-CIP-Einheitsaufnahme

What's at stake in the K–12 standards wars: a primer
for educational policy makers / ed. by: Sandra Stotsky.
–New York; Washington, D.C./Baltimore; Boston; Bern;
Frankfurt am Main; Berlin; Brussels; Vienna; Oxford: Lang.
ISBN 0-8204-4490-1

Cover design by Nona Reuter

The paper in this book meets the guidelines for permanence and durability
of the Committee on Production Guidelines for Book Longevity
of the Council of Library Resources.

© 2000, 2001 Peter Lang Publishing, Inc., New York

All rights reserved.
Reprint or reproduction, even partially, in all forms such as microfilm,
xerography, microfiche, microcard, and offset strictly prohibited.

Printed in the United States of America

Contents

Contributors vii

Preface: Sandra Stotsky xiii

I. Questions of Content and Pedagogy

IN MATHEMATICS

1. **Hung-Hsi Wu**
   The 1997 Mathematics Standards War in California 3

2. **Ralph A. Raimi**
   Judging State Standards for K–12
   Mathematics Education 33

3. **Paul Clopton, Wayne Bishop, and David Klein**
   Standards-Based Mathematics Assessments:
   Appearances May Be Deceiving 59

IN SCIENCE

4. **Stan Metzenberg**
   National Science Standards:
   Where is the Evidence Supporting Them? 79

5. **Alan Cromer**
   The Science Standards Wars:
   What Is the Basis for Scientific Inquiry? 99

6. **Paul R. Gross and Sandra Stotsky**
   How Children Learn Science: Do We Now Know? 115

IN HISTORY AND ECONOMICS

7. **Sheldon M. Stern**
   Why the Battle over History Standards? 149

8. **Robert M. Costrell**
   Discipline-Based Economics Standards:
   Opportunity and Obstacles 169

IN THE ENGLISH LANGUAGE ARTS

9. **Thomas Carnicelli**
   The English Language Arts in American Schools:
   Problems and Proposals 211

10. **Sandra Stotsky**
    The State of Literary Study in National and State English
    Language Arts Standards: Why It Matters and What
    Can Be Done about It 237

11. **Jeanne J. Smoot**
    Toward Improved English Language Arts Standards
    for K–12: What a College Professor Wishes
    Her Students Had Read 259

II. The Influence of Federal Purse Strings

12. **Mary Campbell Gallagher**
    Lessons from the Sputnik-Era Curriculum Reform Movement:
    The Institutions We Need for Educational Reform 281

13. **Michael McKeown, David Klein, and Chris Patterson**
    The National Science Foundation Systemic Initiatives:
    How a Small Amount of Federal Money Promotes
    Ill-Designed Mathematics and Science Programs in
    K–12 and Undermines Local Control of Education 313

Contributors

Wayne Bishop is professor of mathematics at California State University, Los Angeles, where he served two terms as department chairman. He is co-author of *Elementary Linear Algebra,* now in its fourth edition. He has also served as an advisor to California's Commission for Teacher Education, as a member of the state's Mathematics Task Force in 1995, as a mathematics textbook reviewer, and as an advisor to the Core Knowledge Foundation. He is currently a member of the Mathematics Content Review Panel that is making recommendations to the California State Board of Education for approval of K–8 mathematics materials. He taught high school for three years and received his Ph.D. from Western Michigan University.

Thomas A. Carnicelli is professor of English and humanities and director of the English Teaching Major at the University of New Hampshire. His teaching and scholarly interests include old English, medieval literature, English grammar, and the teaching of secondary school English. He is the author of *King Alfred's Version of St. Augustine's Soliloquies* (1969) and of numerous articles on literary and pedagogical subjects. He served on the Professional Standards Board of the State of New Hampshire from 1994 to 1996, and has been a member of the York, Maine, school board for 16 years. He received his Ph.D. in English from Harvard University.

Paul Clopton is a research statistician with the Research Department of the Veterans Affairs San Diego Healthcare System, where he works in conjunction with the faculty of the University of California, San Diego School of Medicine, in the design and analysis of various biomedical research projects. He is a co-founder of Mathematically Correct, a national mathematics education advocacy group based in San Diego. He has provided service to California through his work on various educational committees, including drafting the Mathematics Framework, developing the augmented STAR statewide mathematics assessments, recommending mathematics textbooks for statewide adoption, and advising the State Board on educational technology. In his local district, he served on the Mathematics Standards committee and on various textbook adoption committees.

Robert Costrell is professor of economics at the University of Massachusetts at Amherst (on leave) and Director of Research and

Development in the Massachusetts Executive Office for Administration and Finance. His early research focused on macroeconomic theory, growth theory, and finance; his more applied work examined employment shifts from high-wage industries to lower-wage industries. In recent years, he has published on the economic theory of educational standards and college admission standards. He is currently working on the economic theory of income distribution and testing (in collaboration with Glenn Loury). He served as president of the parents' group that successfully restored A.P. European History to the curriculum of Brookline High School, as recounted in Richard Bernstein's book *Dictatorship of Virtue*. In 1997, Massachusetts Governor William Weld appointed him to serve on the legislature's Taxation Alternatives Commission, on financing K–12 education; his minority-of-one report recommended property tax reform and expansion of inner city school choice to promote educational accountability. He received his Ph.D. in economics from Harvard University.

Alan Cromer is professor of physics at Northeastern University. Since 1989, he has participated in professional development programs for middle-school science teachers. More recently, he has developed middle-school science curricular materials. He is the author of *Uncommon Sense: The Heretical Nature of Science* (1993) and *Connected Knowledge: Science, Philosophy, and Education* (1997).

Mary Campbell Gallagher is a writer based in New York. A graduate of Barnard College in philosophy, she holds degrees from Harvard Law School (J.D.), Hofstra University (M.S. in education), and the University of Illinois (Ph.D. in linguistics). From 1963 to 1966, she wrote curriculum materials and taught demonstration classes in the Curriculum Reform English Project at the University of Illinois. Recipient of a number of scholarly awards, she is also co-author, with Thomas J. Brown and Rosemary Turner, of *Teaching Secondary English: Alternative Approaches* (1975), to which she contributed the sections on the Curriculum Reform approach to teaching English. Her *Scoring High on Bar Exam Essays* appeared in 1991. She owns Gallagher Law & Essay Training Schools, a business that prepares candidates for the bar examination.

Paul R. Gross is University Professor of Life Sciences, emeritus, University of Virginia. At Virginia, he was Vice President and Provost, later Director of the Shannon Center for Advanced Studies and the Markey Center. He has been a trustee of Associated Universities, Inc., and of the University of Rochester, and is currently a trustee of the American Academy for Liberal Education, Washington, DC. His scientific work has been in molecular, cell, and developmental biology, subjects he taught at New York University, Brown University, Massachusetts Institute of Technology, and the University of Rochester. From 1978 until 1988, he was Director and President of the Marine Biological Laboratory, Woods Hole. In recent years he has published widely on science in culture and on science education. Among his books is *Higher Superstition: The Academic Left and Its Quarrels with Science* (1994), co-authored with Norman Levitt.

David Klein is professsor of mathematics at California State University, Northridge, where he teaches undergraduate and graduate courses in mathematics, including teacher training courses in mathematics. He has published articles on mathematics and mathematical physics in mathematics and physics journals, and has also written on K–12 and university mathematics education. He served on the 1999 Content Review Panel for the California State Board of Education to review K–8 mathematics textbooks submitted for adoption by the state of California. He received his Ph.D. in mathematics from Cornell University.

Michael McKeown is a co-founder of Mathematically Correct, a nationwide organization of parents, mathematicians, and others concerned about mathematics education. Dr. McKeown served on the committee that wrote the California Mathematics Program Advisory and on the committee that wrote the San Diego Mathematics Content and Performance Standards. Dr. McKeown also participated in the early stages of the writing of the California Science Standards. He has testified by request before committees of the California Assembly and Senate, and was invited to Washington, D.C., to speak with Secretary of Education Richard Riley and his staff on issues related to mathematics education. He works as a biomedical researcher in San Diego, using molecular biology and genetics to study development and behavior in complex organisms. He also teaches graduate courses in genetics at the University of California, San Diego.

Stan Metzenberg is assistant professor of biology at California State University, Northridge, specializing in the molecular biology of infectious diseases. In 1998, he was a science consultant for the California Commission for the Establishment of Academic Content and Performance Standards, and currently serves on the Advisory Board of the California Science Project. He received his Ph.D. from the Universtiy of

Wisconsin-Madison in molecular biology and was a postdoctoral fellow at the University of California, San Francisco.

Chris Patterson is a public policy analyst and executive director of the Education Connection of Texas. She has published numerous reports about education reform of primary and secondary schools, including: "Mathematics Textbook Selection for Elementary and Middle Schools," "School-to-Work: The Coming Collision," "Texas Social Studies Textbook Selection in Public Schools," "Texas Essential Knowledge and Skills: Action Guide for New State Curriculum Standards," "Design for Mediocrity: A Report on Current Education Reforms in Texas Public Schools," and "Parents' Handbook for Academic Success." She received a B.A. in psychology from the New York State University College at Oneonta, and post-graduate certification from the Cornell University School of Management and Labor Relations.

Ralph A. Raimi is professor emeritus of mathematics at the University of Rochester. Following military service as a radar maintenance officer in World War II, he received a B.S. in physics and a Ph.D. in mathematics at the University of Michigan. He has served as chairman of the University of Rochester Department of Mathematics, and of its Department of Sociology, and has been Associate Dean for Graduate Studies. Besides his research papers in mathematics, he is the author of numerous other essays, some of which are gathered in his 1982 book, *Vested Interests*.

Jeanne J. Smoot is professor of English and comparative literature at North Carolina State University. A former Woodrow Wilson, Fulbright, and National Endowment for the Humanities Young Humanist Fellow, she has held positions in numerous professional associations, among them the International and Southern Comparative Literature Associations and the Association of Literary Scholars and Critics. From 1983 to 1988, she was director of the Office of Academic Programs, U.S. Information Agency, where she managed the worldwide Fulbright academic exchange program. Author of *The Poets and Time: A Comparison of Plays by John Millington Synge and Federico Garcia Lorca*, and numerous articles in professional journals, she holds her Ph.D. in comparative literature from the University of North Carolina at Chapel Hill.

Sheldon M. Stern has been historian at the John Fitzgerald Kennedy Library in Boston since 1977. He was in charge of the John F. Kennedy Oral History Program until 1989, conducting interviews on domestic and foreign topics. He has been director of the American History Project for High School Students since 1993, working with teachers to help students use primary sources and learn to separate historical evidence from mere opinion or speculation. He is especially interested in the responsible teaching of history in secondary schools and the effective use of historical evidence. He has taught United States history at several colleges and universities and is the author of numerous articles and reviews in United States history and historiography. A specialist in politics and the presidency, he earned his Ph.D. in history from Harvard University.

Sandra Stotsky is Deputy Commissioner for Academic Affairs and Planning at the Massachusetts Department of Education. She is also a research associate at the Harvard Graduate School of Education. In 1996–1997 she served as co-chair of the committee that developed English language arts/reading standards for Massachusetts, and from 1997–1999 she served on a successor committee to develop and monitor assessments based on these standards for grades 4, 8, and 10. The author of many research reports, essays, and reviews in the English language arts/reading, her most recent book is *Losing Our Language: How Multicultural Classroom Instruction Is Undermining Our Children's Ability to Read, Write, and Reason* (1999). From 1991 to 1996, she served as editor of *Research in the Teaching of English*, the research journal sponsored by the National Council of Teachers of English. She received her Ed.D. from the Harvard Graduate School of Education.

Hung-Hsi Wu is professor of mathematics at the University of California, Berkeley. He is the author of several books in differential geometry, including *General Relativity for Mathematicians* (with R.K. Sachs). He became interested in K–12 mathematics in 1992 and has written many articles on current mathematics education reform since then. He is at present writing a monograph on the teaching of fractions for teachers in grades 5–7.

Preface

Despite wide public support for the development of standards for K–12, conflicts have regularly erupted over one or another set of standards since the inception of the standards-writing movement about a decade ago. The disciplinary and pedagogical issues at the core of these conflicts have varied, depending on the particular subject areas in dispute, the governor of the state, and the composition of the state legislature, the state board of education, the staff of the state department of education, the committees selected to develop the standards, and the leadership of groups with professional or political interests in their content. However, the disciplinary and pedagogical issues driving the conflicts in the major subject areas in the K–12 curriculum are not just a matter of a more rather than a less inclusive curriculum or of one or another set of teaching methods. They are also a matter of how much students ultimately learn, thereby affecting the development of a responsible citizenry capable of analytical thinking and informed participation in civic life.

The standards-writing movement began in most states in 1989, soon after the federal government began to stimulate the development of voluntary national standards for every major school subject—to serve as models for states and local school systems. Standards were perceived as an important way to begin to solve one of the most daunting problems that this country faces—the low level of academic achievement of its young people. How can standards help raise student achievement? To begin with, standards provide all parents, teachers, and students in a state with clear expectations of what all students should learn. They also contribute to coherent educational practices when teachers align their instructional methods and materials with assessments based on these standards. Further, they establish relevant guidelines for teacher preparation, professional development, and certification. Finally, and perhaps most important, standards that reflect high expectations for all students in a state contribute strongly to the goal of equity.

This collection of essays on disciplinary and pedagogical issues in national and state standards arose from a one-day conference on K–12 standards at Assumption College, Worcester, in May 1998, sponsored by the New England affiliates of the National Association of Scholars. Thomas Carnicelli and I, the organizers of the conference, presented papers at it, as did Sheldon Stern, Ralph Raimi, Alan Cromer, and Mary Campbell Gallagher. I later solicited the other essays appearing in this volume because of their relevance to the subject of national and state standards. The reason for the conference, and for papers on K–12 standards by scholars, was the (often deliberate) exclusion of academic scholars from participation in the development of many of the national and state standards.

As a matter of policy, literary scholars were excluded from participating in the development of the national English language arts and reading standards; to judge by the almost total neglect of literary content in most state standards documents, few literary scholars were involved in the development of these standards as well. Mathematicians were also almost totally excluded from any real influence on the content of national and state standards in mathematics, even though they are the ones who define the content and structure of their discipline through their research and scholarship. Very few if any academic or research scientists took part in the writing of the two sets of national science standards, and it is not clear how many academic or research scientists have participated in the writing of state science standards. Although economists did develop national economics standards, they have not always been invited to participate in the development of state standards in the social sciences. In the field of history, academic historians were clearly in charge of the national standards for K–12, but, ironically, it was the skewed work of the particular historians who created the first set of national history standards that set off the highly publicized battle over the history standards in the early 1990s, causing attention to shift to the importance of state standards.

Thus, this volume is a first in two ways. It is the first set of essays analyzing in specific detail the disciplinary and pedagogical issues that confront those writing, revising, or evaluating K–12 standards in science, mathematics, the English language arts/reading, history, and the social sciences. It is also the first set of essays in which the disciplinary and pedagogical issues affecting standards-writing in the major subjects taught in K–12 are analyzed by scholars in these disciplines. Some issues are similar across subject areas, but there are important differences as well. The main thrust of this volume is to clarify exactly what is at stake in the often invisible battles still taking place over national and state standards and the assessments based on them from the perspective of those who know the content of those disciplines in depth.

Preface

Educational policy makers need to learn what disciplinary and pedagogical issues literary scholars, historians, economists, scientists, and mathematicians see in current K–12 standards because of the nature and thrust of an educational philosophy that has influenced most national and state standards. Often termed a "constructivist" approach to learning, it may base what is to be studied more on the student's interests than on a curriculum planned by the teacher; it favors 'interdisciplinary' (or holistic) approaches to learning in order to make connections across subject areas and, in effect, reduces the amount of disciplinary content taught to students; it may privilege topics for study generated by social and political issues rather than by the structure of a discipline; it encourages practical problem solving rather than abstract or deductive thinking; it promotes student-led small group activities rather than whole class instruction; and it all too often places much of the responsibility for teaching the less able students in a class on the more able students in the class rather than on the teacher. Although a constructivist approach to learning is allied today with a multicultural approach to curriculum and pedagogy, it deals more with what it presumes are the motivating conditions for learning rather than with the specific content of the curriculum. Nor, in itself, does it seek to inculcate specific attitudes and feelings on social or political issues, as does a multicultural approach.

The explicit claim behind standards reflecting this educational philosophy is that poor student achievement in K–12, especially in mathematics and the sciences, is due to an overstuffed curriculum with no relevance to the "real world," taught by teachers who do little more than lecture and "drill on skills," and who expect students to learn mostly through rote memorization. Constructivists believe that the current obstacles to higher academic achievement lie chiefly in the structure and content of the traditional curriculum and in the use of unmotivating pedagogical strategies, rather than in low academic expectations for *all* students or in the number of teachers who are not fully knowledgeable in their subject matter. They seem to ignore the possibility that a curriculum based on student-initiated inquiry may require for successful implementation more highly knowledgeable teachers than we have at present or are ever likely to have. A constructivist philosophy has dominated the thinking of educators in our schools of education and the training of many K–12 teachers in recent years. It has had a very strong influence on current national and state standards in mathematics and science in particular.

As readers will see, the conflicts over these standards documents have raised a crucial question, phrased in different ways by different commentators. What kind of standards enables a state to best fulfill its responsibility to all its citizens? Content standards that are designed to raise the academic achievement of all students but give teachers pedagogical and curricular flexibility in how they help students achieve the standards? Or constructivist standards that implicitly or explicitly require teachers to use particular instructional methods, classroom grouping arrangements, and ways to organize disciplinary content for all students even though there is no large, consistent, and credible body of research evidence that these pedagogical and curricular approaches can raise academic achievement in all students or minority students in particular? The essays in Part One of this volume elucidate the various issues affecting the authors' own academic disciplines, higher education in general, and our civic culture as these issues have emerged in national or state standards "wars" over the second kind of standards.

The first three chapters address the national and state standards in mathematics. In "The 1997 Mathematics Standards War in California," mathematician Hung-Hsi Wu sets forth the differences between the two sets of mathematics standards at the center of the 1997 "standards war" in California. One set was a draft based on current pedagogical thinking, the other a draft delineating the content that mathematicians believe K–12 students should learn. What was at issue was the centrality of mathematical content to a mathematics education. After describing the differences between the two drafts in their content and the pedagogical thinking behind them, Wu evaluates the final version approved by the State Board of Education and discusses its implications for mathematics textbooks and other K–12 mathematics curricula in this country.

In "Judging State Standards for K–12 Mathematics Education," mathematician Ralph Raimi documents the negative influence of the national mathematics standards on state standards for mathematics. He finds most state standards documents vague and pretentious, frequently omitting important mathematical content and offering mischievous curricular advice. This is the case, in large part, he believes, because none of the authors of the national standards document was a mathe-matician, nor were most of the authors of the state standards documents, so far as he could determine. Raimi's essay points to the need for much greater cooperation between mathematicians and mathematics educators in further development or revision of mathematics standards at the national and state level.

Preface

As important as the mathematics are in a set of mathematics standards, they are even more so in the statewide assessments based on those standards. Although a fully developed assessment system based on a state's standards might imply high academic demands, it turns out that much depends on the level of the content specified in the standards, the design of the tests, and the reporting mechanisms used by a state department of education. In "Standards-Based Mathematics Assessments: Appearances May Be Deceiving," three mathematicians report the results of their analysis of the content and rigor of the statewide mathematics tests used in Texas for grade 10 and Algebra 1 from 1995 to 1998. Paul Clopton, Wayne Bishop, and David Klein found most items on the tests used in these four years too easy for the grade levels assessed, in part because the state's standards were not demanding enough at all grade levels, especially at grade 10. In their comments on the model that Texas seems to be using for improving mathematical learning, they raise questions about the real impact on K–12 mathematics curricula of tests that are in essence minimal competency tests and thus insensitive to high levels of achievement.

Chapters 4, 5, and 6 present critiques of the national science standards and the research base for the pedagogical methods and curricular orientations promoted in these documents. The current standards-writing movement in science began in the late 1980s with the project supported by the Association for the Advancement of American Science (AAAS). It sought to define the core content that all adults should have learned in K–12. Written primarily by science educators and published in 1993, *Benchmarks for Science Literacy* emphasizes the teaching of big ideas or themes in science and downplays the learning of detailed facts and concepts. Nevertheless, as biologist Stan Metzenberg demonstrates in "National Science Standards and the Evidence Supporting Them," the document does not point to credible research evidence to support the pedagogical and curricular approaches it recommends. Metzenberg points out various flaws in the peer-reviewed studies cited in the section for biological and physical sciences in the AAAS standards document, proposing that the failure of a standards document in science to point to a sound and substantial body of evidence as support for its pedagogical approach to science education ought to raise doubts about its educational worth. He raises the question whether standards should serve chiefly as baseline expectations for all students (i.e., as minimum competencies) or whether they should serve as a way to challenge the majority of our students to do better, even if all students cannot meet them.

The standards document issued in 1996 by the National Research Council (NRC) of the National Academy of Sciences, titled *National Science Education Standards*, has probably had the most influence on state efforts to write standards. In "The Science Standards Wars: What Is the Basis for Scientific Inquiry?" physicist Alan Cromer shows how it lacks logical coherence and promotes non-scientific inquiry, in effect, bordering on anti-science. As an example of its effects on state science standards, he describes its influence (through its early drafts) on the 1995 Massachusetts Science and Technology Curriculum Framework. He concludes with a brief account of the conflict that took place over California's new science standards between those who wanted student-initiated inquiry at the center of the science curriculum and those who wanted a clear delineation of the essential science content to be learned grade-by-grade, devoid of pedagogical mandates. He, too, raises questions that beg for wider discussion: Is there a fundamental conflict between "raising standards" and a "science for all" philosophy? A question that must be answered, Cromer believes, is whether and when secondary school students deeply interested in science will be able to take science courses matched to their abilities and interests in a curriculum guided by the latter philosophy.

Using as our point of departure the claim of those supporting the national science standards that "we now know how children learn science," biologist Paul R. Gross and I explore the research base for the learning theory inspiring the pedagogical and curricular recommendations in the national science and mathematics standards documents. We also investigate the empirical support for the presumed effectiveness of these recommended pedagogical and curricular strategies in K–12. Examining major reviews of the research, summaries of their findings, and current, individual studies in peer-reviewed educational research journals, we find neither a convincing research base for a developmental/constructivist learning theory nor empirical support for the pedagogical strategies and curricular configurations now touted for science and mathematics education, such as cooperative learning, real-world problem solving, integrated science or mathematics instruction, and the use of technology. We also find no body of evidence for the efficacy of "systemic reform"—a generalized plan for the reform of science and mathematics education in this country that embeds these pedagogical and curricular methods and this learning theory. In our judgment, the chief problems to be addressed in the K–12 curriculum are the decline in trained science and mathematics teachers and the small number of trained teachers now teaching science and mathematics.

Teacher competence in subject matter looms as a major factor in chapters 7 and 8, which deal with standards in history and economics. In "Why the Battle over History Standards?" historian Sheldon Stern suggests three reasons for the current struggle over history standards, state and national. First, the largest proportion of teachers with neither a major nor a minor in the field they are teaching are history teachers. Thus, a long-standing failure to put substance first in history education has left a shaky foundation for serious reforms in history education in the schools. A second reason relates to the impact of multiculturalism on the teaching of history and the efforts to write history standards. In Stern's view, multiculturalism is not about "new and truthful historical scholarship"; rather, it is about turf, power, patronage, and money. The third reason relates to the curious politics of the standards debate. What is at issue here is the very notion of historical truth. Both political extremes want only their own version of historical truth taught and use the claim that there are no facts, only interpretations, to dismiss information or ideas that might undermine their respective versions. This divisive context has made the writing of strong history standards at the state level extremely difficult, and Stern sees no easy solutions to the current conflicts.

An entirely different set of issues affects the adoption and use of the Voluntary National Content Standards in Economics, released in January 1997. As economist Robert Costrell points out in "Discipline-Based Economics Standards: Opportunity and Obstacles," the few public controversies over economics standards that have occurred do not reflect disagreements within the profession itself over its content or between research economists and economics educators over how it should be taught. The controversies seem to reflect suspicion if not dislike of the discipline of economics on the part of non-economists. In his essay, Costrell addresses the major questions that are apt to be posed to those seeking to incorporate strong economics standards into the K–12 curriculum: Is economics too difficult? Is it amoral or immoral? And, can it be best taught within other disciplines, especially history? Using as a case in point the way in which economics was dealt with in the 1997 Massachusetts History and Social Science Curriculum Framework,

Costrell points to the many contingencies that policy makers need to consider in the development of state and local standards and assessments if they want serious discipline-based economics instruction to take place in K–12. Chief among these contingencies is the extent to which the average history or social studies teacher has a sound background in the central concepts of economics and can teach them.

Chapters 9, 10, and 11 address the interests and concerns of those in the English language arts, the basic subject in the K–12 curriculum. In "The English Language Arts in American Schools: Problems and Proposals," Thomas Carnicelli critiques the educational theories and professional forces he identifies as current influences on the teaching of the English language arts in our schools. From his perspective as a literature teacher and literary scholar, director of the English Teaching Major at his university, and member of his local school board for 15 years, he believes that education faculty have made positive contributions to current teaching practices in the area of grammar and composition. In contrast, he finds literary scholars in English departments responsible for the flawed reader-centered theories of literary study now in vogue in K–12 classrooms. Carnicelli offers a list of what he regards as ideal standards for the English language arts and concludes with several practical suggestions for educational policy makers.

The chief purpose of "The State of Literary Study in National and State English Language Arts Standards: Why It Matters and What Can Be Done about It" is to show how the anti-intellectualism that has always been a characteristic of our schools of education has affected state standards for the English language arts and reading. Chapter 10 sets forth the important limitations I found in the 28 standards documents I reported on in a monograph published in 1997 by the Thomas B. Fordham Foundation and then traces the sources of these limitations. The major problem in these documents is a failure to *specify in their standards* the level of difficulty they expect at the grade levels to be assessed and the general literary content they want all students to study. Comparing the statewide reading tests developed in Texas from 1995 to 1998 with those developed in Massachusetts in 1998, I show why specific standards for reading and literary content matter for assessment purposes. In Texas, the failure to specify in its standards desired reading levels for each grade level led to statewide tests that were too easy for the grade levels assessed, even though the state had relatively good English language arts standards in other respects. In Massachusetts, other features of its standards document compensated for the absence of specific reading levels or literary content in its standards. The essay suggests several ways in which those responsible for a state's educational policies can address the absence of specific literary content or desirable reading levels in their state's standards and assessments.

To show educational policy makers the instructional value of specific literary and reading standards in K–12, Jeanne Smoot spins out a dream list of what authors or works she wishes her first-year college students had read before taking her courses, explaining how standards with specifics like these would make a difference to college professors like her. As she observes in "Toward Improved Language Arts Standards for K–12: What a College Professor Wishes Her Students Had Read," if this kind of reading took place in K–12, college literature teachers could again teach reasonably demanding works of literature to first-year students rather than spend their time, and taxpayers' money, in remedial work or in teaching the most elementary introduction to literary discourse—what many of them must do at present. In her essay, Smoot offers her own guidelines for setting literary standards as well as the standards themselves.

The two chapters in Part Two of this volume shed light on the different roles that the federal government has played in K–12 education in the last half of the twentieth century. Mary Campbell Gallagher's essay may give most readers the first account they have ever read of the development and fate of the many K–12 curricula developed in the Sputnik era, almost all supported chiefly by government funding. In "Lessons from the Sputnik-Era Curriculum Reform Movement: The Institutions We Need for Educational Reform," she describes the origins of the movement, the principles that eminent university scientists, mathematicians, scholars in other disciplines, and educators used in designing the innovative K–12 curricula in the Sputnik era, and how these curricula were developed, evaluated, and made available to local school districts. For her account of the first effort by the National Science Foundation and other organizations to improve the academic quality of the entire K–12 curriculum, Gallagher draws on recent interviews with some of the surviving leaders of the Reform Movement, as well as on scattered and fragmentary records, notes, and books on the movement and its founders. Among the lessons she draws for today is the need to pay even more attention to teacher knowledge of subject matter than did the Curriculum Reformers. Although Congress and the public became preoccupied with different educational concerns in the 1970s, chief among the causes of the demise of this reform movement, she concludes, was the lack of teacher knowledge in mathematics and the sciences (as well as in other subjects) and the inability of K–12 teachers *then* to implement a discovery-oriented pedagogy, even with considerable training or retraining.

The final chapter analyzes the role of the National Science Foundation (NSF) in the current national effort to improve K–12 science and mathematics education in this country. Its title—"The National Science Foundation Systemic Initiatives: How a Small Amount of Federal Money Promotes Ill-Designed Mathematics and Science Programs in K–12 and Undermines Local Control of Education"—indicates the conclusions that Mike McKeown, a molecular biologist, David Klein, a mathematician, and Chris Patterson, a public policy analyst, have drawn from their examination of a program designed by NSF to make "fundamental, comprehensive, and coordinated changes in science, mathematics, and technology education through attendant changes in policy, resource allocation, governance, management, content, and conduct." Their chapter addresses two concerns that need far more open discussion than they have so far received. The first is the federal government's unpublicized assumption of what have historically been local educational responsibilities and the way in which it is assuming them. The second is the educational value of the particular discovery-oriented science and mathematics programs, policies, and curricular materials that this NSF program expects state and local school districts to adopt as the condition for securing its funds. Using the Los Angeles Systemic Initiative as an example of an Urban Systemic Initiative, and the Texas Statewide Systemic Initiative as an example of a State Systemic Initiative, the authors document the various ways in which this NSF program enables employees of a federal agency to foreclose further state and local educational decision making on matters of curriculum and pedagogy without broad public examination and discussion of their educational philosophy. They also describe deficiencies in the content of the instructional programs and materials that NSF is promoting. They question the appropriateness of a federal agency insisting on the adoption of an exclusionary and dogmatic educational philosophy by all school systems in this country as the condition for its funds, especially in the absence of strong and consistent empirical support for its efficacy.

Preface

The preparation of this volume was made possible by grants from the National Association of Scholars, the Thomas B. Fordham Foundation, and the Massachusetts Association of Scholars. I am grateful to these organizations for their support. As the editor of this volume, I deeply appreciate the willingness of all its contributors to address an audience that they have rarely addressed, if at all, in their professional writing—educational policy makers. The essays all deal with matters that are the legitimate responsibility of state governments—standards, assessments, and guidelines for teacher training and professional development. I believe these essays provide educational policy makers with much food for thought about these crucial matters.

> Sandra Stotsky
> Brookline, Massachusetts
> October, 1999

I.

Questions of Content and Pedagogy

Chapter 1

The 1997 Mathematics Standards War in California

Hung-Hsi Wu
University of California, Berkeley

The controversy discussed in this essay has its origin in the 1992 Mathematics Framework for California Public Schools (the 1992 Framework).[1] Published three years after the Curriculum and Evaluation Standards of the National Council of Teachers of Mathematics (the NCTM standards),[2] the 1992 Framework has come to symbolize the more extreme of the practices of mathematics education reform initiated by the NCTM document. Its overemphasis on pedagogy at the expense of mathematical content knowledge spawned several new curricula that so enraged the parents of schoolchildren that grassroots revolt against the reform within California spread like wildfire on a hot summer day. Eventually, the Californian legislature bowed to the inevitable and called for an earlier-than-expected writing of a new Framework. It was also decided for the first time in the history of California that there should be a set of mathematics standards. By law, these standards have to be set at a level comparable with the best in the world. The California Academic Standards Commission (the Commission) was created by the California legislature for the purpose of writing the standards.

In October 1997, the Commission submitted to the State Board of Education (the Board) a draft of Mathematics Content Standards which took the Commission more than a year to complete.[3] Under normal circumstances, the Board would approve such a document with no more than minor changes. However, a preliminary review of the Commission's standards by several well-known research mathematicians was so devastating that the Board broke precedent by commissioning a group of Stanford University mathematics professors to revamp the Commission's draft. Within ten weeks, the Board issued the revised standards, first the portion on grades K–7 and then that on 8–12.[4] The reaction to the new version was swift and violent:

> [The Board's set of Standards] is 'dumbed down' and is unlikely to elicit higher order thinking from the state's 5.5 million public school students.
> Delaine Eastin, Superintendent of Public Instruction
> as reported in the *New York Times*

> I will fight to see that California Math Standards are not implemented in the classrooms.
> Judy Codding, Member, Academic Standards Commission
> as quoted at a National Council on Educational Evaluation conference

> The critics claimed the Board's 'back-to-basics' approach marked a return to 1950s-style methods... Opponents characterized the [Board's] Standards as a 'return to the Dark Ages.'
> as reported in the *San Diego Union*

The interest engendered by these two sets of standards remained unabated in the ensuing months. For example, in the February 1998 issue of its *News Bulletin*, NCTM weighed in with unflattering comments about the Board's standards.[5] Because education is a very political issue, it is expected that opinions would be delivered without relation to facts. However, a set of *mathematics* standards for schools also deserves a critical inspection from a mathematical as well as an educational perspective, one that is based on facts, not hyperbole. With this in mind, this essay proposes to take a close look at both sets of standards from a scholar's perspective.

In the first section I suggest why the California mathematics standards war should be of national interest. The second section gives an overview of the comparison between the two versions. The third details some of the mathematical flaws in the Commission's standards, and the fourth contrasts these flaws with the clarity and overall mathematical soundness of the Board's revision. The fifth section discusses the problems that are in the Board's standards and indicates whether and how these are addressed in the new California Mathematics Framework that was approved in December 1998.[6] Should the appearance of the new framework in a discussion of the standards come as a surprise, let it be noted that, in the state of California, the standards were not designed to stand by themselves. Rather, the standards and the framework are required by law to function as a single unit in providing a blueprint for

California's mathematics education. The final section summarizes what we have learned from this battle.

Why the California Mathematics War Is of National Interest

It may be asked why a dispute within the state of California should be of interest to the rest of the nation. There are several reasons. One is that California, the most populous state of the nation, has been in the forefront of the current mathematics education reform. In the opinion of people outside California, "as California goes, so goes the nation." A second reason is that the inadequacy of mathematics education in this country has held a firm grip on the public's attention in the recent past, and the very visible act of groping for a solution in California adds enormously to cement this grip. Also the timing is just right: the Californian squabble came right in the midst of the revelation about the nonperformance of American students in the Third International Mathematics and Science Study (TIMSS). The California situation thus offers other states a glimpse of what to look forward to in their own battles to save mathematics education.

A third reason that makes the dispute between the two sets of standards interesting to other states lies in the very nature of the dispute. The pervasive lack of precision in the Commission's standards is symptomatic of a larger trend in contemporary mathematics education, which is to minimize the technical precision inherent in the discipline in order to make it more accessible to a wider audience. Would a state be fulfilling its basic mission in mathematics education if it promotes such a modified version of mathematics in order to reach out to a higher percentage of its students? California answered this question in the negative in 1998 when the Board's revision restored the precision and the technical materials. This very likely ensures California's ability to continue to produce a robust corps of scientists and engineers. Whether or not it will also succeed in raising the mathematical achievements of the lower 50% of its students will be a matter of intense public interest. Other states would do well to look at the details of this dispute before they too fight the same battle in the near future.

The fourth and final reason is perhaps the most important because of its enormous practical consequences: the Board's standards will generate a completely new set of mathematics textbooks by 2001. According to the latest information (December 1998) from the California Department of Education, there is more publisher interest, *by far*, in this new round of textbook adoption than in any other that has ever been conducted in this state. This means that by 2001 the nation will have a plethora of alternative textbooks that heed the call, not of the NCTM standards but of the California Mathematics Standards and Framework. The debate within California will become a national debate in a matter of two years.

An Overview of the Two Sets of Standards

No critical inspection of the two sets of standards, the Commission's and the Board's, should engage in hairsplitting in order to search for perfection. Social documents generally do not fare too well when subjected to this kind of treatment. We expect flaws in both versions, and we shall find flaws aplenty. Yet, there is a fundamental difference between their flaws, and it is this difference that is our major concern.

The Commission's standards is a thoughtful document. In both the Interim Report from the Commission Chair to the State Board and the Introduction to Mathematics Standards, one sees clearly the care that went into the enunciation of the goals, the work that had been done to achieve them, and the work that was envisioned in their implementation. Even if one disagrees with some of the details, one can applaud the overall soundness of purpose and the conscientious effort that went into the writing. The good intentions, however, are not abetted by flawless execution. Some parts of the document are controversial, such as the omission of the division algorithm in the lower grades,[7] the omission of the Fundamental Theorem of Algebra in the upper grades, or the mixing of pedagogical statements with statements on content.

There is also a pervasive ambiguity of language that makes the document unreadable in many places, e.g., the word "classify" has a precise meaning in a mathematical context which is not consistently respected. Or, what is a 7th grade teacher to make of "identify, describe, represent, extend and create linear and nonlinear number patterns"? But the most striking impression it makes on a mathematically knowledgeable reader would likely be the numerous mathematical errors that almost leap out of the pages.

The Board's standards do not suffer from mathematical errors.[8] Mathematical accuracy thus assured, one can proceed to find fault from a higher perspective. It should be fairly obvious to experienced eyes that the standards for each grade are not very "idiomatic": They are more like marching orders from an outsider than sure-handed utterances by a veteran of the classroom. There are occasional (though very rare) linguistic ambiguities. There is an overemphasis on pure mathematics in grades 8–12. The geometry curriculum in grades 8–12 is too much tilted towards synthetic Euclidean geometry. And so on. But perhaps the one quality of the document that stands out is its overall jaggedness; the various standards don't fit together too well. Is there an obvious explanation?

According to R. James Milgram—one of the Stanford mathematicians who helped revise the Commission's standards—the revision was carried out under many constraints. The goals had been set for them: to rid the Commission's standards of all the mathematical errors, to re-arrange the existing standards to make better sense of them, and, above all, to clarify what was in there. There was also a strict order not to add anything new unless it was *absolutely* necessary because the Board itself was under the same pressure. Milgram also added that, in fact, the Stanford mathematicians would not have minded if the standards were a little less inclusive, but the choice of deleting the existing standards was not open to them or to the Board. Retrofitting a set of standards is much more difficult than writing a new one, and it showed.

In spite of the controversy surrounding these two standards, the verdict among mathematicians has been overwhelmingly in favor of the Board's version.[9] Could this be no more than a case of closing of ranks behind their own colleagues? At least one mathematician would venture the opinion that such is not the case, and that it is more a matter of triumph of substance over form, and clarity over vagueness.

The Board's standards have the unmistakable virtue of being clear, precise, and mathematically sound overall. They describe clearly and precisely what is expected of students' mathematical achievement at each level, and the mathematical demands thus imposed conform to the conception of mathematics of most active working mathematicians. The qualities of clarity, precision, and correctness are the *sine qua non* of any mathematical standards worthy of the name, but the sad truth is that very few of the existing mathematics standards of other states can lay claim to any of them.[10]

Even the influential NCTM standards are no exception.[11] These qualities will come to the fore in the comparison between the Commission's and the Board's standards in the next two sections. At the end, there should be little mystery as to why, notwithstanding its flaws, the Board's set of standards is the preferred version by far.

It may be puzzling to some as to why there is this great emphasis on the soundness of the mathematics in a set of mathematics standards. No doubt part of the puzzlement comes from a belief that the experts in mathematics education should be able to get the mathematics right. We know that such is not the case—as evidenced by the discussion of the Commission's standards in the next section—and this discrepancy between perception and reality points to a serious problem in contemporary mathematics education: the divorce of mathematics from education. Too often mathematics educators and administrators lose touch with mathematics. Perhaps the publication of the Board's standards and the publicity engendered by the accompanying fracas will inaugurate a new era of reconciliation between the two disciplines.

The large number of mathematical errors in the Commission's standards also points to an intellectual problem far removed from the political fray. As the errors begin to pile up, they send out the unmistakable message that these standards were written by people whose mathematical understanding is inadequate for the task, and whose vision is therefore unreliable as a guide to lead students of California to a higher level of mathematical achievement. Such being the case, the so-called "conceptual understanding" embedded in this document is thus of questionable value at best.[12] The politicians and educators who rallied around the Commission's standards and praised it for its emphasis on "conceptual understanding" were most likely unaware of this fact.

Local Flaws

The mathematical flaws in the Commission's standards are of two kinds: local and global. The *local* ones are those obvious errors that can be corrected without causing damage elsewhere. A colleague has estimated that there are over a hundred of these, and that is a conservative estimate. Since it is impossible to be exhaustive, only a few that are easily understood even when taken out of context will be discussed. Starting with the glossary at the end, one finds for example:

> Asymptote: a straight line to which a curve gets closer and closer but never meets, as the distance from the origin increases

Since this definition of an asymptote does not specify that the distance between the curve and the straight line has to decrease to zero, it would make the line $y = 1$ an asymptote of $y = 1/x$ for $x > 0$.

> Axiomatic system: system that includes self-evident truths; truths without proof and from which further statements, or theorems, can be derived

By dictating that the axioms of an axiomatic system must be "self-evident truths," this definition excludes the axioms for non-Euclidean geometry from being an axiomatic system. After all, the statement "given a line and a point not on the line there are infinitely many lines from the point not intersecting the given line" is certainly not a "self-evident truth."

> Recursive function: in discrete mathematics, a series of numbers in which values are derived by applying a formula to the previous value

This term has a precise technical meaning in symbolic logic, and its definition is nothing this simple. Perhaps the authors had in mind "recurrence relations" instead. Assuming this to be the case, then the correct definition would change "the previous value" to "previous values." Otherwise, even the Fibonacci numbers would not fit this description.

It has been argued by some people that it is inappropriate to criticize the glossary with such mathematical precision because phrases such as "closer and closer" and "self-evident truths" are merely intended to be comprehensible to the layman in the same way a dictionary definition is. This kind of argument does not take into account the fact that an official state document on *mathematics* education which addresses not only the lay citizen but also the professional—the mathematics teacher—has the duty to aim higher than merely being informally correct. Moreover, for the case at hand, it is easy to be both informal *and* correct: just change "closer and closer" to "arbitrarily close" and "self-evident truth" to "statements to be taken on faith."

Next, we turn to the Commission's standards proper and look there at some representative local flaws. It may be noted that the following examples do not include any that might have been the result of carelessness, such as that about the asymptotes of a polynomial (*Clarification and Examples* for Standards 1.1 and 1.2 in Algebra and Functions).[13]

> **Grades K–8** Problem Solving and Mathematical Reasoning
> 2.1 predict outcomes and make reasonable estimates.

It is not common to equate "predict outcomes" with mathematical reasoning. Could the authors have in mind "Make conjectures and provide justification"? One would gladly overlook this as an inadvertent error but for the fact that the same sentence appears nine times in grades K–8:

> **Grade 3** Problem Solving and Mathematical Reasoning
> Clarifications and Examples: Your friend in another classroom says that her classroom is "bigger" than yours. Find the answer, and prove that your solution is correct using mathematics you have learned this year. (Note: Students should be able to approach this task using concepts of perimeter and area.)

This passage is supposed to *clarify* the content of the standards, but it has achieved the opposite effect by obfuscating it. It would take many pages to write an analysis that does this passage justice, so here is a very abbreviated account.[13] First of all, mathematics deals with precise statements, and to the extent that we try to educate our children about mathematics, we would do well to teach them the necessity of eliminating the inherent vagueness in many everyday utterances before transcribing them into mathematical terms. "Her classroom is bigger" is clearly a case in point. Faced with such a statement, a set of mathematics standards has the responsibility to instruct children of grade 3 to make sense of the word "bigger" before proceeding any further. If they *interpret* "bigger" to mean "more area," then they should measure the respective areas. If they *interpret* "bigger" to mean "longer perimeter," then measure the perimeters. The basic message is therefore that each answer would be correct according to whichever interpretation is used.

Furnishing such an explanation would seem to be the minimum requirement of a mathematics education for the young. Now look at the passage above: it tells teachers and students alike to accept an instruction that has no precise meaning ("bigger") and immediately proceed to "find the answer," and worse, "prove that your solution is correct using mathematics." If a teacher in an English class shows students a black box without telling them what is inside other than that it is an expensive piece of jewelry, and asks them to write an essay to describe the latter and

The 1997 Mathematics War

justify why their description fits the object, there would be an uproar. Yet when the same thing happens in a set of mathematics standards, we have people leaping to its defense and calling it "world class." Why is that?

> **Grade 4** Measurement and Geometry
> Students understand and use the relationship between the concepts of perimeter and area and relate these to their respective formulas.
>
> **Grade 5** Measurement and Geometry
> Students understand the relationship between the concepts of volume and surface area and use this understanding to solve problems.

The trouble with both standards is that there is no general relationship between perimeter and area, or between volume and surface area, except for the isoperimetric inequality. However, the latter would be quite inappropriate for students at this level. Moreover, how are students supposed to "use" this nonexistent relationship to help relate to the "respective formulas" of perimeter and area? What could the authors have in mind?

> **Grade 5** Number Sense
> Clarifications and Examples: What is the fractional value of each of the tangram pieces to the whole set of tangrams? Determine equivalences between one or more pieces and other pieces, based on the fractional values that you have determined.

What does "fractional value" refer to in this case? Does each piece count as one unit, or is the area of each piece being sought in proportion to the whole area? What kind of "equivalence" between the pieces is intended here and why has it not been clearly defined?

> **Grade 6** Number Sense
> Clarifications and Examples: Emphasize how fractions and ratios as well as operations involving them are similar and how they can differ.

Since a fraction is a ratio of integers, how can there be any difference between them with respect to their mathematical operations? Some educators, it is said, have begun to advocate that fractions are not ratios. If so, then we must redouble our efforts to produce better informed mathematics educators and not allow such ideas to creep into any mathematics standards.

Grade 6 Measurement and Geometry
1.2 Determine estimates of pi (3.14; 22/7) and use these values to estimate and calculate the circumference and the area of circles.

There is no explanation of how a sixth grade student could "determine estimates of pi" with this kind of accuracy, 3.14 or 22/7, especially the latter value. Is such a precise estimate even remotely conceivable?

Grade 7 Algebra and Functions
Clarifications and Examples: Order of operations may be helpful when evaluating expressions such as $3(2x+5)^2$. Recognizing the structure of the algebraic notation may be more helpful when evaluating $3(2x+5)$; both should be included as techniques.

The order of operations to evaluate algebraic expressions is a matter of *definition* and is not a technique. Moreover, to say in a mathematics standards document that knowing the simple definition of the notation is more helpful in the situation of $3(2x+5)$ than of $3(2x+5)^2$ is to undercut the credibility of the statement.

Grade 8 Algebra and Functions
Clarifications and Examples: Record and graph the relationship between time and the height of water in a cylindrical container when a drain on the bottom of the container is open and determine an equation which generalizes the situation.

One would *guess* (although that is asking a lot of the general reader of the standards) that the "relationship between the time and the height of water" means that height is a well defined function of time. This function happens to be quadratic, but what could it mean to find an equation that would *generalize* the situation?

Grades 9/10 Algebra and Functions
Clarifications and Examples: Students should understand the fact that equations in one variable (e.g., $(x-3)(x+1)(x-1)=0$, $3^{x-2-8}1=0$) have related two-variable counterparts (e.g., $(x-3)(x+1)(x-1)=y$, $3^{x-2-8}1=y$) and use this fact to solve or check the original equation and analyze the graph.

If the intended message is that the zeros of a given polynomial can be approximated by examining the intersection of its graph and the x-axis, then this statement is very poorly phrased. If the intended message is something else, then this statement needs to be completely rewritten.

Global Flaws

Next we examine global flaws. Their corrections would involve changes in several related parts. The first such example occurs in grade 7:

> **Grade 7** Measurement and Geometry
> 3.2 understand and use coordinate graphs to plot simple figures, determine lengths and areas related to them, and determine their image under simple transformations in the plane.

Now grade 7 is not the usual place to find references to "simple transformations" in the plane and their "images." What is meant by "simple transformations"? Has it been defined? Has the image of a transformation been discussed? It turns out that "simple transformations" are defined nowhere in the standards, but one could guess from related comments that the authors had in mind "reflections" and "translations." It is difficult to decide whether the authors were unaware of the need to fulfill the minimum mathematical requirement of clarity or simply considered such matters unimportant. Could such negligence be merely a momentary lapse? Not likely, because one also finds in grades 9/10 another reference to "transformations" in the plane with no explanation:

> **Grades 9/10** Algebra and Functions
> 1. Students classify and identify attributes of basic families of functions (linear, quadratic, power, exponential, absolute value, simple polynomial, rational, and radical).
> 1.4 demonstrate and explain the effect that transformations have on both the equation and graph of a function.

A pertinent related issue in connection with the above standard in grade 7 is how much coordinate geometry has been developed up to that point so that students may appreciate such a discussion. The answer appears to be "not enough." The first introduction of coordinates in the plane takes place in the fourth grade under, of all places, Algebra and Functions:

> **Grade 4** Algebra and Functions
> 1. Students use and interpret variables, mathematical symbols, and properties to write and simplify expressions and sentences.
> 1.4 understand and use two-dimensional coordinate grids to find locations, and represent points and simple figures.

Special attention should be called to the fact that the important idea of "algebraicizing" the geometric plane occurs here almost as an afterthought in a discussion on variables and mathematical symbols. Since it is now fashionable to talk about "conceptual understanding," one can say unequivocally that such a set of mathematical standards displays a lack of conceptual understanding of mathematics.

But, to continue with the present discussion, in the standards of grade 5, one finds "write the [linear] equation and graph the resulting ordered pairs of whole numbers on a grid" (*Algebra and Functions*, 2.2) and that, in grade 6, more graphing of linear functions and "single variable data" is called for in *Algebra and Functions* and *Statistics, Data Analysis and Probability*. This would seem to be the extent to which students have been exposed to coordinate geometry before they are asked to contemplate the image of a transformation in the plane.

Consider now a second example, which is the way the Commission's set of standards approaches the Pythagorean Theorem, a fundamental result in school mathematics. The first mention of this theorem is in grade 7:

> **Grade 7** Measurement and Geometry
> 3.3 use the Pythagorean Theorem to find the length of the missing side of a right triangle and lengths of other line segments, and check the reasonableness of answers found in other ways.
>
> Clarifications and Examples: Help students understand the relationship between the Pythagorean Theorem and direct measurement. Experience with both measurement tools and measurement on a coordinate grid should be included.

One's first reaction to "Experience with" in the last sentence is: How very Californian! This standard certainly makes it sound as though the Pythagorean Theorem is a tool already familiar to the students. Yet, in fact, this is the first time the theorem is discussed. One could bend over backward to give a benign interpretation of this standard as: "State the Pythagorean Theorem and verify it empirically by direct measurements." Few readers, however, would recognize that this is the intended message. Because this theorem is so surprising to a beginner, one would expect a demonstration of its truth early on. For example, the so-called "tangram proof" using four congruent right triangles nestled in a square is so elementary that it could be presented to fourth or fifth graders. One finds instead that when the theorem is mentioned again in grade 8 and for the first time in grades 9/10, no proof is mentioned:

The 1997 Mathematics War

Grade 8 Measurement and Geometry
1.3 use the Pythagorean Theorem to determine distance and compare lengths of segments on a coordinate plane.
   Clarifications and Examples: Include using the Pythagorean Theorem to confirm accuracy of scale drawings and contexts involving coordinate graphing.

Grades 9/10 Measurement and Geometry
2.4 use the Pythagorean Theorem, its converse, properties of special right triangles (e.g., sides in the ratio 3–4–5) and right triangle trigonometry to find missing information about triangles.

It should be obvious that this standard in grade 8 merely repeats what is already in grade 7. What purpose does this serve? In addition, is it good education to ask students to believe in the converse of this theorem in grades 9/10, as indicated above, without first giving them a proof of the theorem itself? It remains to point out that only later in Standard 4.4 of Measurement and Geometry, grades 9/10, do we find: "prove the Pythagorean Theorem using algebraic and geometric arguments."

It was mentioned earlier that the Commission's set of standards omits the long division algorithm in the early grades except for the case of a single digit divisor (grade 4). With that in mind, let us look at what happens in grade 7.

Grade 7 Number Sense
1.3 describe the equivalent relationship among representations of rational numbers (fractions, decimals, and percents) and use these representations in estimation, computation, and applications.
   Clarifications and Examples: Students should understand the relationship between terminating and repeating decimals and fractions.

Yet, the mere fact that a fraction yields a repeating decimal depends on the understanding of the sequence of remainders in the division algorithm. How are students going to *understand* that terminating and repeating decimals represent fractions without first knowing this algorithm by heart? Furthermore, in grades 11/12, we have:

Algebra and Functions
Clarifications and Examples: Graphing calculators, long and synthetic division may be used to factor polynomials and rational equations to verify attributes of the equation and graph.

Perhaps not enough thought was given to the fact that, without learning the division algorithm for integers, it would be difficult to teach synthetic division for polynomials. Incidentally, the preceding two examples from the Commission's standards show an all-too-common sloppiness of language: "equivalent relationship among...," "relationship between terminating and repeating decimals...," and "attributes of the equation and graph" are too vague for a set of mathematics standards.

As a final example, let us look at how the Commission's set of standards handles the concept of a function. The term "functional relationship" is used already in grades 4 and 5 ("the functional relationships within linear patterns" in grade 4, and "solve problems involving functional relationships" in grade 5). Now, there is nothing wrong with an informal discussion of a formal concept before a precise definition, but it is pedagogically untenable not to make it very clear that only an informal discussion is intended. (The Board's set of standards simply deletes all such references.) Next, in grade 6 of the Commission's standards, one finds:

Grade 6 Algebra and Functions
2. Students analyze tables, graphs, and rules to determine functional relationships and interpret and solve problems involving rates.
2.1 identify and express functional relationships in verbal, numeric, graphical, and symbolic form.

Since it calls for a direct confrontation with the concept of a function itself, this standard is less likely to be ignored and the potential damage is consequently greater than before. Are students to learn about the definition of a function, or are they not? That is the question. The hazy conception of mathematics itself as exemplified in this instance (and elsewhere too, of course) is unnerving to the mathematically informed. If one cannot resolve this issue here, what about the next one in grade 8?

Grade 8 Algebra and Functions
1.1 identify the input and output in a relationship between two variables and determine whether the relationship is a function.
   Clarifications and Examples: Students should be able to identify key ideas when a relationship is expressed through a table, with symbols, or through a graph.

Because this explicitly asks students to distinguish between a "relation" and a "function," nothing short of a full-scale investigation of the functional concept would suffice. But should one do this in grade 8? And

The 1997 Mathematics War

is this really what the authors had in mind? The answers seem to be supplied, however indirectly, by the following standard in grade 9:

Grades 9/10 Algebra and Functions
2. Students demonstrate understanding of the concept of a function, identify its attributes, and determine the results of operations performed on functions.

It would appear that here is the first time that students learn what a function is. If this is to be believed, then what is one to make of all the rumblings on these topics in grades 6 through 8? But if not, *i.e.*, if a function is supposed to have been defined earlier, then what is such a standard doing in grades 9/10?

I hope the foregoing gives some idea of the magnitude of the problems besetting the Commission's standards. At the same time, it should be pointed out that these problems are probably not detectable by someone who is not mathematically knowledgeable. The criticisms of the Board's standards coming from educators and politicians are therefore understandable to a certain degree. By the same token, this gap in mathematical knowledge then imposes on professional mathematicians the obligation to serve as intermediaries between major decisions in mathematics education and the public. May the mathematics community as a whole take this responsibility seriously.

The Board's Standards

Now a brief look at the Board's standards.[14] Some of the flaws of this document will be discussed in the next section. The main aim of this section is to contrast the mathematics here with the Commission's standards. Let us first start with grades K–7. This portion is *very* close to the Commission's standards, and the only difference between the two is that the Board's version eliminates the ambiguous and superfluous, corrects the erroneous, and deletes the *Clarifications and Examples* in the right-hand column of the original. I will have more to say about this last concern presently, but let us sample some of the differences. It was mentioned above that in grade 4 the Commission's set of standards incorrectly asks for "the relationship between the concepts of perimeter and area." By comparison, the Board's version now reads:

Grade 4 Measurement and Geometry
1. Students understand perimeter and area.

1.1 measure the area of rectangular shapes, using appropriate units (cm^2, m^2, km^2, yd^2, square mile).
1.2 recognize that rectangles having the same area can have different perimeters.
1.3 understand that the same number can be the perimeter of different rectangles, each having a different area.
1.4 understand and use formulas to solve problems involving perimeters and areas of rectangles and squares. Use these formulas to find areas of more complex figures by dividing them into parts with these basic shapes.

It is clear, and it is correct. More than that, 1.2 and 1.3 anticipate students' possible confusion, and 1.4 emphasizes the importance of applications and the general principle of progressing from the simple to the complex.

Another example is the Board's correction of the error committed in the Commission's version regarding the introduction of coordinates in the plane in grade 4. Now it is accorded a standard all its own and is placed correctly in the strand on Measurement and Geometry.

Grade 4 Measurement and Geometry
2. Students use two-dimensional coordinate grids to represent points and graph lines and simple figures.
2.1 draw the points corresponding to linear relationships on graph paper (e.g., draw the first ten points for the equation $y = 3x$ and connect them using a straight line).[15]
2.2 understand that the length of a horizontal line segment equals the difference of the x coordinates.
2.3 understand that the length of a vertical line segment equals the difference of the y coordinates.

Note that Standard 2.1 pays special attention to the *tactile* aspect of learning mathematics: use graph papers and draw ten points (by hand). We should be grateful that it does not say: "Enter these data in a graphing calculator and watch the graph emerge on the screen." Moreover, Standards 2.2 and 2.3 again anticipate students' confusion by singling out two key points for discussion. There is no question that this is an education document that truly tries to educate.

As a final example, let us look at how the Board's version discusses in one instance the issue of mathematical reasoning:

Grade 4 Mathematical Reasoning
3. Students move beyond a particular problem by generalizing to other situations.
3.1 evaluate the reasonableness of the solution in the context of the original situation.

3.2 note method of deriving the solution and demonstrate conceptual understanding of the derivation by solving similar problems.
3.3 develop generalization of the results obtained and extend them to other circumstances.

In plain, readable English, this standard lays out a step-by-step method of doing mathematics. Educational writing can be no better than this.

It is improvements of this nature that make the Board's standards a superior document over the Commission's standards in grades K–7. Yet, intense criticisms were already pouring in as soon as the K–7 portion of the Board's standards appeared. Looking at the facts, how does one presume to claim that this set of standards is "basics only," or that it "cuts out almost everything that is not related to computation and the memorization of formulas"? Obviously not on account of the standards themselves. But one explanation is that some people reacted strongly to the deletion of the *Clarifications and Examples* that are in the Commission's standards.

It was pointed out earlier that whereas in other states mathematics standards must stand alone as the sole guide-post for mathematics education, California has two documents: the Standards *and* the Framework. In this arrangement, the curricular comments on the Standards, including examples, properly belong to the Framework, which at the time of the controversy was yet to be approved by the Board. It serves no purpose to criticize the absence of examples in the Board's standards when they have merely been moved to a companion document.

Let us complete our brief survey of the Board's standards by looking at grades 8–12. There is a basic change of format here, in that the grade-by-grade account in the Commission's version is replaced by a listing of topics in the traditional strands across the grades: Algebra I, Geometry, Algebra II, etc. The justification is that since at present an overwhelming majority of the schools teach mathematics in the traditional manner while others do so in an integrated manner, listing only the content of each subject would provide maximum flexibility.[16] Instead of prescribing one particular approach to the curriculum, it throws the door open to many approaches. Such a change is a defensible one, and is in any case not one to make a lot of fuss about. With this understood, one can immediately appreciate the clear and uncompromising demand that the Board's standards places on students' all-around mathematical competence—not the formula-laden, rote-learning variety, but the genuine one. Students must be technically proficient, and they must know what they are doing.

For example, consider the discussion of the quadratic formula in Algebra I (which contains twenty-five standards):

> **Grades 8–12** Algebra I
> 14. Students solve a quadratic equation by factoring or completing the square.
> 19. Students know the quadratic formula and are familiar with its proof by completing the square.
> 20. Students use the quadratic formula to find the roots of a second degree polynomial and to solve quadratic equations.

It does not say: "Derive the quadratic formula and use it to solve all quadratic equations." Instead, it makes students learn the important technique of completing the square first. Then it asks for a derivation of the formula. It is only after this that it mentions *using* the formula to solve equations. Does a document that handles the learning of a formula in this manner strike anyone as a "back to basics" document that emphasizes memorization and computation?

Next, a similar example in a different subject:

> **Grades 8–12** Geometry
> Students write geometric proofs, including proofs by contradiction.
> 3. Students construct and judge the validity of a logical argument. This includes giving counterexamples to disprove a statement.
> 4. Students prove basic theorems involving congruence and similarity.

The unequivocal demand on students' ability to write down proofs and counterexamples is important in this day and age of diminished standards when proofs produce allergic reactions in many education circles. One can quibble with the precise meaning of Standard 4—and more of this later—but that is not the same as insinuating that these standards axe the development of mathematical understanding in the students. My personal opinion is that these are thoughtful standards, but their virtues are by no means apparent to the general public. Perhaps for this reason, the torrent of abuse heaped on these standards took over the front pages of many newspapers for several weeks. Here are some reminders:

> I think [the Board's standards are] half a loaf. We went from a world-class set of standards to one that cannot be characterized as world-class... The reality is one set of standards had basics and problem-solving and conceptual understanding but what the Board adopted was the basics only.
>
> Delaine Eastin
> Superintendent of Public Instruction

The 1997 Mathematics War

> When the State Board took a knife to the Commission's standards, it cut out almost everything that was not related to computation and the memorization of formulas. What was gained? Nothing... What the State Board deleted or weakened were standards intended to make sure students understand the key concepts underlying mathematics.
>
> Judy Codding, Member
> Academic Standards Commission

> While emphasizing important basics and memorization, [the Board's set of standards] axes development of understanding, applications and critical thinking skills students will need to live in the 21st century. In one stroke, the Board discards the last three years' hard work and reasoned consensus among math professors and teachers, college professors who use math in their teaching, science and business, and public representatives.
>
> James Highsmith, Chair
> Academic Senate, California State University
> Letter to the Editor, *Los Angeles Times*

> The Commission's standards are the best set of mathematics standards in the U.S. ... The Board's standards are most disappointing, [and are nothing more than] a "back-to-basics" document that emphasizes memorization and computations.
>
> William Schmidt, Executive Director
> U.S. Center for TIMSS

> The wistful or nostalgic "back-to-basics" approach that characterizes the Board standards overlooks the fact that the approach has chronically and dismally failed. It has excluded youngsters from engaging in genuine mathematical thinking and therefore true mathematical learning.
>
> Luther Williams, Director for Education and Human Resources
> National Science Foundation
> Letter to the California State Board of Education

It may be noted that the NCTM editorial of February, 1998, endorsed the preceding statement by Luther Williams,[5] and that *none* of the preceding writers is a mathematician.

One may ask, in light of all the flaws in the Commission's standards and the obvious emphasis on mathematical understanding in the Board's version, how people could bring themselves to make indefensible statements about the high quality of the former and the unworthiness of the latter. There are probably political and psychological reasons that are beyond my power to probe. But as an educator, I would like to offer a speculation on how this has happened. I believe there is a fundamental misconception about mathematics education that has sprung up more or less in the past decade, which is that there are *conceptual understanding* and *problem solving ability* on the one hand and *basic skills* on the other. Furthermore, this misconception is based on the assumption that one can acquire the former without the latter. Thus when the Board's standards explicitly call for fluency in basic skills, all kinds of red flags went up. Were these standards not set up by elitists to thwart students' "mathematical empowerment"?

One *can* acquire some appreciation of mathematics without mastering technical skills, in much the same way that one can learn the main melodies of an opera by listening to recordings of "operas without the human voice" and even enjoy them to some extent.[17] But if we wish to educate students properly about the art of the opera, using such recordings "without the human voice" is not recommended. In the same way, a correctly written set of mathematics standards should not just talk about "the conceptual understanding in mathematics" without getting the mathematics straight. It must start and end with 100% correct mathematics, and will therefore be more like the Board's version rather than the Commission's. Mathematical understanding *goes through technique*, and technique is built on understanding. That is the way it is.

The New Framework

What are the problems with the Board's standards? Without trying to be comprehensive, I will describe a few obvious ones and, at the end of the section, will look into how the new framework addresses them.

First, the terse statements of the Board's standards need examples to clarify them. For example, Standard 4 in Geometry (grades 8–12)— "Students prove basic theorems involving congruence and similarity"— means many things to many people. Should one only assume *SAS* and prove *SSS* and *ASA*, or should all three be assumed for simplicity? Should the *AA* theorem for similar triangles be proved? Or take the case of the introduction of negative fractions and decimals in elementary school: Exactly when should this take place?

The preamble of the standards in grade 5 states: "Students increase their facility with the four basic arithmetic operations applied to positive and negative numbers, fractions, and decimals." Is this to be taken literally so that "fractions" and "decimals" mean (as usual) *positive* fractions and *positive* decimals, or does it mean "positive and negative numbers, positive and negative fractions, and positive and negative decimals"? It does not help that this linguistic ambiguity persists in the subsequent enunciation of the detailed standards in both grades 5 and 6.

We must remember that these standards are pioneering something new in California, and pioneers have to be transcendentally clear at each step or they run the risk of having no followers on their trail. I wish to drive home this point by comparing with what I consider a very admirable set of mathematics standards, the 1990 mathematics standards of Japan.[18] There the statement about similarity (in grade 8!) is equally terse:

> To enable students to clarify the concepts of similarity of figures, and develop their abilities to find the properties of figures by using the conditions of congruence or similarity of triangles and confirm them.
> a. The meaning of similarity and the conditions for similarity of triangles.
> b. The properties of ratio of segments of parallel lines.
> c. The applications of similarity.

There is a big difference, however. The Japanese change their standards every ten years and, because they already have a well established tradition, the changes are gradual and minor by comparison with the kind of sea change we have over here. Moreover, they have excellent textbooks already in place, so there is no great need to spell out everything.[19] By contrast, we are almost starting anew in California, especially in these turbulent times in education. There is, therefore, a very great need for the Board's standards to be absolutely clear.

Second, the Board's standards intentionally eschew any prescription on how to teach students in grades 8–12, whether in the traditional way or the "integrated" way.[19] The intention for greater flexibility was admirable, except that, in the absence of a tradition, the added flexibility could be a curse. For example, the standards specify that each discipline (Algebra I, Geometry, etc.) need not "be initiated and completed in a single grade." It would appear that this specification makes it possible to describe the desirable content of each discipline without undue regard to the time limitation of fitting everything into exactly one year. Perhaps for this reason there are more topics in Algebra II than can be reasonably completed in a single year. How to teach this material in more than two semesters then becomes a challenge which few schools could meet. Also, Algebra I asks that "students [be] able to find the equation of a line perpendicular to a given line that passes through a given point." No matter how this is done, it would involve theorems about similar triangles. Does it then imply—contrary to the traditional curriculum—that Geometry may be taught simultaneously with Algebra I?

Third, the forthcoming tenth or eleventh grade statewide mathematics test was to include some statistics. The Board's set of standards does not suggest ways of teaching statistics in the early part of secondary school if the traditional curriculum is followed.

Fourth, considerations of this nature bring out the fact that the traditional method of offering year-long sequences for algebra and geometry is too rigid to be educationally optimal. While none of the current "integrated" models in this country seems to be entirely successful, the argument cannot be ignored that we should pursue the kind of integrated mathematics education that has been in use in Japan or Hong Kong for a long time.[20] The framework might fulfill its basic function if it could nudge California in this direction in a forceful manner.

Fifth, an idea that undoubtedly occurred to many people is how much the Board's standards for grades 8–12 read like a "Manual for Pure Mathematics." One almost has the feeling that this document could not bring itself to face the relationship between school mathematics and practical problems. Thus the framework needed to restore the balance between the pure and applied sides of school mathematics. While it is true that the reform exaggerates the role of "real-world" problems in mathematics, ignoring them altogether is for sure not a cure either. We would do well to remember that the overwhelming majority of school students will be *users* of mathematics, and that as future citizens they need to be shown the power of mathematics in the context of daily affairs. But all through grades 8–12, I seem to see only three explicit references to applications:

Algebra
15. Students apply algebraic techniques to rate problems, work problems, and percent mixture problems.
23. Students apply quadratic equations to physical problems such as the motion of an object under the force of gravity.

Trigonometry
19. Students are adept at using trigonometry in a variety of applications and word problems.

I hope I am not overusing the Japanese model if, again, I look at the corresponding situation in the 1990 Japanese standards. The description of the *content* of the Japanese standards is every bit as abstract and "pure" as the Board's standards, but *The Construction of Teaching Plans and Remarks Concerning Content* after each of grades K, 1–6, 7–9, and 10–12 pays careful attention to the bearing of "daily affairs" on the curriculum. For example, here is what is said after grades 7–9:

> In the [8th and 9th] grades, problem situation learning should be included in a total teaching plan with an appropriate allotment and [implementation] for the purpose of stimulating students' spontaneous learning activities and of fostering their views and ways of thinking mathematically.

Here, "problem situation learning" means the learning to cope with a problem situation, appropriately provided by the teacher so that the content of each domain may be integrated or related to daily affairs. The tone makes it abundantly clear that this is no mere lip service to applications, but that the applied component is central to the whole curriculum.

A final problem concerns the contentious subject of technology. From K–12 in the Board's standards, I could detect only the following two references to technology:

> **Grade 6** Algebra and Functions
> 1.4 solve problems using correct order of operations manually and by using a scientific calculators.
>
> **Grade 7** Statistics, Data Analysis and Probability
> 1. Students collect, organize and represent data sets…both manually and by using an electronic spreadsheet program.

This reticence is a *de facto* confession that we, as educators, do not know what the proper role of technology is in mathematics education. The reality is that computer and graphing calculators are here to stay, and the younger generation is besieged on all sides by them. It would not be an effective education policy to retreat and abdicate responsibility exactly when we were supposed to come forward to provide guidance. We do not want any kind of technological debauchery in the mathematics classroom, but neither do we want to make technological prudes out of our students. What we want are students who are technologically informed, especially about the role of technology in mathematics, but we won't get them if we continue to pretend that technology does not exist. I am being intentionally suggestive in my use of language in order to force the comparison with sex education. In both situations, it is better to keep our students informed than to let them pick up the wrong information in a state of prevailing ignorance.

Allow me to cite for the last time the 1990 Japanese standards. Part of *The Construction of Teaching Plans and Remarks Concerning Content* also deals with the technological issue after each of grades K, 1–6, 7–9, and 10–12. Here is what is said after grades 1–6 and 10–12, respectively.

> At the 5th Grade or later, the teacher should help children adequately use "soroban" or hand-held calculators, for the purpose of lightening their burden to compute and of improving the effectiveness of teaching in situations where many large numbers to be processed are involved for statistically considering or representing, or where they confirm whether the laws of computation still hold in multiplication and division of decimal fractions. At the same time, the teacher should pay attention to provide adequate situations in which the results of computation may be estimated and computation may be checked through rough estimation.

> In teaching the content, the following points should be considered. The teacher should make active use of educational media such as computers, so as to improve the effectiveness of teaching. In the teaching of computation, the teacher should have students use hand-held calculators and computers as the occasion demands, so as to improve the effectiveness of learning.

The Board had already wisely decided that no standards-based state test in grades K–12 would use calculators. This general policy on technology, sensible as it is, needed to be supplemented by a more comprehensive one which gives guidance not only on when *not* to use it but also on *when* to use it. For example, encouraging teachers to use problems with more natural—and therefore more unwieldy—numerical data by enlisting the help of calculators is a beginning. In the presence of the no-calculator-in-tests rule, students would get a clear perspective on what they need to know regardless of technology, and on how they can use technology to their benefit when the need arises. Encouraging students in calculus to use a calculator to estimate the limits of sequences while also holding them responsible for proofs of convergence is another example. Doubtlessly, thoughtful educators could formulate similar specific recommendations in other situations. As the preceding passages from the Japanese standards indicate, we need to make *active* use of calculators and computers to improve the effectiveness of teaching and learning.

With all this said, it is time to look at the new framework to see how it managed to address the foregoing problems in the Board's standards. In this context, the foremost accomplishments of the new framework would seem to be as follows: It gives a detailed guide on how to teach the standards in each grade of K–7, and for each discipline in grades 8–12. In particular, the ambiguities regarding the introduction of negative fractions and negative decimals have been cleaned up. It also adopts a policy on the use of technology in the classroom that is as comprehensive as the available research allows. For example, it essentially recommends against the use of calculators in grades K–5, but encourages its judicious use starting with grade 6. Further, a conscientious attempt is made in the new framework to emphasize applications in grades 8–12.

Thus almost all the major concerns regarding the Board's standards have been removed. *Almost*, except for two of them. It fails to directly address the issue of how to teach statistics in the traditional curriculum before grade 11. More seriously, it does not even take up the question of how to give Californian high school students a more integrated kind of mathematics education along the line of the Hong Kong or Japanese model.[20] These failures are blemishes in the new document to be sure, but considering how far it has outdistanced its 1992 predecessor in terms of mathematical coherence and accuracy, one can afford to be philosophical about these blemishes. Social changes are rarely accomplished all at once. They take time.

What Have We Learned?

It is often forgotten in the war of words that mathematics education has a substantive component: mathematics. We have seen how a choice between the two versions of the Mathematics Content Standards in California came down to a mathematical assessment of the documents. The scant attention given to this component in the mathematics standards of an overwhelming majority of the states, as pointed out in the Fordham Foundation monograph, is nothing short of scandalous.[10]

One positive outcome of the current mathematics education reform may very well be the revival of the idea that mathematics is important in discussions of mathematics education. The battle over the standards is a stunning illustration of this fact.

If there is anything that the Californian experience can teach policy makers in the other states, it is that without solid mathematical input, it would be impossible to have a sound policy on mathematics education. California happened to benefit from such input through entirely fortuitous circumstances. The accidental confluence of a group of enlightened state board members and a group of knowledgeable mathematicians who are also educationally informed led to the writing of a set of quality standards and a framework that is equally promising. So, what can other policy makers do in order to bring about comparable results?

One can try to seek out mathematicians who are dedicated to the cause of education, but by itself this is not without risk. It suffices to recall that the New Math of the sixties was spearheaded by a small group of well–intentioned mathematicians.[21] A safer recommendation would be that policy makers cultivate standard channels of communication within the mathematical community as a whole and seek consensus in that community at each major step of decision making. Back in the age of the New Math, much anguish and frustration would have been avoided had this guideline been followed.[22] The mathematical community, especially research mathematicians, should likewise do their share and make an effort to stay informed about mathematics education. Fortunately, recent events have proven that at least the latter seems to be taking place. Let us hope that in the near future, mathematicians will be alongside educators in formulating major decisions in mathematics education.

It goes without saying that having a set of good standards and curriculum framework is only the first step towards improvement in education. The far more difficult issues of getting qualified teachers and administrative support for the implementation of the standards lie ahead in California. However, these would be subjects of a different essay.

Finally, let us return to the battle of the standards for a moment. Few would disagree that this so-called math war is entirely senseless, but in the context of human affairs, it may be necessary. Destruction often has to precede progress. Needless to say, not everybody shares this view. When news of the U.S. twelfth-grade performance on TIMSS was released on February 34, 1998, the President of NCTM at the time, Gail Burrill, made the following comment on the TIMSS result: "What's important is that we are working together toward a common goal of excellence in mathematics. The recent math wars have done nothing to improve mathematics education." These are sobering statements. On the one hand, Ms. Burrill's optimistic view that we are already working together toward a common goal in mathematics education could not have been based on the reckless public condemnations of the Board's standards that had just transpired. NCTM's editorial did not exactly contribute to promoting harmony either. On the other hand, the math war in California did manage to reverse the disastrous trend initiated by the 1992 framework.

While much work remains to be done to achieve a balanced mathematics education in California, this achievement disproves the assertion that the math wars have done nothing to improve mathematics education. When all is said and done, educational reconstruction should be the common goal of all parties at this juncture, and the battle over the standards is, in this light, nothing but a distraction. In his address before the Joint Annual Meeting of the American Mathematical Society and the Mathematical Association of America on January 8, 1998, Secretary Richard W. Riley sounded the same theme of reconciliation: "This leads me back to the need to bring an end to the shortsighted, politicized, and harmful bickering over the teaching and learning of mathematics. I will tell you that if we continue down this road of infighting, we will only negate the gains we have already made—and the real losers will be the students of America."

In all our education activities we should think of our children first. No, we *must*. If there is a main lesson to be learned from the battle of the standards, it is that we should all learn to look at the facts and keep in mind the welfare of the students before we air our opinions.

Author's Note: I could not have written this essay without the support of Henry Alder, Dick Askey, Wayne Bishop, and especially David Klein. Subsequent corrections by Roger Howe also contributed significantly towards an improved presentation. Sandra Stotsky's editorial advice was decisive in the final stage of preparation of this manuscript.

Notes

[1] *Mathematics Framework for California Public Schools*, California Department of Education, Sacramento, CA, 1992.
[2] *Curriculum and Evaluation Standards for School Mathematics*, National Council of Teachers of Mathematics, Reston, 1989
(http://www.enc.org/online/NCTM/280dtoc1.html).
[3] California Academic Standards Commission, *Mathematics Content Standards*, October 1, 1997 (http://www.ca.gov/goldstandards).

[4] *The California Mathematics Academic Content Standards* as adopted by the California State Board of Education, February 5, 1998 (http://www.cde.ca.gov/board/board.html).

[5] "New California Standards Disappoint Many," *NCTM News Bulletin*, Issue 7, 34 (1998), 1 and 5.

[6] *Mathematics Framework for California Public Schools, Kindergarten Through Grade Twelve*, 1998 (http://www.cde.ca.gov/cilbranch/eltdiv/mathfw.htm).

[7] According to Commissioner Williamson Evers, "the omission of long division with two or more digit divisors was a conscious decision" by the Commission. See *California Mathematicians Respond*, (http://www.mathematicallycorrect.com).

[8] Unless one counts editorial howlers such as "1 square foot = 12 square inches" in standard 2.4 of Grade 7, Measurement and Geometry.

[9] There was some dissent, of course, but on February 2, 1998, an open letter to California State University Chancellor Charles Reed signed by over 100 mathematicians was released to the public; it expresses sentiments in support of the Board's standards. See *California Mathematicians Respond* (http://www.mathematicallycorrect.com).

[10] See the survey of mathematical standards of 47 states in R. Raimi and L.S. Braden, *State Mathematics Standards*, Fordham Report, Volume 2, No. 3, Thomas B. Fordham Foundation, Washington D.C., 1998.

[11] H. Wu, "Invited Comments on the NCTM Standards.," (http://math.berkeley.edu~wu).

[12] Mathematicians are only concerned with whether students *understand* mathematics, *i.e.*, whether they know why something is true, why it is of interest, how to apply it, what its implications are, and whether something more general is still true. However, educators introduce the term "conceptual understanding" and make it one of the three pillars of a so-called balanced curriculum (the other items being "problem solving" and "basic skills"). To my knowledge, the meaning of "conceptual understanding" is as yet unclear.

[13] The Commission's standards are published in a two column format which displays the mathematics standards on the left and the *Clarifications and Examples* on the right.

[14] But see H. Wu, "The Role of Open-Ended Problems in Mathematics Education," *Journal of Mathematical Behavior* 13 (1994), 115–128.

[15] There is an unfortunate linguistic slip here: "draw ten points" is undoubtedly what is meant. Subsequently this error was corrected.

[16] The meaning of this word has to be carefully qualified because there are several "integrated" approaches to mathematics in secondary schools.

[17] A popular undertaking by conductors such as Carmen Dragon and André Kostelanetz in the 1950s and 1960s.

[18] *Mathematics Programs in Japan*, Japan Society of Mathematics Education, 1990.

[19] Cf. K. Kodaira, ed., *Japan Grade 7 Mathematics*, *Japan Grade 8 Mathematics*, *Japan Grade 9 Mathematics*, The University of Chicago Mathematics Project, Chicago 1992; K. Kodaira, ed., *Mathematics 1*, *Mathematics 2*, *Japan Grade 11 Mathematics*, American Mathematical Society, Providence 1997; and K. Kodaira, ed., *Algebra and Geometry*, *Basic Analysis*, *Japan Grade 11 Mathematics*,

American Mathematical Society, Providence 1997. The publication date of the Japanese original of these texts is 1984.

[20] Cf. e.g., the texts cited in the preceding endnote.

[21] However, the common perception that mathematicians were solely responsible for the New Math debacle is wrong. In fact, NCTM was also behind the New Math.

[22] See, for example, "On the Mathematical Curriculum of the High School," *American Mathematics Monthly*, 69 (1962), 189–193. This open letter was co-signed by 75 of the foremost mathematicians in this country.

Chapter 2

Judging State Standards for K–12 Mathematics Education

Ralph A. Raimi
University of Rochester

In the summer of 1997, Lawrence Braden and I were commissioned by Chester E. Finn, Jr., president of the Thomas E. Fordham Foundation, to conduct a survey of the mathematics standards published by each of the states of the Union. Our report was issued by Fordham in March of 1998, along with or following corresponding reports, written by corresponding specialists, for state standards in English, history, geography and science.

Lawrence Braden is a mathematics teacher at St. Paul's School in Concord, New Hampshire, and I am professor emeritus of mathematics at the University of Rochester. We are thus at first glance an unlikely pair for such a job, as neither of us has any credentials in mathematics education. To understand our enterprise one must know that "math education" is not to be confused with mathematics on the one hand, nor with teaching on the other. Systematic mathematics is at least four thousand years old, and teaching is surely older than that, but mathematics education is strictly a 20th century phenomenon. This specialty is the domain of professors in the education colleges, members of the state and federal education departments, officers of the teachers' unions and professional associations, and writers, consultants, and editors of school textbooks and books designed for use in teachers' colleges as well. Many of those one calls "math educators" also conduct research in methods of mathematics education, but this is not the same as research in mathematics itself, which is also abundant, though necessarily arcane. There is some apparent overlap between the three categories (mathematicians, teachers of mathematics in the schools, and math educators) in that a given person might move from one to another during his lifetime, but that person cannot simultaneously be an active member of more than one of these groups. The jobs are simply different.

For the Fordham Foundation analysis of the state standards in K–12 mathematics then, Braden, a teacher, and I, a mathematician, temporarily took on a task more usually associated with math educators, those whose business it is, or should be, to compose and analyze such documents and their use. Our main results are only partly contained in the grades we assigned to this or that state, though these judgments were the primary purpose of our study. While the details will be given below, there is no need to conceal, even at the outset, that those grades were terrible.

More important for the long run, I believe, was our more general conclusion that the divorce of the math education community from that of the mathematicians, and to some degree of the teachers too, has led to a disastrous decline in our traditionally low expectations for student performance in school mathematics, as evidenced in the state standards we read and judged; and that this division contributes to the miserable standing of American students on international assessments such as the recent TIMSS (Third International Mathematics and Science Study). We further concluded that to reverse this trend, the nation requires an unprecedented increase in the participation of mathematicians in what is today regarded as the domain of math education specialists, both in the establishment of curricula for the schools and in the education of the cadre of teachers needed to understand and use such improved curricula.

As with every other problem, the improvement in school mathematics, that is, in the mathematical education of children in the Kindergarten through high school levels (K–12), is a problem with a history, which will be outlined in the first section. This history is more than background, for it helps explain the nature of the problem, not just its past, and it contains elements that are already illuminating its future.

The present, too, is much misunderstood. The second section deals with today's math education community's influence on present-day curricula and pedagogy, for this is essentially the subject of our actual findings concerning the state standards we studied. Those standards were largely written by math educators and certainly inspired by the earlier writings of that group. To the attitudes implied by these writings, we oppose the criteria by which our own judgments were formed; and as will be seen, they are quite different. Examples given here should illustrate the points; many more will be found in the Fordham Foundation report itself.

The third section will describe some parallel assessments of the state standards which were made by two other organizations, the Council for Basic Education (CBE) and the American Federation of Teachers (AFT), and will explain why their conclusions differed so from those we made for the Fordham Foundation. Fundamentally, the Fordham Foundation report reflects a view from outside the math education community, while the other two represent the currently predominant philosophy of the National Council of Teachers of Mathematics—and the state education departments being judged. State standards judged by their own writers, in effect, are like the famous lawyer who argues his own case. His case is a winner with his family, but open court is another matter.

In conclusion, the fourth section will return to the recent history of the relationship between the two domains, of mathematics itself on the one hand, and school curricula and teaching on the other, and some consequent recommendations for the future.

From "New Math" to "Reform Math" (1951–1989)

Before about 1900 there was nothing special about mathematics education in the schools. One presumed that a teacher, whether in mathematics, history, or Latin, merely taught what he knew, using textbooks written by those who knew even more. In the case of mathematics in the American public schools, practical arithmetic was the norm, and only a small minority went to high school at all. For the upper levels, the universities' entrance requirements pretty well dictated what the high schools (most importantly, private "prep schools") were to teach.

With the great changes due to immigration and technologically driven increases in the standard of living in the new century, however, the high schools of this century were no longer for only a privileged few, and the earlier grades had to take account of a possible high school future for their grade 8 graduates. For mathematics this presented a special problem, since its more advanced levels—algebra, geometry, trigonometry—were not the stuff of daily life; nor was the average product of a normal school (as teachers' colleges were once styled) equipped to teach it. Before World War II mathematicians (university professors mainly) were very few indeed, and remote from the schools in distance as well as interest.

Thus what inevitably grew up was what William Duren, a mathematician influential during the middle of this century, called the

"PEB," meaning Professional Educational Bureaucracy. Someone had to govern the teaching of mathematics in the schools, with due regard to the new constraints and demands, and this group, which had not existed before, emerged to perform that task. That they did not do it well is not a reflection of their labor and dedication, for the problem had many dimensions and amounted to raising a nation by its own bootstraps.

By 1940 it became something of a public scandal that army draftees knew so little of mathematics that the army itself had to undertake their training in the arithmetic necessary for even the most mundane bookkeeping and gunnery; and by 1945 the deficiency became even more evident when the wartime developments in radar, navigation, operations analysis, cryptography, rockets, and atomic weapons (among others) showed the extent of mathematical accomplishment needed for a modern society, at war or at peace. "Practical" mathematics was not just arithmetic and interest rates any more, and whatever it was, America didn't have it. About 1950 there arose the beginnings of an attempt at reform (generated by some previously indifferent mathematicians among others), an attempt that burgeoned when the Soviet Sputnik of 1957 plunged Congress into shock.

Thus there arrived the one brief period in the history of mathematics education when professional mathematicians did come to exert some influence, and that was this era of the New Math, which can be placed between the establishment of Max Beberman's University of Illinois project in 1951 and the gradual discrediting of all New Math projects, with loss of Federal grant support in the early 1970s. The (temporary) prestige of science and mathematics during this time emboldened mathematicians, who had always found school mathematics preparation of college students inadequate anyhow, to organize projects to rewrite curricula and train teachers in different ways; but these reform efforts would have had no more effect than earlier ones had not Sputnik goaded Congress into financing such projects on a hitherto undreamed-of scale.

The exact nature of these failed reforms makes a long story; so do the reasons for that failure. For the present purpose it is enough to say that the intent of the reform was to introduce the essentials of mathematical reasoning, of logic and rigor, into all parts of the curriculum, on the hypothesis that this was necessary if the later teachings were to be more than a drill in mindless algebraic abracadabra. The main hypothesis underlying those attempts were that essentially all children could be taught these things and would ultimately learn more sophisticated mathematics with less time and effort than by any other means.

Another hypothesis, this one totally unrealistic, was that teachers could be trained overnight (as Congress seemed to expect) to accomplish all this—for the whole nation—once a group of mathematicians could construct the correct curriculum and test it out. This last requirement was nearest the truth, for such curricula were indeed constructed, if not perfectly at least by very competent mathematicians, and with the help of practicing and experienced school teachers. But though testing was as thorough as time permitted, it appears that this was mainly done by specially trained teachers who would have had a hard time failing whatever curriculum they used.

In some places and in some small part the mathematicians were able to accomplish a good bit, but it was still only experimental, and only a beginning, on a task destined for the generations. Nonetheless, the popular desire to be up with the times immediately generated a flood of commercial textbooks affecting to be New Math, and school boards and superintendents were swept along with a meretricious tide of puffery. The result was far from what the experimenters had arrived at, imperfect though that already was. The public made no distinctions, however; in a few years the entire enterprise was judged to have failed, and the country clamored for a return to the familiar: "Back to basics" became the motto of the 1970s.

Actually, the true attempts at reform hadn't traveled very widely, and despite the incessant journalistic debates concerning New Math and its successes and failures, the great majority of students never saw more than the slogans. "Back to basics" in 1975 was therefore business as usual for most schools anyway, and for the others the residue of the experiment was rather slight, with the exception of some changes in the senior high schools for college-preparatory students, changes that would have taken place anyway.

From 1970 to 1990, then, the schools were not far from 1950 in their math programs, with one sad exception—though an exception that had already been under way before the Sputnik-induced revolutions: The total collapse of deductive Euclidean geometry, to which at least lip service had been given before the New Math. Geometry was already only a carryover from 19th century high school practice, and in pre-New Math times a last remaining beacon of reason in school mathematics. But as the tenets of progressive education gained currency in all fields in the early years of this century, the writers of geometry texts, too, were increasingly slighting what was geometry's principal value, and were themselves becoming downright ignorant of the logical structures of mathematics itself.

Like Latin, history, and rhetoric, geometry had been a liberal art in the 19th century, studied mainly by those intending a university education. Nobody then regarded Euclid as a practical guide to carpentry or navigation; it was an intellectual exercise. Abraham Lincoln was proud to have studied the first six books of Euclid during the years he was also studying for the bar, though he had no intention of becoming a carpenter. During the more egalitarian 20th century, however, geometry gradually became downgraded in favor of what was deemed more practical and more in alignment with the "felt needs" of schoolchildren.

Such a development was convenient for those who didn't understand Euclid anyway. Some Euclidean geometry, with some formal constructions and proofs, remained in some schools, but textbooks were increasingly taking the attitude that geometry was a sort of science of description of natural objects, with mensuration formulas its goal. By 1950 there were very few children getting the real thing, though even today one may sometimes meet an old-timer (non-scientist) who remembers Euclidean geometry as one of the thrills of an otherwise drab school experience of long ago. The New Math reforms did attempt to deal intelligently with geometry, but it was difficult, and the form in which the commercial world of publishers then took it up was a travesty. By 1975, Euclid was dead in the schools.

With the decline and fall of the New Math, the mathematicians went home to their universities and their researches, and the PEB tried to make sense of "basics." Parents might have been mollified for a while by the fact that their children were no longer bringing home weird tales of "set intersections" and "truth tables" as they had done in the 1960s. But their accomplishment in terms of such national assessments as the National Assessment of Educational Progress continued to show the American children no better off in mathematics—even in "basics"—than they had been in 1950. The federal government established a National Institute of Education in 1972, intending it to conduct research towards improvement; and little by little the professional educators, who had by and large tried to celebrate and participate in the New Math projects while they seemed popular, recovered their nerve and reassumed direction of school mathematics.

Judging State Standards for K–12 Mathematics Education

In 1980 the National Council of Teachers of Mathematics (NCTM), their principal professional organization, issued a brief report, "An Agenda for Action," announcing that school mathematics should have "problem solving" as its primary focus. Other features of this manifesto, which showed no signs of mathematicians' influence, are also of interest, but apart from its emphasis on the calculator or computer as a tool for the future, all of it could have been written before 1950. In particular, the Agenda did not portray mathematics in any way as an intellectual adventure, or as a preparation for scientific studies, or as a thing of beauty.

That the document urged "understanding" of mathematics over memorization and routine did not reflect an attachment to the sort of reasoning one finds in either Euclid or the New Math axiomatic systems for algebra. Earlier educators, both traditional and those attempting reform, had always exalted "understanding." Who would not? But the profession's understanding of "understanding" seems to shift with the times. The new "understanding" was to be the relationship of mathematics with the "real world" rather than with reason. And with the interpretation of "real world" now being given, not much mathematics could be made relevant. In short, a dumbing-down was in process, mathematics to be made palatable by a diminution of content, accompanied by a sugarcoating labeled improved pedagogy.

Over the next decade the NCTM formed committees to fill in the specifics, culminating in the 1989 publication of the rather large and ambitious *Curriculum and Evaluation Standards for School Mathematics*. This volume was actually only one of three allied "standards" reports, the others more narrowly concerning pedagogy and testing, but the 1989 volume is the one commonly referred to as "the NCTM standards," and the one that was to have a decisive influence on the developments Lawrence Braden and I were to study in 1997.

The National Science Foundation, following publication of the NCTM standards (which had not been federally financed but was the product of NCTM alone), undertook to help finance a similar study on the part of every state that would itself create a similar document for use in that state. Some states, of course, had long had standards in one form or another, to guide school districts in their choice of textbooks and curricular emphases, and in many cases as syllabi for statewide examinations. But with the federal legislation of the 1980s came a wholesale production of such standards, many of them in avowed imitation of the one produced by NCTM, though generally much shorter, and different in other ways.

The American tradition of local control of education more or less forbids a national curriculum, except *de facto* in some degree. These state standards, though federally encouraged and supported, are supposed to be each state's vision of the future, of what mathematics education ought to be. Some were apparently written by enormous committees of teachers and math education specialists, but the final texts obviously were assembled and organized at the state education department level, sometimes with the help of one of the regional educational "laboratories" set up and financed by the U.S. Department of Education. Despite the regional differences, the influence of NCTM and these laboratories has imparted a certain sameness to many of the state standards we ended up studying. Almost all of them had publication dates of 1996 or 1997.

The Judgment of the State Standards

Braden and I got the documents, we read them, we graded them. We could grade only 47, counting D.C., as three were incomplete drafts we could not cite or quote, and Iowa on principle does not produce one. Our grades were divided by criteria of our own devising, of which there were four: their Clarity, their demands for mathematical Content, their demand for what we call Mathematical Reasoning throughout the curriculum, and their freedom from the Negative Qualities we called False Doctrine and Inflation. Each criterion had parts, that is, subcriteria, but our overall judgment gave equal weight to these four groupings, producing a grade of A, B, C, D, or F (for "failure").

In all, 16 states got an F and 12 more got a D, making a clear majority at the more melancholy levels. Not that the C and B states were admirable. There were only three grades of A: North Carolina, Ohio, and California.

Japan got an A, too, but not as a 51st state. When we decided to include the Japanese document, our copy of which was dated 1990, we hadn't yet known that any American ones would receive a good grade, and we wanted to make sure our report contained some good examples for comparison's sake. In truth, the Japanese document (despite its high grade) could not really be used verbatim by any of our states, even if it were better translated, because of cultural differences that allow Japan's standards a rather allusive, if not cryptic, style, one that would not easily

Judging State Standards for K–12 Mathematics Education

explain itself to American school systems. Just the same, it is well worth study by every one of our states, and some of the best American standards were written by states that had avowedly considered the Japanese model during their deliberations.

To our minds, anything less than a grade of A should be unacceptable. Grades of B and C are counted respectable for college students and children, but states are different. States can and should hire their best talent to write their papers, something frowned on in rich and lazy undergraduates but which in a state is not plagiarism. Nor can a state be excused for lack of sleep the night before the exam, or an attack of mononucleosis. Under these circumstances, the overall failure of all but (generously) thirteen of our states, those graded A or B, to produce a sensible document that simply and adequately delineates even what it hopes for in its citizens' mathematical education, must be considered a national disaster.

We didn't have to look hard to find faults; they hit us in the face. First off was the bloated language, which even in mathematics can only be called Educationese. It was our duty to read it anyhow; perhaps it was only an unfamiliar jargon which, once penetrated, does in fact make sense. Every trade has its jargon, after all. We persevered, we penetrated, but we found no bottom to it. This sort of thing we downgraded as Inflation, a gentler word than our in-house use of "blather." Now one can say that blather is really only a matter of style; was there anything really wrong about what was written in these standards? Well, yes, there was. Some of what we read did make sense, but in places we would rather it had not, for the sense it made was too often destructive of mathematical learning. Such things we called False Doctrine, a telling example of which we shall come back to later in some detail. For now, the principal false doctrines we found prevalent in state standards were these:

1. The denial of the value of memorizing anything, especially the basic definitions and facts of arithmetic, and their computational algorithms; also the concomitant notion that since the hand calculator and computer largely replace the computational skills of the past in daily life, they should do so during the arithmetic learning process as well.

2. The urging of "real-life" experience as the touchstone of value in mathematical knowledge, i.e., that mathematical ideas without imme-

diate physical realization should not be imposed on children, or cannot.

3. The idea that whatever cannot, or apparently cannot, be taught to all children should be taught to none.

Not every failing state exhibited all of these doctrines at every turn, and certainly never in so bald a statement of principle as here summarized, though the philosophy is plain enough: "rote learning" should give place to "real understanding of concepts," for example. Rather than say all mathematical truths of value must have a physical realization, the state will prescribe "manipulatives" such as "algebra-tiles," and team projects such as measuring playgrounds, so insistently that mathematics can no longer be seen as an intellectual adventure. And, rather than say that the curriculum is to be limited to what average and below-average students of previous generations seem to have been able to accomplish, states combine the language of inclusiveness and equity with the omission of everything difficult in order to accomplish that end quietly. Other false doctrines will be considered in their turn, below. ("Manipulatives" are objects designed to teach mathematical lessons by analogy. Kindergarten blocks are an example, and for the early grades many other devices are convenient and instructive, but the genre has recently passed all bounds, both intellectual and financial, with the enthusiastic advocacy of most states' standards. One state even mentions the possible purchase, for educational purposes, of a Pascal's Triangle; but we have not yet seen advertisements for Occam's razors.)

Overlying each false doctrine there is usually a fog of reference to high-sounding psychological theories of cognition, learning-style differences, and the like, making it sound as if the mathematical contents of a program are quite unproblematical, and that the only real problems are how to transmit or cause the student to discover a well–understood body of mathematical material. That the relevant body of mathematical material is not so well understood by the educators themselves can be seen from the multitude of mathematical solecisms and errors with which so many of the state standards are sprinkled, and the vagueness of much of the rest. A small selection of these are quoted, though with minimal explanation, in our report for the Fordham Foundation. Alas, the cited errors are not mere oversights or misprints but represent a genuine reservoir of mathematical ignorance.

Judging State Standards for K–12 Mathematics Education 43

Our second criterion, Content, was split three ways: primary school, middle school, high school. There has long been a traditional content in American schools: arithmetic for primary schools, geometry and algebra for the high schools, and time-wasting reviews, usually called "ratio and proportion," or "business applications," for the middle schools. Fitful and shifting reforms since 1950 have, we found, improved things somewhat in some directions, especially for college-intending high school students, but have degraded geometry on the whole, and have unreasonably delayed the introduction of algebra in the middle schools in most states.

Reason was our third criterion of judgment. Euclidean geometry is not its only home in school mathematics, of course, and the New Math of the era 1955–1975, led by mathematicians, had made the attempt to introduce rigorous reasoning throughout the curriculum, and genuine algebra earlier than high school. The "back to basics" movement of the 1970s and 1980s therefore generated a tragedy of its own, for it helped render the community of mathematicians suspect and even excluded by the mathematics educators of the generations since. And not just the mathematicians but the lessons of mathematics itself.

In today's most widely used textbooks, the logical structures of algebra have disappeared, though some few items of vocabulary remain. The emphasis on problem solving has exalted the linear equation and its uses to a veritable definition of algebra, with such things as the binomial theorem and the quadratic formula downplayed or omitted. Euclidean geometry is in practice regarded by most state standards as a sort of empirical study of the shape of the world around us, dimensions of playgrounds and soup cans, augmented by some exercises (aided by computer software) in naming symmetries and looking at things in mirrors. While geometry as a deductive system has had some small staying power in actual classrooms, present math-education philosophy, as expressed in most state standards, would guarantee that in another generation no teachers will be left us who are competent to handle the Euclidean system.

Reason in other parts of the school curriculum, especially in algebra, became so discredited during the New Math era that it is only sporadically visible today. "Deductive and inductive reasoning" may be a mantra in standards-land, but by "inductive reasoning" is mostly meant extrapolating number sequences and playing with geometric manipulatives. Most states in most contexts, moreover, confuse mathematical, i.e., deductive, reasoning with the process by which real-life problems are converted into algebraic equations, a process better described as mathematical modeling. So, led by the bellwether NCTM standards of 1989, most state standards lump "problem solving" with "mathematical reasoning" under a single rubric, which might be termed the burial shroud of the New Math.

Comparing 1998 with 1948 overall, as seen in the content of the state standards taken together, there are visible a few, but very few, noticeable effects or legacies of the intervening reform efforts. One of these is the presence of some of the ideas of statistics in the school mathematics curriculum, and another is the recurrent attempt to leap-frog the time-wasting of the middle school by "acceleration," at least for the better students, leading to Advanced Placement calculus in the 12th grade. This is not much, and not entirely to the good, either, for it has often been accomplished by some curricular thinning in other directions.

Furthermore, the ignorant descriptions the new topics (along with the old) are so often given in the state standards betoken a national cadre of math educators unable to lead the nation's teachers to a suitable intellectual plane. For example, the definitions given mathematical terms in the glossaries that so many standards (unnecessarily) include are sometimes real howlers. This one from Tennessee, for example, exhibits the straining after "humanistic" values in mathematics education that someone who didn't understand its really humanistic values was forced to invent:

> Algebraic Thinking: thinking skills which are developed by working with problems which require students to describe, extend, analyze, and create a variety of oral, visual, and physical patterns (such as ones based on color, shape, number, sounds) from real life and other subjects such as literature and music.

Nobody will be particularly misled by this definition when preparing for examinations, of course, but a later definition from the same glossary is more characteristic:

> Equation: two mathematical expressions joined by an equals sign.

While this describes the physical appearance of an equation, it omits the essence, that an equation is a sentence, or clause in a sentence, helping make a statement of a certain sort. Students and teachers who take this definition's attitude cannot learn to make use of equations, except to pass certain multiple choice examinations.

Judging State Standards for K–12 Mathematics Education

Today's NCTM-led movement to a "reform" math runs along different lines from either New Math or the "back to basics" that succeeded it. It would replace what it calls "mindless drill" by "real understanding of concepts." But "mindless drill" is a straw man and characterizes bad teaching rather than a bad curriculum. Meanwhile, today's touted "concepts" are little connected with mathematical reasoning and instead said to be connected with "problem solving" and the "real world." This new attitude, which has been relentlessly propagandized by the NCTM, underlies the main substantive failings in the standards we were reading and judging last fall.

One difficulty in invoking "the real world" as a touchstone of value in school math is that the real "real world" is one quite unknown to children and generally of little interest. A real-world arithmetic problem might concern the amount of paint to order for the redecorating of an office building. What could be more tedious and unenlightening for a child learning to multiply numbers? Children are imaginative and in fact can become more interested in the decomposition of an integer into primes than in any amount of schoolyard measurement.

Other so-called "real-world" problems are too often strained attempts to attach names to old routine exercises. "A candy store sells $n(n+1)$ boxes of candy on the nth day..." Why a candy store? Because the author can't think of any other real-world application of the equation he plans to introduce. Any child will see this is not even sugar-coating of the algebraic pill; it is saccharine. Genuine quadratic equations are actually more interesting than phony candy stores.

The 1989 NCTM standards document (which was not one of the documents graded in our Fordham Foundation report but is their progenitor) is longer than almost every set of state standards we read. It is not too hard to write state standards that resemble the NCTM document, and most states tried. The difficulty is this: NCTM is very vague about a lot of things and doesn't make it entirely clear what the content should be at each stage of schooling. One would think a set of standards should tell a new teacher what to teach in each grade, or at least what a student should know at the end of, say, grades 6, 9, and 12, if not year by year.

Instead, NCTM offers aspirations of a more general sort, though still classified by year or range of years. Here is an example (p. 81):

> In grades 5–8, reasoning shall permeate the mathematics curriculum so that students can:
>
> recognize and apply deductive and inductive reasoning;
>
> understand and apply reasoning processes, with special attention to spatial reasoning and reasoning with proportions and graphs;
>
> make and evaluate mathematical conjectures and arguments;
>
> validate their own thinking;
>
> appreciate the pervasive use and power of reasoning as a part of mathematics.

These points are typical of NCTM rhetoric in that however many times I read them I cannot remember all five, even in paraphrase, and would fail any test on the whole statement. I invite any amateur (or professional) actor reading these words to try to memorize them; they rival *The Bald Soprano* and most of the works of Gertrude Stein in their structureless difficulty.

The quoted standard is followed by examples of problems—classroom exercises meant to illustrate some of these demands; but it does not outline or even suggest a coherent program. Following the five points quoted above, one example concerns tiling a plane, a second concerns the search for prime integers, and a third shows how a graph can represent a plot of speed against time for a pictured roller coaster.

All worthy exercises but in context typical of an unworkable current dogma, which is to have all the possible threads of mathematics appear in some form in each year of schooling. Tiling a plane might be called geometry, study of the primes might be called number theory, graphing speed against time might be called analysis (or "pre-calculus" in the schools). Placing three such diverse examples under one rubric is here a deliberate NCTM invitation to "integrate" the curriculum. But the straining for integration leads more often to mathematical incoherence. In an outline for a mathematics curriculum one should invoke some system, something memorable, as, for example, Euclidean geometry does by the very ordering of its theorems. The examples for Reason should, as in the Japanese standards, be organized by subject matter or by year to exhibit a progression of skill in reasoning; it is not something to be isolated as a subject of its own, to be illustrated by random examples.

Judging State Standards for K–12 Mathematics Education 47

Almost all the state standards imitate NCTM in this regard, though usually rather more dangerously than the national organization. The result has been characterized by one critic as a curriculum that is "a mile wide and an inch deep." Some of the standards we read have something called "algebra" in every grade, K–12, but manage to end the series (as Connecticut does) without the quadratic formula, without geometric series, and without the binomial theorem: a triumph of nomenclature over substance. Such algebra should rather be called "algebra appreciation" unless, as in some "reform" textbooks, it is also tricked out with today's political virtues and may better be called, to quote an unfriendly but accurate critic, "rain-forest algebra."

NCTM, and hence most states, have taken up another popular doctrine, which is that children should "discover," maybe even construct, knowledge for themselves. They should not be told things; the teacher is to be a "guide on the side" rather than a "sage on the stage." This Rousseauean idea has gone through many generations of educational theorists, including our own John Dewey and his followers. In the legendary case of Mark Hopkins and a log, it has some validity; but in the schools of middle America it leads to such absurdities as the "discovery" of the Pythagorean Theorem by children instructed exactly how to spend their hours communally cutting out appropriately shaped pieces of paper.

Certainly children do not learn by having knowledge laid upon them like a blanket, and if we do not participate in our own educations we will learn nothing. But this obvious insight has been elevated into a doctrine that in practice often excuses the teacher from ever bringing a lesson to a conclusion, or even knowing the answers.

As another example, New Jersey's 1996 Framework, avowedly "built on" the 1989 NCTM standards, contains, in addition to its own content standards, a great deal of amplifying educational philosophy and pedagogical advice, some of it revealing in this regard. Under Number Sense (Standard 6: "All students will develop number sense and an ability to represent numbers in a variety of forms and use numbers in diverse situations"), the Framework offers extra advice according to grade level. For grades 5 and 6, it explains,

> Models are essential for the continued exploration of fraction meaning... Fraction circles and Fraction Bars help children... establish rudimentary meaning for fractions but have the drawback of using the same size unit for all the pieces. This is a fairly serious drawback leading to the misconception, for instance, that 1/3 is

> always less than 1/2 without regard to the units in which these fractions are expressed; students need to be aware, for example, that 1/3 of a large pizza is frequently larger than 1/2 of a small one.

This might sound like a deep insight to someone but certainly not to a mathematician, for whom 1/3 has always been less than 1/2 and always will be. New Jersey is for some reason deliberately confusing the numbers 1/2 and 1/3 with the use of their names as adjectives in practical applications. If there is any point to the study of mathematics, it is exactly in the distinctions it draws between objects one might wish to eat and numerical abstractions which can partially describe them. Certainly mathematics does not take account of flavor and material, and only somewhat of shape and weight; but if a child is ever to make use of the properties of fractions, what is truly "essential" is not the use of manipulatives like "fraction circles," but rather the distinction between "1/3" and "1/3 of a large pizza."

The person who wrote about "the misconception that 1/3 is always less than 1/2" was suffering from an overdose of Piaget, the psychologist who most perceptively wrote of the development of number sense in small children. Children develop concepts of "large" and "small," "few" and "many," by stages, and their early perceptions sometimes lead them to believe, or say, e.g., that an apple divided in two parts is thereby diminished. There may even be a sense in which the division does lead a child to prefer the whole, or to call it "bigger" (or is it "smaller"?), and there is no denying that such perceptions slow the child's early understanding of the mathematician's vocabulary of halves and thirds. But this does not make 1/3 greater than the number 1/2—ever. The child will simply have to learn that while the third part of a very large pizza, or of a galaxy, still lacks two parts of the whole, we are not thereby insisting it is "small" compared to half a banana. We are duty bound to explain the meaning of the words—a restricted meaning, to be sure, but a necessary one. It is for the child to learn the world's conventions and the world's science, and not for the world to defer to the child's initial imaginings, even though understanding the sources of a child's difficulties is of high importance in teaching. The notion that "in this case one third is greater than one half" is simply mischievous, an exaltation of psychological insight and sympathy over the demands of reason.

In passing, it is a pity that students at the sixth grade level are not yet, and not only in New Jersey, weaned from such material objects as the

Judging State Standards for K–12 Mathematics Education

"fraction circles" prototypes of simple fractions. Of course, a child begins life with material experiences: in number, in vocabulary, in the study of ethics for that matter. But the genius of mathematics is that it organizes raw experience by means of a universe of ideals whose manipulation is for some purposes easier and more illuminating than living the experiences themselves. Yet, rather than giving life to the abstractions, a process essential in every science, the New Jersey standards counts it "essential" that the objects themselves be used in the classroom and indeed confounded with their numerical abstractions. Their only caution in the present case is that all the pieces marked "1/3" are unfortunately the same size, as if that were a hindrance to the truth of their representation of numbers. It is not a hindrance. The day will come when the mere symbol "1/3" will have to replace even the "fraction circles" in describing pizzas and galaxies alike.

Another example of a mathematically mischievous doctrine deriving from a pedagogical insight that has become all but forgotten in the transition is found under New Jersey's Standard 4, Reasoning: ("All students will develop reasoning ability and will become self-reliant, independent, mathematical thinkers"). The "K–12 Overview" section under Reasoning contains the following philosophical note:

> Multiple solutions. There is no single "best" solution; rather, there are many solutions, each with costs and benefits.

Solution to what, one might ask—to a *mathematical* problem? Surely twice two hasn't become ambiguous in recent times? No, the examples show that no such thing is meant. New Jersey offers in this context a "vignette" of a second grade classroom exercise: "Can a dinosaur fit in this room?" Children are to make or find appropriate measurements, define "fit in the room," etc. It looks like a pleasant enough exercise, which teaches among other things that dinosaurs come in several sizes, as do classrooms; and it certainly has no single "best" solution. But the question is not a mathematical one. Even at the second grade level, the mathematical component of a problem should be separated from the empirical part; such separation is later essential in all science, though it is hard in a brief space to indicate its importance. That the "many solutions" doctrine is correct in many human endeavors is plain obvious, and nobody needs to be taught that. But this lesson is not mathematics.

Yet this false (mathematical) doctrine has a history in pedagogy that goes beyond today's unreasonable emphasis on "real-life" problems. In the days of the Three R's, legend has it, children were lined up in rows and taught to shout *viva voce*, or write on their slates, the answers to an interminable list of identical exercises. "Drill and kill" is the derisory phrase used by today's pedagogy to describe this sort of teaching, and if one looks at a common textbook of the year 1910 one does see pages grey with routine exercises of this sort. Whether this implies that classroom activity was equally rigid is hard to say; certainly the other legend, that of the one-room schoolhouse for all grades, implies otherwise. However that might be, the picture is certainly that of "one question, one answer," and the object of most mathematics reform efforts of the past century has been to avoid catechism and to open the mind.

One observable aspect of most non-trivial reasoning is that there is often no single road to the answer. A proof of a Euclidean proposition should not be memorized as if it were a simple fact, for example, but should be analyzed and understood; and a student who finds an alternate proof is deserving of praise. The same is true of all sufficiently complicated problems, and not only in mathematics. But this idea of several roads to a (mathematical) solution of a (mathematical) problem has become conflated with the idea of several solutions to a non-mathematical problem, resulting in the confused notion that mathematical problems may have several answers.

The NCTM insistence on this theme, visible in many state standards, has led to the creation of whole curricula where students are not only invited to create their own mathematical methods but are not told whether what they have created is right. And while the students struggle to create their own rivals to the algorithms mankind has developed over the centuries, they do not get to take advantage of the efforts of their ancestors. While it is true that a rote memorization may be unaccompanied by understanding, it does not follow that it is the cause of mindlessness. Beethoven didn't have to invent the well-tempered scale— it was taught to him; but his imagination survived this quite well. Learning how mankind has already arrived at the single correct solution to a certain well-defined problem is not necessarily going to cripple the math student's imagination. To insist otherwise is false doctrine.

John Adams (1735–1826), a schoolmaster before he took up the law, wrote in his Diary the following entry:

Judging State Standards for K–12 Mathematics Education

> June 1, 1756 Drank Tea at the Majors. The Reasoning of Mathematicians is founded on certain and infallible Principles. Every Word they Use, conveys a determinate Idea, and by accurate Definitions they excite the same Ideas in the mind of the Reader that were in the mind of the Writer. When they have defined the Terms they intend to make use of, they premise a few Axioms, or Self evident Principles, that every man must assent to as soon as proposed. They then take for granted certain Postulates, that no one can deny them, such as, that a right Line may be drawn from one given Point to another, and from these plain simple Principles, they have raised most astonishing Speculations, and proved the Extent of the human mind to be more spacious and capable than any other Science.

Adams was certainly aware that the law employs reason in somewhat the same way, and that a carpenter must measure and calculate elaborately from a simple set of tools. But he shows his astonishment at the extent to which a single line of reason can lead, in this case in the single science of Euclidean geometry. Such an appreciation is lost in a splintered curriculum of the current dispensation. NCTM's standards has no place for an edifice so great as that which astonished Adams and which no classroom full of cooperative children is likely to "discover," even when aided by a guide on the side. First a bit about tilings, then a bit about primes, and then some measurements in the schoolyard, all in the name of "integrating" the strands of a diverse mathematical education.

Other Judgments of the Standards of the States

Well, Braden and I arrived at our list of grades, and the results have been published. Two other organizations have also produced comparable studies of state math standards: the American Federation of Teachers and the Council for Basic Education. Their grades differed from ours. Michigan got a C from AFT, a B+ from CBE, and an F from us (Fordham). A Michigan State official remarked wryly, for the newspapers, that standards seem to be in the eyes of the beholders, as if to say he had no cause for anxiety if the experts could not agree. New Jersey, which got from the CBE the only pure grade of A it gave, received only a C from us, and a D from AFT.

Thus our grades were not merely lower than the others on average, they showed a different spectrum entirely. For another example, where CBE graded New Jersey and New York A and B+, respectively, our Fordham report gave them C and B, respectively. CBE gave Alabama a C (and it gave very few grades that low) where we gave them a B, one of the few states scoring that high. AFT gave Alabama a B as well, though it was quite free with grades that high. Why? There is clearly a difference of "expert" opinion across the country; is it idiosyncratic, principled, careless?

In the case of the AFT we are unable to analyze the reasons for the grades it gave, except to say that it apparently valued most highly the seriousness with which each document was prepared, its definiteness and suitability as a guide to statewide evaluations, and so on, but has little to say about actual curricular or content choices, at least in mathematics. We may also note that the AFT evaluators were few and "in-house," with mathematicians having no hand in the judgment.

In the case of the Council for Basic Education we can say much more because CBE has published its method of judgment in a separate report. CBE says it collected a panel comprising "subject specialists, teachers, parents, and business representatives to help to 'develop' CBE's definition of rigor in standards..." The definition was in fact written by an in-house group apparently called "CBE." There were 81 items it ended with (51 at the eighth grade level and 30 at the twelfth), but rather than being *criteria* by which to judge standards, they were actual statements of content or pedagogical desiderata, of the sort one might expect to find as *entries* in a standards document. These were avowedly drawn from a combination of the two most authoritative sources in the country: the 1989 NCTM standards and the NAEP guidelines for the periodic national diagnostic tests at certain grade levels. The ultimate author of all these statements, for all that CBE winnowed them out a bit, is the math education community, not including mathematicians.

Some of the entries were exactly the sort of thing Braden and I considered unhelpful or vague, though others were reasonable. For example, from the eighth grade level: "Add, subtract, multiply, and divide with rational numbers." This isn't really bad but avoids the question of how far the required algorithms are to be carried. Braden and I downgraded states that insisted on calculator calculations whenever one of the factors was of more than two digits; CBE had no way to notice such a subtlety and in fact found that almost all states satisfied the CBE standard in this case. (CBE's own explanatory text states that it will consider the use of calculators in its next such evaluation.) Others of CBE's 81 items were much more vague: "Ask clarifying and extending questions related to mathematics"; and (under "reasoning"), "Make and test conjectures."

Judging State Standards for K–12 Mathematics Education 53

As a four-word summary of the purpose of all science and philosophy, this last demand, "Make and test conjectures," is not bad. As a guide to teachers and test-makers it is impossibly broad; it won't do without further guidance. In the NCTM standards that phrase appears on page 143 (for grades 9–12) and (slightly varied) on page 61 (for grades 5–8). NCTM follows these headlines with a good deal of commentary, but the CBE evaluators, according to their explanation of method, would give full marks on that "reasoning" item for the four words alone, provided they appeared at the twelfth grade level. At the eighth grade level, also under "reasoning," the following words produce another four-point (full marks) score: "Make and evaluate mathematical conjectures and arguments."

Their scoring method was this: CBE trained panels made up entirely of teachers or former teachers to judge the state standards, giving instructions designed to make the procedure almost automatic and in any case uniform in result when two different panelists graded the same document. The 81 statements, three of which have been quoted above, were taken as a template, and if a state contained one of them verbatim, or essentially verbatim though perhaps divided into parts appearing in different parts of the document, it received a full 4 points. If the corresponding statement, or combination of desiderata, in a state document asked a bit less than CBE did in its own formulation, the state got 3 points. And so on, down to zero if the state standards contained nothing mentioned in the template statement. Finally, the points were added and grades assigned.

Had the system worked perfectly, any state repeating the 1989 NCTM standards plus NAEP benchmarks would have got a near perfect score. CBE did not make any independent judgment second-guessing the experts as to the desirability of these items, though it had necessarily to omit or combine some of the many items to be found among the NCTM and NAEP guidelines and standards. But, even so, the system didn't work perfectly. How imperfect the judgment was, even by template standards, we can only judge by the few examples the CBE report gave to illustrate the way 4, or 3, or 2, or 1, or no points might be given to a standard intended to cover a template item.

One example was this: Under the rubric Data Analysis, Statistics, and Probability is found the twelfth grade benchmark, "Model real-world situations to determine the probabilities of dependent and independent events and compare these experimental probabilities with what would be expected based on theoretical models." Any state essentially repeating this benchmark gets 4 points. A state whose corresponding standard "omits one of the essential concepts or skills or a few minor components," or which "aligns with the framework benchmark, but is written at a lower degree of sophistication," receives a 3. Here the CBE document gives as an example of what would be worth 3 points rather than 4: "Model real world situations to determine the probabilities of dependent events and compare these experimental probabilities with what would be expected based on theoretical models."

Now the 3-point benchmark differs from the template benchmark by omitting only the two words "and independent." That's all. Anyone unacquainted with probability theory might be fooled into thinking something was thereby left out of the shorter statement, but this is not so. It is impossible to understand or use the phrase "dependent events" without also understanding and being able to use the phrase "independent events;" thus, while it is not usual to say it this way, to ask a student to understand and use formulas and insights concerning "dependent events" is asking no less than did the original formulation.

The degree of ignorance or carelessness demonstrated in considering the second of these two formulations less inclusive (or "rigorous") than the first is exhibited even more strikingly in a (doubtless hypothetical) example that CBE said it would have awarded 2 points: For example, the CBE document says, "Explain the difference between a dependent and an independent event and..."

Two points? There is no such thing as an independent event or a dependent event. Dependence is a property of sets of events, not of events singly. Hence any state writing "Explain the difference between a dependent and an independent event..." should be scored zero on grounds of ignorance, carelessness, false doctrine, and pretence of understanding. In this case, having most of the words right is something like omitting a "not" when quoting a theater reviewer for advertising purposes. The conjectured 2 point "standard" would be a positive disservice to its users.

Thus the system of scoring employed by the CBE misses its target in two ways: First, in choosing as benchmarks those published by the authoritative mathematics education establishment of the day, rather than collecting its own judges and having them begin the process from the beginning, using criteria for genuine judgment rather than template exhortations for imitation; and second, in imagining that subjective standards of judgment can be eliminated by its "quantitative" evaluation

Judging State Standards for K–12 Mathematics Education 55

of adherence, item by item, to its own model benchmarks. If the NCTM and NAEP model of standards is accepted without further debate there is no need for state standards at all, and every state would score well by reprinting the relevant parts of documents already in print. But even if this model of judgment were taken as informative, an ignorant judgment of the intellectual distance between a benchmark being judged and the template (as in the case of the notion of "an independent event") renders the numerical scale untrustworthy even as measured against the template. A judgment of whether a mathematical statement makes sense, or is in a correct context, or is worth teaching, can only be made by persons who understand the mathematics in question. The ultimate lesson of the CBE judgments is that they fail because the judges didn't know enough mathematics.

The Need for Mathematicians in School Mathematics

Knowledge of mathematics makes a difference, even in the prescriptions for the earliest grades. This statement needs defending, for it is hard for a member of the general public to believe, concerning such elementary things as the fourth grade rules for arithmetic or the sixth grade calculations with fractions, which everyone knows, that the educator's mathematical ignorance can be a factor in the educational program. Since the arithmetic of the primary grades apparently presents no great intellectual or philosophical challenge, one might imagine the problem of the schools to be a matter of good teaching style, small classes, discipline, and so on, but not a question of what is truth concerning fractions or multiplication.

There are two considerations allied here. As to "what is truth," I would like to assure the reader that fractions are more complicated than one might remember, and that calculators don't render their understanding and applications a whit easier, except for the mindless part of the computations. But more important than the mathematical content of such elementary lessons is their intellectual setting in the classroom. That will critically affect future understanding. In the earliest grades are developed, for example, the baneful reflexes of "getting the answer" from key words of standardized questions and explanations, reflexes that are actually generated by teaching that has no regard for future progress because it proceeds from its own ignorance of what that future can contain. A piano teacher who has never actually played Chopin (let alone

Prokofiev) will give misdirected lessons in finger placement, arpeggios, and scales, and teach "shortcuts" that will return a year or two later to cripple the student's sincerest efforts. That analogy with arithmetic is precise.

Among other things, there is today, despite lip service to the contrary in the NCTM standards and most state standards, a sad misapprehension of the role of deductive reasoning in school mathematics. Teachers and their own mentors in the schools of education all too often consider rigorous mathematics, based on careful definitions and using logically structured arguments, to be "difficult," and *a fortiori* too difficult for the children they will be teaching. But people untaught in mathematical reasoning are not being saved from something difficult; they are, rather, being deprived of something that makes easy all that follows. And this observation applies to children having difficulty with their lessons in fractions even more than to children who begin their intellectual lives with every advantage of educated parents and peaceful environments.

That a proper intellectual setting is needed beyond the mere facts of mathematical information transmission is, of course, realized by the math education community, too; but its estimate of proper intellectual setting is in too many cases faulty through lack of a sufficient understanding of mathematics itself. The standards documents we awarded low grades could not possibly have been passed by any mathematician at the local state university, although their solecisms and inappropriate prescriptions were passed through a multitude of reviews (according to their Introductions) by certified math educators.

That the general public does not appreciate the difference between a mathematician and a math educator choosing curriculum for a school district is understandable, but the difference is enormous and should be understood by the educator and made use of. Mathematicians by definition don't teach in the schools, nor can they administer a school district; but to do either without the scrutiny of mathematicians is like building a house with skilled carpenters and no architect.

Every state has a state university with mathematicians in it, almost across the street from the state education department in many cases. Is it not unconscionable that a governor or a board of education wanting advice on a mathematics curriculum doesn't pick up the telephone and give it a call? They go, if at all, to the school of education, thinking this the obvious place where advice is to be had when in-house experts in the department of education seem to want it.

But in the school of education, most math educators have retreated into a culture of their own, with a language of their own, devoted to pedagogy as if it were a skill that could be applied irrespective of subject. As evidenced in the standards they have been writing, this attention to just one part of the educational process will not do. That this division between the mathematicians and the math educators is partly the legacy of the failed intervention of mathematicians in the era of New Math doesn't make it correct. Every other course has failed too, after all; that is why we are where we are today.

Since the publication of the Fordham Foundation report on mathematics standards, I have received several invitations to review a new edition of the standards whose earlier drafts were the subject of our study, or from states not included in our report. Some I answered, but as I could not participate in every case, and since there is nothing unique about my own expertise anyway, I answered a couple of the others in this way:

> If your standards were composed without the significant participation of mathematicians, let me advise you to go down to your best state university and find a professor of mathematics, at least 40 years old, who is willing to help you. He need not have heard of Piaget and Bruner, and he might very well be of such a personality that you would never trust him in a fifth grade class, but he should be an English-speaking American who himself has gone through our public school system, and he should be a genuine mathematician who has published at least a handful of research articles in the refereed professional journals of pure or applied mathematics. (Not journals of math education; you have such people in your department of education already.) Find out that this mathematician is willing to devote a few days to your project. Give him a copy of the Fordham Foundation report on the state standards to read, with particular attention to the criteria for judgment contained therein, and give him copies of the printed school mathematics standards of California, Ohio, North Carolina, and Japan. (These were the ones we counted best in our report.) Then give him a copy of your own state's draft standards and ask for a written commentary. Then use it.

It is not possible to put school mathematics education in the hands of the mathematicians. If we did, they would cease to be mathematicians. Theirs is another trade. But mathematics education in the schools, while conducted by school teachers, must still be done in a climate of mathematical understanding. At the present time and for the foreseeable future this understanding is insufficient among those who need it. The reasons are complex and are not unique to the present generation, either; they constitute a whole story of their own, and they may never be satisfactorily repaired. But one should not deduce from this that the educators should be exterminated and replaced by mathematicians, or even that mathematicians' ideas of what and how to teach should automatically be credited and put into practice at once.

However that may be, the education community cannot get along without the advice of the mathematicians, and many more mathematicians than now do should learn something of the problems of school mathematics and stand ready to provide that advice. Among other things, the teaching of mathematics to future teachers is done in colleges or universities, but not enough of it is done by mathematicians, who today take more care with the teaching of future engineers and scientists than future teachers, and who today almost never see future elementary school teachers at all. College textbooks in algebra and geometry, and more advanced topics for undergraduates as well, are written by mathematicians. But not enough of them are written with sufficient attention to the needs of future teachers.

To repair all of this is the work of generations. What is most serious at the present time is that the math education community demonstrably needs more such advice now, today, than it thinks it needs. A quick mathematical fix, a Fordham Foundation Report, even a brilliant textbook, will of course not suffice, but beginnings are necessary if never sufficient.

In one of Edgar Allan Poe's stories there is recounted an anecdote about the famous 18th Century Scottish physician, John Arbuthnot. At a dinner party he was seated next to a lady who at some length described to him her symptoms, ending with, "Well then, Doctor, what should I take?" "Take?" said Arbuthnot, "Why, take advice, of course."

Chapter 3

Standards-Based Mathematics Assessments
Appearances May Be Deceiving

Paul Clopton
Research Department, Veterans Affairs San Diego Healthcare System

Wayne Bishop
California State University, Los Angeles

David Klein
California State University, Northridge

Large-scale, standards-based assessments in mathematics have the potential to improve student achievement at a low cost. They enable students to judge their strengths and weaknesses and to monitor their own progress. They can help educators identify successful instructional methods and curriculum materials. They also provide an objective way to determine the worth of a high school diploma and compensate for the effects of years of grade-inflation and social promotion on the utility of traditional indicators of academic success.

However, a fully developed and coordinated assessment system based on standards of learning in mathematics does not guarantee substantial achievement gains. Much depends on the specificity and difficulty level of the standards themselves at each grade level assessed, as well as the design of the assessments and related reporting mechanisms. Tests that emphasize low-level content may not stimulate significant overall student improvement and may even mask a lack of high-level performance. This possibility is suggested by the findings and conclusions of a landmark report issued by the American Federation of Teachers (AFT) in July 1998, *Setting Higher Sights: A Need for More Demanding Assessments for U.S. Eighth Graders*. This report compared the content and rigor of five eighth grade mathematics tests used in the

United States (three commercial tests and two designed for states—one for Texas and one for New York) with the content and rigor of tests used at this educational level in Japan and France.[1] The AFT's findings and conclusions deserve repeating:

> The United States does appear to have a de facto national test in mathematics that is visible in current mathematics test content. Large percentages of students across the country take the same or similar tests of math achievement.
>
> Those tests assess low-level content and difficulty at the eighth-grade level.
>
> Existing tests are incapable of providing information about high-end performance because such performance is not tested.
>
> Since existing tests drive what gets taught and what mathematics materials get published, they cannot move us to achieve our goal of being first in the world.

Our analysis of the content and rigor of the Texas Assessment of Academic Skills (TAAS) mathematics tests used from 1995 to 1998, as we reported earlier,[2] corroborates the findings and conclusions of the AFT report. We analyzed the content and rigor of the Texas mathematics tests for grade 10 (the high school exit test) and the Algebra 1 end-of-course tests, and can now comment more broadly on the Texas assessment system. Its mathematics assessment system has important features. Its design links assessments to achievement standards and curriculum materials. School textbooks align with the contents of the tests. In addition, private industry provides study materials and instruction tailored to the exams. The purpose of this chapter is to present the results of our analysis of the content and rigor of the high school exit tests and the Algebra 1 end-of-course tests used from 1995 to 1998 to describe the model that Texas seems to be using for improving mathematical learning, and to raise questions about the real impact of this model on the mathematics curriculum and student achievement.

Test Policy Issues

Before we turn to our analysis of the items on these tests, we need to comment on the influence of public policy decisions on test construction. Whether or not the effects are explicitly noted, policy decisions that

Standards-Based Mathematics Assessments

guide test development can have a dramatic impact on the level of achievement measured by the tests.

One important policy decision that affects test content is the stipulation that test items represent content offered in current curriculum materials. The rationale is reasonable enough—students are not to be tested on material they have not had the opportunity to study. However, this stipulation may interfere with a criterion-referenced test design (that is, assessments can potentially be kept from addressing what assessors might want to see tested). The stipulation limits the capability of assessments to drive advancements in student learning. Implementation of such a policy decision tends to perpetuate existing deficiencies in the curriculum. Indeed, during the screening of potential TAAS items, a review was conducted to insure that item content was reasonably well addressed by the existing curriculum in Texas.

Another important policy decision is a legislative mandate that state assessments must measure a state's learning or achievement standards. In Texas, the TAAS system had to be designed to measure the achievement indicators in the Texas Essential Elements, the grade-by-grade standards in force until 1998, when they were superseded by newer ones. In effect, this placed an upper limit on the achievement levels measured by the Texas assessment system. A detailed analysis of the mathematics standards cannot be provided here, but we do provide evidence later to suggest that the tests address mathematics at lower levels than in high-achieving countries.

The TAAS design also seems to have achievement goals that are below the grade level expectations of the Essential Elements in mathematics. To judge from the Texas Education Agency's own cross-reference between the grade-level expectations of the Essential Elements and TAAS's Instructional Targets, the Instructional Targets typically map onto grade-level standards that include the standards for the two prior grade levels.[3] For example, the Instructional Targets for grade 8 mapped onto Essential Elements standards for grades 6 and 7 as well as for grade 8. This means that, on average, the test specifications for a particular grade-level test center roughly on standards that are one grade lower in difficulty.

Worse yet, according to this cross-reference provided by the Texas Education Agency (TEA), the items in the TAAS grade 10 exit exam map onto learning standards that are not significantly different from those for the grade 8 test. The relationships between the test objectives and the learning standards in the Essential Elements are summarized in Figure 1.

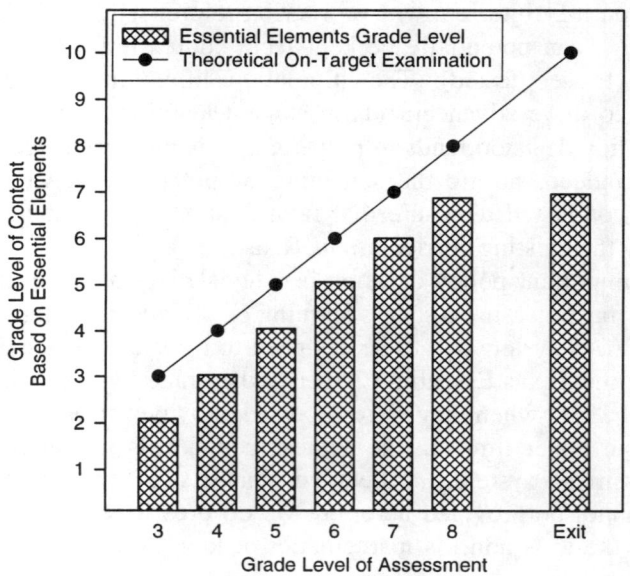

Figure 1

Thus, relative to the Essential Elements, the TAAS grade 8 tests appear to be below grade level and the grade 10 exit tests appear to be similar to the grade 8 tests. However, this observation is based upon information provided by TEA's documents and addresses only the relationship between the Essential Elements and the TAAS tests. This observation does not speak to how use of the Essential Elements may improve overall achievement, and it does not clarify the actual difficulty level of item content. For a better understanding of the expectations embedded in the tests, we provide a detailed analysis of the content and rigor of the grade 10 high school exit tests and the Algebra 1 end-of-course tests.

The TAAS Grade 10 Exit Tests

The high school exit test in mathematics is first given in grade 10, and students must pass it as a requirement for graduation. By law, items in the tests are released to the public after use. Thus it is possible to inspect and evaluate actual item content. Our inspection of 240 test items—60 per year for four years of tests—revealed several areas of mathematical knowledge weakly represented or missing; answers requiring minimal mathematical knowledge; and items too easy for the grade level assessed. Here are examples of the problems we found in each of these three areas.

Areas of Mathematical Knowledge Not Represented or Underrepresented
Since we reviewed tests from four years, any content area with fewer than four items found means that the content area was not tested at all in some years. The omission or paucity of examples in the areas below clearly suggests the limitations in the mathematical content of the exit tests.

- We found only six items requiring the addition or subtraction of fractions with unlike denominators. In each case, the denominators were simple small integers.

- We found no instances of the multiplication of two fractions. There was only one instance of the division of a mixed number by a fraction.

- We found no items on the relationship between repeating decimals and fractions.

- We found no items directly addressing factors of numbers, prime and composite numbers, greatest common factor, or least common multiples.

- For powers, roots, and exponents, we found only two items calling for the squares of integers (15 and 40). Only one item required finding two consecutive integers that bound the root of a number.

- We found only two items dealing directly with the distributive property and asking for the equivalence of two expressions.

- We found no items involving absolute value. Only one item required sorting signed integers; only one asked for the distance between two altitudes, one of which was below sea level; and only one required evaluating an expression containing a sum in which one addend was negative.

- Regarding area and volume, we found only one item asking for the lateral surface area of a cylinder (although the formula was supplied). There was one item asking for the volume of a rectangular prism.

- We found only one item asking for a median, none for a mode.

- Only two items required the solution of an equation. The equations to be solved were: $1.5x - 6 = 4.5$ and $c = \$15 + \$7.50p$ when c is $\$45$.

Answers Requiring Minimal Mathematical Knowledge
Multiple choice items are often difficult to write because students can work backwards to the right answer by using a process of elimination. In other cases, correct answers can be found by methods other than those intended; sometimes too much information is given in the item. The result is that the mathematical knowledge an item is intended to test is not drawn upon by the students. Here are some examples from the TAAS exit tests:

- Students were asked for the ordered pair that represents the intersection of two lines given by linear equations. However, the lines were clearly graphed. This problem thus only required being able to identify a point on a coordinate grid.

- Students were told that two ladders are leaning against a building at the same angle. They were given the lengths of both ladders and the distance from the base of the longer ladder to the wall. (A figure showed that the ground forms a right-angle with the wall.) Students evidently were expected to use similar triangles and proportions to determine the distance from the base of the shorter ladder to the wall. Unfortunately, only one answer choice was reasonable, given the illustration that accompanied the problem. In fact, all incorrect choices exceeded the length of the shorter ladder.

- To solve for unknown lengths of the sides of a right triangle, three items appeared to require the use of the Pythagorean theorem or, at least, the recognition and application of Pythagorean triples. However, the figures were drawn reasonably close to scale and only one response choice for each item was reasonable, given the figure. Thus, students were likely to employ simpler solution strategies than those intended in some of the most difficult content areas addressed in the TAAS exit tests.

Items Too Easy for the Grade Level Assessed

The items discussed above were among the most advanced TAAS items with respect to content. To illustrate the lower end of the spectrum, we list below some of the items showing the lowest level of mathematics content.

> The total attendance recorded at the 1984 Summer Olympic Games in Los Angeles, California, was 5,797,923. What is this number rounded to the nearest thousand?
>
> Mrs. Ramos has a plastic cube on her desk that holds photographs. There is a picture on every face of the cube except the bottom. How many pictures are displayed on the cube?
>
> What is the approximate length of a new pencil before it is sharpened? (Response choices are 1.9 millimeters, 19 millimeters, 19 centimeters, and 1.9 meters.)
>
> Devon's house is on a rectangular block that is 330 yards long and 120 yards wide. What is the distance around his block?
>
> Kenyon is 5 feet 6 inches tall. His sister Tenika is 7 inches taller than he is. How tall is Tenika?
>
> At a restaurant Steve ordered food totaling $6.85. If he paid with a $20 bill, how much change should he receive?

Certainly every high school graduate should be able to solve problems of this nature easily. However, these items do not reflect the kinds of skills and knowledge appropriate for testing high school students. These items are more appropriate for tests in the elementary grades.

Comparisons with the Content of Tests in Japan

In Japan, 12-year-old students are given a mathematics examination that consists of 225 story problems. These items show a depth of content that is striking in contrast to the TAAS exit test items. Some of these items have been translated into English and we reproduce them by permission.[4]

> Jenny wanted to purchase 2 dozen pencils and a pen. Those items cost $8.45 and she did not have enough money. So she decided to purchase 8 fewer pencils and paid $6.05. How much was a pen?
>
> Hose A takes 45 minutes to fill the bucket with water. Hose B can do the same in 30 minutes. If you use both hoses, how long will it take to fill the bucket?
>
> A job takes 30 days to complete by 8 people. How long will the job take when it is done by 20 people?
>
> Bob, Jim, and Cathy each have some money. The sum of Bob's and Jim's money is $18.00. The sum of Jim's and Cathy's money is $21.00. The sum of Bob's and Cathy's money is $23.00. How much money does each person have?
>
> Tom's mother is 30 years old. The three children are 5, 3, and 0 years old. 12 years later, the total age of Tom's mother and father is twice as much as the total ages of all three children. How old is Tom's father?
>
> Ellen baked cookies for the neighborhood children. She gave each child 6 cookies and she had 7 cookies remaining. So, she gave one more cookie to each of the children until she ran out of cookies. She was one cookie short. How many cookies did she bake in total?
>
> It is 6 miles between Joe's house and Larry's house. Joe and Larry started to walk to each other's houses at noon, meeting at 12:30. Joe walked 2 miles per hour faster than Larry. How fast did Larry walk?

Grade Level Ratings of the Items on TAAS's Exit Exams

To assess the target grade level of the TAAS exams against external criteria, individual exit exam items were evaluated for their grade level based on the newly established California Mathematics Standards.[5] These standards provide a desirable benchmark for several reasons. They are perhaps the most highly detailed of all the sets of state mathematics standards, greatly facilitating item evaluation. And they have been judged as the best available mathematics standards among all sets of state standards, even better than those from Japan.[6]

Two of the authors of this chapter independently judged the grade level of every item on the TAAS mathematics exit exams for 1995 to 1998 using California's mathematics standards as the external criterion. There was a high level of rater reliability (r = .813). When they disagreed on the grade level of an item, the grade levels were averaged. The average distribution of the grade levels for all the items is shown in Figure 2.

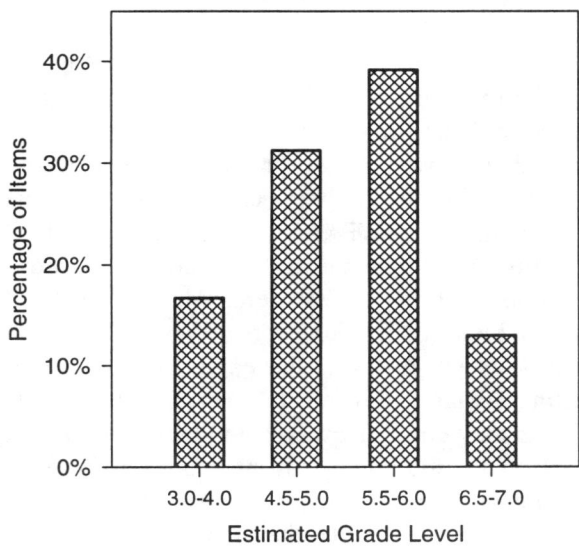

Figure 2

Use of California's Mathematics Standards as the criterion yielded a mean grade level of 5.3 for the items on TAAS's exit exams over the four-year period. The most advanced items on the TAAS exit tests were judged as equivalent to the California grade 7 standards. Admittedly, the California Standards are set at a high level and are roughly equivalent to those in Singapore and Japan. Nonetheless, the low mean grade level of the items on the Texas tests is striking. Moreover, it should be noted that California's standards are designed to complete the content of pre-algebra by grade 7, so that students are ready to study algebra and geometry in grades 8 and above.

The low mean grade level we estimated for the items on the TAAS exit tests raises the possibility that students could pass the TAAS exit test in grade 10 and still not be ready for the study of algebra. This possibility is consistent with the fact that Texas students do better on the TAAS exit tests exams than a more exclusive subset of students do on the Algebra 1 end-of-course test. The problem of a low mean grade level for the items on the TAAS exit tests leads to their insensitivity to high achievement levels.

Insensitivity to High Achievement Levels

The distributions of actual student scores on the TAAS exit exams are given in Figure 3 for three test years. These show strong negative skews, meaning that most students score near the top of the scale range. The presence of a negative skew is not surprising, given that a majority of students get more than 70% of the items correct. However, the skewing is sufficient to confirm that the TAAS tests cannot identify high achievement levels. This means that the tests cannot tell us how well the most able students do, or if there are students who do very well at all. In effect, these tests are blind to high achievement.

There is no way as yet to know the extent to which these ceiling effects are affecting actual achievement—that is, keeping able students from going as far as they could. However, the lack of sensitivity to high achievement levels in the tests does call into question TAAS's capacity to motivate high levels of achievement or instructional objectives. By emphasizing low-achievement levels, they may serve to lower the level of instructional objectives or at least prevent them from advancing.

The use of test scores to address equity issues is also negatively affected by this distribution of scores. There is an incessant relationship between socio-economic status and achievement in mathematics that bodes poorly for the disadvantaged. However, the strength of this relationship will appear to decrease if the top of the achievement distri-

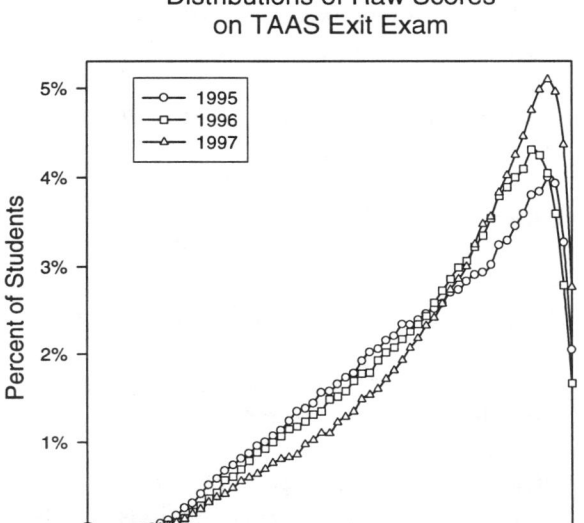

Figure 3

bution is truncated by the use of a test that is too easy. The inherent risk is that data generated by the assessment system would be misleading with respect to equity issues in education.

The Algebra 1 End-of-Course Exams

Students enrolled in introductory algebra must take the Algebra 1 end-of-course test and may use a passing score on this examination to fulfill their high school graduation requirement in mathematics. Our analysis of these tests indicated problems similar to those we found on the grade 10 exit tests—omission of significant content and problems that could be answered with minimal mathematical knowledge.

How the Algebra Items Were Rated

In order to comment on both the content coverage and difficulty level of the Algebra 1 end-of-course exams, we evaluated all the exam items for the four-year period. To accomplish this, we prepared a list of common algebra concepts and skills by looking at several standard pre-algebra and Algebra 1 textbooks and the tests themselves. This list gave us a means to identify objectively the content of each item. Each item also received a 1–5 rating with the following identifiers:

1. *Prior to Pre-Algebra*: roughly fourth or fifth grade mathematics competence without algebra readiness implied.

2. *Pre-Algebra*: standard pre-algebra, as judged against standard texts.

3. *Low Difficulty Algebra*: standard but easy algebra, the level of algebra mastery that might be universally expected.

4. *Moderate Difficulty Algebra*: a more sophisticated level of algebra competence for solution, such as clearing fractions and then solving a linear equation, or finding an obvious least common multiple of the denominators of two rational functions and adding them.

5. *High Difficulty Algebra*: even more sophisticated but still appropriate for a broad screen, end-of-course algebra test, such as clearing the fractions and then solving a resulting quadratic equation, or solving an equation involving radicals that requires squaring both sides twice.

Generally speaking, an item was rated at the pre-algebra level if it appeared that an algebra-ready student who had not yet studied the subject could solve the problem by simply looking at it or by eliminating wrong answer choices rather than using actual algebraic techniques. That was especially true if a student could solve a problem, for example, without clearing fractions, squaring both sides, or factoring as algebraically indicated. Some of the items received higher ratings if response grids rather than a multiple choice format were used.

Standards-Based Mathematics Assessments

How Items Were Distributed

The distribution of item ratings for the Algebra 1 end-of-course exams is indicated in Figure 4. The mean rating across all items was 2.46 on the 5-point rating scale. This means that the exams are a combination primarily of pre-algebra material and easy algebra material.

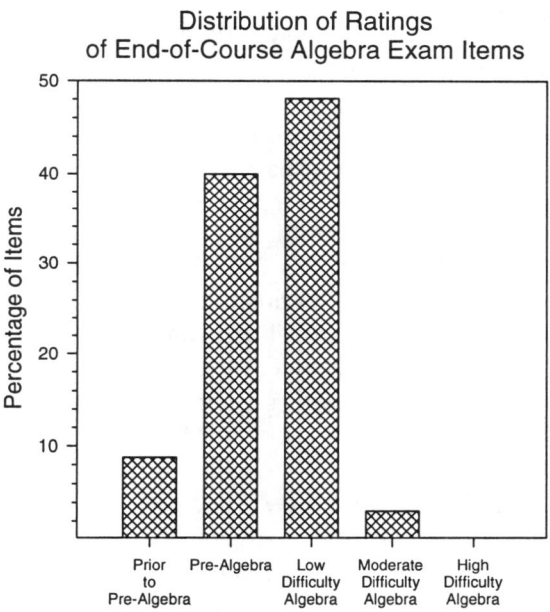

Figure 4

Approximately 14% of the items would have received higher ratings had alternative, less-advanced solution strategies not been available for the item in context (mostly if response grids could replace the multiple choice format). If these alternative solution strategies were not available, the mean rating would increase to 2.62 on the 5-point rating scale.

Missing or Weak Algebraic Content

It is disturbing to see almost no factoring required in the tests. In fact, almost no competency in algebraic simplification or arithmetical operations was tested. Factoring appears to be intended in several items on each test, but it is always possible to get around it, sometimes trivially, as in solution checking, or by using pictures ("factoring blocks") that give the actual factorization in an artificial form. The ability to factor simple polynomial expressions is very helpful in subsequent algebra courses. The omission of factoring in these tests may signal to the state's algebra teachers that symbolic manipulation skill does not matter.

Poorly set up problems constitute another shortcoming. Many problems do not require algebraic understanding for solving them. For example, one item on the 1997 test asks, "What are the solutions to the equation $x^2 + 5x = 36$?" One of the answer pairs offered is "$x = 4$ and $x = -9$." Checking these values by substitution, the student can immediately conclude that this answer pair is correct without solving the equation.

Direct and inverse variation problems such as asking students to find a constant without a given model to follow, or problems such as "How much water should be added to 20 quarts of a 30% solution to obtain a 14% solution," have strong practical application in science and would have been useful questions to include. Integer number problems like the following also test algebra skills in greater depth: "The quotient of the successor of an integer number and one-third of the number is 4. What is the number?"

Standard questions involving linear equations and properties of lines are important but poorly done in the Algebra 1 end-of-course test. Much space on the exam is devoted to graphs and pictures attached to problems which probe only the most superficial understandings of linear equations and their graphs. Much better assessment items for this essential topic are easily available. For example, without graphs or pictures, students could be given two distinct points and asked to find the slope, the y-intercept, and the x-intercept of the line containing them. A more demanding problem would provide coordinates for two pairs of points and require students to find where the respective lines determined by these two pairs of points intersect. Carefully constructed questions of these types would not easily lend themselves to shortcuts such as eliminating wrong answer choices. Moreover, the skills tested by these kinds of questions are fundamental prerequisites for more advanced high school and college courses.

Standards-Based Mathematics Assessments

The following weaknesses were also noted:

- Too many formulas are given. Many, such as the area of a rectangle or the slope of a line, should not be provided.

- There is almost no confirmation of standard algebraic manipulation skills at all, such as by reduction of fractions involving products of monomials.

- Simple applications of the distributive property, such as factoring polynomials, do not appear.

- Word problems whose solutions require the use of algebra are inadequate in number and in depth.

- Test items on linear equations and their graphs are numerous but superficial to the point of being vacuous. No items involving the relationship of slopes of perpendicular lines appear, for example.

- Many items can be answered by eliminating given answer choices or by inspection. Even the simple inclusion of a "none of the above" response choice would improve some items.

- No test item requires students to use the Pythagorean Theorem or even the special case of the distance formula. Correct answers may be deduced by testing the answer choices until the correct one is found.

- No items requiring the simplification of radical expressions were found.

- Scattergram questions are trivial.

- Even when there is an exact and correct answer among the choices, "Which BEST describes..." language is used in the stem.

- The response-grid format (machine-readable numeric response) is insufficiently used. It was down to one item in 1998.

In summary, the tests for the end of Algebra 1 are more algebra readiness tests than they should be. There are no items that require more than the most trivial symbolic manipulation, and many of the items do not actually require any algebra at all. The statistics and probability questions are not at algebra level even with the most generous interpretation.

The Model Used in the Texas Assessment System

To judge from our analysis, Texas has a relatively stable mathematics assessment system in place. That is, the kinds of items tested and their distribution are similar across the four years we examined. There is also evidence to suggest there has been some improvement in student achievement in mathematics. The percentage of students meeting minimum expectations on the TAAS tests has been rising, and the mathematics scores for Texas students in grades 4 and 8 on National Assessment of Educational Progress tests look promising relative to the rest of the country.[7] Because the tests are stable, we may conclude that this improvement is real. But, to judge from international comparisons like the Third International Mathematics and Science Study (TIMSS), this may not be saying much.[8]

An Anecdote

> It was a warm evening in Arizona, and some of the vacationers at the hotel were lounging by the Jacuzzi. A 14-year-old from Texas chanced to strike up a conversation with a math instructor from California. The instructor asked the teenager about the TAAS exam in Texas. "Oh, that..." replied the youth, "well, the math is very easy and that's all they teach us, so it gets pretty boring."

As our analysis consistently shows, Texas assesses mathematics achievement at a low level. Indeed, the content of the high school exit test is more appropriate for the sixth grade. Grade 10 students could pass this test and yet have difficulty with the national exam given to 12-year-old Japanese students. Whether the use of low-level content items on high school level tests stimulates higher overall achievement in mathematics is a critical strategic question. The consequences for many students may be similar to the experience of the teenager in the anecdote above. Use of low-level content items is not consistent with the high expectations for mathematics achievement that are being called for throughout the country.

The risks inherent in using low-level content items in a state assessment seem to be compounded in Texas by its particular emphasis on minimal competence in reporting test results. The TEA uses several methods for reporting TAAS performance data. These include average scale scores, Texas Learning Index scores, Texas Percentile Rank scores, Normal Curve Equivalents, and the percentage meeting minimum expectations. However, the primary focus is on the percentage of students meeting minimum expectations, which is bound to affect the instructional focus in the schools.

The low expectations embodied in the test items for the grade 10 exit test and Algebra 1 test, and the fact that instruction is geared toward these exams, are cause for concern. The results of the analysis of Texas's grade 8 tests (the AFT judged 98% of the items on the grade 8 test as easy) amplify this concern. Moreover, the level of the grade 8 tests suggests that the entire mathematics curriculum up to that point is not demanding enough to promote meaningful achievement in Algebra 1 and in higher level mathematics courses. Algebra is often referred to as a gateway course. Without it, a wide spectrum of career opportunities that depend on mathematics will be denied to students. A recent report from the U.S. Department of Education articulated the need to:

– Provide all students the opportunity to take algebra 1 or a similarly demanding course that includes fundamental algebraic concepts in the 8th grade [to enable students to take] more advanced math and science courses in all four years of high school.

– Build the groundwork for success in algebra by providing a rigorous curriculum in grades K-7 that moves beyond arithmetic and prepares students for the transition to algebra.

– Ensure that all students, parents, teachers, and counselors understand the importance of students' early study of algebra as well as continued study of rigorous mathematics and science in high school.[9]

To judge from our analysis (and that of the AFT), the mathematics assessment system in Texas is not designed to meet these objectives.

Concluding Remarks

The mathematics assessment system in Texas is a comprehensive model but is too highly focused on minimal achievement. The incentives for improvement that accompany the assessment system do not emphasize high achievement sufficiently. The design of the assessments does not permit measurement of high achievement levels. Without a substantial adjustment in the content of the exam items themselves, it seems unlikely that the assessment system will promote development of the curriculum and instruction necessary for students to obtain a rigorous mathematics education.

As the report from the American Federation of Teachers suggests, the shortcomings of mathematics assessment in Texas resemble similar problems across the country. There is no evidence to suggest that a model which focuses on minimal competency can drive overall achievement higher. There is certainly no reason to believe that such a design can help us to catch up to our international competition.

Notes

[1] American Federation of Teachers. *Setting Higher Sights: A Need for More Demanding Assessments for U.S. Eighth Graders*, Washington D.C.: American Federation of Teachers, July, 1998
(http://www.aft.org/Edissues/standardsmathgap/index.htm).

[2] Clopton, P., Bishop, W., & Klein, D. "Statewide Mathematics Assessment in Texas," November 9, 1998 (http://www.mathematicallycorrect.com/lonestar.htm).

[3] Texas Education Agency. Texas Student Assessment Program Technical Digest for the Academic Year 1996–1997
(http://www.tea.state.tx.us/student.assessment/techdig.htm).

[4] *Japanese Math Challenge*: 20 Story Problems Translated from Japan's Junior High Math Tests, Pacific Software Publishing, Inc., Redmond, Washington, 1996
(http://www.japanese-online.com/math/index.htm).

[5] California State Board of Education. The California Mathematics Academic Content Standards for Grades K–12, Prepublication Edition, February 2, 1998
(http://www.cde.ca.gov/board/mcs_intro).

[6] Raimi, R.A. & Braden, L.S. *State Mathematics Standards*, Fordham Report Volume 2, Number 3, March 1998 (http://www.edexcellence.net/standards/math.html).

[7] Shaughnessy, C.A., Nelson, J.E., & Norris, N.A. *NAEP 1996 Mathematics Cross-State Data Compendium for Grade 4 and Grade 8 Assessment*, Washington D.C.: National Center for Education Statistics, January 27, 1998
(http://nces.ed.gov/nationsreportcard/96report/98481.pdf).

[8] Mathematics Achievement in the Primary School Years (June 10, 1997), Mathematics Achievement in the Middle School Years (November 20, 1997), and Mathematics and Science Achievement in the Final Year of Secondary School (February 24, 1998), TIMSS International Study Center (http://wwwcsteep.bc.edu/TIMSS1/Achievement.html).

[9] "Mathematics Equals Opportunity" (White Paper Prepared for U.S. Secretary of Education Richard W. Riley), U.S. Department of Education, October 20, 1997 (http://www.ed.gov/pubs/math/).

Chapter 4

National Science Standards: Where is the Evidence Supporting Them?

Stan Metzenberg
California State University, Northridge

In December 1998, newspapers reported a remarkable corporate acquisition: The company that publishes *Cliff's Notes* was being acquired by the company that publishes the *"For Dummies"* books for $17.2 million.[1] *Cliff's Notes* are the small yellow and black booklets that explain literary works and are widely available in college bookstores. For example, Hemingway's *Old Man and the Sea* is condensed to about 50 pages in the *Cliff's Notes* series, and Tolstoy's *War and Peace* is distilled to a little over 100 pages. What a tremendous refinement! I must confess to having used a few of these study aids in school myself, partly to overcome being mystified by literary criticism, but mostly so that I might devote more time to more exciting subjects, such as science and mathematics. The *For Dummies* books are also yellow and black but consist of titles such as *DOS For Dummies*, *The Internet For Dummies*, and *Everyday Math For Dummies*. The people buying them are not "dummies," but they may want to devote more time to other educational pursuits, such as literary criticism.

All adults use academic crutches from time to time, whether it means purchasing an English translation for *The Iliad*, using a calculator to compute a simple sum, or relying on a spelling checker. Bringing *Cliff's Notes* and the *For Dummies* books under the same publishing roof brings a bit of symmetry to the world and underscores the fact that all of us have academic frailties. None of us can remember, or can expect to remember, everything that was taught to us as children, but, oddly, that has been the core of a significant and long-lasting debate in science education. It has again become fashionable to decry the amount of time that is supposedly wasted in K–12 on the detailed facts and concepts that few people remember when they are adults. For example, many high school students learn how to balance chemical reaction equations, but few are likely to have retained the requisite knowledge and skill twenty years later. It is not obvious to many people that analytical thinking as well as understanding a particular body of knowledge are developed by the formal study of chemistry or other sciences, and that students are bettered by such study, whether or not they remember everything they have learned.

A pitched battle has been waged for years by science educators in schools of education who believe that recall of facts plays too large a role in the science curriculum and who want more emphasis on the understanding of large concepts. The distinctions are largely artificial, however, because scientific concepts must be constructed on a foundation of fact, and a familiarity with at least a few specific details is necessary to trigger understanding of scientific principles. The amount of factual detail needed for science learning is something many students dislike, and the words of an 1832 essay by John Stuart Mill might ring true for some today:

> Modern education is all *cram*—Latin cram, mathematical cram, literary cram, political cram, theological cram, moral cram. The world already knows everything, and has only to tell it to its children, who, on their part, have only to hear, and lay it to rote (not to *heart*). Any purpose, any idea of training the mind itself, has gone out of the world.[2]

In his essay, Mill celebrates the genius of Aristotle and Plato (e.g., "wisdom was not something to be prattled about, but something to be done") and indicts nineteenth-century men for finding it easier to remember than to think. In Mill's view, students should study nature directly. If he were alive today, one might assume that he would be a strong advocate of "hands-on" science in the classroom. It is doubtful, however, that Mill would approve of modern attempts to water down the curriculum, to substitute "big ideas" and "themes" in science for a solid foundation of substantive content, or to think one can get to the big ideas without the foundation. A science standard, such as "By the end of the 5th grade, students should know that [in] something that consists of many parts, the parts usually influence one another,"[3] would probably strike Mill as philosophical prattle. As he stated in 1867, "It is surely no small part of education to put us in intelligent possession of the most important and most universally interesting facts of the universe, so that the world which surrounds us may not be a sealed book to us, uninteresting because unintelligible."[4]

One reason that educational combat may never cease is that the middle ground is muddy and unstable. In his 1956 *Taxonomy of Educational Objectives*, the cognitive psychologist Benjamin S. Bloom attempted to bring precision to terms such as knowledge, comprehension, and analysis.[5] Interpretations of Bloom's *Taxonomy* often treat knowledge, as expressed by the verb "to know," as a fairly worthless and lower-order form of recall. Bloom's position was less judgmental: "The intellectual abilities represented in the taxonomy assume knowledge as a prerequisite."[6] To put it another way, one cannot engage in higher-order thinking—by analyzing, evaluating, or applying ideas—before one *knows* the specifics, terminology, and facts of a field.

In recent years, science education has become a casualty of rhetoric. The moderate position that students should have laboratory experiences in school, a matter upon which most scientists would agree, is twisted by educators into the dogmatic prescription that all learning should be "hands-on" and that direct instruction has no value. The reasonable notion that students should be actively engaged in class, not asleep, is distorted into radical constructivism, a view that scientific knowledge can emerge only from the learner's personal experience and is therefore not independent of the observer. The traditional goal of wanting students to become capable of critiquing scientists' ideas is reshaped into postmodernism, a philosophy that disputes the truth of scientific knowledge itself. A stress on "higher-order" thinking is used as a way to undercut the need for foundational knowledge. It is difficult to chart a reasonable course through waters so badly muddied. Even with a clear direction in mind, it is easy to misunderstand friend and foe alike.

The influence of the utilitarian thinking exhibited by those who oppose the learning of details is apparent in the national science standards created by Project 2061 of the American Association for the Advancement of Science (AAAS). Its document, entitled *Benchmarks for Science Literacy*, emphasizes the teaching of "big ideas" or "themes" in science and avoids mention of such instructional practices as direct instruction that promote the learning of detailed facts and concepts.[7] Nevertheless, the document does not point to credible research evidence to support the approach it does recommend. The flaws in the research used to support the AAAS standards document will be the focus of this chapter. A standards document in science that fails to offer a substantial body of evidence to support its pedagogical approach to science education ought to raise doubts about its educational worth.

The Problematic Research Base for the AAAS Standards

The AAAS Project 2061 sought to define the core scientific facts and concepts that all adults should have learned and to reduce the science curriculum for all K–12 students to just those concepts and facts. This principle is stated in its *Benchmarks for Science Literacy*, a document written primarily by science educators: "Curriculum reform should be shaped by our vision of the *lasting* knowledge and skills we want students to acquire by the time they become adults... If we want students to learn science, mathematics, and technology well, we must radically reduce the sheer amount of material now being covered."[8] These educators believe that if students are taught only what they supposedly need to know in science, there would be a savings in curriculum time that could be better spent developing *true understanding*. With fewer "factoids" to memorize, so their theory goes, students' understanding and enjoyment of science would also increase. The important question for science curriculum developers, school administrators, and other educational policy makers to ask is whether the AAAS standards document points to a solid base of research evidence as support for this theory and their standards.

Benchmarks for Science Literacy claims that "research on students' understanding and learning bears significantly on the selection and grade placement of the benchmarks."[9] However, over half of the citations in the sections of the document encompassing the physical and biological sciences are not of peer-reviewed studies. Of the 92 separate citations in these sections, 42 are of chapters in books. Five others are of sources unavailable to the public, either because they were presentations at educational conferences or in one case because the journal is not listed in international library databases.[10] Fewer than half (45) are of peer-reviewed studies published in professional journals. Further, as I show below, most of the peer-reviewed studies cited in these sections are flawed, albeit in different ways. My discussion in this chapter of the peer-reviewed research used by the AAAS to support its standards for the physical and biological sciences is based on an examination of 41 of the

45 cited journal articles; the remaining 4 articles could not be obtained. I discuss them according to the chief flaw I found in them.

Little pedagogical value in the knowledge explored
In a number of studies, the kind of scientific knowledge the authors sought to explore in students has little instructional value. In a New Zealand-based study, for example, a few dozen adolescent students were shown cards during interviews and asked whether the illustrations were of animals and how they could tell.[11] Shown a picture of a cat, for example, students readily identified it as an animal, giving a variety of informal reasons, such as it "has four legs," "has fur," "is a pet," or "makes noise." Some students did not apply the word "animal" correctly in a formal sense (e.g., by limiting the term to four-legged, land-dwelling mammals), although, as the author points out, the term has both everyday and scientific uses. When the author extended the study to adults at a teachers' college, many of the same misstatements and misidentifications were recorded. The problematic aspect of this study is not that some adolescents and adults incorrectly believe that spiders are insects, or that insects are not animals, or that humans are not animals, but rather that the kind of scientific knowledge explored by the author is not pedagogically very useful. It would have been far more valuable to find out whether students knew some basic facts about the diets, habitats, and behaviors of a variety of animals as the basis for further learning of anatomy, physiology, and ecology. Moreover, although the author was trying to explore these students' understanding of classification schemes—the study is cited in *Benchmarks for Science Literacy* as showing that "upper elementary-school students tend not to use hierarchical classification" and "may have difficulty understanding that an organism can be classified as both a bird and an animal"—the data in the study are not inconsistent with an understanding of hierarchical classification. It is likely that many students in the study misinterpreted "animal" because of the differences between its colloquial and scientific meanings. This type of error has little significance for instruction and does little to illuminate the long-term needs of students.

Testing students on their understanding of "animal" is a popular research exercise because the question is so simple on the face of it. It assumes that a person who does not come up with the precise answer expected by the author (e.g., that an animal is a heterotrophic, multicellular organism having cells lacking a cell wall) has a profound gap in their understanding. In a study of 42 fifth- and eighth-grade students, the authors asked the question: "Can you name five animals?"[12] Most students replied with everyday examples, such as dog, cat, bird, horse, and rabbit. The authors of the study concluded: "In the case of the concept 'animal,' students of all age groups tend to subscribe to a highly restricted viewpoint, applying the label principally to familiar vertebrates." Apparently, students were judged to have a "highly restricted viewpoint" because they had not answered with a diverse list, such as starfish, tapeworm, butterfly, snail, and wolf. But even if every student had delivered such a clever answer as this, it is highly doubtful that the students would have been praised for having a broad conceptual understanding. The animal kingdom cannot be adequately described with any five examples, and one suspects that the authors would then have objected that sponges, anemones, earthworms, nematodes, and lobsters had been entirely neglected! I found in my own informal survey that professors of biology at several universities usually answer the "five-animal question" as schoolchildren do (i.e., dog, cat, bird, horse, and rabbit)! It may be important to test a young child's ability to name five animals, but fifth- and eighth-grade students are well beyond that point. More important, the question had a nuance that the authors did not reveal to their subjects—that the five animals in the answer should come from more than one phylum.

In some cases, the questions posed in studies cited by *Benchmarks for Science Literacy* seem designed not for their potential instructional value but for promoting a different educational philosophy. College students in Australia, for example, were asked why they thought fire was not alive, and their responses were categorized as passive, behavioral, functional, structural, or environmental. The author was critical of students who provided passive or glib responses and were not able to "use their knowledge." She commented:

> These observations suggest that the majority of these students have rote-learned characteristics of living things. Perhaps if they had been specifically asked to plan an experiment to test for the presence of respiration, or to name the molecule which is capable of self-replication [sic], these students would have been able to do so. But do such questions reveal meaningful scientific learning? The difficulty these students appear to have is not in 'knowing' but in being able to 'use' their knowledge, out of the context of schools, exams, and textbooks.[13]

Most teachers would be pleased if their students could answer a question on a test asking them to "plan an experiment to test for the presence of respiration," but the author's belief that such questions do not reveal "meaningful scientific learning" is especially problematic, given that her research question, "Why is the fire not alive," seems to be viewed as a superior alternative. Suggesting what is meaningful scientific learning can be useful to others, but the author has not set a standard that would be widely shared by scientists.

Questions that ignore the difference between the scientific and colloquial meanings of words
Many questions used in the studies cited in the AAAS document are problematic because they are informally stated and use key words with differing scientific and colloquial meanings. Informal questions are unlikely to be answered in a way that is scientifically accurate and acceptable to the researchers, even though students may understand the underlying science. The following questions illustrate this problem.

> How do you define "food" for a bean plant?[14]
>
> Can you name five animals?[15]
>
> What does energy mean to you?[16]
>
> To begin with, out of the 'things that surround us in the world,' which are matter and which are not?[17]
>
> If you were to walk for many days, would you ever reach the end of the earth?[18]

A student may struggle with the definition of "food for a bean plant," for example, because "plant food" is a supplement one can buy at a store. "Food" as a scientific concept, however, has a different meaning. "Earth," too, has several meanings. It is defined in the dictionary as both "the planet on which human beings live, the third planet from the sun," and "the land surface of the world; ground; soil; dirt." If a student is thinking of one of the latter meanings, then walking to the end of the earth may mean nothing more than taking a trip to the beach. On the other hand, a question such as "What does energy mean to you" begs for an informal response and is unlikely to evoke a scientific answer.

Questions that may elicit a philosophical interpretation
Some questions, such as the following examples, seem to encourage a philosophical interpretation rather than a scientific response. It should be noted that the question about the nature of a shadow was asked of children.

> Do you know what shadow is? Could you tell me whether it is material or not?[19]
>
> Do you believe the theory of evolution to be truthful?[20]
>
> [Agree or disagree] Human beings are different from nonliving things because they possess a soul.[21]

Questions that are unanswerable
At times, students are presented with questions that cannot be answered, as in the examples below:

> An electric drill, working at a rate of 500 watts, is used to drill a hole in a piece of wood. How much work could it do in 20 minutes?[22]
>
> [Interview task] Point in the direction you would look to see people in far-off countries like China.[23]

The question about the electric drill cannot be solved with the information given, since both work and heat will be generated by the electrical energy; in the discussion of this problem, the author appears to have taught children to use a mental model that violates the Second Law of Thermodynamics. It is also absurd to ask a child to point in the direction he would look to "see" people who cannot possibly be seen.

Questions with more than one correct interpretation
In some studies, students are presented with questions for which multiple answers are possible, even though the researchers considered only one as correct. For example, in one study students were tested on a question that the researchers posed as a case of biological adaptation:

> The Arctic Fox lives well at very low temperatures. It has a thick coat of fur, which is obviously very useful in the fox's survival. Can you explain how you think this came about originally?[24]

National Science Standards

The researchers saw a slow evolutionary process as the answer. But another answer is plausible. Dog fanciers know that it is cruel to suddenly put huskies outside on a cold night in January if they have not been gradually exposed to the weather over a period of months. The extent of fur growth in huskies (and foxes) is a matter of accommodation to the cold, much as humans accommodate to sunlight by suntanning. And we see this reasoning reflected in the explanation for the arctic fox's coat provided by a student in the study:

> Well, it's just preparing itself to leave its mother and live in the cold itself... and when it's old enough to leave it needs something to keep it warm, so it grows a thick coat, so it can keep warm while it's out looking for food.

The authors criticized explanations which had the foxes responding to adverse environmental conditions, but these answers were scientifically accurate.

Researchers' misconceptions

Some authors of research papers appear to hold scientific misconceptions themselves, even though children's misconceptions are the usual object of study. In a previously cited example, the author seems to hold the erroneous view that DNA is a self-replicating molecule.[25] Another author explored the following question: "Every living thing (including ourselves) uses oxygen. How is it that the oxygen is never used up?" This author was ignoring anaerobes.[26]

In another study, a group of grade 10 students in Germany were asked to discuss the cooling of a hot piece of metal. The researchers observed in their article that:

> Some students appeared to be unaware that every cooling process requires an interaction partner. It appears that they held the idea that bodies may cool spontaneously without other (colder) bodies being involved.[27]

The researchers are incorrect. Objects may cool by infrared radiation, but this phenomenon does not require any form of "interaction partner." For example, when a person feels the warmth of the sun on his cheek, it is because his face has absorbed a bit of energy radiated by the sun. There is no requirement, however, that before the sun can release infrared light there must be an exposed cheek (or other "interaction partner") to absorb the energy. The German syllabus indicates that the students had learned about heat radiation in seventh grade, so they may well have been prepared for the question.

Interestingly, the error in the study was repeated in *Benchmarks for Science Literacy*, which in citing the study states:

> Middle- and high-school students do not always explain heat-exchange phenomena as interactions. For example, students often think objects cool down or release heat spontaneously, that is, without being in contact with a cooler object.[28]

Errors in interpretation

In a study testing the knowledge of a group of first-year physics students at Monash University in Australia, students were given a scenario in which a spring balance is being used to weigh a bucket of sand at different altitudes (i.e., near sea level *vs*. the top of Mt. Everest).[29] The students were asked to indicate how the position of the balance pointer might change on a scale, and the authors favored an answer in which the weight of the sand decreases slightly with altitude. Although that principle is correct, the actual percentage change in weight upon moving to the top of Mt. Everest would be too small for the student to mark on the scale provided with the answer sheet.[30] In *Benchmarks for Science Literacy,* this study is cited with the following comment: "Even after a physics course, many high-school students believe that gravity increases with height above the earth's surface."[31] This citation is doubly misleading because no students expressed such a misconception about gravity in their written comments in the original study as published, and none of the students in the study was in high school!

Students' understanding of inheritance has also been misinterpreted in the research literature and misrepresented in *Benchmarks for Science Literacy.* It states: "It may not be until the end of 5th grade that some students can use arguments based on chance to predict the outcome of inherited characteristics from observing those characteristics in the parents."[32] There are three citations following this allegation. The first two are studies of student understanding *prior* to instruction and are therefore not informative about what students can learn.[33] One may wonder whether the students understood all the questions in one of them. In it, students were presented with a task in which they were shown six photographs of beagles with variations in coat color and marking, following which the students were asked the question: "Do similar differences occur in plants?" The authors drew the following conclusion:

National Science Standards

> The interview transcripts show quite clearly that almost all students in the study recognized that variation among animals of the same species was quite "normal," quite "usual." However, a sizeable proportion (17%) of responses indicated that variation in plants does not occur as a normal rule; this finding confirms an observation by Okeke and Wood-Robinson (1980) that 40 per cent of their sample of 16–18 year olds did not seem to believe that plants were capable of sexual reproduction.[34]

This was a great opportunity for a misunderstanding. Even if a student did not think that plants could vary in the same way as beagles, perhaps never having observed a plant with a fur coat, it is not logical to conclude that he also doesn't believe plants capable of sexual reproduction!

The third citation related to students' understanding of inheritance was a study based on interviews with Canadian children between the ages of 7 and 13. Two of the interview questions, asked in sequence, are as follows:

> 14. If a white male dog and a black female dog have six puppies, what colour would the puppies be?
> 15. Which one of the parent dogs do you think will give more colour to the puppies?[35]

Students answered Number 14 in a variety of ways, usually reporting that the puppies would be a mixture or combination of black and white, or all black. A geneticist would not attempt to answer such a question without knowledge of the genetic loci and alleles involved in the problem, but the student responses are certainly reasonable. Most of the students answered Number 15 by saying the mother dog would give more color to the puppies, which is also forgivable considering that the male dog is identified as being white. What is not forgivable is the authors' interpretation of these answers. The authors generalized their findings (i.e., went beyond the specific context of white male and black female dogs) to say that "a large number of the children thought the mother would contribute more to the genetic make-up of the offspring than the father." If the white dog had been female and the black dog male, one suspects that the authors would have come to the opposite conclusion!

Questions whose answers may be misinterpreted
Many of the research papers cited in *Benchmarks for Science Literacy* rely on highly subjective interpretations of student responses gathered from open-ended interviews. Even if the question to the student is

reasonable, misinterpretation of the answer is a constant danger in this type of methodology. In one study, a student's casual reply that "the sun goes down in the West" as an explanation of why it gets dark at night might mark the student as someone who believes the medieval idea that the sun goes around the Earth each day.[36] In her article, the author writes: "I describe those theories that children use to account for a number of the easily observed astronomical events and indicate how these theories can resemble ideas supported in the Middle Ages and how they can undergo a similar evolution during their development."

The summary comment in another study further illustrates this danger:

> Lest we forget: the pupils participating in this study had all been routinely examined on completion of the topic, and teachers had been reasonably satisfied. Nevertheless, an unorthodox method of testing for concept formation opened up a 'veritable can of worms' of misconceptions and dysfunctional information.[37]

In this study, students were asked: "What is the function of water in the living body?" The following answers were recorded as "inadequate" by the authors.

1. Water is the source of energy.
2. There are many enzymes in water and that is why one must drink great amounts.
3. The body is held firm by the pressure of water (something like turgor).
4. Everything in the cell is floating in water and can function only when floating in water.

These student answers are clearly informal, but one could make a more carefully stated argument for nearly every one. The first answer probably reflects the student's informal use of the word "energy," since a sip of water may make his body feel more energetic. On the other hand, water must be present in a body for chemical bond energy to be collected from digested food, and so it might not be unreasonable to label water as a "source" of energy. Speculation about such nuances of language should contribute to the authors' conclusions and the readers' interpretation of the results. Since the study was conducted in Israel, and the questions and answers were probably originally in Hebrew, it is reasonable to wonder whether the English translation is a faithful representation of the students' concepts. The second student answer above is a misconception that would have been revealed by traditional testing methods, but the third and fourth student answers are perfectly valid, though informally stated. The research question is fundamentally flawed because of its level of generality. One might just as easily try to answer such a question as "What is the function of the vowel letters in literature?" Water is involved in nearly every process at a molecular, cellular, and organismal level, and so a general question about its "function" is more philosophical than scientific. A clever student of biochemistry might provide an equally general answer, such as "hydrogen bonding is the function of water in the living body," but this would probably be viewed cynically as an indication of "rote-learning." Although the authors' goal was to uncover misconceptions that would not be revealed by traditional testing, the selection of research questions whose answers are not clearly interpretable as "inadequate" lessens the credibility of the results.

The open-ended interviews in many of the research studies are modeled after the clinical interview methodology of Jean Piaget. Piaget's methodology and conclusions have been questioned by many researchers.[38] For example, in his well-known experiment on number conservation, Piaget assembled two identical rows of objects, such as marbles or bottles, with each row containing the same number of objects spread out in the same way. When three- to four-year-old children were asked whether the (identical) rows were the same or whether one had more, they tended to answer correctly. When the pattern was then changed, by adding objects to one of the rows while pushing the objects closer together (so that the more populous row was the narrower one), the same question posed to the child yielded an incorrect answer. To Piaget this result was an indication that the children did not have a sense of number and helped him develop his theory that children pass through discrete developmental stages of cognition.

Stanislas Dehaene reviewed research on whether students really understand questions of the type posed by Piaget and cited an example in which palatable treats (M&Ms) were substituted for marbles in the number conservation experiment. When children were allowed to pick and consume one of the two rows, they were usually not fooled and selected the row with the greater number. Dehaene commented on the probability of error in the interpretation of Piaget's original experiment:

> Let us suppose for a moment that the numerical equality of the two rows is obvious to [the children]. They must find it quite strange that a grown-up would repeat the same trivial question twice. Indeed it constitutes a violation of ordinary rules of conver-sation to ask a question whose answer is already known by both speakers.

> Faced with this internal conflict, perhaps children figure out that the second question, although it is superficially identical to the first, does not have the same meaning.[39]

Some questions in the studies cited in the AAAS document may have unintentionally caused the same type of conflict in the students' thinking. Here are several examples: "Is the fire an animal?"[40] "Which is larger: a dog or an elephant?"[41] "What is below the earth? Which way do we look to see the earth?"[42] Any of these may strike young children as a peculiar questions to be asked by an adult, and they may assume that the obvious answer is incorrect. Children may have far more sophistication than they are given credit for.

The questioning of children in an interview setting may also be a source of intimidation. In one study, the following "conflict" is established:

> The child is given a folded sheet of paper on which to draw a picture of himself standing on the ground. The paper is then turned over, and the child is asked to draw the earth in space, showing the sun, moon, and stars. Then the interviewer opens the paper and asks, 'Why did you draw the ground flat here and the earth round there?' If the child fails to relate the flat ground and ball-shaped earth, the response is classified as Shape Level 1.[43]

If the children (some of whom were in the third grade) did not defend their drawings during interrogation, the authors classified their belief as "Shape Level 1," which was translated as "the earth is flat." All but two of the children said that the earth was round or ball-shaped, and their most commonly-cited evidence for this was pictures of the earth taken from outer space. What is astonishing is that the authors discounted this knowledge, commenting: "Since this question required only recall, it was not used to characterize how the children actually reasoned about the earth's shape." As a consequence of the scoring rubric, 30% of the third grade students (N = 30) were classified as holding the belief that the earth is flat.

Perhaps recall was discounted by these researchers because it was based on pictures, culturally shaped information now considered as a source of bias by postmodernists. We find this way of thinking in another study that sought to "investigate the nature of children's intuitive knowledge about the shape of the earth and to understand how this knowledge changes as children are exposed to the culturally accepted

National Science Standards 93

information that the earth is a sphere."[44] Most scientists would not feel the need to insert the qualifier "the culturally accepted information" to any statement that "the earth is a sphere," believing that the shape of the Earth does not depend on culture. But postmodernism is not unknown in science education today.

Piaget's theory has an unfortunate corollary. Since children are allegedly unable to comprehend matters that are beyond their developmental stage, teaching the material prematurely can only lead to unpleasant results. This philosophy is foundational for *Benchmarks for Science Literacy*: "Overestimation of what students can learn at a given age results in student frustration, lack of confidence, and unproductive learning strategies, such as memorization without understanding."[45] The philosophy also pervades many of the studies in their research base. For example, in a study on the ideas about matter that are held by children between the ages of 6 and 13, the author comments:

> It seems that there is no point in teaching the particulate nature of matter when students don't know what we mean by matter and don't believe that gas, for example, is material... There is also no point in teaching biological concepts such as photosynthesis, breathing, nutrition, etc., when students don't regard biological objects as material.[46]

Piaget's influence on science educators does not seem to lead to or support high academic expectations for all children.

The students used in the research

The numbers of students used in studies cited in *Benchmarks for Science Literacy* tended to be extremely low. In the previously mentioned genetics paper, only 12 students were below grade 5. Among the 41 papers reviewed for this chapter, representing nearly the entire collection of cited peer-reviewed publications, there were just over 4000 research subjects in grades K–12, with a median number of 60 subjects per study. Many of the studies were conducted on college-age students, though they are cited misleadingly in *Benchmarks for Science Literacy* as representing younger students. Approximately three quarters of the research subjects were from countries other than the United States (Israel, New Zealand, Australia, England, Germany, Italy, and Canada), and thus the cultural and schooling backgrounds of the students may be a significant factor. There were only four papers using U.S. children in the K-5 grade span, and in total they represented only 276 research subjects.

It does not seem reasonable to design a national education policy for the elementary schools in the United States using such sparse and inadequate information.

Concluding Remarks

Finding reliable research on which to base educational policy in science is an extremely difficult task.[47] The U. S. House of Representatives Committee on Education and the Workforce released a report entitled *Education at a Crossroads: What Works and What's Wasted in Education Today* that decried the extensive number of federal education programs (approximately 760) and the lack of data on their effectiveness.[48] This point was reiterated by a major science policy report from the U.S. House Committee on Science entitled *Unlocking Our Future— Toward a New National Science Policy*, which estimated that only 0.01% of federal education expenditures are for research in education.[49] The reliability of the research being generated through that funding is a matter that was not discussed, but it is critical.

Not only are the AAAS standards based on predominantly flawed research, so, too, by implication are the National Science Education Standards (NSES), the final version of which was issued in 1996 as the fruit of a collaborative effort between the National Science Teachers Association (NSTA) and the National Research Council (NRC).[50] That is because the NSTA and NRC used *Benchmarks for Science Literacy* as a model and adopted much of its philosophy. The NSES document has had a large influence on state and local standards documents. Moreover, both standards documents are strongly supported by the National Science Foundation through its "systemic reform" programs. Yet, neither standards document presents a body of credible evidence that meaningful scientific literacy is possible without knowledge of many scientific facts and concepts. The research they cite does not show that students can develop a meaningful understanding of big ideas or themes in a science curriculum that has de-emphasized the learning of detailed facts and concepts.

Educational policy makers need to consider these national science standards documents with a critical eye. In devising local and state standards, it is important to decide what scientific knowledge and skills all students should possess and to define them clearly. To do so, it is perhaps more important to decide whether standards should serve chiefly as baseline expectations for all students (i.e., as minimum competencies) or whether they should serve as a way to challenge the majority of our students to do better, even if all students cannot meet them. In addition, although well-designed research can help identify science topics not easily learned by students, studies should be viewed with suspicion if they suggest that teachers should draw on only a few specific instructional approaches and not the full range of pedagogical approaches available. Policy makers should save their deepest level of skepticism for national movements in science education that claim to represent the best interests of all students but show no body of credible research evidence to support their claims.

Notes

[1] Gross, E. "Classic Purchase." *New York Daily News*, December 9, 1998, p. 39.
[2] Mill, J.S. "On Genius." *In Autobiographies and Literary Essays by John Stuart Mill*, ed. J.M. Robson. Vol. I. Toronto: University of Toronto Press, 1981, pp. 329–339.
[3] American Association for the Advancement of Science Project 2061. *Benchmarks or Science Literacy*. New York: Oxford University Press, 1993, p. 264.
[4] John Stuart Mill's 1867 Inaugural Address to the University of St. Andrew, quoted in: G.E. DeBoer, *A History of Ideas in Science Education*. New York: Teachers College Press, 1991, p. 8.
[5] Bloom, B.S. *Taxonomy of Educational Objectives, Handbook I*, Cognitive Domain. New York: David McKay Co., Inc., 1956.
[6] Bloom, p. 33.
[7] *Benchmarks, Op. Cit.*
[8] Ibid, p. xi.
[9] Ibid, p. xiii.
[10] An article in the journal *Chemica Didactica* is cited in *Benchmarks for Science Literacy*, but the journal is not listed in either the PubList, which consists of 150,000 international journals, or OCLC WorldCAT.
[11] Bell, B.F. "When Is an Animal Not an Animal?" *Journal of Biological Education* 15 (1981): 213–218.
[12] Trowbridge, J.E. & J.J. Mintzes. "Students' Alternative Conceptions of Animals and Animal Classification." *School Science and Mathematics* 85 (1985): 304–316.
[13] Brumby, M.N. "Students' Perceptions of the Concept of Life." *Science Education* 66 (1982): 613–622.
[14] Anderson, C.W., T.H. Sheldon, & J. Dubay. "The Effects of Instruction on College Nonmajors' Conceptions of Respiration and Photosynthesis." *Journal of Research in Science Teaching* 27 (1990): 761–776.
[15] Trowbridge & Mintzes, *Op. Cit.*

[16] Kesidou, S. & R. Duit. "Students' Conceptions of the Second Law of Thermodynamics—An Interpretive Study." *Journal of Research in Science Teaching* 30 (1993): 85–106.

[17] Lee, O., et al. "Changing Middle School Students' Conceptions of Matter and Molecules." *Journal of Research in Science Teaching* 30 (1993): 249–270.

[18] Vosniadou, S. "Designing Curricula for Conceptual Restructuring: Lessons from the Study of Knowledge Acquisition in Astronomy." *Journal of Curriculum Studies* 23 (1991): 219–237.

[19] Stavy, R. "Children's Ideas About Matter." *School Science and Mathematics* 19 (1991): 240–244.

[20] Bishop, B.A. & C.W. Anderson. "Student Conceptions of Natural Selection and its Role in Evolution." *Journal of Research in Science Teaching* 27 (1990): 415–427.

[21] Lawson, A.E. & W.A. Worsnop. "Learning About Evolution and Rejecting a Belief in Special Creation: Effects of Reflective Reasoning Skill, Prior Knowledge, Prior Belief and Religious Commitment." *Journal of Research in Science Teaching* 29 (1992): 143–166.

[22] Solomon, J. "Learning About Energy: How Pupils Think in Two Domains." *European Journal of Science Education* 5 (1983): 49–59.

[23] Sneider, C. & S. Pulos. "Children's Cosmographies: Understanding the Earth's Shape and Gravity." *Science Education* 67 (1983): 205–221.

[24] Clough, E.E. & C. Wood-Robinson. "How Secondary Students Interpret Instances of Biological Adaptation." *Journal of Biological Education* 19 (1986): 125–130.

[25] Brumby, *Op. Cit.*.

[26] Stavey, R., Y. Eisen, & D. Yaakobi. "How Students Aged 13–15 Understood Photosynthesis." *International Journal of Science Education* 9 (1987): 105–115.

[27] Kesidou & Duit, *Op. Cit.*

[28] *Benchmarks*, p. 337.

[29] Gunstone, R.F. & R.T. White. "Understanding of Gravity." *Science Education* 65 (1981): 291–299.

[30] One additional fact that confounds the conclusion is that atmospheric pressure provides buoyancy to objects (such as buckets of sand), relieving some of their apparent weight on a scale. The authors' question was therefore impossible to answer with the information given.

[31] *Benchmarks*, p. 340.

[32] Ibid, p. 341.

[33] Clough, E.E. & C. Wood-Robinson. "Children's Understanding of Inheritance." *Journal of Biological Education* 19 (1985): 304–310; Deadman, J.A. & P.J. Kelly. "What Do Secondary School Boys Understand About Evolution and Heredity Before They are Taught the Topics." *Journal of Biological Education* 12 (1978): 7–15.

[34] Ibid.

[35] Kargbo, D.B., E.D. Hobbs, & G.L. Erickson. "Children's Beliefs About Inherited Characteristics." *Journal of Biological Education* 14 (1980): 137–146.

[36] Baxter, J. "Children's Understanding of Familiar Astronomical Events." *International Journal of Science Education* 11 (1989): 502–513.

[37] Dreyfus, A. & E. Jungwirth. "The Cell Concept of 10th Graders: Curricular Expectations and Reality." *International Journal of Science Education* 10 (1988): 221–229.

[38] For example, Bybee, R.W. & R.B. Sund. *Piaget for Educators*. Second ed., Columbus: Charles E. Merrill Publishing Co., 1982. Rodger Bybee is Executive Director of the Center for Science, Mathematics, and Engineering, National Research Council.

[39] Dehaene, S. *The Number Sense—How the Mind Creates Mathematics*. New York: Oxford University Press, 1997.

[40] Bell, *Op. Cit.*.

[41] Smith, C., S. Carey, & M. Wiser. "On Differentiation: A Case Study of the Development of the Concepts of Size, Weight, and Density." *Cognition 21* (1985): 177–237.

[42] Vosniadou, S. & W.F. Brewer. "Mental Models of the Earth: A Study of Conceptual Change in Childhood." *Cognitive Psychology* 24 (1992): 535–585.

[43] Sneider & Pulos, *Op. Cit.*

[44] Vosniadou & Brewer, *Op. Cit.*

[45] *Benchmarks*, p. 327.

[46] Stavy, *Op. Cit.*

[47] Hirsch, E.D., Jr. "Research Based Education Policy." In *What's Gone Wrong in America's Classrooms*, ed. W. M. Evers. Stanford: Hoover Institution Press, 1998, pp. 165–178.

[48] Committee on Education and the Workforce, Subcommittee on Oversight and Investigations, United States House of Representatives. *Education at a Crossroads: What Works and What's Wasted in Education Today*. July 1998 (http://www.house.gov/eeo/oversight/crossroads.htm).

[49] Committee on Science, United States House of Representatives. *Unlocking Our FutureToward a New National Science Policy*. September 1998 (http//www.house.gov/science/science_policy_report.htm).

[50] National Research Council, *National Science Education Standards*. Washington DC: National Academy Press, 1995.

Chapter 5

The Science Standards Wars
What Is the Basis for Scientific Inquiry?

Alan Cromer
Northeastern University

The current standards-writing movement began in the late 1980s as part of a national effort to reform science education. Major national organizations, such as the National Academy of Sciences, the American Association for the Advancement of Science, and the National Science Teachers Association, mounted independent efforts to try to be the voice of K–12 science education in the United States. The document published by the National Academy of Sciences, entitled *National Science Education Standards* (NSES), has probably had the most direct influence on state efforts to write their own standards.[1] Its final version was published only in 1996, but many states followed earlier drafts in writing their own standards.

Although the public might well think that a set of science standards developed by the National Academy of Sciences would be above reproach in the eyes of scientists themselves, this is not at all the case with NSES. It is a highly flawed document, conceptually and pedagogically. This essay will point out some of its major flaws and demonstrate its baleful influence on the 1995 Massachusetts science standards as an illustration of its effects on state standards.

Advocacy of Non-Scientific Inquiry

The intent of NSES, in its own words, is "science standards for all students." As NSES explains, "the phrase embodies both excellence and equity. The *Standards* apply to all students, regardless of age, gender, cultural or ethnic background, disabilities, aspirations, or interest and motivation in science." This highly political agenda, I will argue, requires a redefinition of science that borders on anti-science. Indeed, in its first printing in 1992, in a discussion of the intellectual foundations of the standards, it stated that the standards would reflect the "postmodernist view of science" that "questions the objectivity of observations and the truth of scientific knowledge."[2] This was said to be the opposite of logical positivism, which it disparaged as being "characterized by arguments for the objectivity of scientific knowledge." After protest from the scientific community, those were removed from later printings of the document, other changes were made, and the final version of NSES has a more moderate statement of the nature of science.

Nevertheless, NSES is still a radical document. In a speech given in 1996, Bruce Alberts, a distinguished scientist and president of the National Academy of Sciences, was very open on this point:

> This is a revolutionary document... All those who have kids in school recognize that we're far from anything like this... its not like the post-Sputnik revolution. This is science for everybody. This is to make the country vital and competitive, not to produce scientists. And [it's not] the science that we're testing in SAT2 exams... It's science as inquiry-based learning. And that's a major revolution.[3]

In his speech, Alberts complains of an eighth grader in a private school who was turned off science because he had to memorize parts of a worm. Then, in his next breath, Alberts speaks of schools "vitalizing" interest in the world around us. "It's exciting. The world's a wonderful place to investigate." Yes it is. It's the most interesting place I know. And worms are an important part of it. The study of their anatomy—usually through dissection—would seem to be totally aligned with NSES's own Grade 5–8 Life Science Standard: Structure and Function in Living Systems. But such study isn't there because technical vocabulary and specialized knowledge have been as thoroughly eliminated by the NSES revolutionaries as they were by the Pol Pot revolutionaries. The NSES revolution is about science for the least engaged students, not the most engaged.

Table 1 shows how NSES divides the content of science into seven categories, burying basic science in a stew of peripheral matters. James Shea, the editor of the *Journal of Geoscience Education*, writes in an editorial that this categorization "is virtually guaranteed to produce misconceptions, fragmentation, and fog, rather than clarity and comprehension."[4]

The Science Standards Wars

Table 1. NSES Science Content Categories

- Science as Inquiry
- Physical Science
- Life Science
- Earth and Space Science
- Science and Technology
- Science in Personal and Social Perspectives
- History and Nature of Science

Science as inquiry presents a special problem. NSES says, "Inquiry into authentic questions generated from student experiences is the central strategy for teaching science. Teachers focus inquiry predominantly on real phenomena..." The document also says, "Although the *Standards* emphasize inquiry, this should not be interpreted as recommending a single approach to science teaching." NSES further says, "Conducting hands-on science activities does not guarantee inquiry, nor is reading about science incompatible with inquiry." This isn't as balanced as it appears, however, because NSES doesn't mean by "inquiry" what a scientist might think it means. Inquiry in the sense understood by NSES must be inquiry "into authentic questions generated from student experiences." It thus is very different from traditional laboratory-based science, in which students learn to systematically use methods and equipment appropriate to ends determined by the curriculum. In a hypothetical example called "Funny Water," students begin "a unit that would include the development of students' understanding of the characteristic properties of substances such as boiling points, melting points, solubility, and density." The unit begins with students observing and commenting on a layered column of different colored liquids. All comments are accepted, from "It's pretty," to "The atoms in some are heavier than the ones in others." The students are then given the liquids in small cylinders and asked to find out what they can about them. No systematic method of investigation is taught, nothing is said about density as the ratio of mass to volume, of buoyancy as a force, of forces in equilibrium, of reasoning from principles. Instead, as the teacher demonstrates more confusing phenomena, students are encouraged to "write down any ideas they had about what was happening." Then it is on to boiling points.

Table 2 reproduces in its entirety Table 6.1 of NSES on Science as Inquiry Standards. Most notable is the absence of any characterization of how the skills and knowledge of scientific inquiry are to be developed progressively over 13 years of study. The 1995 *Massachusetts Science and Technology Curriculum Framework*, which is based on NSES, is honest about the nonscientific character of inquiry: "Before there was science or technology, there was inquiry." Inquiry to educators includes activities that most scientists would consider pre-science, and even anti-science.

Table 2. Science As Inquiry Standards (NSES Table 6.1)

LEVELS K–4	LEVELS 5–8	LEVELS 9–12
Abilities necessary to do scientific inquiry	Abilities necessary to do scientific Inquiry	Abilities necessary to do scientific Inquiry
Understanding about scientific inquiry	Understanding about scientific Inquiry	Understanding about scientific Inquiry

As another example of inquiry, the 1995 Massachusetts *Science and Technology Curriculum Framework* outlines a unit entitled "How Do Objects Fly?" "Middle school students' study of flight begins with building and informally testing different types of gliders. Students explore features that make flight possible..." The students then go on to pursue further inquiries based on their own questions, such as "What impact does air traffic have on people and organisms in communities near an airport?"[5]

The difference between this "inquiry" and a scientific investigation of flight couldn't be starker. The distinctions among a projectile, a glider, and powered flight are never made, or even suggested. There is no inquiry into lift, or Bernoulli's principle. Nothing about these critical matters can be learned from "informally testing different types of gliders." Middle school students can't make any meaningful inquiry into the impact of air traffic; all they can do is read about complaints of abutters and environmentalists. Who decides that this sort of reading is compatible with inquiry in science but that structured experiments on pressure and Bernoulli's principle are not? What contribution does reading about complaints of airplane noise make to a student's understanding of how airplanes fly? It merely disguises a social science exercise as a science exercise. This often turns out to be the real meaning of "real world phenomena."

The Science Standards Wars 103

A Lack of Logical Coherence

NSES recognizes three major divisions of science and gives specific standards for each. Table 3 shows the Physical Science Standards for Grades 5–8, and Table 4 shows the Earth and Space Science Standards for Grades 5–8.

Table 3. NSES Physical Science Content Standards (Grades 5–8)

Properties and changes of properties in matter
    A substance has characteristic properties...
    Substances react chemically in different ways...
    Chemical elements do not break down during normal laboratory reactions...

Motions and forces
    The motion of an object can be described by its position, direction of motion, and speed...
    An object that is not being subjected to a force will continue to move at a constant speed in a straight line.
    Unbalanced forces will cause changes in the speed or direction of an object's motion.

Transfer of energy
    Energy is a property of many substances and is associated with heat, light, electricity, mechanical motion, sound, nuclei, and the nature of a chemical.
    Energy is transferred in many ways.
    Heat moves in predictable ways.
    Light interacts with matter by transmission (including refraction), absorption, or scattering (including reflection)...
    Electrical circuits provide a means of transferring electrical energy...
    In most chemical/nuclear reactions, energy is transferred into or out of a system.
    The sun is a major source of energy for the changes on the earth's surfaces.

Unfortunately, these standards, in spite of their overarching subtitles, lack any logical coherence. For example, refraction is included under energy transfer (Table 3). Is there to be a unit on geometrical optics, or is refraction merely to be thrown out as an isolated concept? Are students to express their own opinions as to why light bends, or do they do a systematic study of the phenomenon?

Chemical reactions, nuclear reactions, and elements are included, but atoms, molecules, and atomic structure are not. How is one to talk about nuclear reactions and not discuss atoms and nuclei? All middle school textbooks currently teach atoms and mention molecules when discussing biology. But NSES explicitly rules against this:

> It can be tempting to introduce atoms and molecules or to improve students' understanding of them... However, use of such terminology is premature... Elements and compounds can be defined operationally from their chemical characteristics, but few students can comprehend the idea of atomic and molecular particles.[6]

Table 4. NSES Earth Science Content Standard (Grades 5–8)

Structure of the earth system
- The solid earth is layered with a lithosphere...
- Lithosphere plates on the scales of continents and oceans constantly move at rates of centimeters per year...
- Land forms are the result of a combination of constructive and destructive forces.
- Some changes in the solid earth can be described as the "rock cycle."
- Soil consists of weathered rocks and decomposed organic material...
- Water, which covers the majority of the earth's surface, circulates through the crust, oceans, and atmosphere in what is known as the "water cycle."
- Water is a solvent. As it passes through the water cycle it dissolves minerals and gases and carries them to the oceans.
- The atmosphere is a mixture of nitrogen, oxygen, and trace gases that include water vapor...
- Clouds, formed by the condensation of water vapor, affect weather and climate.
- Global patterns of atmospheric movement influence local weather.
- Living organisms have played many roles in the earth system...

Earth's history
- The earth processes... today... are similar to those... in the past.
- Fossils provide important evidence of how life and environmental conditions have changed.

Earth in the solar system
- The earth is the third planet from the sun in a system that includes the moon, the sun, eight other planets and their moons, and smaller objects.
- Predictable motion... explains such phenomena as the day, the year, phases of the moon, and eclipses.
- Gravity governs motion in the solar system.
- Seasons are due to the tilt of the earth's rotation on its axis.

NSES is correct that students will have misconceptions at the beginning. And it is also true that many middle school textbooks give more details of atomic structure than can possibly be meaningful to most students. But the introduction of atomicity and atomic structure has to begin somewhere. It is radical in the extreme to postpone this until high school. A Daltonian notion of atoms and molecules can be given in seventh grade, some atomic structure developed in eighth, and nuclear structure described in ninth. Over three years, most students will develop a "good enough" concept of atoms.

Also missing from the middle school standard is the topic of pressure in fluids, which is central to many topics in both life science and earth science. Pressure must be developed in seventh grade if later standards are to be meaningful. This in turn requires an understanding of forces in equilibrium, another topic that NSES omits.

The choice of topics included in NSES does not form a logically connected set of ideas. This should not be surprising since the ability to reason from principles is not itself a standard. NSES claims it is setting the criteria to judge the quality of what students know and are able to do. But as Shea points out:

> There seems to be no place in the "Standards" where it says directly and unequivocally that "students will know" anything in particular or "students will be able to do" anything; instead, what we find is the weaseling assertion that "students will develop an understanding of..."
>
> For example, the "Standards" mentions "rocks" repeatedly, but never once specifies "sedimentary," "igneous," or "metamorphic" rocks. The word "mineral" appears only once as far as I could determine, and not even one specific mineral is named. The word "processes" is used many times, but, incredibly the authors do not seem to know what processes are, because "the presence of ozone and greenhouse gases in the atmosphere" and "cloud cover" are explicitly identified as processes rather than conditions, whereas most geological processes aren't even mentioned. Just for example, "crystalization," "lithification," and "metamorphism" are never mentioned, nor are "glaciation," "percolation," "folding," "faulting," "intrusion," "extrusion," etc., etc., etc. The list of omissions is too long to do more than give examples here.

Massachusetts's Science and Technology Standards and Assessments

Following this dismal lead, most states have undertaken the arduous task of writing their own standards. Here we find all the errors of NSES, plus a few new ones. As an example I use the 1995 *Massachusetts Science and Technology Curriculum Framework* and the 1998 state assessments based on it.

Like NSES, the Framework is divided into a number of major categories, as shown in Table 5. The three technology standards comprised 25% of the 90-minute Science and Technology test taken by all fourth, eighth, and tenth graders. This left 75%, or approximately 30 questions, to cover the other four categories.

Table 5. The 1995 Massachusetts Science Content Categories
- Inquiry
- Physical Science
- Life Science
- Earth and Space Science
- The Design Process
- Understanding and Using Technology
- Science, Technology, and Human Affairs

Table 6 summarizes the scope of the three domains of science. The three science domains contain 58 topics, many of which encompass whole fields of knowledge. Note that Massachusetts follows NSES in dividing physical science into matter, force and motion, and energy transformation, but adds a division on the particulate model of matter. It doesn't go as far as NSES in avoiding the topic, but neither does it go so far as dictating any specific particulate model. Any particulate model of matter that a child can think of will do. The test, however, was on the standard model.

The main problem with the Framework is that it is too wide-ranging in scope and content to be the basis for the development of a coherent, teachable curriculum. As a consequence, the Massachusetts science assessments for eighth and tenth grade, which were based on the Framework, can neither drive education reform nor reliably assess individual student attainment in science. Indeed, testing 58 fields of knowledge with 30 questions sent precisely the opposite message of what education reform is all about. Such thin testing gives no incentive to districts to cover material in depth. Moreover, it's simply impossible to assess an individual student's knowledge of a topic like electricity with a single question. Table 7 gives a few bullets from the physical science standards to illustrate this point.

Table 6. Keyword Summary of the 1995 Massachusetts Science Content Standards

I. Physical Sciences
A. *Properties of Matter*
   1. Measure density
   2. Elements and compounds
   3. Chemical change
   4. Conservation of mass
   5. Pressure and temperature (gas law)
B. *Particulate Model of Matter*
   1. Atomic model
   2. a. Atoms, molecules, and ions
      b. Arrangement of atoms in solids, liquids, and gases
   3. Conservation of atoms in chemical reactions
C. *Motion and Changes in Motion*
   1. Force
   2. Addition of forces
   3. Position and speed of as functions of time
D. *Transformations of Energy*
   1. Conservation of energy
   2. Heat transfer
   3. Electromagnetic radiation
   4. Light
   5. Energy transformations
   6. Electrical circuits

II. Life Sciences
A. *Characteristics of Organisms*
   1. Cell
   2. Kingdoms
   3. Animal and plant cells
   4. Cell replication and growth
   5. Life processes
   6. Specialization of cells
   7. Systems of cells
B. *Diversity/Adaptation of Organisms*
   1. Effects of environmental changes
   2. Evolution
C. *Heredity, Reproduction, Development*
   1. Sexual and asexual reproduction
   2. Haploid and diploid cells
   3. Segregation and recombination
   4. Genetic variation

III. Earth and Space Sciences
A. *Interactions and Cycles in the Earth System*
   1. Earth's interior
   2. Heat flow and convection within the earth
   3. Sedimentary, igneous, and metamorphic rocks
   4. Soil
   5. Water cycle
   6. Shape and rotation of the earth
   7. Oceanography
   8. Climate
   9. Weather
   10. Insulation
   11. Pollution
   12. Hydrology
   13. Human effects on the environment
B. *Earth's History*
   1. Continental drift
   2. Evolution
C. *Earth and Space*
   1. Pattern of stars
   2. Telescope
   3. Planetary motion
   4. Solar system
   5. Sun, and the Milky Way
   6. Galaxies in the universe
   7. Moon
   8. Universal gravity
   9. Sun's energy on earth

Table 7. Sample Physical Science Learning Standards, Grades 5–8; Massachusetts Science and Technology Framework

A. Properties of Matter
5. Measure and predict changes in the pressure, temperature, or volume of a gas sample when changes occur in either of the other two properties.

B. Particle Model of Matter
1. Describe a particulate model for matter that accounts for the observed properties of substances.

C. Motions and Changes in Motion
2. Show and describe how forces acting on objects as pushes or pulls can either reinforce or oppose each other.

D. Transformations of energy
1. Demonstrate principles of electrical circuits. Use wires, batteries, bulbs, and instruments to measure and analyze electrical energy, resistance, current, and power. Use electrical currents to produce electromagnetic coils of wire, and, conversely, use a moving magnet to generate a current in a circuit.

The electricity standard (D.1 in Table 7) shows just how much material is crammed into each of the 58 bullets. The gas law standard (A.5) requires a sophisticated understanding of pressure, but there is no explicit stand-alone standard on pressure itself. This sends the message that it is okay to use scientific concepts without developing any understanding of them as long as they have common English names.

Both NSES and the 1995 *Massachusetts Science and Technology Curriculum Framework* are so deficient in their outlining of a coherent science curriculum that they hinder the development of a sound science curriculum. I have watched as school districts struggle in vain in come to grips with these flawed mandates. To date, I know of no program that can be described as even remotely implementing them.

The 1998 California Science Standards

In February 1998, I spent three days in Los Angeles working on the first draft of the California Science Standards. The politics of this is a long story, but parts of it are relevant here. Two groups had submitted proposals to the California Academic Standards Commission in response to its RFP to write the state's science standards. One group, headed by Bonnie Brunkhorst, a professor of science and mathematics education, was pro-NSES, and the other, headed by

The Science Standards Wars 109

Stan Metzenberg, a biology professor, was anti-NSES. After a bitter dispute, both proposals were rejected, and Brunkhorst and Metzenberg were asked to be consultants to the Commission. Glenn Seaborg, an eminent scientist, Nobel laureate, former chancellor of the University of California system, and a member of Metzenberg's group, was appointed to the Commission and became chairman of its science subcommittee.

The Commission sponsored a three-day standards-writing conference in February 1998, to which Brunkhorst and Metzenberg could each invite their "experts." There was much jockeying over who could invite whom, but in the end a combined group of pro- and anti-NSES people was assembled. My two principal goals at this conference were: 1) to prevent NSES from being given special authority in our discussions, and 2) to prevent inquiry from being made a separate component, or strand, of the document.

There were about seven people in the physical science group, mostly university-level chemists and physicists. Although some of us had been invited by Metzenberg and some by Brunkhorst, there were no ideological divisions among us. Our first meeting began with the suggestion that we break into three subgroups according to the NSES subdivisions of physical science—matter, force and motion, and energy transformations. But since motion is inseparable from energy, the group preferred to split the topics into chemistry and physics. The chemists worked on standards related to chemical reactions, atoms, and molecules, and the three physicists worked on the standards related to everything else. We also decided not to get involved with promulgating overarching themes like "energy transformations." Instead we tried to organize the physical science standards into teachable units, with the standards describing the essential components of the units.

Our work passed through several layers of editing and internal review by the Commission before it was released for public comment in April 1998. Table 8 shows some excerpts from the final document, which was approved by the State Board of Education in November 1998.[6]

Table 8. Excerpts from the 1998 California Science Standards: Physical Science Grades 6 and 7

Grade 6: Heat moves in a predictable flow from warmer objects to cooler objects until all objects are the same temperature. As basis for understanding this concept, students know:
a. Energy can be carried from one place to another by heat flow, or by waves including water waves, light and sound, or by moving objects.
b. When fuel is consumed, most of the energy released becomes heat energy.
c. Heat flows in solids by conduction (which involves no flow of matter) and in fluids by conduction and also by convection (which involves flow of matter).
d. Heat energy is also transferred between objects by radiation; radiation can travel through space.

Grade 7: Physical principles underlie biological structures and functions. As a basis for understanding this concept, students know:
a. Visible light is a small band within a very broad electromagnetic spectrum.
b. For an object to be seen, light emitted from it must enter the eye.
c. Light travels in straight lines except when the medium it travels trough changes.
d. How simple lenses are used in a magnifying glass, the eye, camera, telescope, and microscope.
e. White light is a mixture of many wavelengths (colors), and that retinal cells react differently with different wavelengths.
f. Light interacts with matter by transmission (including refraction), absorption, or scattering (including reflection).
g. The angle of reflection of a light beam is equal to the angle of incidence.
h. How to compare joints in the body (wrist, shoulder, thigh) with structures used in machines and simple devices (hinge, ball-and-socket, and sliding joints).
i. How levers confer mechanical advantage and how the application of this principle applies to the musculoskeletal system.
j. Contractions of the heart generate blood pressure, and heart valves prevent backflow of blood in the circulatory system.

California's 1998 science standards break with NSES in a number of important ways. First, the document doesn't confuse methods and goals. It doesn't say how science is to be taught but only what is to be learned. Inquiry is not touted as the "central strategy for teaching science." Second, it doesn't confound the teaching of science with the burden of teaching sociology, history, philosophy, and technology as well. (Although I favor including history and technology in science whenever possible, I don't want to see them made a requirement. Doing so dilutes already limited resources.) Third, the physical science part is organized into teachable units, with detailed descriptions of the expectations of each unit. This is very helpful for designing curricula and allocating time.

Life Science is not organized this way, and the whole matter is controversial.

Defenders of NSES, including Bruce Alberts, actively campaigned against the document before it was approved by the State Board of Education precisely because student-initiated inquiry is not central to it. Yet ironically, the crowning achievement of the document, applauded by all sides, is the development of a progressive Investigation and Experimentation standard in place of the dreadful "Science as Inquiry" of NSES (Table 2). Table 9 gives the Grades 6–8 Investigation and Experimentation standards. This is the first state standards document that explicitly links science to mathematics. It is also the first attempt to list explicit skills in order of increasing complexity.

Table 9. California Standards for Investigation and Experimentation

Perform all previous investigative skills [Grades K–5].
Develop a hypothesis.
Plan and conduct a scientific investigation to test a hypothesis.
Select and use appropriate tools and technology (including calculators, computers, balances, spring scales, microscopes, and binoculars) to perform tests, collect data, and display data.
Utilize a variety of print and electronic resources (including World Wide Web and CD-ROMs) to collect information as evidence as part of a research project.
Differentiate variable and controlled parameters in a test.
Communicate the logical connection among hypotheses, science concepts, tests conducted, data collected, and conclusions drawn from the scientific evidence.
Recognize whether evidence is consistent with a proposed explanantion.
Construct appropriate graphs from data and develop quantitative statements about the relationships between variables.
Differentiate between linear and non-linear relationships on a graph of data.
Construct scale models, maps, and appropriate, labeled diagrams to describe scientific knowledge (e.g., motion of earth's plates, or cell structure of an organism).
Communicate steps and results in an investigation through written reports and verbal presentations.
Evaluate the accuracy and reproducibility of data.
Apply simple mathematical relationships to determine one quantity given the other two (including speed = distance/time, density = mass/volume, force = pressure x area, volume = area x height).
Recognize the slope of the linear graph as the constant in the relationship as $y = kx$ and apply this to interpret graphs constructed from data.
Use triangulation to determine the position of a point from data.
Read a topographic map and a geological map for evidence provided on the maps.
Interpret events by sequence and time from natural phenomena.
Identify changes in natural phenomena over time without manipulating the phenomena (e.g., a tree limb, a grove of trees, a stream, a hillslope).

Concluding Remarks

The National Science Education Standards is a radical postmodern document that replaces focused investigation with student-initiated inquiry in order to define a fingerpainting version of science accessible to all. This movement has been met head-on by the movement to make schools accountable through statewide testing. The logic of testing requires standards that are far more specific than NSES supporters find acceptable. Brunkhorst complained that the California "standards have too much detailed content and too much technical jargon at all grade spans." Yet details and specific vocabulary are absolutely necessary if the standards are to be the basis for statewide testing.

I am hopeful that the California science standards will open discussion on issues of substance. Are its physical science standards too specific? Can anything less specific be the basis for state testing? Can we realistically expect all students to learn this much science? At what grade will students interested in science be permitted to take science courses matched to their abilities and interests? Is there a fundamental conflict between "raising standards" and a "science for all" ideology?

Notes

[1] National Research Council, *National Sciences Education Standards*, National Academy of Sciences, Washington, D.C., 1996
(http://www.nap.edu/bookstore/isbn/0309053269.html).

[2] National Research Council, *National Sciences Education Standards: A Sampler*, National Academy of Sciences, Washington, D.C. 1992. As it turned out, although this draft was supposed to represent the consensus of teachers and other science educators, scientists, and the general public, and although the lists of those supposedly involved in the preparation of this draft included the names of some of our most respected scientists, they did not write the report, as physicist Gerald Holton noted in an essay describing the problems he saw in that draft and in a subsequent draft ("Science Education and the Sense of Self," *Partisan Review*, 1996, 63 (2): 205–214).

[3] Bruce Alberts. "Critical role of professional development in science and mathematics reform," NISE Conference Speech, 1996
(http://teech.terc.edu/modes/lectures/alberts_nise96.cfm).

[4] James Shea, "More Progress(???) on Science Education Standards," *Journal of Geoscience Education* 46 (1998): 118.

[5] Massachusetts Department of Education, *Massachusetts Science and Technology Curriculum Framework*, Department of Education, Malden, MA 1995 (http:www.doe.mass.edu/doedocs/frameworks/science5.html).

[6] California Academic Standards Commission, 1998 (http://www.ca.gov/goldstandards/Drafts/Science/SciContents.html).

Chapter 6

How Children Learn Science
Do We Now Know?

Paul R. Gross
University of Virginia

Sandra Stotsky
Harvard University

> Although the new theories of science are interesting and provocative, the evidence for their soundness is much too flimsy to warrant accepting them as a tentative, let alone a definitive, template for describing whole disciplines or sub-disciplines... All these projects rest on the assumption that recent accounts of the character of natural science are sound, or at least pretty close to the mark. Yet we have no reason whatsoever for making that assumption, either about Kuhn's theory or about its more recent rivals.
> —Donovan, Laudan, and Laudan, *Scrutinizing Science,* 1992[1]

Very rare are the senior college faculty, especially in the natural sciences and mathematics, who would deny that there has been a decline among high school graduates in their factual knowledge and basic skills, as well as in their general preparation for systematic inquiry (which is what "science" means). Of course, one needs decades of teaching experience to see or to imagine such changes. But on average and over some decades, a decline in student competence and performance, especially in the later school years, is not imaginary. It is a fact, not a nostalgia; age is not the cause of seeing it. The decline is evidenced by—among many indicators—the history of the Scholastic Aptitude Test since 1960, and by the performance of American twelfth graders in national and international tests in science and mathematics.[2] The brute fact of deficiency cannot be camouflaged by recurring efforts on the part of those with a stake in good news on education to "spin" the data.[3] It helps explain why most colleges in the U.S. find today that significant numbers of admitted students need remedial instruction. Before any attempt at college work, these students must learn what they didn't learn in K–12. Remedial studies in college often extend over several years, if they succeed at all. It is easy to understand the hobbling effect of this on the scientific achievement to which these young people can aspire.

After the national shock of Sputnik, everybody agreed that scientific education in the U.S. required a boost. We needed, it was urged, more scientists and engineers. That, catalyzed by a bonanza of federal dollars for innovation in science teaching, led to a broad range of educational initiatives, especially at the secondary school level and in introductory college courses. Doubtless some lasting improvements resulted and some insights were gained. But despite the magnitude of the investment, hard evidence of gains on any large scale remains astonishingly lacking. Most of the big curricular innovations of this period seem to have been abandoned. This is justly deplored by the mathematicians and scientists, as well as the many schoolteachers, who gave time and effort to designing the programs.[4] The earliest Sputnik-era programs, in what we should recognize as the first phase of a national response to deficient science education, were improvements and enrichments to existing offerings. They sought to push *more* science and mathematics content into the curriculum, along with broader, more theoretical implications of that content (as, for example, in the unlamented New Math). A clearly different, second phase has taken its place. This one responds to stimuli very different from the originals (which were the "Space Race" and the "Missile Gap"), and to anxieties different from those of competing with the Soviet Union. There is now evidence of mediocre and even declining performance by American schoolchildren in science and mathematics relative to their age-peers in other developed societies, and of especially poor showings, on average, among some minority groups as well as among the most able American students.[5] Today's problem, almost everyone agrees, is less how to train scientists or mathematicians than how to educate all students to a respectable level of scientific literacy.

A new wave of educational commentary has succeeded the earlier one. Prescriptions for radically revised pedagogies and standards dominate professional and public writing on the subject and have become a chief product of consultancy businesses. Methodological fixes are implemented on a large scale with the blessings and funding of state and federal agencies, the largest charitable foundations, and corporate and other private donors. Many of these fall under the mandate of "systemic reform," which we discuss in detail later. The specialized research that in principle justifies these methodologies, pedagogies, and standards grows exponentially. Since some, but not all, of the problems are problems not just in the U.S. but in the West generally, this literature is multinational. It is no surprise, therefore, that those who are not professionally familiar with it but are sympathetic toward its purposes and hopes—a group that includes school boards, parent groups, community leaders, legislators, and nearly all working scientists—think that we have today important new knowledge of how children learn science. They believe that studies cited in support of this or that new pedagogical strategy, professedly based upon such knowledge, have established the effectiveness of the strategy—at all grade levels and with all students.

Understanding as we now do how children learn science, the argument continues, we are in a position to relieve the science-learning ills from which too many of them suffer. What is the proposed therapy for the deficiency in science learning? Well, there isn't just one. Many have been proposed, each one a little bit different from the others, and each one claimed to be implicit in the results of the new research on how children learn. These pedagogies go by such names as cooperative learning, hands-on learning, real-world problem solving, integrated science and mathematics, and inquiry-based learning. To be sure, the principle—that a knowledge of physiology is normally required for an effective attack on pathology—is perfectly sound. Thinking by analogy alone, people concerned about the ineffectiveness of science teaching in K–12 can be confident: if we understand now how children learn science, can effective treatment of learning failure be far behind? Is there any reason why all children should not be, as at Lake Woebegon, above average?

Unfortunately (at least in the case of schoolchildren learning science), such confidence is unfounded. The proposed theories of learning and the well-advertised therapies based upon them have no better empirical grounding, we will argue, than do the fashionable theories of knowledge and science itself to which the philosopher-authors of our epigraph refer, and to which the newest educational theories give respectful lip-service.[6] Belief of well-meaning and otherwise sophisticated people in the existence of a solid empirical base for these new pedagogies was at the core of an attempted intervention by a few noted scientists and science educators in the process that had been established for the design of K–12 science standards in California.[7] The story is a goldmine of anecdotes for contemporary cynics: it seems to support their quotidian claim that nothing, not art, not science, not even epistemology is more than a form of politics. But, for the national effort to reverse a long history of mediocrity in science education, for the effort to equip our children to do better if not to be the best, the conflict attending the intervention was unfortunate.

The "Blast" from "a Dozen Scientific Societies"

On September 9, 1998, the distinguished biomedical scientist, Bruce Alberts, wrote to the members of the California State Board of Education a letter that began: "I write as the president of the National Academy of Sciences, a private organization founded in 1863 under a Congressional charter signed by Abraham Lincoln..." (see the Appendix). Thereafter came his credentials, and strong ones—a Californian, a father of children who had attended San Francisco's public schools, and a citizen long active in the improvement of public education in science. The Board had nearly finished its consideration of a new set of science standards for K–12, standards that seemed a shoo-in to become official. Of all the credentials listed in Dr. Alberts's letter, the most important was the first: no member of the Board had any reason to doubt that he was writing on behalf of, as the voice of, the history- and prestige-laden National Academy of Sciences. But he was not speaking for the members of that society. Nor for the members of other societies. He was speaking, eloquently enough, to be sure, for himself. Among other indictments, he offered this:

> The authors of the draft [California] standards have pushed down the teaching of abstract concepts such as atoms and molecules to fifth, and even third grade. We know that it will be nearly impossible for children at this age to do more than memorize terminology about these concepts... Finally, the draft standards have neglected the strong recommendation in the National Science Education Standards that major effort be made to tie school science to the science that students hear about on television and experience in their lives.

Thereby hangs the tale. The underlying events, those that generated the heat of the controversy, are discussed elsewhere in this volume.[8] During the main period of public contention in California, details were examined at length in the California media and in national newspapers.[9] Suffice it to say that there *was* controversy. At first it was over the selection of a contractor to write the required standards. That was settled in due course by what appears to have been an intelligent compromise. The resulting standards, which were approved later in 1998, are a concurrence, to which members of both the originally competing groups contributed. Chairman of the team finally organized to draw up the standards was the late Nobel laureate chemist, Glenn T. Seaborg. A feature of these standards is that they do not subscribe to the pervasive educational philosophy of the *national* science standards that had emerged earlier, over a period of years, in multiple drafts, and with major support from the federal government. These came in two forms: the *National Science Education Standards* proper, from an operating arm of the National Academy of Sciences (the National Research Council, or NRC), and a long document on science-learning benchmarks from the American Association for the Advancement of Science (AAAS). Both organizations are housed in Washington, D.C.

These two sets of putatively national standards are preoccupied with pedagogy driven by an educational philosophy that stresses *developmental appropriateness* (what children are supposedly able to learn—and unable to learn—at particular ages) and by a doctrine about learning, "constructivism," according to which, for optimum learning to take place children must "construct" knowledge about the topic under study from their personal experience and to the greatest extent possible without teacher intervention.[10] According to this doctrine, *transmission* of knowledge is not really possible. Knowledge must be *developed* by the knower (or learner) in the context of the learning environment. Also, and importantly, the first draft of the NRC national standards was explicitly and proudly "postmodernist" in its epistemology, that is, in its view of scientific knowledge.[11] That claim was later withdrawn (without much change otherwise) after complaints from scientists who had actually read and understood its nihilist implications for the goals of objective thought. It is not surprising, therefore, that on matters of substantive scientific content, the national standards tend to be general and sometimes even ambiguous. They are the creation, despite suggestions to the contrary, primarily of science teachers and educational theorists rather than of scientists.

In the eyes of Dr. Alberts and the other objectors, the sins of the proposed California science standards were two. First, they ignored the theoretical pleadings and strong pedagogical commitments of the national standards, emerging instead with emphasis upon specific scientific content that California students were to acquire grade-level by grade-level. Such emphasis is today scorned in schools of education. It is considered to be undesirable in itself and is disparaged as employing, for the learning strategy, nothing but memorization. Second, by emphasizing specific content and deliberately leaving the choice of instructional method to the school districts and individual teachers, the new California standards were ignoring—as the complaints came to be summarized in the newspapers—"everything we have learned about how children learn." From Washington, *that* was communicated to the public as the besetting sin.

Readers in a hurry but interested in the *dramatis personae* of the attack could do worse than to read the succinct account of it that appeared that September in *The Chronicle of Higher Education*.[12] It reported that "A dozen U.S. scientific societies... blasted California's proposed standards for science curricula in public schools and offered a panel of six nationally known scientists in the state to rewrite the requirements." A key voice in this "blast" was that of Ramon E. Lopez, an education officer of the American Physical Society, who is quoted as saying that "the proposed standards fly in the face of much of what is known about how children learn, and they are at odds with national consensus."

Now, the "U.S. scientific societies" referred to are Washington-centered. And in none of them—including the National Academy of Sciences—was there, so far as we have been able to determine, a vote of the organization's membership on the California or any other K–12 science standards. Thus there is so far nothing that can be considered a "national consensus." Dr. Alberts, whose complaints about the California standards seem to have been taken in the news media as representating the views of the National Academy's membership, could not have known that his views were, literally, representative. His denunciation of the California standards was his own, unquestionably sincere, opinion—an opinion shared by some colleagues and some other society officers. In essence, the public attack upon the California standards was *ab initio* a response from officers of some of the science societies (presumably those who were available to the person rounding up endorsements for the "blast"). Nor is there as yet any evidence of knowledgeable agreement among scientists on the issues. It would be surprising if there were, given

How Children Learn Science

the long tradition of indifference on the part of professional and university science to goings-on in K–12 education.

On the contrary, there is some reason to suppose that most members of the National Academy of Sciences know little about these things and don't care much about them. For example, in 1996 Dr. Alberts and the Academy staff conducted a comprehensive survey of the membership, "in order to determine [their] familiarity with the programs of the Academy and the National Research Council..."[13] Some 60 percent of the members responded. Among questions on activities of the NRC, one asked about member familiarity with the NRC's Center for Science, Mathematics, and Engineering Education. Eighty-five percent of those responding said that they were *not* familiar with it. Of those 15% who did admit to some familiarity with this most relevant operating branch, 35% expressed satisfaction, 11% expressed dissatisfaction, while 54% reported "no opinion." Taken *in toto*, those numbers measure the proportion of scientists likely to have had any interest in the NRC undertakings vis-a-vis K–12. It is small. They present a picture different from the assurances of spokesmen for the "dozen U.S. scientific societies." There is no consent on the national standards for K–12 or on the California standards (which most of the membership of those societies could not have seen at the time of the "blast"). The absence of consensus has been noted in the reporting on this issue in professional science magazines such as *Science*.

Clearly, however, there *are* issues of educational philosophy at the heart of this conflict, and strong disagreements about them. Dr. Alberts is right: The eventual decisions on how to teach school science in California will be influential, if for no other reason than the impact they must have upon the textbook business. Given the vast financial resources and the organizational prestige already invested in the NRC and AAAS standards, an observer making the effort to judge the arguments objectively or even as postmodernists do (for them there is no such thing as objectivity)[14] must wonder about gored oxen and their owners. In any case the key public complaint was that *a body of sound knowledge on how children learn science, acquired through educational research, exists; this knowledge provides imperatives for the design of standards, curriculum, and pedagogy; and the new California standards ignore them.*

It behooves us, therefore, to examine the claim of new and definitive knowledge about how children learn and about how they are best taught science (and mathematics). No such examination seems to have been made by the spokesmen for the "dozen U.S. scientific societies." During the public phase of the conflict, none of the objectors to the California standards made specific reference to the research findings upon which the national science standards rely, although there are abundant citations thereto in the national standards documents. Yet those commentators, among whom are some important scientists, clearly believe that a high-quality research base with concrete implications for curriculum and pedagogy is available. But, so far as we can tell—and we have tried hard to tell—there exists neither a convincing research base for the learning theory inspiring the pedagogical and curricular recommendations in the national standards documents, nor sound empirical support for their effectiveness in K–12 classes.

We have made our own attempt to determine "what is known about how children learn." What we found were: (1) serious limitations in the developmental/constructivist theory that guides current thinking about science and mathematics learning; (2) absence of a sound, consistent body of evidence from studies of science (and mathematics) education in this country to support the pedagogical and curricular methods most prominently recommended (cooperative learning, the redesign of laboratory instruction, real-world problem solving, integrated science and mathematics instruction, and the use of technology); and (3) a remarkable dearth of evidence that would testify to the efficacy of "systemic reform"—a generalized plan for the reform of science and mathematics education in this country that embeds these pedagogical and curricular methods and this learning theory. In order to maximize the range of published research we needed to explore, we examined major reviews of the research on these topics, summaries of their findings, and many current, individual studies in peer-reviewed educational research journals.

The Status of the Theory Underlying Inquiry-Based Learning

The logical point of departure for inquiry into "what is known about how children learn" is the status of the dominant learning theory on which the present "inquiry-based" methods for science teaching are based.[15] For decades, the most powerful influence on teacher educators and curriculum developers in elementary school science has been the work of Jean Piaget, the Swiss pioneer of developmental psychology who spent many years investigating the "natural" (and by clear implication, the universal) development of intelligence in children.[16] For Piaget, language development was inextricable from and dependent upon general intellectual development up to the time of adolesence. Only at the time of adolescence could language influence thought directly and thus allow the formalization of concepts.

Piaget's observations and claims about stages of individual development, based on painstaking empirical research (to a considerable extent with his own children and with the indispensable collaboration of his psychologist-wife, Valentine Chatenay), have had an extraordinary influence on educators.[17] Piaget proposed that children's thinking naturally evolves through discrete stages, from the sense-based thinking of infants, to the intuitive thinking of pre-schoolers, to the concrete, experience-based thinking of elementary school students, and to the formal, logical thought of which adolescents are (in principle) capable.[18] Piaget's was a theory about the dominant mode of thought in children at different stages in their development—essentially, how they understand the world around them and what the limitations in their thinking are at each stage.

Clearly, the ability to engage in formal, logical thinking does develop over time. And no one would deny that cognitive capacity and strategies change as we grow up and mature. However, many educators accept Piaget's theory at face value: that these stages are discrete, inevitable, and predictable for all children by age-group. And they have understood it to mean that they must follow the putative evolution of children's thinking through these discrete stages in designing appropriate curricular content and pedagogy, even though Piaget himself had noted

> that environment can play a decisive role in the development of the mind; that the thought content of the stages and the ages at which they occur are not immutably fixed; that sound methods can therefore increase the students' efficiency and even accelerate their spiritual growth without making it any the less sound.[19]

In fact, cross-cultural research has failed to establish the universality of Piaget's stages.[20] Many of his specific claims, including the stage-like characterization of cognitive development, have been questioned or dismissed by linguists and psychologists.[21] These investigators find, for example, little support for the claim that large qualitative changes occur as intelligence develops. Instead, the generally-held position today is that cognitive changes are gradual and cumulative, but also uneven. That is, development does not proceed equally across a range of cognitive skills. And students may regress—often temporarily—in their approach to a new topic because of the difficulty or novelty of what is being learned.

An important critique of Piaget's research on intellectual development (and indirectly of the educational philosophy it inspired) came from the Russian developmental psychologist, Lev Vygotsky.[22] Emphasizing the role of language in learning from pre-school on, Vygotsky insisted that *instruction,* by its conveyance of scientific concepts—the major feature of the language of formal schooling—is one of the principal resources for the schoolchild's intellectual development. To Vygotsky, imparting "systematic knowledge" to the child means teaching him "many things that he cannot directly see or experience." Vygotsky argued that the "formal discipline of scientific concepts gradually transforms the structure of the child's spontaneous concepts and helps organize them into a system." Moreover, because instruction given in one area "can transform and reorganize other areas of child thought, it may not only follow maturing or keep in step with it but also precede it and further its progress."

Hence, in Vygotsky's view, and in contrast to the curricular and pedagogical implications that many educators teased out of Piaget's work, "instruction precedes development." Vygotsky maintained that "studying child thought apart from the influence of instruction, as Piaget did, excludes a very important source of change and bars the researcher from posing the question of the interaction of development and instruction peculiar to each age level." Because Piaget did not consider the role of instruction in cognitive development, Vygotsky argued, the "gauge of the child's level of development [in Piaget's research] is not what he has learned through instruction but the manner in which he thinks on subjects about which he has been taught nothing."

Also influenced by Piaget was Jerome Bruner, the cognitive psychologist who chaired the seminal conference at Woods Hole, Massachusetts, in 1958 that brought together scholars and teachers guiding the development of the Sputnik-era curricula in the sciences and mathematics. At first, Bruner strongly advocated "discovery learning"— the role of experience and intuitive thinking in the educational process. And, clearly, the scientists and teachers who developed the Sputnik-era curricula did want students to engage in inquiry. But they wanted inquiry as scientists and mathematicians do it, that is, within the conceptual and structural frameworks of their disciplines. They had laid out these frameworks with great care in the curricula they designed. Indeed, Bruner remarked at one point that the "effectiveness [of the good intuiter] rests upon a solid knowledge of the subject, a familiarity that gives intuition something to work with."[23] In his 1961 essay in the *Harvard Educational Review* on the "act of discovery," Bruner commented: "There are many ways of coming to the arts of inquiry. One of them is by careful study of its formalization in logic, statistics, mathematics, and the like. If a person is going to pursue inquiry as a way of life, particularly in the sciences, certainly such study is essential."[24]

Later Bruner came to have some doubts about "discovery as the principal vehicle of education."[25] As he observed: "it seems...unlikely, given the nature of man's dependency as a creature, that this long period of dependency characteristic of our species was designed entirely for the most inefficient technique possible for regaining what has been gathered over a long period of time, that is, discovery." Bruner also argued that a critical weakness in Piaget's theory is its "intrinsic anticulturalism." "A theory of development that specifies nothing about intervention," he declared, "is blind to culture."

Remarkably, despite the many critiques of Piaget's stage theory, the lack of an unambiguous body of evidence to support its important details (see Metzenberg's discussion in this volume), and the formulation of alternative theories of cognitive development, his "universal/ constructivist perspective," as one major textbook on child development describes it,[26] has inspired many a curriculum in the elementary school in which there is little or no skills practice or direct instruction in abstract concepts. In these curricula, children's intellectual development is supposed to be guided chiefly by their own curiosity and experiences as they explore the use of "manipulatives" in concrete activities. In the past decade, the pedagogical implications educators have derived from Piaget's theories have spread ever more deeply into elementary school science and mathematics and steadily upward into secondary school science and mathematics curricula. Thus the NRC science standards make no educational distinctions when they proclaim that "inquiry into *authentic questions generated from student experiences* is the central strategy for teaching science. Teachers focus inquiry predominantly on *real phenomena*..."

Although the NRC document does not identify the *unreal* phenomena and *inauthentic* questions that are being taught in standard science courses and should now be dropped, its approach to learning may account for the absence of specific, grade-by-grade content in the proposed standards. "Discovery learning," originally a kind of inquiry-based learning in a curriculum framed by the concepts and structure of a discipline, seems thus to have been transformed since the 1980s into classroom activity rooted only loosely in planned curriculum, oriented more toward the construction of student *opinion* than the reconstruction of disciplinary *knowledge*.[27] That is why the science standards developed for the California State Board of Education were made to contain grade-by-grade specification of concepts and principles of science, to be learned by all students, sequenced in a cumulatively meaningful way. However, student inquiry, the direct study of natural phenomena, remains an important part of that program, through a "strand" on investigation; it is not just memorization.

Not only is there no general assent from psychologists to the stage theory that Piaget formulated to account for the growth of children's intelligence; there is little if any evidence in educational research for the *efficacy*, however measured and whatever its theoretical justifications, of student-centered inquiry as the basis for a complete science curriculum. We could find no studies comparing science learning based on student-centered inquiry over a long period (that is, a full curriculum determined chiefly by the students' interests) with science learning based on a teacher-planned curriculum over a long period (that is, a curriculum providing substantive, sequenced direction for study and inquiry within it). It is possible that there are none and that there will be none: Each approach to learning necessarily entails a different approach to assessment (to be blunt: the tests are different!) and to the role of instruction. One scientist-educator who has examined with great care the *difference* between these two approaches characterizes it as the vast discrepancy in the fraction of available time given to purely student-initiated inquiry *versus* time given to planned, focused instruction.[28] More time spent on student-centered inquiry means, for him and many others, not only less time for focused instruction but also greater difficulty in planning for such instruction in any time that may be left free for it.

Evidence on Cooperative Learning

Available evidence for a cooperative learning strategy is inconsistent. In a 1994 essay on small-group interaction,[29] Elizabeth Cohen reported that a 1985 review of studies in mathematics education found "significant differences favoring cooperative versus traditional methods of instruction in a third of the studies; the remaining studies showed no significant differences according to type of instruction."[30] That is, it didn't matter in most studies whether the teacher used cooperative learning groups or "traditional" methods of instruction. This finding alone should signal much less support for the strategy of cooperative learning than that with which advocates credit it. In any event, the finding is not surprising, given the amount of time teachers must invest in teaching students how to conduct useful small-group discussions on particular topics. Cohen further observes that, although a 1987 review of secondary level studies across the curriculum concluded that "68% favored cooperative learning over traditional forms of instruction,"[31] another review published in 1987 noted that the results of cooperative learning "sometimes differed according to the ethnic or racial group of the student."[32] An authoritative review of the research, published in 1995, pointed to only two studies finding large effects for black students, and neither study concerned mathematics or science.[33] The author of this review has argued over the years that "cooperative learning is effective only when group rewards and individual accountability are present," two features that were rarely present, as four other researchers found, when in a study published in 1998 they asked a large group of teachers about how they structured cooperative learning groups in their classes.[34]

Aside from the uncertain picture of the effectiveness of this particular strategy, in general and in science and mathematics classes in particular, it seems that productivity in cooperative learning is defined in different ways by different researchers. Most commonly it is defined, in Cohen's words, as "conventional academic achievement"; but it is also defined as "conceptual learning and higher order thinking" (by which Cohen means the sharing of "ideas, hypotheses, strategies, and speculations"), or, most commonly, as equal participation within groups by "students of different academic statuses." Indeed, the latter is the *gravamen* of her own argument, which advocates the use of "ill-structured problems" for small groups in order to produce more equal interaction between more and less academically able students. Thus, not only is enhanced academic knowledge not necessarily an outcome when this strategy is used, it is also not necessarily what is *intended* as an outcome.

Cooperative learning seems to appeal to teachers and educational researchers because of its egalitarian and synergetic implications. It draws, in principle, on the ability of the most able students in the class to improve the learning of the least able. Importantly, cooperative learning also removes the teacher from the center of the instructional process and frequently diminishes (or eliminates) the teacher's role as determiner of what is to be learned or as judge of what has been learned. These last two features seem to be taken, in education schools, as glad tidings of cooperative learning. The "intrusive" or "controlling" teacher is one of the *bêtes noires* of current educational thinking. Indeed, one of the most troubling aspects of cooperative learning, as reflected in recent studies we have examined, is the implication that teachers are no longer to provide whole class instruction. For example, a study published in 1995 comparing grade 9 biology students working in triads with students working completely alone on a unit about photosynthesis seems to suggest that instructional choices are limited *either* to student work and learning in peer groups *or* to students working and learning entirely on their own. Nothing in between. The evidence, not surprisingly, indicated that learning in peer groups was somewhat better than learning independently.[35]

Even if one viewed all the advertised features of cooperative learning positively, a close reading of key studies suggests that two problems in the use of this strategy beg for open discussion. The most able students, regardless of educational level, may be shortchanged by *not* being allowed, for the sake of "equity," to work with one another during instructional time or during performance assessments. That may be the practical implication of a recent study titled "Equity Issues in Collaborative Group Assessment: Group Composition and Performance," dealing with 21 seventh and eighth grade science classes. According to this 1998 article, performance assessment projects have been devised as a way to link assessment more closely to classroom instruction. From a comparison of the outcomes of groups formed in a variety of ways, the study found that "high-ability students generally performed better when they worked in homogeneous groups (that is, with other high-ability students) than when they worked in heterogeneous groups," but that "heterogenerous groups provide a greater benefit for below-average students than they impose a detriment on high-ability students..."[36]

Of even greater concern is that serious commitment to common forms of cooperative learning is quite likely to entail reduction in the substantive content to be covered in a course. This was discussed candidly by the authors of two studies using it for problem solving in community college physics classes.[37] Reduction in substantive content is apparently an inevitable consequence of the time needed for the formation and maintenance of well-functioning small groups. Teachers must devote time and work to insure positive group dynamics. And the forms of insurance required can differ from one topic to the next. Available time, on the other hand, is a constant: the content is inevitably reduced, and the question of how much content can reasonably be sacrificed to comity in the group is *not* reasonably discussed in the literature we have surveyed.

Evidence on the Use of Technology

Despite the promotion of "technology" by the proponents of systemic reform, from kindergarten on, its utility as a guarantor of improved learning in K–12 classrooms remains uncertain. The authors of a 1998 report to the President on the use of technology to strengthen K–12 education concluded that a large-scale program of rigorous, systematic research is necessary to insure its efficacy and cost effectiveness.[38] The authors noted: "Regarding the extent to which widely usable constructivist applications of computing and networking in fact achieve desirable educational outcomes in a cost-effective manner... we are not yet able to answer this question (nor indeed, even to define it precisely) with the degree of certainty that would be desirable from a public policy viewpoint."[39] Indeed, they seem to doubt that truthful evaluations are possible. As they comment, "the widespread current acceptance of the central tenets of constructivism within the educational reform movement... should perhaps lead us to be especially vigilant in guarding against an ideological (rather than a scientific) approach to the evaluation of educational applications of technology."[40] They are not alone in urging a go-slow approach to the introduction of more "technology" into K–12 (meaning, essentially, more computers in the classroom). A large-scale study on gender and science learning in high school, published in 1997, also concluded that a "blanket call for more computers in science is unwarranted."[41]

The discussion of technology use is often befogged by claims of inequities in the availability of machines or of access to various computing services. Some educators believe that it does make a difference in achievement and that students in wealthier school districts have an advantage over those in poorer or urban school districts. Yet, according to a nationally-publicized 1998 report on computer use and achievement in mathematics by fourth and eighth grade students, students who spent more time with computers in school actually scored worse on mathematics tests than students who spent less.[42] This study was conducted by the Educational Testing Service using 1996 NAEP data on more than 13,000 students. It also found no difference in *school* use of computers between schools with disadvantaged students and schools with other students, and little difference in *computer* use between advantaged and disadvantaged groups in fourth grade. However, it did find "great differences in eighth grade... [where] minority, poor, and urban students are more likely to find themselves learning lower-order skills than their white, nonpoor, and suburban counterparts; disadvantaged students are also less likely to find themselves learning higher-order skills."

To counter the strong implication that teachers in urban schools are somehow, on purpose, restricting computer use to the teaching of lower-order skills and deliberately avoiding the use of computers for teaching higher-order skills, we must note that the data in this study and others like it are purely correlational. Conclusions as to cause and effect are neither implied nor justified. It could be the case (although we have no knowledge that it *is*) that the disadvantaged eighth graders in this study actually needed more lower-order skills training than did their suburban peers. Whether or not that is so, solid evidence justifying large investments in technology for the purpose of enhancing learning in K–12 has not been forthcoming.

Evidence on Integrated Science and Mathematics Instruction

Integrated curricula are another highly-recommended contrivance for improving science and mathematics education. Yet a survey of international efforts to implement or continue implementation of integrated approaches to science teaching revealed the grave difficulty of evaluating such curricula.[43] According to this 1990 UNESCO report, there "appears to be little agreement on what constitutes integrated science curricula, on how to assess learning in relation to standardized tests that are content-specific, and on the ratio of science process and science content in instructional time allocations." These kinds of complexities suggest that the usual kinds of comparisons of differently configured curricula may not be meaningful.

The concerns in the UNESCO report also hint at the possibility that at least some science content is sacrificed in such curricula. We clearly need much more discussion of this question: how much content *is* displaced by the new emphases on process? This is especially important to know because of the lack of evidence to date that emphasis on process, regardless of other values it might have, is intellectually beneficial. One 1998 study we examined raises the further concern that integrated curricula might even achieve the opposite of what they intend.[44] This study compared the organization in concept maps made by high school students in an integrated algebra-physical science class with the organization of concept maps made by students in a discipline-specific physical science class. Contrary to expectations, the maps generated in the integrated class exhibited a more compartmentalized view of science and mathematics than did those of the students in the discipline-specific class.

Evidence on Laboratory Instruction

No serious scientist or science teacher deprecates laboratory experience for students. To do so would be asking for the scorn of one's peers. Yet the conclusions of a review of research on the role of the laboratory in science teaching, published in 1982, are sobering. It noted that there are "insufficient data to confirm or reject convincingly many of the statements that have been made about the importance and effects of laboratory teaching. The research has failed to show simplistic [*sic*] relationships between experiences in the laboratory and student learning."[45]

Nor is it clear that newer approaches to the design of the laboratory experience make a difference, overall, in student thought about the subject toward which the laboratory experience is directed. Indeed the absence of effect is suggested by a well-designed study published in 1997 which distinguished student-designed laboratories, called in the report, with evident admiration, "open-inquiry," from those designed by textbook publishers (that is, by teacher-authors), named, pejoratively, "confirmation labs."[46] The study compared the thought processes of two groups of eighth graders, one of them given a series of open-inquiry labs, the other a series of confirmation labs. It found student-designed labs no more productive of apposite thinking than teacher-designed labs. That is, there were no significant differences in the frequency of the various distinguishable, content-relevant thought-processes; the dominant process exhibited by both groups was—quite appropriately—information-gathering. There were some differences between the two types of lab experiences in what stimulated students' thinking. But thinking elicited by the design of inquiry and thinking elicited by the data gathered would seem to be equally valuable, so that it is not clear why one type of lab would be preferred over the other.

The results of an evaluation of four alternative introductory physics courses taught at nine colleges and universities in the early 1990s provide some insight into the value of the laboratory experience as the students see it, and the problems in its organization.[47] The authors of this report, published in 1998, found from a review of all available assessment information that students in courses that included labs preferred mini-labs to full labs. In fact they ranked laboratory work least valuable, and lectures and assigned problems most valuable, for learning—what, presumably, they thought they were expected to learn.

Evidence on Problem Solving and Reasoning

Problem solving has always played an important role in science and mathematics learning. Teachers have traditionally taught concepts, rules, formulas, and procedures by statement and example, and then given the students, for practice and reinforcement, problems to solve that require the application of those concepts, rules, and procedures. Today, however, in the educational reform literature, problem solving seems to be related to two other pedagogical imperatives, each allied to constructivist educational philosophy but with different sources for the problems the students are to solve. These imperatives are strongly endorsed as necessary features in the reform of the K–12 curriculum, and they are firmly embedded in the national mathematics and science standards.

In one approach, disciplinary understandings and procedures are the source of the problems to be worked out. According to a 1996 article in a leading journal on educational research, "reform in curriculum and instruction should be based on allowing students to problematize the subject. Rather than mastering skills and applying them, students should be engaged in resolving problems."[48] That seems to mean, as a general teaching strategy, withholding some disciplinary knowledge when it is

How Children Learn Science

available and asking students to work it out for themselves, in order to break down the distinction between acquisition and application. It involves different mixtures of "telling students and letting them discover." The claim is that students will acquire the skills they need, and a deeper conceptual understanding of disciplinary content, by being allowed to problematize what is usually taught through demonstration and repeated practice (for example, how to compute with multidigit numbers). Although the eight co-authors of this article focused on mathematics, they believe that the "principle" they propose is "relevant for all school subjects." Curious to discover the empirical research basis for this belief, we examined the article for references to studies showing support for its efficacy. Some ten studies were cited. To judge by their titles and descriptions, most deal with problem solving in first and second grade.

We then examined the references cited in a section titled "How Effective Are the New Programs?" of a 1999 article on the relationships between research and the standards produced by the National Council of Teachers of Mathematics (NCTM).[49] This piece was in the notable *Journal for Research in Mathematics Education* and was written by the senior author of the 1996 article just mentioned. About a dozen studies were cited here, most of the ten studies cited in the 1996 article among them. Assuming for the sake of argument only that all these studies were well-designed and the evidence from them convincing, one must nevertheless wonder how the results of a small group of studies on beginning arithmetic could have justified, and could continue to justify, overhaul of the entire school curriculum in science and mathematics. Reading between several lines of the author's conclusion, intended to support the learning goals in the NCTM standards, one can hardly avoid thinking that there are *no* studies at higher grades to support this approach. The author writes:

> Although the primary evidence comes from elementary school, especially the primary grades, there is no inconsistent evidence. That is, there are no programs at any level that share the core instructional features, have been implemented as intended for reasonable lengths of time, and show that students perform more poorly than their traditionally taught peers. (p. 16)

No citations appear after these statements. One may infer either that no programs beyond the primary grades sharing the desired features have been implemented *and* show that students perform better than peers taught traditionally, or that such as have been implemented are no worse than the others. Surely this would mean, however, that there *are* programs that have attempted to implement the desired and theorized pedagogy, have failed to produce better results than "traditional" approaches, but can be excused on the grounds that the precise conditions necessary for showing their superiority over "traditional" approaches weren't met. There is the gnawing doubt that *any* "problem solving" program failing to show superiority over "traditional" teaching will ever be judged to have been fairly tested.

In the other approach to problem solving in the K–12 curriculum, the source of the problems to be solved is not disciplinary content or procedure but rather the so-called real world. Indeed, "real-world problem solving" is a term astonishingly prevalent in the educational literature today, implying that what students have learned from problems that teachers or textbooks offered in the past was of little use, practical or otherwise. This kind of problem solving often comes with ideological baggage, as we can see in a 1991 report by the National Center for Improving Science Education, titled "The High Stakes of High School Science."[50] Charging that high school science courses have traditionally been aimed at the select few, it seeks a core curriculum in grades 9 and 10 featuring heterogeneous grouping of students and organization of course content around contemporary social, civic, and personal issues— so as to address the needs of "women, minorities, and low-income and non-college bound youth." We can find *no* relevant studies to support the charge or the prescription. Nor can we think of any reason, theoretical or practical, why high school science courses centered on contemporary social issues and based on heterogeneous groupings of students should be better for women or minorities than discipline-centered courses, whether or not students are in heterogeneous or homogeneous groups.

In the studies we have read, problem solving is frequently set in the context of an "inquiry-based approach" on grounds that it leads to the optimal development of reasoning skills as well as to conceptual understanding. Nevertheless, our reading of a representative group of studies emphasizing the development of reasoning skills through inquiry-based problem solving suggests that: (1) students *always* need teacher guidance in solving problems; (2) reasoning ability depends as much on content knowledge and its manipulation as on the students' presumed level of intellectual development; and (3) the conclusions drawn from them too often depend less on the actual results than on a desire by the authors to promote inquiry-based, problem solving learning. Example: a 1998 study on the relative effects of college students' reasoning ability and prior knowledge on biology achievement in two types of classes, one providing "inquiry" instruction, the other providing "expository" instruction (that is, lecture classes with "verification" labs) found, unexpectedly, that "reasoning ability was a better predictor of achievement in expository classes than in inquiry classes." Failing to consider the possibility that students acquired more information from the lectures and "verification" labs than they had from "inquiry" and, thus equipped, could "reason" better on the final exam, the authors concluded that "the present results imply that college students would be better served by courses that teach by inquiry and focus on the development of scientific reasoning and the acquisition of fewer concepts."[51] (Can one "focus on" the acquisition of fewer concepts?)

Of course, it is not at all clear how one could conclude from any ordinary educational experiment that reasoning skill, *not* knowledge, needs instructional prioritizing, or that low achievement is caused by limited reasoning skill, *not* limited knowledge.

The Effects of Systemic Reform

For almost two decades, reformist voices have endorsed systemic educational reform as the primary cure for poor learning in K–12 mathematics and science. One very important reason for the shift toward systemic reform was the belief that the "current system does not adequately provide for the needs of poor and minority students."[52] Systemic reform, or standards-based reform as it is often called, refers to educational policies that seek to bring about and enforce consistency in goals and content across curriculum frameworks, textbook selection, teacher training, instructional strategies, and assessment practices. As one researcher describes it, proponents of systemic reform believe that "better teaching of mathematics and science will result when all elements of the system that bear most directly on the classroom—especially those dealing with what is taught, how it is taught, how learning is assessed, how teachers are prepared and supported, and how they are held to account for student performance—are aligned with challenging standards, applicable to the full range of students, embedded in a coherent... vision of reform that reflects professional consensus among scientists and educators."[53]

As desirable as standards-based reform—so ambiguously described as that—might be, however, not only have the national science standards developed in the early 1990s been severely criticized for their *lack* of challenge, so too have the national mathematics standards. At first the NCTM standards, developed in the late 1980s and early 1990s, were praised for emphasizing challenging content for all students and for advocating early introduction of more advanced topics, such as geometry, probability, and pre-algebra. In the late 1990s, however, as their effects on textbooks and the curriculum became clearer, the NCTM standards came to be criticized, for example, by the American Mathematical Society,[54] by the Mathematical Association of America,[55] by the authors of a critical report issued in 1998 on the mathematics standards in 46 states,[56] and by Harold Stevenson, the director of the Ethnographic Case Studies Project of the Third International Mathematics and Science Study.[57] In Stevenson's words:

> The NCTM standards present a vague, somewhat grandiose, readily misinterpreted view of what American children should learn in mathematics. Moreover, the view fails to meet what we would consider to be the meaning of 'standards.' Standards should involve a progression of accomplishments or competencies that are to be demonstrated at defined times in the child's schooling. The NCTM standards give no indication (beyond four-year intervals) of the sequence with which the content is to be presented and are not helpful to the classroom teacher in designing lessons that meet the standards.

Most states have by now developed standards for science and mathematics, but those, too, are of uneven quality. Indeed, most of them were rated poor by the authors of two comprehensive reports on state science and mathematics standards.[58] In addition to the reviews of state standards issued by the Fordham Foundation, the American Federation of Teachers and the Council for Basic Education conducted their own review of state standards documents and also rated many of them poor.[59] A common problem of the state standards documents is lack of specificity and of clarity sufficient to enable teachers and test developers to interpret the standards in the same way for purposes of curriculum development, instruction, and assessment.[60] Two other issues have surfaced with respect to national and state standards documents in science and mathematics. First, the articulation of standards, in the eyes of many people, practicing scientists among them, was not intended to entail particular instructional methods and curriculum configurations;

rather, standards documents were to establish what students should know and be able to do, not how the curriculum should be packaged and taught. Yet, many educators or departments of education have used the development of content standards as a license for enforcement of particular pedagogical strategies and curriculum configurations. The science standards conflict in California is simply the most recent, visible, and publicized conflict of this kind. The pedagogical issues were clear to Dr. Seaborg when he was appointed to direct development of the science standards later approved by the California State Board of Education. He was quoted as seeking "an emphasis on basics and fundamentals... not so much emphasis on trying to relate science in unmeaningful ways to modern life and not so much emphasis on educating teachers in methods of teaching rather than in subject matter."[61]

Second, it has also become quite clear that the national standards are meant to prescribe a "basic literacy," as Andrew Ahlgren, Associate Director of the standards project for the AAAS, put it. In testimony to the House Subcommittee on Science, he stated that "the majority of students would be expected to learn far more." Dr. Alberts confirmed that description in testimony of September 24, 1997, stating that "the [AAAS and NRC] standards are minimal standards." In other words, the national science standards were not by themselves intended to provide adequate grounding in science for students wishing to study some science in college, as most college students do. Thus the issue is whether *minimal* competencies plus a great deal of shaky educational philosophy (including current sociology of science notions, to which it relates) are what the public and lawmakers expect as science standards, and whether minimal competencies expressed as standards can increase academic expectations for all students.

We doubt, therefore, the wisdom of binding education reform tightly to current versions of national science and mathematics standards or to most current state standards. Moreover, there is "considerable disagreement and confusion over exactly what systemic reform means in theory and in practice."[62] The scholar who reflected thus notes further that there is little "conclusive evidence on what combination of local, state, or federal factors are necessary for stimulating and maintaining school reforms." Indeed, he finds that little or no scientifically-acceptable evidence has been brought forward to support systemic reform as a stimulant for local school changes.[63]

Nor is there a body of persuasive evidence that systemic reform, however it may be described in particular cases, improves student achievement. One summary report discussing the "emerging evidence from instances of systemic reform" points to a study in California that showed what *three* elementary school teachers learned over a four-year interval of the reform process—a study that led its authors to suggest that the state's systemic reform efforts "could be judged a success, in some respects."[64] One is inclined to question whether even that slightly enthusiastic conclusion is justified by such evidence. Moreover, the study itself, in its discussion of statewide results, indicated that "when the district received the CLAS scores in Spring 1993, the fourth grade results showed that only 6.5% of district students scored at the desired levels 4–6 on the CLAS test in mathematics..."[65]

Even more recently, a five-year study of the National Science Foundation's Statewide Systemic Initiatives Program by an independent evaluator, SRI International, found that the program's impact "has been extremely hard to measure and that evidence of improved test scores as a direct result of the SSI reforms is even more tenuous." As the results of this evaluation were described in an extensive report in the December 4, 1998, issue of *Science*, "after seven years and nearly $600 million spent on the three programs (SSI and two other reform programs for urban and rural schools), officials are still a long way from knowing whether systemic reform works—or even what constitutes success."

In Short: We Don't Really Know

Our reading of the educational research literature has uncovered two key problems that should be explored more intensively in any complete review of research on science (or mathematics) teaching. Such a review is beyond the scope of this chapter, but we can confidently identify the problems. The first is the increasingly common trade-off between process and content. We are concerned that what is called educational reform, whether it refers to the use of specific pedagogical strategies, textbooks, changes in individual courses, or an entire curriculum, seems commonly to entail more class time and emphasis on group processes (and on non-substantive matters such as the interactions among science, technology, and society)[66] and less class time and emphasis on substantive science and mathematics content. This dichotomy emerges starkly from an analysis of seven currently used high school chemistry textbooks, which noted that *CHEM Study*, a text first published during the Sputnik-era reforms, had the most disciplinary content (91.3%), while the text with the least amount of content, published in the 1980s, had only 25.7%.[67]

It is not clear what this trade-off in K–12 or the beginning college years means, in the long run, for the development of independent thinking and informed citizenship. Nor is it clear what it means for high-level professional training. The professional schools have heretofore relied upon a certain level of competence in science and mathematics among their admittees, and research- and work-oriented facilities have done likewise. The trade-off of content for process *may*, for all we know now, be justified; but it has certainly not received justification in the educational writing we have reviewed. And it is unlikely that we have overlooked a body of excellent, analytical work on this question.

The second problem is the lack of critical attention to faults we found in much of the published research on science and mathematics teaching. To enumerate them: concern with changes in students' or teachers' *attitudes, skills,* and *processes* rather than with effects, if any, of the particular "reform" under discussion on student or teacher content *knowledge*; failure to account for the extensive training of teachers in the "reform" as a variable biasing the results of the study when the control group of teachers has received no training in whatever *it* is doing; failure to note that the contents of the "new" test may favor the "reform" and thus be biased in its results; failure to note that many (perhaps most) teachers may not be capable of carrying out the kind of "reform" advocated in the study because they need more structure, support, and knowledge than we can reasonably expect them to have under present conditions; a remarkable lack of candor about what precisely is meant by "conceptual" knowledge and "higher-order thinking" as distinguished from "factual" knowledge or "lower-order thinking"; the citing of anecdote or simply unapologetic advocacy instead of primary research data; and the distorting of what earlier studies actually found as the research base or rationale for a study. There *may well be* some well-designed and well-conducted studies showing support for the new pedagogies at the very lowest educational level and perhaps at scattered higher grade levels, but one must ask whether scientists and mathematicians should support, without informed discussions in their own professional organizations, standards advocating transformation of the entire curriculum in science and mathematics on the basis of just these few studies.

Given the limitations in the design, methodology, and conclusions of many of the individual studies we have examined, and the absence of abundant, sound, and consistent evidence at all educational levels to support the pedagogical or curricular strategies now recommended in schools of education, it is not reasonable for educational policy makers at the state or local school district level to demand systematic adherence to the current versions of the NCTM, AAAS, or NRC standards, or to a constructivist epistemology as now defined in schools of education. *We do not see that there have been breakthroughs in our understanding of how children learn science.* On the other hand, it is reasonable for policy makers to seek ways to address what clearly *is* a major problem if not *the* major problem, the solution to which would surely do more to remedy deficiencies of K–12 science and mathematics education than any set of standards, pedagogical stragegies, curricular configurations, or textbooks: That is, the steady decline of qualified science teachers in K–12, and the pitifully small number of qualified science teachers now in our public schools. According to National Science Foundation officials, as reported in a March, 1999 article in *Education Week,* "75% of science and math teachers in the United States did not major in the field that they are teaching."[68] Surely that is one of the real causes of the growing crisis in science and mathematics education.

Appendix

National Academy of Sciences
2101 Constitution Avenue, NW
Washington, DC 20418

Office of the President
September 9, 1998

California State Board of Education
721 Capitol Mall, Room 532
Sacramento, CA 95814

Dear Board Members:

I write as the president of the National Academy of Sciences, a private organization founded in 1863 under a Congressional charter signed by Abraham Lincoln, and directed to help bring the benefits of science and technology to the American government and the American public. I am a long-term resident of California. My four children attended the San Francisco public schools, and my two grandchildren are students there now. Before I left for my current position in Washington, DC, I helped to start an ongoing, very effective partnership between my university, the University of California, San Francisco (UCSF), and the San Francisco Unified School District. This partnership continues to play a major role in science education and the professional development of teachers in San Francisco.

In 1991, the Academy through its operating arm, the National Research Council, was asked to lead a coalition of scientific societies and national teacher organizations to prepare the first-ever National Science Education Standards for the United States. The development process proceeded through a series of public drafts, which were widely disseminated to over 30,000 individuals and reviewed at yearly intervals. The final Standards document of 250 pages was published in 1996 and offered as a guide for states, school districts, teachers, and parents: it has been acclaimed around the world. Forty members of the National Academy of Sciences contributed their efforts to this document, along with many hundreds of others around the nation. The four-year process succeeded in combining the expertise of scientists, professional science educators and science teachers—and we all learned a great deal from each other. Most importantly, the outcome was a national consensus document designed to set a direction and define expectations for the science learning of all students.

The National Science Education Standards are consistent with similar documents that have been prepared by the American Association for the Advancement of Science in emphasizing the critical importance of active learning. These documents are based on the view that students benefit from engaging in carefully structured scientific investigations in which they also learn to make observations, pose questions, make predictions, propose explanations, and communicate results—as part of the process of learning science. Acquiring critical thinking skills through such scientific inquiry is a crucial component of science teaching and learning, and it will prepare the type of citizens that California needs if our state is to prosper in the years ahead.

The current California State Science Education Standards apparently have been drafted with a very different attitude towards science in mind. The press has reported that they were drafted by a group of Nobel Prize winners: in fact, except for Glenn Seaborg, the much-advertised Nobel Prize winners were not involved. In the interest of making science education more "rigorous," the authors of the draft standards have pushed down the teaching of abstract concepts such as atoms and molecules to fifth, and even third, grade. We know that it will be nearly impossible for children at this age to do more than memorize terminology about these concepts. Throughout, acquiring knowledge through rote learning is overemphasized, and understanding it is underemphasized; in fact, knowledge with understanding is what matters. Finally, the draft standards have neglected the strong recommendation in the National Science Education Standards that a major effort be made to tie school science to the science that students hear about on television and experience in their lives.

The science standards that are adopted for California will influence textbooks, teaching, and testing across the nation for many years. I fear that they will have a direct and detrimental effect on millions of children who are likely to view science facts that they are being asked to memorize as unrelated to their lives. These students will leave school with the same feeling about science that most adults now have: that science is something mysterious and incomprehensible, accessible only to an elite few. This is not good for science, and it is not good for California. Moreover, to the degree that California provides leadership for other states, I fear that these standards have the potential of diminishing our national progress in science education in the years ahead.

For these reasons, I urge the members of the Board to refrain from implementing the current draft of the California State Science Standards until they have been revised to be in closer alignment with the National Science Education Standards.

Sincerely yours,
(signed)
Bruce Alberts
President

Notes

1. Donovan, D., Laudan, L., & Laudan, R. (1992). *Scrutinizing science: Empirical studies of scientific change*. Baltimore: Johns Hopkins University Press. Originally published by Kluwer Academic Publishers, 1986.
2. See, for example, Marci Kanstoroom, What do the 1988 SAT scores really show? *Thomas B. Fordham Foundation. Selected Readings on School Reform*, Vol. 2, No. 4, Fall 1998, 107–108; William H. Honan, SAT scores decline even as grades rise. *The New York Times*, September 2, 1998; and Pascal D. Forgione, Jr. U. S. Commissioner of Education Statistics. Achievement in the United States: Progress since *A Nation at Risk?* U.S. Department of Education, National Center for Education Statistics (http://www.nces.ed.gov). Key summarizing statements: (1) "Data from the Third International Mathematics and Science Study suggests that the relative international standing of U.S. students declines as they progress through school. In both subject areas, our students perform above the international average in grade 4, close to the international average in grade 8, and considerably below it in grade 12." (2) "In twelfth grade, the achievement scores of both our overall student population tested on general mathematics and science knowledge, and of our more advanced students tested in mathematics and physics, were well below the international average." Full report presented at the convocation "Fifteen Years and Still *A Nation at Risk*," April 3, 1998, Washington, D.C., the Willard Hotel.
3. For some recent and egregious examples of such spin, see Diane Ravitch, See all the spin. *The Washington Post,* March 23, 1999, A17.
4. For example, McDermott, L. C. (1991). What we teach and what is learned—closing the gap. *American Journal of Physics 59, 301–315.*
5. See Forgione, cited in Note 2, especially the NCES Web pages.
6. A short and sharp explanation of this lip service can be found in Alan Cromer, *Connected knowledge: Science, philosophy, and education*, Oxford: Oxford University Press, 1997, 10–15.
7. The document can be accessed at www. Ca.Gov./goldstandards. For a reader with general knowledge of science and its classroom teaching, a comparison of this document with the *National Science Education Standards* of the National Research Council will say more than can a lengthy partisan argument (www.nap.edu/readingroom/records/0309053269.html).
8. See Cromer's chapter in this volume.
9. Examples: Deborah Anderluh, Educators ask how much science study is enough, *Sacramento Bee*, March 15, 1998; Paul R. Gross, Science without scientists, *The New York Times,* December 1, 1997, A27.
10. The Piagetian constructivism prevalent in schools of education is neither the constructivism of mathematics philosophy nor the much more common doctrine to which most philosophers and social scientists refer nowadays. The latter is a sociological statement about knowledge, according to which "knowledge" (*hence* "truth," which thus deserves its scare-quotes) is "constructed" as a *social process* rather than by individual acquisition. Under social constructivist doctrine, knowledge is arrived at by processes such as conflict, negotiation, and bargaining (i.e., by politics) rather than by instruction, analysis, or discovery through experience. This is

contrasted with the (rejected) "positivist" view that truth is discovered by appropriate epistemic strategies operating upon experiential evidence under constraints of nature. The term "constructivism" as used by educators, refers therefore to Piaget's own word for the synthesis he claimed to have made of the thesis of pure innatism and the antithesis of pure environmentalism. His hypothesis was a sequential, individual "construction" of intelligence. Piaget's dialectic was in turn derived from Hegel and Marx. The modern educator's version of constructivism—that children's knowledge is constructed, not from their teachers' offerings but from the active deployment of their own cognitive resources while interacting with appropriate objects—is a severe simplification of Piaget's transactional "genetic epistemology." Needless to say, the distinction between Piagetian constructivism and contemporary social constructivism is more often than not missed or glossed over by teacher educators.

[11] Holton, G. (1997). Science education and the sense of self. In P. Gross, N. Levitt, & M.W. Lewis (eds.), *The flight from science and reason.* Baltimore: Johns Hopkins University Press. pp. 551–560.

[12] Basinger, J. (1998). Coalition lashes out a California's proposed science education standards for schools. *The Chronicle of Higher Education,* September 3.

[13] NRC's standards are the product of one of its many grant-funded projects; most contributors to such projects are not members of the Academy.

[14] The first draft of NRC's standards document applauded the questioning of "objectivity" and the "truth" of scientific knowledge. See Holton, *Op. Cit.,* and Cromer, this volume.

[15] See, for example, Peter Gega's introduction to his *Science in elementary education* (New York: John Wiley), which had at least three editions: 1996, 1970, and 1977.

[16] Piaget was an evolutionist, albeit a Spencerian and Lamarckian rather than a Darwinian. That is, he held to the inheritance of acquired characteristics and denied that "chance mutations" alone could play the role attributed to them in standard evolutionary biology. He was convinced that his theory of the development of *individual* human intelligence from infancy to adulthood would reveal details of the evolution of cognition in the human species *as a whole*. Piaget's evolutionary ideas were flawed by the unwarranted leap from individual development to the evolution of whole populations, and by his failure to understand what was already known of genetics. Like Spencer's and Lamarck's, his massive output did not, in the end, have much impact upon biological science.

[17] For a very general but incisive (and admiring) examination of Piaget's thought, and of objections to it, see Pat Duffy Hutcheon, *Leaving the cave: Evolutionary naturalism in social-scientific thought,* Waterloo, Ontario, Canada: Wilfrid Laurier University Press, 1996, 361 ff.

[18] He also proposed two mechanisms to account for the internalization of knowledge: assimilation and accommodation. Disequilibrium is triggered when the child senses a discrepancy between his current concepts and the experiences he is undergoing. The operation of these mechanisms helps him achieve a new equilibrium that includes understanding of new concepts.

[19] Piaget, J. *Science of education and the psychology of the child.* NY: Orion Press, 1970, p. 173. This quotation appears in E.D. Hirsch, Jr., *In the Schools We Need and Why We Don't Have Them,* NY: Doubleday, 1996.

[20] As Michael Cole and Shelia Cole observe in *The development of childhood,* 2nd ed. (NY: Scientific American Books, 1993), "contrary to classical Piagetian theory, not everyone proves capable of solving Piagetian formal operational tasks, even in adulthood. In some societies, virtually no adults can solve these problems. Non-Piagetian versions of formal operational thinking occur in some contexts in all societies, however" (p. 649). They also note that "recent studies seem to show that young children are not so limited in their ability to appreciate alternative points of view as Piaget thought" (p. 324), and that one reason why Piaget "underestimated the cognitive competence of young children" was because his research techniques relied heavily on verbally presented problems and verbal justifications of reasoning" (p. 328).

[21] Anderson, P., Reder, L. & Simon, H. (1998). Radical constructivism and cognitive psychology. In D. Ravitch (Ed.), *Brookings papers on education policy 1988.* Washington, D.C.: Brookings Institute, 227–278.

[22] Vygotsky, L. (1962). *Thought and language.* Cambridge, MA: MIT Press. Although Piaget and Vygotsky are both considered developmental "constructivists," Piaget is seen as espousing an individualistic form of constructivism (implying to many educators that the child should be "left alone" in a cognitively rich environment to direct his or her own learning), while Vygotsky is seen as a social constructivist (wrongly implying to many educators today that children should be left alone in heterogeneous peer groups in a cognitively rich environment to direct their own learning). Vygotsky talked about the "scaffolding" for learning that could supplied by an adult or more able peer, but he never intimated that heterogeneous peer groups could substitute for a teacher's instruction.

[23] Bruner, J. (1966). *The process of education.* Cambridge, MA: Harvard University Press.

[24] Bruner, J. (1961). The act of discovery. *Harvard Education Review,* 31, 21–32.

[25] Bruner, J. (1973). *The Relevance of Education.* New York: W.W. Norton. Chapter 4: Some elements of discovery.

[26] See Cole & Cole, *Op. Cit.,* p. 574.

[27] This is a sub-phenomenon within the broader fading, in our culture, of any distinction between knowledge and opinion.

[28] Cromer, A. (1998). The math and science wars. *Features.* Northeastern University Magazine. May, 49–52.

[29] Cohen, E.G. (1994). Restructuring the classroom: Conditions for productive small groups. *Review of Educational Research,* 64, 1–35.

[30] Davidson, N. (1985). Small group learning and teaching in mathematics: A selective review of the research. In R. Slavin et al..(Eds.), *Learning to cooperate, cooperating to learn.* New York: Plenum.

[31] Newmann, F., & Thompson, J.A. (1987). *Effects of cooperative learning on achievement in secondary schools: A summary of research.* Madison, WI: University of Wisconsin-Madison, National Center on Effective Secondary Schools.

[32] Widaman, K.F., & Kagan, S. (1987). Cooperativeness and achievement: Interaction of student cooperativeness with cooperative versus competitive classroom organization. *Journal of School Psychology*, 25, 355–365.

[33] Slavin, R. (1995). *Cooperative learning: Theory, research, and practice*, 2nd ed. Boston: Allyn & Bacon.

[34] Antil, L., Jenkins, J., Wayne, S., & Vadasy, P, (1998). Cooperative learning: prevalence, conceptualizations, and the relation between research and practice. *American Educational Research Journal, 35, 419–454.*

[35] Lumpe, A.T., & Staver, J.R. (1995). Peer collaborations and concept development: Learning and photosynthesis. *Journal of Research in Science Teachings, 32,* 71–98.

[36] Webb, N., Nemer, K.M., Chizhik, A., & Sugrue, B. Equity issues in collaborative group assessment: Group composition and performance. *American Educational Research Journal,* 1998, 35, 607–651.

[37] Heller, P., Keith, R., & Anderson, S. (1992). Teaching problem solving through cooperative grouping. Part I: Group versus individual problem solving. *American Journal of Physics,* 60, 627–636; Heller, P., & Hollabaugh, M. (1992). Teaching problem solving through cooperative grouping. Part 2: Designing problems and structuring groups. *American Journal of Physics,* 60, 637–644.

[38] Shaw, D.E. & PCAST Panel on Educational Technology. (1998). Report to the President on the use of technology to strengthen K–12 education in the United States: findings related to research and evaluation. *Journal of Science Education and Technology,* 7, 115–116.

[39] Shaw & PCAST, p. 117.

[40] Shaw & PCAST, p. 118.

[41] Burkham, D., Lee, V., & Smerdon, B. (1997). Gender and science learning early in high school: subject matter and laboratory experiences. *American Educational Research Journal,* 34, 297–331.

[42] Wenglensky, H. (1998). *Does It Compute? The Relationship between educational technology and student achievement in mathematics.* Princeton, NJ: Educational Testing Service.

[43] Chisman, D.G. (Ed.) (1990). *New trends in integrated science teaching.* Fleurus, Belgium: UNESCO.

[44] Westbrook, S.L. (1998). Examining the conceptual organization of students in an integrated algebra and physical science class. *School Science and Mathematics,* 98, 84–92.

[45] Hofstein, A., & Lunetta, V.N. (1982). The role of the laboratory in science teaching: Neglected aspects of research. *Review of Educational Research,* 52, 201–217.

[46] Shepardson, D.P. (1997). The nature of student thinking in life science laboratories. *School Science and Mathematics.* 97, 37–44.

[47] Coleman, L.A., Holcomb, D.F., & Rigden, J.S. (1998). The introductory university physics project 1987–1995: what has it accomplished? *American Journal of Physics,* 66, 124–137.

[48] Hiebert, J., et al. (1996). Problem solving as a basis for reform in curriculum and instruction: The case of mathematics. *Educational Researcher,* May 1996, Vol. 25, No. 4, 12–21.

49 Hiebert, J. (1998) Relationships between research and the NCTM standards *Journal for Research in Mathematics Education.* Vol. 30, No. 1, 3–19.

50 The National Center for Improving Science Education. (1991). *The high stakes of high school science.* Washington, D.C.: Office of Educational Research and Improvement, U.S. Department of Education.

51 Johnson, M.A., & Lawson, A.E. (1998). What are the relative effects of reasoning ability and prior knowledge on biology achievement in expository and inquiry classes? *Journal of Research in Science Teaching*, 35, 89–103.

52 Vinovskis, M. (1996). An analysis of the concept and uses of systemic educational reform. *American Educational Research Journal*, 33, 53–85.

53 Knapp, M. (1997). Between systemic reforms and the mathematics and science classroom: The dynamics of innovation, implementation, and professional learning. *Review of Educational Research*, 67, 227–266.

54 The report is at http://www.ams.org/government/nctm2000.html.

55 Two reports with specific criticism of the NCTM standards are available from this association: http://www.maa.org/past/maanctm2.html and http://www.maa.org/past/maanctm3html.

56 Raimi & Braden, *op.cit.*

57 See http://mathematicallycorrect.com/hwsnctm.html for Stevenson's full statement.

58 Raimi & Braden, *op.cit.*, and Lerner, L.S. (1998). *State science standards: An appraisal of science standards in 36 states.* Fordham Report Vol. 2, No. 4, March. Washington, D.C.: Thomas B. Fordham Foundation.

59 Gandal, M. (1997). *Making standards matter: An annual fifty-state report on efforts to raise academic standards.* Washington, D.C.: American Federation of Teachers; Joftus, S., & Berman, I. (1998). *Great expectations? Defining and assessing rigor in state standards.* Washington D.C.: Council for Basic Education.

60 Although it has been argued that vague standards allow for local control, the reality is almost always the opposite. Vague standards allow state test developers to interpret the standards as they wish, making statewide assessments the tail that wags the curriculum dog in local schools. And it stands to reason that even the most conscientious teachers are unlikely, in present circumstances, to create higher and more focused standards of achievement than those handed down to them as official. The deeper problem is that because of test security, only test developers and staff members of the state department of education know what the academic expectations really are in each subject, even though the major reason for developing standards is to provide public accountability as to exactly what was expected and to increase academic expectations for all students.

61 Interestingly, the TIMSS report notes that grade 8 Minnesota students had among the highest scores in science, second only to Singapore in science and tied with Singapore on earth science. The authors of the TIMMS report attribute these achievements to a coherent statewide science curriculum that focused on earth science and to the special training teachers had in earth science.

62 Vinovskis, *Op. Cit.*, 73.

63 Vinovskis, *Op. Cit.*, 70.

64 Knapp, *Op. Cit.*

[65] Grant, S. G., Peterson, P.L., & Shojgreen-Downer, A. (1996). Learning to teach mathematics in the context of systemic reform. *American Educational Research Journal,* 32, 509–541.

[66] This is not to suggest that such interactions are unimportant. They are very important; but they are not science. They are civics, or politics, or social science, or whatever, and can be taught as such.

[67] Chiappetta, E.L., Sethna, G. H., & Fillman, D. A. (1991). A quantitative analysis of high school chemistry textbooks for scientific literacy themes and expository learning aids. *Journal of Research in Science Teaching,* 28, 939–951.

[68] Portner, Jessica. *Education Week,* Vol. 18, No. 26, p. 7 (http://www.edweek.org/ew/current/26sci.h18).

Chapter 7

Why the Battle over History Standards?

Sheldon M. Stern
John Fitzgerald Kennedy Library and Museum

This essay attempts to probe beneath the heated rhetoric of the national and state history standards debate by exploring several factors which have distorted efforts to reform history education in American schools. It examines the impact of multiculturalism on curriculum and teaching, the political and educational co-dependency of reactionary zealots and multicultural extremists, and the widespread acceptance of deconstructionist attacks on the existence of a knowable historical reality. As readers will infer from the examples discussed in this essay, there are no easy ways to combat the influence of these three factors on the K–12 history curriculum.

Once upon a time, there was a nation called the Very United States. Late in the 20th century, historians, political leaders, teachers and parents, alarmed by poor student performance in history in the schools, called for higher standards and expectations for students from K–12. Several commissions were formed, testimony was heard across the nation, and an achievable plan for improving the training of history teachers and the quality of history teaching was approved without serious opposition. The program was carefully implemented, and within a decade the most intellectually gifted college graduates were choosing history teaching careers in record numbers, test scores were rising sharply, and the number of young Americans studying history in high school and college had reached an all-time high.

This fantasy assumes that developing higher standards and improving the teaching of history are simply educational tasks. In the real world, of course, they depend, especially in the critical areas of teacher accreditation and staffing, on the criteria formulated by political bodies such as boards and departments of education. In that context, Diane Ravitch's recent research has documented what many observers of history in our schools have long suspected: 81.5% of American social studies teachers had neither a major nor a minor in history and the majority do not have degrees in any academic field. The situation in history is only slightly better: 55% of high school history teachers had neither a major nor a minor in history. In other words, well over half of American students are studying history with a teacher who, Ravitch concludes, "was not sufficiently interested in the subject to study it in college. Of all subjects taught in school, history has the largest proportion of teachers who are teaching 'out of field.'" This is a shaky foundation on which to build serious history standards for genuine reforms in history education.

In addition, history teachers are not generally encouraged, evaluated, or rewarded for their historical knowledge. I have worked with many terrific teachers over the years, because those participating in the Kennedy Library American History Project are a self-selected group with a real commitment to history. One excellent history teacher, for example, recently described his department's annual performance evaluations as "a farce" in which they discussed "everything but history." The evaluation has nothing to do with content, he charged, with what he knows and teaches. He suggested the following question to the evaluation committee: "What are the last five books you read in your field, and how have they changed your views and influenced your teaching?" After some awkward looks and rolling eyes, the suggestion was quietly dropped.

By knowing history, of course, I mean much more than just the mastery of chronology and facts, but also the understanding of historical methodology, the grasp of the connection between evidence and conclusions and the awareness of how historical interpretation evolves and changes in the context of the time and place in which it is written.

The development of history standards turned out to be even less educationally driven than the certification and staffing of history teachers. In the real world of education, the clash over history standards inevitably got tangled up in changes in American life, from popular culture to the academic world, and in struggles between interest groups and institutions at all levels of American society. Several of the factors which have made the struggle over standards so contentious have become clear to me from my work with teachers and students in Massachusetts since 1980.

The Impact of Multiculturalism on Curriculum and Teaching

The first factor is the impact of multicultural extremism in our schools. Multicultural history should mean exposing American students to a full recognition of our rich and diverse past. Only a fool would deny that such recognition is necessary and long overdue. Samuel Eliot Morison's 1965 best-selling *Oxford History of the American People*, for example, essentially ignored the story of three-fourths of those people. Unfortunately, in the rush to discard these old distortions, multicultural extremists in the contentious world of American schools have often simply substituted new distortions. Theories and rhetoric aside, multiculturalism often operates in schools much like Newton's Third Law of equal and opposite action and reaction: inclusion of the previously excluded is never enough; exclusion of the previously included is also essential. For more than a decade, as a case in point, I received as many as a dozen invitations to speak during Black History Month (a subject I taught for ten years on the college level). A program director who had invited me each year from 1982 to 1986 was replaced in 1987, and told me that her successor wanted future programs to be "more multicultural." I think that was the first time I had ever heard the term. It's been eleven years since my last invitation to speak during Black History Month. Multicultural inclusion/exclusion works on many levels: a friend who had written a book for young people on Nat Turner and was planning a study of the slave trade was told by his publisher, off the record, that they no longer accept books by whites about blacks.

In the recent controversy in the San Francisco schools over setting a quota requiring minority authors, it was hard to tell whether the real agenda was to include books by minorities or to exclude "outside" writers and subjects. The most revealing words in that discussion, which could serve as the poster slogan for multiculturalism as it operates in the real world of American education, came when school board members insisted that the *Diary of Anne Frank* was irrelevant, especially during Black History Month. As Mark Twain wrote toward the end of his life, "In the first place God made idiots. That was for practice. Then He made school boards."[2]

My experience suggests that the very idea of definable national standards for *all* students is anathema to militant multiculturalists. Gary Nash, Charlotte Crabtree, and Ross Dunn, in *History on Trial*, their recent book on the "war" over national history standards, cite the following exchange during a 1992 discussion of multiculturalism by members of the national council reviewing the proposed standards. Chester Finn cautioned:

> We must teach about diversity, to be sure, but must never lose sight of what binds us together as a nation, the great unifying Western ideas of individual freedom, political democracy, and human rights... We agree wholeheartedly that in the past schools did not present history in a very balanced way... But the solution to this problem is not... to turn things around 180 degrees and blame, or even worse, ignore, Western tradition. Mollifying factions who come to the table at education meetings isn't the same as developing standards for history that will have an impact upon how it is learned around the country.[3]

These remarks set off a firestorm of charges of a hidden agenda to exclude native Americans, blacks, and women—a political ploy to preserve traditional history by raising the specter of balkanizing American society.

Nash and his colleagues then quote, with obvious approval, several of the critics who responded to Finn's remarks. Adelaide Sanford, a member of the New York State Board of Regents, for example, argued that traditional history contributed to the oppression of people who had been marginalized and ignored. Inclusivity is important, Sanford stressed, but nothing is more important than *"the quality of the history that is included—its truthfulness and its reflection of the new historical scholarship..."* [emphasis added].[4]

Two years earlier, when Diane Ravitch criticized the anti-white, anti-European bias in a proposed New York State "Curriculum of Inclusion" written by Leonard Jeffries of the City University of New York, the same Adelaide Sanford responded angrily: "Your grandparents owned my grandparents." When Ravitch replied that her grandparents came to the U.S. with nothing from a tiny village in Poland, Sanford countered, "They owned the slave ships that brought my ancestors here." Ravitch protested that her grandparents were poor and did not own slave ships. Sanford then retorted, "I am speaking ethnically."[5]

Sanford's version of "truthful historical knowledge and new scholarship" is rooted in the Nation of Islam's anonymously written book, *The Secret Relationship Between Blacks and Jews,* which argues that Jews—including "the Jewish Pilgrim fathers"—financed the Atlantic slave trade and controlled slavery in the United States. Henry Louis Gates, director of African American Studies at Harvard, in a lengthy critique in the *New York Times,* called the book "one of the most sophisticated instances of hate literature yet compiled" and charged that it "massively misrepresents the historical record largely though a process of cunningly selective quotations from historically reputable sources."[6] Historians of slavery, black and white, have condemned the book, particularly its use of Nazi-like notions of inherited racial guilt. Even the American Historical Association took the rare step of publishing an explicit denunciation. Nevertheless, Adelaide Sanford, who is still a New York State Regent, evidently accepts such nonsense as "new and truthful historical scholarship." Just as illuminating, Nash and his colleagues are comfortable quoting her as an authority on history education.

In this context, we should never lose sight of the fact that extreme multiculturalism is also about turf, power, patronage, and money—it is a very lucrative business. In New York State, for example, students learn that the Iroquois Confederacy was as influential as the Enlightenment and the American colonial experience in shaping the Albany Plan of Union, the Articles of Confederation, and the Constitution. There is, of course, no evidence to support this view. It was adopted in multicultural deference to the state's Iroquois lobby. Here in Massachusetts, at a local parochial school which hired a "diversity director," teachers bitterly complained about the multicultural awareness sessions which faculty and students were compelled to attend in order to purge their racism. The teachers were willing to tell me about the situation confidentially, but no one would say anything publicly. This discussion occurred four years ago and the "diversity director" is still there. Viewed in this sense, multiculturalism is a kind of ideological Tammany Hall.

The Political and Educational Co-Dependency of the Extremes

The second factor in this story is the curious politics of the standards debate. Defenders of multicultural history are eager to cite the attacks on history reform by right wing extremists like Rush Limbaugh, Gordon Liddy, and Oliver North. There is clearly much support, financial and otherwise, from rightist extremists who fear inclusion, who don't want to tell the whole American story by including the history of women and minorities, who believe that archaic history equals patriotism and still hope to roll back a generation of revisionist scholarship.

Ironically, however, militant multiculturalists and the extreme right desperately need each other. They are, my experience suggests, involved in a curious dance—feeding off each other in order to justify their own excesses. Nash and his colleagues, for example, in *History on Trial,* argue that the extreme Right was primarily responsible for the resistance to the standards and thus make no genuine effort to analyze the criticism by serious scholars and historians. To illustrate this symbiosis of extremes, when Diane Ravitch publicly criticized the 1994 draft of the national history standards, a co-director of the UCLA National Center for History in the Schools, in a not very subtle attempt to intimidate critics, wrote to warn that she would be judged by the company she keeps, the racist, anti-Semitic, anti-pluralist, and neo-nativist enemies of the standards on the authoritarian right.[7] This phenomenon appears, to borrow some psychological jargon, to be a case of political and ideological co-dependency. They really do need each other!

The Attack on the Existence of a Knowable Historical Reality

These two factors, the impact of extreme multiculturalism in the schools and the co-dependency of the extreme left and right, provide the context for my final point: the battle over history standards, in large part, reflects an escalating attack on the very notion of historical truth. Not long ago, the denial of the existence of a knowable historical reality was confined to the largely inconsequential backwaters of academic deconstructionism and postmodernism. Today, these views are seeping into every level of American popular culture, society, and education. Several years ago, when a colleague discovered a bizarre "interpretation" of the JFK assassination on the Internet, which claimed that aliens were involved, I requested the evidence to back up this claim. Within twenty minutes I received the following reply, "Evidence! Evidence! All you people talk about is evidence!"

More than half a century ago, George Orwell wrote: "I know it is the fashion to say that most of recorded history is lies anyway. I am willing to believe that history is for the most part inaccurate and biased, but what is peculiar to our own age is the abandonment of the idea that history can be truthfully written." In the past, Orwell concluded, people still believed

Why the Battle over History Standards? 155

that "the facts existed and were more or less discoverable."[8] Well George, you ain't seen nothin' yet!

In the 19th century, Leopold Von Ranke proclaimed that historians could reconstruct history as it actually happened (*wie es eigentlich gewesen ist*). Original sources, used judiciously, could avoid both the Scylla of relativism and the Charybdis of judgmentalism. As naive and unattainable as this notion may be, today we are seeing a 180 degree turn—nothing is true, nothing has meaning, only the subtexts count. Beethoven's Ninth Symphony, we are told, was written as "a paean to rape." The whole situation suggests something akin to the early 19th century Romantic attack on Enlightenment reason and rationalism and the glorification of subjective and individual emotion.

Something very serious is going on here—it is not a joke. When historians reject inductive reasoning and insist that truth and knowledge are completely relative and determined entirely by language and culture, are they still historians? As Keith Windschuttle put it in *The Killing of History*, the notion that there are no facts, only interpretations, is not new and goes back at least to Nietzsche. What *is* new is the *widespread* popularity such ideas now enjoy among historians and teachers of history. As Windschuttle remarks:

> Many historians have been exposed as mistaken, opinionated, and often completely wrong, but their critics have usually felt obliged to show that they were wrong about real things, that their claims about the past were different from the things that actually happened. In other words, the critics still operated on the assumption that the truth was within the historian's grasp. Today, these assumptions are widely rejected, even among... historians themselves. [Many believe] that it is impossible to tell the truth about the past or to use history to produce knowledge in any objective sense at all. They claim we can only see the past through the perspective of our own culture and, hence, what we see in history are our own interests and concerns reflected back at us. There is no fundamental distinction any more between history and myth.[9]

In April 1992, for example, the *American Historical Review* published three essays evaluating director Oliver Stone's film, *JFK*, as history (including a full-page photo of actor Kevin Costner in the leading role). One reviewer, the only historian, asserted that "Historians do not, of course, approve of fiction, aside from the underlying fiction that the past can be truly told in neat, linear stories."[10] He defended Stone's "invention of incidents and characters because historical events rarely occur with the kind of shape, order, and intensity that will keep an audience in its seats. Inventions move the story forward, keep emotions high, and order complex series of events into plausible structures..." Apparently, the reviewer was either unaware or unconcerned that one of Stone's key technical advisers, and the source for the most important bogus character in the film, "General X," has for decades been promoting the notion of a vast conspiracy of government "power brokers," which began at "Iron Mountain" in the Hudson Valley of New York in the 1960s. The meeting never happened—satirist Leonard Lewin's *Report from Iron Mountain* was, in reality, a spoof and a brilliant hoax. The reviewer nevertheless concludes that *JFK,* which Stone himself conceded was a "counter-myth," "has to be among the most important works of *American history* [emphasis added] ever to appear on the screen." This approach to evidence characterizes so many of the "studies" programs which have proliferated in American schools and colleges. Touted as "cross-disciplinary," they are, in reality, often anti-disciplinary and openly contemptuous of the very idea of historical truth.

The Influence on the Schools

Does all this have any relevance in the practical, everyday world of teaching history in American schools and writing history standards for American students? My experience suggests that the answer is definitely yes. A key example has been the struggle to teach the whole story of the history of slavery in Africa. The original national history standards, for example, extolled the great African kingdoms at the time of European contact—their "importance and influence," "settlement patterns and trade," "attitudes toward nature and the use of land," and the influence of "Islam and Muslim culture." There was an especially glowing account of Mansa Musa, the early 14th century King of Mali—"the social customs and wealth of his kingdom," its trade "in gold and salt," the "achievements and grandeur" of his court, and his great pilgrimage to Mecca in 1324. The facts are more complex: Arab writers reported that Mansa Musa brought 500 servants and 12,000 slaves on the pilgrimage to carry gold staffs and serve as beasts of burden; his wealth was based on trading slaves as well as gold and salt. The pre-European Muslim Arab slave trade is also never mentioned—nor is the role of Africans in enslaving and selling other Africans for centuries before the arrival of Europeans. Indeed, key historians of slavery have concluded that

Why the Battle over History Standards?   157

virtually all Africans brought to the Western Hemisphere in the 17th and 18th centuries were already slaves before they left Africa.

I have tried to explore this issue in schools and workshops for years by discussing my 1994 critique of the national history standards, and more recently by distributing my response to an article in *Time* urging President Clinton to apologize for slavery when he visited the Door of No Return on Goree Island off Dakar, Senegal, during his trip to Africa. The author of the article argued that "the great rift between the races cannot be healed until America seeks forgiveness for one of the most monstrous eras in history" with an official apology at the scene of the crime. I tried to approach the issue with teachers from a broader historical perspective. Was the African slave trade exclusively, or even principally, an American crime? The Moslem Arab slave trade forced millions of Africans into slavery centuries before Western involvement. Likewise, the enslavement of Africans by Africans, particularly by the royal families of the Congo, Benin, and Ashanti, flourished long before the arrival of Europeans. The Atlantic slave trade likely could not have taken root if this system had not existed. White slavers did not have to search for victims, as imagined in Alex Haley's *Roots*; they used African slave markets. "I believe," Ghanaian diplomat Kofi Awoonor has asserted, "there is a great psychic shadow over Africa, and it has much to do with our guilt and denial of our role in the slave trade. We too are blameworthy in what was essentially one of the most heinous crimes in human history."[11]

Any apology for slavery involving the United States should be joined by Portugal, Britain, France, and especially Brazil, which purchased over six times more African slaves than the U.S. and did not abolish slavery until 1888. North America received only 5% of the Africans brought to the New World. In addition, the Moslem Arab states, which imported more African slaves than the entire Western Hemisphere, could confront their past by helping to abolish slavery which persists *today* in Mauritania and Sudan. Forgiveness begins by facing the whole truth about Africa and slavery.

By simply putting this historical material on the table in schools and teacher workshops, I have been involved in confrontations with teachers (both black and white) who refuse to accept the facts. One teacher, now completing a Ph.D., told me that "My African American Studies professor says there was never slavery in Africa before the Europeans." I tried to suggest some reading, but she refused to take the list. In the most disturbing encounter, two teachers responded to the evidence by declaring, "I don't believe that." I told them that it was a question of history and evidence, not belief, and cited the words of Kofi Awoonor. They said that my remarks were offensive and left the room.

In a recent workshop, several teachers conceded that "perhaps" slavery existed in Africa, but explained that it was "benign" or "good" slavery because it was generally not hereditary, making an obviously pejorative comparison to American slavery. Of course, such differences had nothing to do with morality or ethics and everything to do with economic and social reality. In Africa, the potential supply of slaves was unlimited and the cost very low. Hereditary slavery was unnecessary. In the United States, despite some illegal importation of slaves after 1808, the supply was limited and costs high so that hereditary slavery was the most practical solution. One teacher responded to these facts by saying that it was insulting to her to hear slavery discussed in such cold "dollars and cents" terms. After all, she said, with great emotion—slaves were human beings. I saw several teachers roll their eyes, but no one said a word.

A few days later, the discussion turned to another complex fact about American slavery never mentioned in the national history standards: the 1830 U. S. census recorded that 3,775 free blacks owned 12,760 slaves. This time, the same teachers questioned the value of using these statistics because, they declared, blacks bought slaves only in order to emancipate them. The facts, of course, were much more complicated. Most black slave owners lived in the South, but blacks owned slaves in Rhode Island, Connecticut, Illinois, New Jersey, and New York, as well as several border states and the District of Columbia. Most black slave owners held only a few slaves, but some in Louisiana and South Carolina owned as many as eighty. There are some recorded cases in which blacks bought slaves to protect family members or emancipated their slaves (as did some whites), but the evidence indicates that a significant number of blacks who owned slaves did so for the same reasons as whites—economic gain and social status. The teachers glared at me but did not respond. The subject was dropped without further discussion.

In sharp contrast, "Africans in America," the four-part PBS series produced by WGBH in Boston, confronts "America's journey through slavery" clearly and honestly. Viewers discover that slavery was "an ancient business" in Africa. The script draws on the powerful 18th century narrative of Olaudah Equiano, who was captured by Africans and

Why the Battle over History Standards? 159

eventually sold to Europeans, to educate viewers about the African side of the slavery equation. Equiano, viewers discover, was first sold by one African master to another and exposed to a bewildering variety of African languages and cultures which were completely alien to him (in one case, he was sold for cowrie shells). On the slave coast, the script affirms, Africans became absorbed with slave raids and wars, eventually leading to the capture and sale of perhaps 20,000,000 people. Viewers learn that 11,000,000 Africans were eventually shipped to the Western Hemisphere, but only 500,000 (less than 5%) went to the British colonies in North America; the rest went to South America and the Caribbean. The script also discusses the extreme physical brutality of slavery in Barbados.

The "Africans in America" companion book, by Charles Johnson, Patricia Smith, and the WGBH Series Research Team, is even more explicit:

> The white man did not introduce slavery to Africa. The bowing of one human being before another was an accepted notion from the moment man first sensed frailty on the part of a rival. And, by the fifteenth century, men with dark skin had become quite comfortable with the concept of man as property... Long before the arrival of Europeans on West Africa's coast, the two continents shared a common acceptance of slavery as an unavoidable and necessary—perhaps even desirable—fact of existence. The commerce between the two continents, as tragic as it would become, developed upon familiar territory. Slavery was not a twisted European manipulation, although Europe capitalized on a mutual understanding and greedily expanded the slave trade into what would become a horrific enterprise... During this era, Africans and Europeans stood together as equals, companions in commerce and profit... Tribe stalked tribe, and eventually more than 20 million Africans would be kidnapped in their own homeland.[12]

The authors cite Samuel Sulemana Fuseini, a Ghanaian educator and politician descended from African slave drivers, affirming that the great wealth of his forefathers, the Ashanti, was based on slavery.

What is in the Teacher's Guide and the Student Activity guide is a different story, however. The sponsor of these programs, Bankers Trust, declares in the Teacher's Guide prepared for the series, "An understanding of the common history we share as Americans is a strong foundation from which all communities can work together and prosper." Likewise, the Student Activity Guide asserts that an examination of our common history is long overdue: "Our nation's story has the potential to illuminate, to inspire, to heal... The series does not attempt to replace old myths with new ones. By providing a clearer view of our shared past it can help us to provide a better future."[13] But, ironically, the essential "common history" presented in the teaching materials, in sharp contrast to the television series and the companion book, is built on a massive evasion and distortion of the historical record.

Teachers and students are merely told that Africans were "kidnapped," "captured," or "abducted from their homelands" in the "largest forced migration in recorded history"—without any mention of the decisive role of indigenous African slavery and the importance of African royal families, slave dealers, and coastal holding camps in supplying European slave merchants. Students are asked, for example, to locate Olaudah Equiano's homeland (present-day Nigeria) and "brainstorm a list of words they think describe [everyday] life in that part of Africa in the 17th century (e.g., family life, religion, economy)." The word "slavery," the critical element in Equiano's account of his experience in Africa, is missing, promoting the illusion, much like the original national history standards, that Africans lived in a pre-slavery Eden before the advent of the Atlantic slave trade. Students would never guess, as Kofi Awoonor asserts and the PBS script and companion book affirm, that Africans were deeply implicated in facilitating this human catastrophe.[14]

Likewise, the Teacher's Guide completely ignores the larger context of world slavery in which the British-American system took root. Students are left without a clue that the Caribbean and South America absorbed the vast majority of the Africans brought to the Western Hemisphere. Without this information about Africa and the Americas, key questions in the Teacher's Guide—"When and why did slavery in the British American colonies begin?" "What factors made it possible for Europeans to enslave Africans?" "Who profited from slavery?" "Who was dependent on slavery?"—cannot be answered fully or truthfully.[15]

The Teacher's Guide, as a result, squandered a unique opportunity for teaching the skills of historical analysis. Students could have been asked, for example, to assess the fact that Africans enslaved people of their own color, but drew the line at reducing members of their own tribe (or nation) to bondage. Europeans, on the other hand, despite bitter national rivalries, would not enslave people of their own color but had no reservations about making slaves of Africans or sometimes native Americans. The teaching materials make no effort to help students understand why Africans respected nationality over color, but Europeans (and Americans) respected color over nationality. The Teacher's Guide labels as "an American paradox... the enslavement and oppression of one people to provide independence and prosperity to another." But, despite urging teachers "to explore the issue of how and why history has been interpreted—and often distorted—over the years," the authors never mention the paradox of Africans who used the enslavement and oppression of their own people to provide prosperity for themselves.[16]

The television script, on the other hand, makes every effort to educate, explaining, for example, the gradual appearance of racial slavery in 17th century British America as indenture and freedom virtually disappeared for blacks (powerfully illustrated by the story of Anthony Johnson's failed hope for liberty and prosperity for his descendants); exploring the subtle possibility that slavery was not inevitable and that the history of race might have evolved differently in America; and noting the significant fact that bonds between poor whites and blacks were a major cause of the New York slave uprising hysteria of the early 1740s. The episode on the Revolution explores the remarkable story of Venture Smith, a New England slave who, in the context of the "freedom fever" sweeping the colonies, worked tirelessly for decades to make freedom a reality for himself and his family. But, the television script and series scholars also acknowledge that Smith later purchased several slaves and felt "cheated and betrayed" when they ran away and he lost his investment. Finally, the exploration of the coming Civil War discusses Fanny Kemble's encounter with slavery in the Georgia sea islands in context as an example of "the prejudices of her time," emphasizes the importance of abolitionist principles in reinvigorating the "freedom fever" of the Revolution, and acknowledges the critical role of William Lloyd Garrison's *Liberator*, subscribed to mostly by blacks, as the "conscience of the abolitionist movement."

The Teacher's Guide persistently distorts, constructing a tendentious and presentistic portrait of invariably guilty whites and flawless blacks and falling back on evasive double-talk instead of explaining how and why Africans were kidnaped, abducted, or captured in their homelands. In a particularly revealing example, students are asked to "imagine" Venture Smith's arguments in a debate with contemporaries such as George Washington, Thomas Jefferson, and Lord Dunmore over the proposition that "American slavery is an oxymoron," and to discuss "Which side of the debate would each of these people be on and why?" The question clearly demands one-dimensional, no pun intended, black and white responses. The television program, on the contrary, examines Washington's and Jefferson's ambivalence about slavery, emphasizes Lord Dunmore's transparent political and military motives, and reveals Smith's purchase of slaves, making clear that, to varying degrees, they would all have been on *both* sides of the argument.[17] Similarly, in discussing the oncoming Civil War, the teaching guide ignores the importance of Garrison (mentioned merely in passing as Frederick Douglass' mentor) and other white abolitionists and refers instead to the "black abolitionists and their white allies"—a historically misleading term never used in the television script and a classic example of multicultural inclusion/exclusion. The Teacher's Guide, like the original national history standards, consistently resists exposing students to ideologically inconvenient historical complexities.

The television series and book make clear that slavery was the norm in the 17th and 18th century world. The fact that the British colonies in North America became a part of this universal slave network was neither exceptional nor an oxymoron; it would have been remarkable and unprecedented if they had avoided it. The American experience *is* unique because, at the same time, it produced institutions and ideas which eventually helped to destroy slavery itself and extended freedom and citizenship beyond anything imaginable at that time.

Sources at WGBH confirmed that the on-screen scholars, the academic "Series Advisors," and the authors of the companion book had no direct connection to the "Teacher's Guide Advisory Board." The teachers, described as "multiple perspectives educational activists," had access to some preview copies but completed much of the teaching material before the series was finished. One is left to wonder how they deal with the conflict between the programs and the guide in their own classrooms and whether the scholars realize that the teaching materials, publicized at the conclusion of each program, actually undercut the historical integrity and value of this unique television achievement. The American classroom appears to be a safe dumping ground for this politically correct brew of half-truths and evasions, which the scholars rejected in the script and the book and would never include in their own published work.

The pervasiveness of myth-making about African history in American schools is further documented in Richard Bernstein's *The Dictatorship of Virtue*: *Multiculturalism and the Battle for America's Future,* particularly in the section on Molefi Asante's Afrocentric history movement, "which is a booming business in America and he is one of its leading entrepreneurs."[18] Asante has written 30 books with titles such as *The African Presence in Ancient America* and *Africa: Mother of Western Civilization*. When Bernstein and his research assistant Hilary Dunst asked Asante several times for details on his claims about great African figures of the 15th or 16th century (he was not sure which century), he "was unable to provide anything more than the flimsiest sketches of the[se] figures from African history... [and] Hilary and the reference librarian at Columbia University were unable to find any reference to anyone... fitting Asante's description."

The popularity of this ubiquitous mythology spurred Wellesley College classicist Mary Lefkowitz to write *Not Out of Africa: How Afrocentrism Became an Excuse to Teach Myth as History,* in which she brilliantly exposes the origins and development of these false claims about the African roots of Western civilization. In one particularly revealing incident, when a visiting Egyptologist giving a talk on campus insisted that Aristotle had "stolen" most of his ideas from the great library at Alexandria, Egypt, Lefkowitz simply pointed out that the library was likely not built until after Aristotle's death. Angry students surrounded her, denounced her facts, and suggested that her criticism of the speaker was simply racist. One student suggested that if she is an expert, why didn't she know her own subject, and why had she been concealing evidence? Even in her own classes, students asserted that since everyone knows that Cleopatra and Socrates were black, why didn't she mention it?

One of Lefkowitz's colleagues, Anthony Martin, teaches (and "publishes" his findings in a newsletter, "Blacks and Jews at Wellesley News") that Lefkowitz is part of an on-going conspiracy by Jews to falsify history and conceal the fact that they financed the Atlantic slave trade and master-minded slavery in the ante-bellum South. This "history" is, of course, based on the Nation of Islam book mentioned earlier in the Adelaide Sanford incident—and, protected by academic freedom, it is used in "studies" programs all across America.

In some ways, however, the most extraordinary mainstream example of manipulating historical "evidence" for ideological purposes is James Loewen's *Lies My Teacher Told Me: Everything Your American History Textbook Got Wrong,* published in 1995. Loewen argues that American history in schools and colleges today is awash in racism, hero-worship, super-patriotism, and chauvinism. As evidence, he asserts that "As recently as 1950 a text by Samuel Eliot Morison and Henry Steele Commager said: 'As for Sambo, whose wrongs moved the abolitionists to wrath and tears, there is some reason to believe that he suffered less than any other class in the South from slavery.'" As recently as 1950!!! No one could survive ten minutes in a mainstream American high school or college today promoting such trash. Loewen derives his conclusions from a "study" of twelve textbooks: two are over twenty years old, seven are between twelve and eighteen years old, and even the most recent are between seven and eleven years old. And yet, the book gets rave reviews and Loewen is interviewed on radio and TV and was the subject of a lengthy and totally uncritical article in the *Boston Globe*.[19] The old distortions linger on in some conservative backwaters, and may also survive in older texts which poor school districts cannot afford to replace. Nevertheless, Loewen and his supporters seem oblivious to the fact that his observations are completely out-of-date and utterly contrary to what is being taught in the vast majority of American public schools today.

As one of the 1998 *Concord Review* Emerson Prize winners revealed at the award ceremony in Boston, the lecturer in her Harvard Freshman history seminar remarked that he suspected that a colleague had tried to block his appointment because of intellectual differences: "She just has this thing about historical reality," he said with contempt. "She thinks things actually happened in the past in a particular way."[20]

The popularity of such views in history departments is hardly surprising given their currency among historians, particularly those active in drafting the national history standards. Gary Nash, and his colleagues in *History on Trial*, conclude that:

1. All evidence is interpretation and so it is fatuous to argue that there is a "true" and "objective" history which is appropriate for all students or citizens.

2. Historians can never fully detach their scholarly work from their own education, attitudes, ideological dispositions, and culture.

3. As lawyers write briefs, so do historians.

4. It is an absurd fallacy to believe that historical facts exist "objectively and independently of the interpretation of the historian."[21]

Why the Battle over History Standards? 165

Of course, historical interpretations are biased. But, we can recognize that fact and strive to do our best to reach the elusive goal of historical "objectivity," or we can use it as an excuse to abandon the effort entirely in history education. Lawyers present only the evidence which serves their client's interests; historians are obligated to consider and reveal all the evidence and all the facts. Gary Nash, nevertheless, in defending the national standards, declared that young Americans need to be liberated from the "prison house of facts."[22] Such views, curiously, often seem to rationalize less work for their proponents: grades and grading are oppressive and elitist—so why bother? Facts and evidence are relative—so much for expecting students to master research and writing.

This divisive and anti-historical context has obviously made the writing of strong history standards and history curriculum much more difficult. It is not surprising that so many state efforts received dismal ratings in the recent Fordham Foundation evaluation of history standards in 37 states and the District of Columbia. It remains to be seen whether history education in America can flourish in the new century by teaching young Americans that our understanding of the past, which includes the arts, literature, science, and the world of ideas, is nothing more than the politics of today's historians.

Concluding Remarks

More than twenty years ago, NASA included plaques containing mathematical data on the Voyager space probes since it was assumed that the universality of mathematics would be shared by intelligent beings anywhere in the universe. But, in American schools today, extreme multiculturalists advocate a new approach to mathematics education, insisting that the capacity to teach and learn mathematics is racially determined. The director of a program on educational equity and diversity at Wellesley College claims that "the emphasis on right/wrong answers [in math] is a culturally oppressive idea and unfair to minority children." She warns teachers to reject "the mistake of trying to teach black children [math] in the same way they would teach white children, rather than adapting their teaching styles to the 'culture' of African-Americans." There is, of course, not a shred of hard evidence that children of different races learn math, or anything else, differently. Responsible scientists reject the whole concept of fixed and immutable races and racial characteristics. It is only a short and slippery step from this approach to teaching mathematics to the distinction made by Nazi scientists between Aryan physics and Jewish physics. Again, we see the curious symbiosis and co-dependency between the extreme Right and the extreme Left.

The National Commission on Excellence in Education cautioned in 1983, "If an unfriendly power had attempted to impose on America the mediocre educational performance that exists today, we might well have viewed it as an act of war."[23] Content-free state history standards which ask students, for example, to "Assess the long-term consequences of major decisions by leaders in various nations of the world, drawing information from a variety of traditional, electronic, and on-line sources" or to "Compare and contrast varying interpretations of major events in selected periods of time" will not cut it, as Diane Ravitch has warned, in the global society and economy of the 21st century.[24]

David McCullough, after teaching history at several American colleges and universities, has concluded that we are "raising a new generation of Americans who, to an alarming degree, are historically illiterate." In a revealing example, a recent spoof asked major historical figures: "Why did the chicken cross the road?" The mock responses included:

Locke: "Because he was exercising his natural right to liberty."

Marx: "It was a historical inevitability."

Lincoln: "The world will little note, nor long remember, why this chicken crossed the road."

FDR: "This administration will establish an agency—The Poultry Crossing Control Commission—to monitor all road crossings by chickens, for whatever reason..."

JFK: "Ask not why the chicken crossed the road; ask what road you can cross to build a better America."

When I distributed the spoof to advanced placement history seniors at several high schools, they were puzzled and unresponsive; virtually no one laughed or even smiled. Teaching and learning history, as this example suggests, require hard work and mastery of substance, and we have run out of time to accept anything less.

Reliable standards in mathematics and science can often be achieved by resisting the politically fashionable jargon of schools of education and enlisting academic experts in these two subject areas. In history, on the other hand, the clash of ideological points of view among academic specialists is often the problem. Parents, school boards, and legislators must work to achieve a balanced, inclusive, and accurate history curriculum, rejecting both censorship and unsubstantiated myths. It is a challenge which could define the success of American democracy in the twenty-first century.

Notes

1. Diane Ravitch, "Who Prepares our History Teachers? Who Should Prepare our History Teachers?," National Council for History Education, October 18, 1997.
2. Mark Twain, *Following the Equator*, Bliss's American Publishing Co., 1897.
3. Gary B. Nash, Charlotte Crabtree, and Ross E. Dunn, *History on Trial: Culture Wars and the Teaching of the Past*, Knopf, 1997, p. 162.
4. Nash, et al., p. 161.
5. Diane Ravitch to Sheldon M. Stern, February 27, 1998; Professor Ravitch has a tape recording of the meeting corroborating this exchange (Ravitch to Stern, March 1, 1999).
6. Henry Louis Gates Jr., "Black Demagogues and Pseudo-Scholars," *New York Times*, July 20, 1992.
7. Ravitch to Stern, February 26, 1998, March 3, 1999.
8. George Orwell, *A Collection of Essays*, Harcourt Brace, 1981, pp. 197–200.
9. Keith Windschuttle, *The Killing of History*, Macleay Press, 1996, pp. 1–2, 220–221.
10. Robert A. Rosenstone, "JFK: Historical Fact/Historical Film," *American Historical Review*, April 1992, pp. 508, 511.
11. Howard W. French, "On Slavery, Africans Say the Guilt is Theirs, Too," *New York Times*, December 27, 1994.
12. Charles Johnson, Patricia Smith, and the WGBH Research Team, *Africans in America: America's Journey Through Slavery*, Companion to the PBS Series, Harcourt Brace, 1998, pp. 2, 5, 7.
13. *Africans in America Teacher's Guide*, WGBH, 1998, inside front cover; *Africans in America Youth Activity Guide*, WGBH, 1998, p. 4.
14. *Teacher's Guide*, pp. 2, 4.
15. *Teacher's Guide*, pp. 3, 9.
16. *Teacher's Guide*, pp. 2, 3.
17. *Teacher's Guide*, p. 10.
18. Richard Bernstein, *The Dictatorship of Virtue: Multiculturalism and the Battle for America's Future*, Knopf, 1994, pp. 273–276.
19. Jack Thomas, "A Textbook Case of Lying," *Boston Globe*, December 12, 1995.
20. Joelle Novey, "Emerson Prize Remarks," March 5, 1998.

[21] Nash, et al., *History on Trial*, especially pp. 3–24.
[22] *Wall Street Journal*, Editorial, December 30, 1994.
[23] National Commission on Excellence in Education, *A Nation at Risk: The Imperative for Educational Reform*, 1983, p. 5.
[24] Diane Ravitch, "The Controversy Over National History Standards," American Academy of Arts and Sciences, April 9, 1997.

Chapter 8

Discipline-Based Economics Standards
Opportunity and Obstacles

Robert M. Costrell
University of Massachusetts at Amherst and
Massachusetts Executive Office for Administration and Finance

The 1994 Federal Goals 2000 Act expanded the national standards movement to include economics. In fact, economics was the only subject added by that Act to the national goals set previously.[1] This led to the creation of the Voluntary National Content Standards in Economics (VNCSE), which were unveiled in January 1997.[2] The VNCSE is organized around the core principles of the discipline. This now makes it possible for any state that wishes to include economics in its standards to do so in a way that imparts the distinctive, analytically powerful economic mode of reasoning.

Although "standards wars" have not yet broken out in economics, there have been a few public controversies, and also many less visible state efforts with varying degrees of contention. These controversies differ in a striking way from those over other subject standards, discussed in other contributions to this volume. Some of those controversies (e.g., over the history standards) reflect disagreements within the discipline over the content of what should be taught.[3] Other controversies (e.g., those in science and mathematics) reflect disagreements within the discipline (broadly defined to include science and mathematics educators in education schools as well as scientists and mathematicians in disciplinary departments) over how the material should be taught at K–12.

In economics, however, there has been almost no controversy *within* the discipline over the VNCSE: objections have come almost entirely from those *outside* the discipline. There are two reasons for this. First, there is fairly broad consensus within the economics community about the core principles of economics (even though economists are notoriously disputatious on the policy implications), and there is also little or no disagreement between research economists and economics educators about how they should be taught.[4] Second, those who are unschooled in economics nonetheless sometimes believe they have an intuitive understanding of the subject from their everyday experience that trumps the often counter-intuitive views of a vaguely suspect profession.[5]

This latter condition—the sense of a surprising number of laypersons that their intuitive understanding of economics equals or surpasses that of the profession—sharply distinguishes economics controversies from those over science or mathematics. Some of the key arguments raised against the economics standards (e.g., its difficulty or abstractness) have close analogues in science or mathematics but are generally *not* considered decisive in those subjects. These arguments, often demonstrably flawed, nonetheless carry more weight when raised against economics, I contend, because of the different attitude toward the profession in question. Another remarkable implication of this attitude is that a state's economics standards can on occasion be drawn up entirely by non-economists, who refuse and reject professional input. As related in the penultimate section of this chapter, this was the experience in Massachusetts until public controversy forced some accommodation to the profession.[6]

Nationwide, it is too early to tell what effect VNCSE is having on state standards, not to mention K–12 instruction itself. But it is not too early to reflect on the nature of VNCSE and some of the potential obstacles to their full implementation. That is the purpose of this essay.

A Description of the VNCSE[7]

The VNCSE represents a bold statement that real, discipline-based economics should be taught to all students, starting in elementary school. It stipulates that economics should be taught as a set of analytic principles specific to the discipline, such as tradeoffs and opportunity cost, rather than in a non-disciplinary fashion, or from the viewpoint of some other discipline, such as history, or personal finance and business.

The VNCSE was written by a team of economists and economics educators put together by the National Council on Economic Education (NCEE).[8] As John Siegfried and Bonnie Meszaros report, the writing

Discipline-Based Economics Standards 171

committee and several subcommittees generated about ten drafts, which were reviewed by a number of outside organizations and individuals. In addition, a formal review committee provided input after reading an intermediate draft. After a year or so of work, the NCEE unveiled the 46-page VNCSE in January 1997.[9] The hope is that this document, and supporting teaching materials, will inform the work of states and localities as they construct their own standards.

The document consists of a one-page introduction, followed by twenty content standards. Each content standard begins with a basic economic principle that students will be expected to understand (see the Appendix), and a one-sentence general statement of what students will be able to do with that understanding. It is followed by a few paragraphs that provide the rationale for that content standard. Finally, the bulk of each two- or three-page standard consists of more detailed benchmarks for grades 4, 8, and/or 12 of what is to be mastered, along with examples of how that mastery might be demonstrated. Since the document is densely packed with rich lessons, I can only sketch their nature in this limited space.[10]

A quick perusal of the Appendix conveys the general disciplinary approach of the VNCSE. The standards are designed to teach the economic mode of reasoning.[11] That is why the VNCSE is organized around basic principles or propositions. Each principle can itself be broken down into its building blocks, suitable for different grade levels. Clusters of related principles comprise larger themes (e.g., #1–2, #3–6, #7–9, #10–11, #12–15, #16–17, #18–20).

As a concrete example, consider the cluster #7–9, and, specifically, principle #8: "Prices send signals and provide incentives to buyers and sellers. When supply or demand changes, market prices adjust, affecting incentives." If one had to pick a single basic principle that conveys the fundamental insight of economics into how a market economy functions, this would probably be it. This is the principle (along with #7 and #9) that unlocks the mystery of how an unplanned economy manages to come up with something close to the right number of two-ply toilet paper rolls, sushi rolls, and Fruit Roll-Ups in the nation's supermarkets every week, without excess wastage or long lines, such as those that were endemic to the former Soviet Union for basic staples and amenities of life.

It is a principle that can be broken down into its building blocks and taught at various levels of sophistication. The VNCSE asks that grade 4 students understand that high prices lead buyers to purchase less of any given good or service while inducing sellers to produce more of it. By grade 8, students are to have a deeper understanding of the underlying reasons for these relationships. To use the concise language of the basic analytical tools of economics, students are to understand that demand curves generally slope down, supply curves generally slope up, and why. By grade 12, students are expected to use these basic concepts to analyze the consequences of changing conditions of demand and supply in order for them to understand, for example, what to expect in the wake of a freeze in the orange crop. Extending the analysis from product markets to labor markets (in standard #13) helps students understand how various forms of technological progress can differentially affect workers of varying types and levels of skill, an essential lesson to help students understand both their own future and that of society at large.

Grade 12 students who have mastered standard #8 will also understand the often unintended consequences of market interventions such as price ceilings and floors. This helps explain not only the Soviet experience, but, among other things, the U.S. experience (for better or worse) during the oil embargo, rent control in various cities, and farm price support policies. Extending the analysis from product markets to labor markets helps students understand the perennial debates over the minimum wage.

It is worth noting here what is *not* in the VNCSE. For the most part, the standards are designed to convey the principles that have been the mainstay of economics over much of the last century and *not* the new developments of the last decade or two. These developments have tried to broaden the discipline's focus beyond the competitive model toward a richer analysis of strategic interactions (using game theory) and of economic uncertainty or imperfect information. It is fair to say that there is professional disagreement on how fundamentally these developments alter the discipline. Some would stress, for example, that prices do not necessarily serve as the simple allocative signals described in standard #8 when sellers know more about the good's quality than buyers. By contrast, others would argue that professional economists are naturally more interested in these developments on the frontier for their novelty than in the tried-and-true fundamentals that are more relevant for everyday understanding and policy analysis.[12]

Richard Feynman conveys a similar dilemma in teaching introductory physics. Does one teach, for example, the Newtonian "law" that mass is independent of velocity, which is "close enough" for speeds under 100 miles/second? Or does one begin with the more general law, a law that not only gives very different results as we approach the speed of light but, moreover, shows that the simple theory is *philosophically* completely wrong?[13] Feynman gives no general answer to this dilemma. He was brilliant enough, and blessed with freshmen at the California Institute of Technology, to get away with the latter approach occasionally.

The VNCSE, facing different constraints, wisely chose to impart the fundamentals, on which further insights could be built at a later stage of education. But this does come at a cost. A few of the objections that are raised against traditional economics, discussed later, are in fact recognized by some in the field and are the subject of activity on the frontier. It is difficult to respond to such objections by saying, "Yes, we know that, but you need to learn the fundamentals first, and later on, perhaps in college or graduate school, we can get to your objections." And yet, there seems no obvious alternative, just as we teach Newtonian physics to high school students and tantalize them with the mysteries of relativity, to be pursued in higher education.

On the other hand, I do not want to leave the impression that developments on the frontier solve the major problems of economics with the same degree of confidence that we might have in relativity or quantum physics. Indeed, there is a healthy debate within economics as to whether it has become too technical, too austere, too reliant on assumptions of hyper-rationality, and the like. Unfortunately, observers of this debate from outside the profession sometimes bring it into discussions of K–12 economics, where it is really quite irrelevant. That is, even if one thinks that recent economics—as reflected in the profession's often impenetrable journals—has gone off the rails (a judgment I do not share), one may still conclude that K–12 students can benefit greatly from learning the traditional fundamentals in the VNCSE. As I relate below, in the Massachusetts story, there has been some confusion on this distinction between K–12 economics and economics on the frontier.

The main point here is that VNCSE is real economics, designed for K–12. It is, in my view, a major accomplishment. But even among non-economists who clearly distinguish K–12 economics from the more advanced variety, there are still those—notably, some education officials—who raise questions about the difficulty of teaching the discipline's fundamentals at K–12, and about the substance of the material itself. These questions may or may not be widespread, but they have at least been raised in some instances, and they merit a thoughtful examination.

Is Economics Too Difficult for K–12?

There is a perception among some education policy makers that the discipline of economics is simply too difficult to teach at the elementary or even secondary level, and perhaps too difficult for teachers to learn.[14] There are two distinct reasons for this.

The first reason is a rather simple misunderstanding regarding the level of mathematics required in K–12 economics. From time to time, one encounters vastly exaggerated perceptions that real discipline-based economics requires advanced mathematics, such as calculus. Even at the college level this is false: the freshman course rarely uses calculus, and the typical economics major makes little or no use of calculus either. This erroneous notion probably comes from perusing the professional economics journals, where higher mathematics does predominate, as it does in graduate programs.

For college level economics, graphs and elementary algebra are the more common tools of mathematics. Since these tools are taught in K–12, some of them can surely be used by the middle school years. Indeed, it is not uncommon for bar graphs to be introduced as early as kindergarten, so economic concepts can (but certainly need not) be taught graphically at that level, as I have done on invitation to my children's classes. But certainly for middle or high school, the comments of Princeton's Alan Blinder, former vice chairman of the Federal Reserve Board, are apposite:

> Too many American kids are brought up without any basic literacy in economics. I don't mean knowledge of fancy economic theory, I mean fairly elementary things like "demand curves usually slope down."[15]

In short, the math requirement is a red herring. Indeed, the VNCSE presents its twenty basic economic principles in plain English,[16] without any equations or graphs.[17] The general point is that sophisticated disciplines can be taught at K–12 with analytical tools appropriate to the grade. To suggest otherwise would imply that Newton's Laws of Motion cannot be taught in K–12 because they are taught in college using calculus.

There is a second, less easily dismissed reason that students and teachers find economics difficult: the lean and analytical approach that is the discipline's hallmark. Quite aside from the elementary mathematics or graphs involved, K–12 students (and their teachers) can and do find economics too abstract or too theoretical and therefore too difficult or too boring. Of course, they are right about one thing: economic reasoning *is* abstract. It should also be immediately granted that some of the standards *are* too difficult for elementary school or middle school, as the VNCSE clearly indicates,[18] and some of the upper level benchmarks may in fact be too difficult for many high school students as well.

That said, the difficulty students have with abstract reasoning is hardly confined to economics. Algebra and formal logic are surely *more* abstract. If one rejects (as did Massachusetts) the teaching of economics' "timeless abstractions," then by the same logic, Euclidean geometry would also have to be rejected as overly difficult and impractical for K–12 students. And yet, there are good reasons to teach algebra, geometry, and the syllogism at the K–12 level. So too, there are good reasons to teach economics as a set of principles, tied together with logical reasoning.

To teach, for example, the relatively simple lesson that price is almost always inversely related to the quantity of market demand, holding other things equal, is to make an abstract statement. That is so whether the principle is stated verbally or with the aid of a downward-sloping demand curve, the most basic analytical device of economics. Further abstractions are called for in working through the logic of why the demand curve slopes down and the powerful consequences that follow from it. Such abstract analysis can and should be accompanied by illustrative examples, including current events, such as the proliferation of computers as their prices drop, or the effect on teen smoking as taxes are imposed on cigarettes. Historic events can also illustrate, as in the rise in food prices during famines and the historical experience with price controls. But without the abstract analysis, students will be at a loss to answer such questions as the one posed by the controversial 1994 *National Standards for United States History*: "Why did people have to wait in long lines [in the 1970s] to buy gasoline for their cars?"

Abstract principles can be taught at different levels of difficulty with different levels of formalism. We teach young children the difference between necessary and sufficient conditions long before we use these terms and before we introduce them to the syllogism. So, too, young children can be readily taught the elementary lessons of opportunity cost and tradeoffs even if we do not use those terms or formal representations. It seems to me that the objection to economic reasoning as overly abstract is, at one level, part and parcel of the same reaction against deductive mathematics instruction, and abstraction in other parts of the curriculum. The result is that college faculty often find their students to be unprepared for rigorous abstract reasoning, more so, perhaps, than in previous decades. This would suggest that there should be *more* (or better) instruction in abstract thinking, rather than less.

However, there is more to the adverse reaction to the abstract nature of economic analysis. It is arguably more difficult than algebra precisely, and perhaps ironically, because the subject matter is more concrete. A student can pass algebra, at least at a certain low level, by mastering certain rules and applying them consistently to solve algebraic equations. The problem which eventually presents itself is that students often have little understanding of what an algebraic equation means whenever any content is ascribed to the x's and y's.[19] By contrast, economic problems are never so abstract as to be completely devoid of content, as in an algebraic expression. The P's and Q's in economics always refer to something concrete, such as a price or a quantity, even if it is of some unspecified good. As a result, students often get confused or lulled into sloppy thought until they learn to momentarily suspend their everyday personal experience in order to apply rigorous economic logic. Since everyone *thinks* they know economics intuitively, it is difficult to derive and understand results that are often counter-intuitive. This is *not* a problem that applies to learning pure algebra.

Of course, I do not mean to suggest that factual content should be even further stripped from economics to avoid confusing students with the real world. Economics *is* about the real world. Its abstractions are made for a purpose: to reach a deeper understanding about the real world, to learn lessons that are not obvious on the surface. Economic theory is designed to understand empirical reality and cannot be divorced from it. The authors of VNCSE are certainly aware that students need to know certain basic economic facts, such as the size of the economy, the current rates of unemployment, inflation, and interest, but chose not to build any of the standards around them. W. Lee Hansen expresses general approval of the document, but cites E.D. Hirsch's arguments to suggest that perhaps a separate standard on basic economic facts might have been added.[20] It is true that a few economic facts are necessary prior to formal analysis, notably in the area of macroeconomics, as the VNCSE authors note. But for the most part, economic facts are best conveyed through examples that apply economic analysis, and the examples may often be drawn from the newspapers. Economic literacy is truly a matter of reasoning.

Is Economics Ideological, Amoral, Immoral, or Doctrinaire?

What about the substance of economics, its assumptions and implications? What are some of the general lessons of the discipline, and are they welcome in educational circles? There are many who believe that mainstream economics provides an unwarranted defense of free markets, or at least gives short shrift to the case for government intervention. Critics charge that economics serves the interests of the rich and of powerful corporations, wittingly or not, against the less fortunate and the environment. There are those who believe that mainstream economics is obsessed with efficiency at the expense of equity. It is also perceived by some to be an amoral—if not immoral—discipline, based on the assumption of greed, and devoid of ethical considerations.

The reader will not be surprised when I write that many of these charges arise out of a flawed understanding of economics, deeply flawed in some cases. But these sentiments are abroad, and it is worth examining these charges to understand the reasons for such hostility, including some failures of the economics profession itself.

Is Economics Ideologically Pro-Market and Anti-Statist?

It is a fact that the study of the price system generally leads economists and their students to a deeper understanding of the functions served by markets (VNCSE standards #7–9), and under what conditions, as well as a more acute awareness of the unintended consequences of some government interventions. But the lessons of economics hardly stop there. Economic analysis also isolates the conditions under which markets fail—notably in the presence of externalities, such as pollution —thereby providing a firmer and more focused rationale for government intervention than those unschooled in the discipline are often able to provide (VNCSE #16). The extension of economic analysis to government actors also illuminates the conditions under which the cost of intervention can outweigh the benefits, due, for example, to the inefficiencies of interest group politics (VNCSE #17).

The upshot is that there is a wide range of professional opinion regarding the relative strengths of market and non-market mechanisms in different contexts, due to differing assessments of empirical magnitudes, as well as differing personal values used to weigh the tradeoffs society faces. But in general, it is fair to say that even the more liberal economists, advisors to Democratic presidents for example, are more wary of some popular government interventions than the general public. This has been repeatedly demonstrated by polls comparing professional and lay opinion on such matters as the minimum wage, free trade, or environmental regulations. In many cases, economists favor alternative interventions (such as wage subsidies vs. minimum wage, or marketable emissions permits vs. direct pollution controls) which try to use, modify, or even create market mechanisms to better achieve economic and social goals. But such subtleties are lost on those education officials who fear that any curricular space granted to discipline-based economics will result in free-market sectarianism inflicted on our children.[21]

Is "Value-Free" Economics Amoral?

Economics is often thought to be an amoral discipline. This is because it tries to draw as bright a line as possible between the "positive" analysis of how the economy works and what tradeoffs we face, and the "normative" judgments we might make on how to weigh various tradeoffs and evaluate outcomes. Since normative judgments rest on widely varying values, and since economics has traditionally claimed little or no expertise on those values, the profession typically tries (with varying degrees of success) to present the tradeoffs, while leaving the value judgments to politicians, voters, and others.[22] Of course, individual economists have their own values, and these can surely taint their positive analysis as do those of other fallible human beings, but the culture of economics is to at least make the effort, unlike those disciplines that have fallen to the postmodern currents of our day.

This stance is offensive to some. A good example is a recent opinion piece, "God and the National Economics Standards," by Warren E. Nord, Director of the Program in the Humanities and Human Values at the University of North Carolina at Chapel Hill.[23] Nord faults the VNCSE

Discipline-Based Economics Standards 179

and various economics texts for failing to discuss "justice" (particularly religious precepts of justice), and for attempting to be "value free." At a certain level, this is true: textbook economics does not typically presume to pick and choose among the many different notions of justice at play in the polity.

At a more advanced level, it is not true. There has been much advanced work in economics on defining and measuring various notions of justice and fairness—much work on "normative" economics. To take but one example, economists have long been interested in the philosopher John Rawls' 1971 classic, *A Theory of Justice*. A number of economists have seriously engaged Rawls' thought experiment of what kind of distributive system one would choose from behind the "veil of ignorance," prior to being assigned the skills that generate income. The relations between risk and inequality lie firmly in the purview of economics. Should this kind of analysis be brought down to the K–12 curriculum? Perhaps, but at the present state of the art it might require far more technical expertise than most critics of K–12 economics are willing to abide.

Even at a more elementary level, economics does help focus one's thinking on the hard problems encountered in the search for justice. The VNCSE pays fully proper attention, for example, to the distribution of income and to the distributional effects of government policies. Justice cannot be served without an understanding of what the tradeoffs are, if any, between equity and efficiency under any given policy. Is justice served by policies which raise incomes of those at, say, the 10th percentile by $1,000 at the expense of an $X,000 drop for those in some higher percentile? Economics instruction can certainly advance the search for justice by leading students to think about such difficult questions as the size of "X" they would be willing to countenance. Is justice served by minimum wage legislation which raises the income of the working poor while reducing the employment of those with the least skills, as some research indicates, or are there better ways to advance distributional equity?[24] Surely the positive analysis of economics has much to offer students in their thinking about justice, even *if* it left the question of its proper definition to philosophy and religion.

Nord, unfortunately, gives voice to a more widespread misunderstanding when he asserts that the VNCSE gives "no moral weight to the needs of the poor." The VNCSE (and economics more generally) study the income distribution and the distributional effect of government policies (see standards #13 and #16, and their more detailed benchmarks[25]) precisely because they recognize society accords moral weight to the fortunes of the poor; they just refrain from saying what that weight should be. Unfortunately, economists' professional aversion to moral posturing[26] is misinterpreted by some as moral indifference.[27]

Conversely, the normative/positive distinction in mainstream economics is also suspect to some who place the highest value on liberty rather than equality.[28] The Hayekian view is that mainstream economics' focus on the level and distribution of economic welfare is overly consequentialist, and neglectful of the primary value of economic freedom, which is, in turn, a prerequisite for political freedom. This idea is pithily captured in the title of Milton Friedman's 1962 classic, *Capitalism and Freedom*.

Is the "Individualism" of Economics Immoral?

Economics is sometimes viewed as morally suspect because of the discipline's simplifying assumption that individuals act to advance their self-interest.[29] To state what should be obvious, the assumption does not endorse selfishness, it merely analyzes the consequences of such behavior. Nor does the fact that under certain stringent conditions an economy of such individuals reaches an efficient outcome without government intervention (Adam Smith's "Invisible Hand" result) in any way imply that selfishness is prescribed. To the contrary, certain forms of market failure, in the provision of public goods, are a consequence of "free-riding" by selfish individuals. To the extent that economics oversimplifies by assuming selfish behavior, it *overstates* the rationale for government intervention rather than *understating* it, as its critics imply. To take another simple example, if we recognize some degree of altruism among economic actors to explain charitable giving, as we certainly must, then the case for government redistribution is *weakened*, not strengthened.[30]

Closely related (but not quite identical) is the suspicion of economics' methodological individualism. The mode of analysis begins with individual consumers, workers, and firms choosing their actions subject to the constraints they face in the market. The analysis continues by aggregating up to find equilibrium in each market and in the economy as a whole.[31] From this methodology, critics (of whom Nord provides yet another convenient example) jump to the quite unwarranted conclusion

Discipline-Based Economics Standards 181

that "generally speaking, neo-classical theory emphasizes individualism over community." To the contrary, as economist Kenneth Arrow points out, "method and value are distinct."

Analyses based in methodological individualism are used routinely to evaluate social outcomes, both for the community as a whole and for subgroups. For example, racial discrimination is most powerfully analyzed by the concept of statistical discrimination (developed by Arrow, among others), whereby individuals rationally (if unfairly) use intrinsically irrelevant group markers in the absence of perfect information on the individuals they encounter. To assert that an analysis which begins with individuals thereby devalues communities or groups makes no more sense than to argue that modern evolutionary biology, which builds up from the logical imperatives of the "selfish gene," is unconcerned with the species.

What is the alternative to the methodological individualist approach to economics? As Arrow observes, "Whether in Marxist or other forms, such theories relied heavily on disembodied actors, such as classes or national spirits, rather than on the actual persons." While there remain strongly held minority approaches of this type within economics, it is fair to say that the attraction to such class-based approaches as Marxism is greater among some of those outside the profession (for example, among some historians), who have never studied economics, than among those who have.

Is the VNCSE Unduly Doctrinaire?

An overwhelming majority of the profession subscribes to the consensus principles in the VNCSE, as indicated by periodic surveys of professional opinion. This is true, even though economists notoriously disagree on the policy implications of those principles, as well as on the significance of developments on the frontier. As mentioned above, drafts of the VNCSE were widely circulated and externally reviewed. In the end, there were no dissenting opinions or objections from members of the writing committee. As Hansen observes, "This is a notable achievement, because cantankerous economists pride themselves on registering their objections."

Nonetheless, adherents to alternative views from outside the profession consider economics unduly narrow for ignoring them. Nord, for example, fairly thunders at VNCSE's decision to write the standards around the mainstream, or "neoclassical," paradigm of economics to the exclusion of Marxist, socialist, and religious viewpoints.[32] He rejects VNCSE's reason for doing so (given below) as an "appalling" and "profoundly illiberal" rationale for "indoctrinat[ion]."

This is an issue that has a long history in economic standard-setting. In 1986, the Joint Council on Economic Education demonstrated its open-mindedness by convening a two and one-half day conference at MIT devoted to the question of whether the *Framework* (the VNCSE's predecessor) satisfactorily captured the scope of economic thought. The conference began with a keynote lecture by Paul Samuelson, who recounted that the same issue had arisen from a different angle at the time of the National Task Force in 1960, when his textbook was considered "heresy." As he described the shifting landscape:

> It was the tragedy of my teachers' generation that, as they grew older, economics grew more liberal, and even radical. It has been the comedy of my era that, as we grew older, our profession became more conservative.[33]

Each of the six sessions at the 1986 conference was built around an invited paper from a prominent critic of the mainstream, such as Robert Heilbroner, Lester Thurow, James K. Galbraith, and Barbara Bergmann. Respondents found some of the criticisms overblown,[34] but the more common and more telling question was simply "whether the expected benefits of change [in the *Framework*] were worth the opportunity cost..."[35] A decade later, the VNCSE's authors considered this question and concluded:

> Including strongly held minority views of economic processes risks undermining the entire venture. With too many qualifications and alternatives, teachers and their students may abandon economics entirely out of frustration born of confusion and uncertainty.[36]

No doubt the same rationale applies to many fields, since no field is devoid of minority viewpoints. Some of the minority viewpoints might even eventually prevail. Nonetheless, standard-setters usually accord each field its own judgment in such matters. Economics is unusual in that non-economists feel quite strongly about the subject, even if they have not studied it. The only other comparable case that comes to mind is the pressure on biology educators to accord "equal time" to creationism.[37] The dilemma is real. Should parents who believe in creationism, or

Discipline-Based Economics Standards

Christian economics, or Marxism be denied the right to have their children instructed in these minority views? Certainly not. But it is a rather different matter to *require* that all children be instructed in every fringe theory, of which there are quite a few in any given field. In short, the critics' point here is best understood as an argument against having standards at all, and in favor of unfettered school choice.[38] *If* there are to be standards, then choices must be made about what goes in those standards; and *if* there are to be economics standards, with rather limited curricular space, then the professional judgments of VNCSE and the vast majority of the profession must at least be the starting point from which public education officials begin.

Is Economics Best Taught Within Other Disciplines?

Many educators who reject the disciplinary approach to economics in K–12 believe that it is best taught instead from the perspective of another discipline—history, civics, geography—or under the interdisciplinary aegis of "social studies." The argument for doing so is that these subjects must be taught anyway, and since they at least touch on economic topics, they present an opportunity to bring economics into the curriculum. How much economics do the standards in these areas contain, and of what quality?

Stephen Buckles and Michael Watts recently reviewed the economic content of the national standards documents in history, civics, geography, and social studies (817 pages in all).[39] They found a substantial number of economic issues and events raised in these standards. The major problem was that they found very little economic reasoning in the standards that might help students understand the issues and events presented. That is, "they all assume that teachers and students will have or somehow develop an understanding of how market economies allocate resources. It is not always clear that the writers of these volumes have such an understanding themselves..." (p. 166). In terms of the VNCSE, these standards do not convey the principles of microeconomics (standards #7–9) or macroeconomics (standards #18–20).

Since the standards in these subjects do not invoke economic reasoning, it is not surprising that they often seem at odds with the general lessons of the economics discipline. Buckles and Watts provide the following summary assessment:

> We found an uncritical acceptance in these documents for wide-ranging government intervention and planning, little or no recognition of the principle of comparing costs and benefits of alternative public policies, an unbalanced emphasis on the costs of economic growth with little attention to accompanying benefits, and a general failure to recognize the range and efficiency of market functions... If these documents were implemented in their current forms, we believe they would contribute to low levels of economic literacy among those students taking only those courses and confuse students who take a separate economics course. (p. 165)

The point here is not simply that these standards are generally more statist than VNCSE; the point is that these standards provide little basis for analyzing what governments or markets do well, and what they do not, and why. They particularly lack anything corresponding to VNCSE standard #17, analyzing the sources of government failure, to go along with the analysis of market failure (#16). As a result, students would have little basis to understand, for example, why President Clinton would declare an end to the era of big government, let alone whether this was wise or not.

The *National Standards for United States History* provide a particularly striking example of the failure to convey economic reasoning to students through the economic content of another discipline. The main reason for this failure is that the standards were developed with no participation from those economists who specialize in economic history, the economic historians. Economic history has, in recent decades, become more firmly grounded in economic reasoning and has benefited greatly from sophisticated statistical analysis (i.e. econometrics). Unfortunately, there is relatively little contact between the history profession and the economic historians. One is struck by Sheldon Stern's account (in this volume) of the offense taken by history educators at the idea that economic analysis might fruitfully be applied to such topics as slavery. And yet the Nobel Prize in Economics was awarded to economic historian Robert Fogel in large part because of his extensive econometric work on precisely this topic.[40]

The *National Standards for United States History*, produced at UCLA's National Center for History in the Schools, went through two published editions, which I shall refer to as UCLA-I and UCLA-II.[41] UCLA-I, issued in 1994, was highly controversial. The U.S. Senate passed a resolution disapproving of these standards by a vote of 99–1. UCLA-I's economic shortcomings played a small role in the more general criticism they engendered. The NCEE endorsed the standards

Discipline-Based Economics Standards 185

(even though officials there knew of their economic shortcomings) in the hope that they could serve as a vehicle for increasing the economic content of K–12 curriculum.

In the wake of widespread criticism (on non-economic grounds), the standards were revised, and UCLA-II was issued in 1996. Much of the controversy was side-stepped by simply eliminating the teaching examples. But since the teaching examples provided much of the content of UCLA-I, the result is that UCLA-II's economic shortcomings are primarily errors of omission, as Buckles and Watts conclude. Unfortunately, because the textbook writers, curriculum writers, and state standard-setters need to fill in the missing content, they will often refer back to UCLA-I. In fact, its authors report that "When the new edition was imminent, the NCHS found that orders for the first edition surged, notably from teachers who wanted to get their hands on the practical teaching activities before they disappeared from the market."[42] Thus, it is still relevant to consider some examples of the flawed economic content in UCLA-I.

The example that received most attention during the 1994–1995 controversy was UCLA-I's treatment of the causes of the Great Depression,[43] the most closely studied episode in macroeconomic history. Economic historians have spent decades debating what caused the Depression to be so much deeper and longer than other downturns. They have made considerable progress in disproving certain popular theories, developing others, and marshalling supporting evidence. At the risk of oversimplifying a complicated debate, the two main contenders are the monetarist and Keynesian views. The monetarist view is represented by the massive, detailed work of Nobel laureate Milton Friedman and Anna Schwartz, which places heavy responsibility on the failure of the Federal Reserve System to maintain the money supply as banks failed. The Keynesian view, most fully developed by MIT's Peter Temin (though originating with the ideas of Barry Eichengreen and Jeffrey Sachs), gives greater weight to international transmission of deflation by adherence to the gold standard.[44]

UCLA-I's teaching examples on the causes of the Great Depression mention the gold standard in passing, but do not mention the Federal Reserve at all. Herbert Hoover's support for a balanced budget is mentioned, but the money supply is not. Friedman and Schwartz's landmark work, which is probably the most influential analysis of the

Depression among economists, is either unknown to UCLA-I's authors or considered unworthy of inclusion.[45]

Instead, UCLA-I's preferred theories of the Great Depression are those that have been discredited by modern economic research. Chief among these is the idea that the "trickle down" economics of Calvin Coolidge and Andrew Mellon contributed to the 1920s' widening income inequality, which, in turn, led to the Depression. The precise mechanism is not spelled out, but it would seem to be the rather dated "underconsumptionist" argument. Temin's calculations show that this "imagined cause" could not account for more than a minuscule portion of the decline in GDP.[46]

The artfully chosen term "trickle down economics" seems designed to anticipate the Reagan era, where the term originated, and to link that era back to the Great Depression. Indeed, when UCLA-I turns to the subject of President Reagan's economic policies, students are asked to evaluate Tip O'Neill's characterizations of him as "Herbert Hoover with a smile" and "a cheerleader for selfishness." Of course, the economy boomed during most of the Reagan years (unlike the Hoover years), but the standards make no mention of that boom at all. They do, however, draw repeated attention to the relatively brief recession during the Bush administration, which at one point they call "the recession of the 1990s." It is a curious term for the mild eight-month downturn (July 1990- March 1991), associated with Saddam Hussein's invasion of Kuwait.[47]

The revised standards issued in 1996, UCLA-II, omit the teaching examples and thus much of the content attached to the standards themselves. For example, students are expected to "evaluate the causes of the Great Depression." But since none is given, it seems likely that state standard-setters, curriculum writers, and textbook writers will refer back to the flawed UCLA-I for guidance. Students are asked to "evaluate major debates among historians" on this and other economic topics, but economic historians are not mentioned. And as Buckles and Watts point out, the students will not have any analytical background to understand economic history or current economic issues without some explicit standards in economic principles, like those given in VNCSE.

Buckles and Watts summarize the tenor of the stripped-down UCLA-II standards:

> Throughout most of this document, people are seen as overcoming problems that the economic system imposes on them, often with political responses, or sometimes

with more environmentally enlightened or even Luddite responses. Emphasis is based on such concepts as class conflict, exploitation. (p. 160)

A focus on income distribution permeates the standards, especially by race and gender. But without the analytical basis to understand this important issue, the material sometimes reduces to a certain amount of posturing, or even analytical error. The discipline of economics has a lot to say about ethnic and gender income differences. But the UCLA authors are not open to it, perhaps out of hostility to methodological individualism in favor of more "social and historical determinism" (to use Arrow's term) or multicultural and class analysis.

The main lesson from this extended analysis of the history standards is that we simply cannot expect economic principles to be conveyed through such a vehicle. Historians have too much on their hands sorting out the conflicts in their own discipline without trying to convey the principles of a discipline that is rather foreign to most of them and to which many of them are temperamentally hostile.

Can Economics Standards Be Non-Discipline-Based?

Since we cannot expect economic reasoning to be well conveyed through the standards of another discipline, states will have to draft separate economics standards. It might seem logical that such standards would be written by, or least with, economists and/or economics educators. However, curious as it may be, this is not always the case. When economics standards are part of a more general history-social science/studies document, then the team that writes the document may or may not have any economists on it. If not, we are unlikely to get discipline-based economics or other-discipline-based economics, but rather *non*-discipline-based economics. The Massachusetts *History and Social Science Curriculum Framework*, which describes its economics strand as "pre-disciplinary," is a case in point.[48]

The general problems—and lessons for others—can be stated simply, by contrasting the process with the language of the enabling legislation, the 1993 Massachusetts Education Reform Act. That Act mandated the Board of Education to establish K–12 standards in six core subjects, including "history and social science." This meant that economics, the archetypal social science, would be accorded its own set of standards within the document, rather than simply being woven into the history standards. This was in fact the outcome: the document contained an economics "strand" with five learning standards, alongside the fifteen learning standards in the history, geography, and civics strands. Beyond that, however, the process and outcome were at variance with at least the spirit of the legislation.

The use of the term "social science" rather than "social studies" carried the clear inference that economics would be taught as a discipline that at least tries to be scientific. Unfortunately, the Board ultimately chose not to be bound by this language. Indeed, in a meeting immediately prior to the Board's adoption of the standards, the chairman of the Board denounced the economics profession precisely for its "scientific pretensions."

The Act of 1993 also stated that the standards should be drawn up in a process that "may include," among others, "leading college and university figures... in subject matter disciplines..." And yet, economics appears to have been the *only* subject in which no one from higher education was asked to participate, even after some came forward to offer their judgments. Indeed, the standards that were enacted made a point of sharply distinguishing "economics as it is pursued at higher educational levels" from that which the Board deemed appropriate at K–12, a distinction which appears not to have been made in the standards for other disciplines.

Finally, the Act also stated that the standards "shall be constructed with due regard to the work and recommendations of national organizations." Instead, as we shall see, another key Board member openly dismissed the VNCSE. Although professional humility is always in order, it is still noteworthy that economics is the only field in which Massachusetts entirely excluded the professionals from the process, at least until public controversy forced some accommodation, at the very end.

The economics strand evolved through a long process fraught with highly public controversy because it was part of the inevitably controversial history framework. The process extended over more than two years, went through at least ten drafts, and at least three or four different drafting teams. One important lesson can be immediately drawn from this saga: *if* the economics strand had been assigned to a team of economists and economics educators, that strand might have been more insulated from the controversy that swirled all around it. Instead, each time the drafting team was replaced, the economics strand was rewritten

Discipline-Based Economics Standards 189

by a new set of non-economists chosen primarily with an eye to how they would write the history standards.

The first drafts were written over much of 1995–1996 in the state department of education, under the supervision of a career official[49] who favored a "multidisciplinary" approach to economics. The result, not surprisingly, was a non-disciplinary approach. The standards simply used the mandated rubric of "economics" as a crude vehicle to devote more of the curriculum to a hodge-podge of topics favored by the authors, such as the rainforests, early Native American life, African village life, etc. They conveyed a tendentious picture of market economies through the examination of advertising's claims, literary works such as Dickens and Hugo, and the fictional video portrayal of the slave trade in *Roots*,[50] and through teaching children to sing union songs.

The shortcomings of such non-disciplinary "rainforest economics" can be readily grasped by noting that real economic research on the rainforests is based on the principles of externalities (VNCSE #16) that cross national boundaries. Since the draft standards provided no such principles, their treatment of rainforests, and of environmental problems more generally, was devoid of economics. In short, the "multidisciplinary" approach was used to avoid teaching economics rather than to enrich it.

In 1996, Governor Weld appointed a new Board, chaired by John Silber, who brought in a historian to revise the history and social studies standards. As it happens, this historian held strong, idiosyncratic views about how a market economy works, as expressed earlier that year in the *Boston Globe*:

> Having all but eliminated the countervailing powers of labor and government, capitalism is now faced with the problem of how to save itself from itself, by itself. It has never succeeded in doing so before. Now, if ever, is the time for business leaders to confront the danger they pose to themselves and the rest of us...

Naturally, the economics strand remained unburdened by the principles of economic reasoning. Much of what was faulty from earlier drafts was carried over. The new draft was particularly heavy in the area of economic history and suffered from the usual defects, discussed in the previous section. For example, the economically illiterate analysis of the causes of the Great Depression (see note 46) seemed to be in keeping with the author's view that capitalism would destroy itself without government intervention, and ignored the evidence that faulty policy choices contributed greatly to the Depression's depth and length. Throughout the strand, a regulated social democracy was clearly designated as the normative modern economy, but no economic principles were provided by which to understand the costs and benefits of regulation.[51]

In late 1996, the controversy-plagued standards were re-assigned to yet another drafting team, this time a three-person subcommittee of the Board itself.[52] The economics strand was overhauled by subcommittee member James Peyser, who had solid training in economics and was executive director of an influential market-oriented Massachusetts policy think-tank. His final draft, in April 1997, explained the shift in approach:

> Although the ability to apply an economic lens to historical events is important, learning to use the vocabulary of economics and learning to reason about economic issues in a modern market economy have emerged as key goals in the current standard-setting movement.

Peyser and the department of education staff drew explicitly on the VNCSE. The result was a much-improved economics strand. It would doubtless have been improved further yet had Peyser been freer of the constraints of format, organization, and some content handed down to him from earlier drafts. The new draft contained for the first time such basic economic concepts as incentives, opportunity cost, marginal benefit and marginal cost, competition, comparative advantage, GDP accounting, and national income determination. For the first time, supply and demand were included in a serious way, with rigorous teaching examples, instead of simply mouthing the words with no content. In short, after two years of non-disciplinary drafts by previous teams, the draft contained real economics. Nor did it reflect a pro-market or pro-government bias. Students were asked to "evaluate the costs and benefits of government intervention" in various microeconomic and macroeconomic functions and, moreover, were provided the basic principles to make such evaluation.

But in the next twist of the screw, most of these gains were reversed. A new draft was written by yet another subcommittee of the Board, headed by Edwin Delattre, dean of Boston University's School of Education. A moral philosopher by training, Delattre would reveal in due course his aversion to economics. Much of the drafting was returned to the economically unsophisticated hands of the historian whose previous economics strand had received public professional criticism. Unlike

Discipline-Based Economics Standards 191

Peyser's drafting team, no assistance from professional economists was sought, despite advice to do so.

As a result, for the first time in the long saga of the history and social science framework, the controversy over economics became one of the top issues in the debate. Predictably, the draft received "criticisms from several professors of economics around the state," according to Chairman Silber. But the very deep flaws were evident to non-economists as well, especially by comparison with the April draft written by Peyser. The economics strand was singled out for strong written criticisms from three of the nine Board members.[53] Public testimony by several non-economists, including professors of history and political science, also included sharp criticism of the economics strand.[54]

The issue was clearly drawn. Participants on both sides of the debate clearly stated that the question was whether economics would be taught "as a distinct academic discipline" (to quote Peyser) or not. Indeed, the most immediate change made by the drafting team was to expand the introduction in order to explain why it was rejecting the criticisms in favor of its decision *not* to teach much discipline-based economics.

The main rationale given for taking a "pre-disciplinary" approach was that "economics is an inherently difficult subject for students in pre-K–12 grades."[55] After presenting an inflated notion of the mathematical level of college economics, "including calculus,"[56] the standards state:

> A student cannot proceed with study of the formal discipline of economics without first having mastered knowledge and skills typical of a college-preparatory senior high school curriculum.[57]

The standards also reject the discipline's "timeless abstractions" as overly difficult. Instead, the approach taken in Massachusetts is to teach economics by "telling stories," such as "fairy tales," in the early grades. In later grades the idea is to connect "the economic facts, reasoning, and concepts to the work that students are pursuing in history, geography, and civics," i.e., to take the multi-disciplinary approach.

Upon reading the standards and listening to the Board discuss it, one sensed the reason for its non-disciplinary approach was only partly a matter of the subject's perceived difficulty. Some of the Board was animated by an unmistakable antipathy toward the *substance* of the discipline. As I testified to the Board:

> The draft reads as if it were written by people who not only are less than conversant in economics, but indeed seem not to like it.

Chairman Silber had taken the opportunity of the untelevised portion of the Board meeting on the standards to pronounce judgment on the profession's "obscurantism," hiding behind its mathematical modelling and failing to deliver the goods. In the televised portion of the hearings, Chairman Silber continued his attack on some of the profession's "trivia and falsifications." He insisted that he was only speaking of a "small aspect of the field." But if so, one could only wonder why it was deemed important enough to introduce into the discussion.

In any case, for whatever reason, the June 2, 1997, draft standards were a giant step backward for economic literacy over the April 1997 draft prepared by Peyser. Every change of omission and commission was for the worse. Such fundamental concepts as "incentives" (VNCSE #4) were completely excised—neither the word nor the concept appears at all in the June 2 draft. Nor does the marginal principle (VNCSE #2), one of the most important and basic ideas in economics over the last century.[58] The idea of weighing the costs and benefits of government interventions (VNCSE #16–17) was expunged, replaced by a somewhat uncritical statist bias (e.g., "the law of unintended consequences" is introduced but applied only to scientific and material progress and never to government policies). Without such building blocks, it was hardly surprising that the standards contained no coherent account of how the price system allocates resources and coordinates a market economy (VNCSE #7–9), which is the core of microeconomics.

Since the standards were stripped of much of the essence of economics, one might ask what filled the void? Much of it was filled by the authors' idiosyncratic interests (e.g., a rather puzzling item on "obsolescence" in the standard on trade,[59] and a pre-K-4 standard on "gradations and variations in ownership"), a mélange of noble sentiments that have nothing to do with economics (e.g., the value of working together appears three times), an excessive focus on economic history and non-market economic systems (e.g., "utopian communist colonies in 19th century America"), and an occasional flirtation with certain romanticized pre-capitalist ideas.

One standard that raised several eyebrows required students to "understand differences between the price of something [and] its intrinsic worth." This seemed to refer to the medieval doctrine of "just price."[60]

Discipline-Based Economics Standards 193

This suspicion was confirmed by the chairman of the drafting subcommittee, Edwin Delattre, as he defended the standard to the Board:

> Criticism... of the idea of "just price" as devoid of scientific content, even if true, does not show the idea to be devoid of significant content.

As this comment indicates, Delattre was perhaps more interested in the moral content of the economics strand than its scientific content, despite the fact that it was written to meet a "social science" mandate.[61]

Delattre's view of the economics profession was also illustrated by his comment on the VNCSE. In explaining why the VNCSE content was reduced from the Peyser draft to its very minimal representation in his subcommittee's draft, he simply stated, "there were claims made in [VNCSE] that seemed to me false." No further details were provided. Immediately following this judgment, the Board defeated the key motion, to replace his draft with the more discipline-based April draft, by a vote of 5–4.[62]

In the end, the drafting subcommittee did respond to a number of the criticisms raised both by economists and non-economists, as well as by other Board members. After the vote, Delattre solicited the suggestions of Peyser. The drafters added the concept of incentives (but never linked it to the price system, as in the fundamental VNCSE #8). They added the marginal principle to various parts of the document (but never deleted the introductory material that students need not be taught how to economize). They deleted the reference to utopian communist colonies (but retained an inordinate emphasis on non-market systems and economic history). They deleted the unscientific distinction between needs and wants, added the idea that individual effort and competition might also be as valuable as "working together," and slightly reworded a few of the more egregious standards. Some ingeniously chosen "examples" (due to Peyser) were introduced that illustrated sound economic principles rather than the ill-considered standards to which these "examples" were linked. For instance, the standard on price and "intrinsic worth" was effectively undercut by linking it to an "example" on the relation of scarcity to price and the paradox of water and diamonds. Unfortunately, this ingenious use of "examples" to remedy faulty standards may not fully succeed at the district level, since the districts draw mainly on the standards themselves in their curriculum documents and often simply ignore the "examples."[63]

While containing some real economic content, the Massachusetts standards bear the unmistakable imprint of their tortuous evolution and the absence of economists from their creation. The economics strand has something of the character of a shopping list of concepts, some of which are sound economics, and others of which are not. What it lacks is the coherent disciplinary structure that would have required the participation of professional economists.[64] It is certainly not a model for other states to emulate. They should do what Massachusetts never did: get professional help from the National Council on Economics Education[65] and make full use of the VNCSE.

Ultimately, the quality of economics instruction in Massachusetts (as elsewhere) will be driven by the student assessments. A twelve-member assessment committee for history and social sciences was eventually appointed, after the extended controversy in adopting the framework. Since the economics strand constitutes five of the framework's twenty learning standards, one might have hoped that a proportionate share of the committee members—perhaps three of twelve—would have some professional economic expertise. The actual number of seats allocated to economists was zero, not even one seat for an economic historian. It is very hard to understand how such a committee would be able to come up with sound economics test questions or, indeed, how it would be able to choose questions from off-the-shelf tests, such as the NCEE's Test of Economic Literacy.[66]

The fundamental problem in Massachusetts was that although the state law had mandated standards for social sciences, the authorities charged with carrying out that mandate simply did not want much economics in the curriculum, for a variety of reasons. In part, there was an obdurate exaggeration of the level of mathematics required. In addition, Delattre and Silber, two moral philosophers by training, had some aversion to economics' value-free approach and/or its perceived free-market stance. The specific lesson illustrated by the Massachusetts experience is that this obstacle to discipline-based economics transcends simple political categories. It is not only far-left critics who are suspicious of economics but also some social conservatives.

Another, perhaps more fundamental, obstacle was Silber's view that history, geography, and civics are really all the social studies that belong in K–12 and that there is simply no room for economics. I cannot say that he is wrong about K–12 priorities. Since the most fundamental lesson of economics is that life is full of tradeoffs, those of us in the

Discipline-Based Economics Standards

profession certainly understand that people will differ on how to weigh those tradeoffs. Economists, and others with less obvious turf to protect and promote, have made the case for K–12 economic literacy elsewhere.[67] It is for others to decide if that case is persuasive. But unless and until the authorities are clear on that decision, one cannot hope for sound economics standards. Thus, I closed my testimony to the Massachusetts Board with a question that any state board should ask itself before drawing up its standards:

> Does the Board in fact want economics taught in K–12? ... If the Board cannot find people who like economics to write the standards, then perhaps the Board should simply drop the effort entirely, rather than inflict on the children of the Commonwealth something you yourselves do not believe in.[68]

Conclusion

Any state that decides to set discipline-based economics standards using the VNCSE faces some serious implementation challenges: how much economics can fit into the curriculum, in what grades and courses will it be taught, and how will teachers be trained? VNCSE calls for a significant increase in the economics component of the K–12 curriculum at the same time that curricular demands are rising in other subjects, at least some of which merit greater priority.[69] It is, in fact, a legitimate question whether the quantity of VNCSE material is too great to fit into a crowded K–12 curriculum, where economics is accorded only a one-semester high school course, portions of non-economics courses such as history, or scattered units in the elementary social studies curriculum. It is conceivable that a comprehensive curriculum can be designed which at least touches on all twenty standards, but it seems likely that school systems will have to prioritize which standards are to be covered in any depth. VNCSE is not to be faulted for setting out the lay of the land, especially since quite a bit of prioritizing went into the selection of these twenty standards. But further difficult tradeoffs will almost certainly confront most school systems, and they will need sound professional advice from the community of economists and economics educators.[70]

Traditionally, most of the K–12 economics instruction has taken place in a senior year elective. Enrollment in such a course has grown since 1961, reaching about 45 percent by 1990. A good part of this rise occurred during the 1980s, as a number of states began mandating a course in economics for graduation from high school, although the quality and content of such courses has varied widely.[71] But this may be changing. Following the Federal Goals Act, VNCSE sets benchmarks of "competency over challenging subject matter" for grades 4 and 8, as well as 12. Preliminary indications are that in recent years the rise in twelfth grade economics may be reversing itself, as state mandated economics instruction moves to the earlier grades.[72] If so, the addition of economics to the federal goals in 1994 and the creation of VNCSE in 1997 might have the unintended effect of reallocating economics to lower grades and to non-economics courses, rather than increasing the overall economics content of the curriculum.

The reallocation of economics content to lower grades and non-economics courses poses serious challenges for instruction.[73] As is well-known, teacher preparation in economics, which has never been particularly strong even for many twelfth grade economics instructors, is much weaker among elementary and middle school teachers, and non-economics social studies teachers in high school.[74] It will be a tall order to improve the economics training of such a broad spectrum of teachers. Research indicates that non-credit, in-service workshops in economics are ineffective: economic reasoning is a distinctive skill that cannot be casually picked up on the side.[75] It will require either an increase in pre-service, college-level economics, or in-service courses for college credit. If it proves impossible to achieve this result on the broad scale required, then perhaps it will be necessary to move toward a system of economics specialists, analogous to those in art, music, and foreign languages, at the elementary level as well as secondary.

Moreover, research shows that although a high school economics course typically raises student scores on standardized economics tests, there is little or no discernible effect from economics "infusion" into other social studies courses.[76] This negative result probably reflects the more diffuse nature of such courses, as well as the lower degree of economics training among teachers in these other social studies courses.

The implication is very clear: *If* the reallocation of economics into lower grades and non-economics courses is to have any payoff, it *must* be accompanied by strong and effective economics standards. Equally or even more important will be the adoption of strong and effective student assessments that will operationalize the standards and drive the curriculum and teacher preparation. Much depends on the writing of these assessments, and all the issues that arise in the standards debate arise here, too.

Discipline-Based Economics Standards

The VNCSE represents a major step toward discipline-based economics instruction in K–12. It is too early to tell whether the potential created by this nationally recognized set of standards will be fulfilled—there have been other such efforts in the past, and yet economic literacy is still quite low. Many of the obstacles that *can,* but *need not,* arise are illustrated by the cautionary tale of Massachusetts.[77] Other states have done a better job with the help of the economics education community. One thing seems certain: we will not have strong or meaningful economics standards and assessments without the participation of economists in these activities.

I have stressed the resistance of many in the education community to the ideas of economics on their own grounds. But in addition, we should not dismiss the influence of self-interest. We should not be surprised that the leaders of a public education system that is largely sheltered from the forces of competition and heavily influenced by a strong teachers' union are less open to understanding the strengths of the market and the forces of competition than even the general public, let alone the economics profession. This follows from the same principle of understandable self-interest (real or at least perceived) that leads trade unions to favor the minimum wage and to oppose free trade. Indeed, as the debate over market-based education reform escalates, and the education establishment mounts its defense, this may not be the most propitious moment to ask that establishment to introduce the serious study of economics to the curriculum![78]

Nonetheless, it is probably true that low economic literacy, rather than naked self-interest, is the main obstacle to a major upgrading of K–12 economics. That is, unless and until the education community becomes more conversant in economics, there will remain, at best, a certain ambivalence about bringing economics into the curriculum in any serious way. This may be a case of what economists call multiple equilibria. We may be stuck in a low-level equilibrium trap, where low economic literacy on the part of the general public and the education community in particular is itself preventing the steps necessary to an improvement in the next generation's economic literacy.[79] There may be a higher-level equilibrium, where economic literacy is widespread and sustains itself by transmission to the next generation, but we cannot get to that high-level equilibrium from the current low-level one without a large, discrete leap of some kind. If so, this would explain the disappointing results of the last 40 years of organized attempts to improve K–12 economics. It remains to be seen whether the current standards movement, and the VNCSE in particular, will provide enough momentum to make the necessary leap forward.

Author's Note: I would like to thank Sandra Stotsky for her valuable editorial suggestions. I would also like to acknowledge the helpful comments of Dale Ballou, John Clow, Daphne Patai, Diane Ravitch, Roberta Schaefer, Abby Thernstrom, Mike Watts, and Alan Wolfe.

Appendix: Voluntary National Content Standards in Economics [*]

Students will understand that:
1. Productive resources are limited. Therefore, people cannot have all the goods and services they want; as a result, they must choose some things and give up others.
2. Effective decision making requires comparing the additional costs of alternatives with the additional benefits. Most choices involve doing a little more or a little less of something: few choices are "all or nothing" decisions.
3. Different methods can be used to allocate goods and services. People acting individually or collectively through government must choose which methods to use to allocate different kinds of goods and services.
4. People respond predictably to positive and negative incentives.
5. Voluntary exchange occurs only when all participating parties expect to gain. This is true for trade among individuals or organizations within a nation, and usually among individuals or organizations in different nations.
6. When individuals, regions, and nations specialize in what they can produce at the lowest cost and then trade with others, both production and consumption increase.
7. Markets exist when buyers and sellers interact. This interaction determines market prices and thereby allocates scarce goods and services.
8. Prices send signals and provide incentives to buyers and sellers. When supply or demand changes, market prices adjust, affecting incentives.
9. Competition among sellers lowers costs and prices, and encourages producers to produce more of what consumers are willing and able to buy. Competition among buyers increases prices and allocates goods and services to those people who are willing and able to pay the most for them.
10. Institutions evolve in market economies to help individuals and groups accomplish their goals. Banks, labor unions, corporations, legal systems, and not-for-profit organizations are examples of important institutions. A different kind of institution, clearly defined and enforced property rights, is essential to a market economy.
11. Money makes it easier to trade, borrow, save, invest, and compare the value of goods and services.

Discipline-Based Economics Standards

12. Interest rates, adjusted for inflation, rise and fall to balance the amount saved with the amount borrowed, which affects the allocation of scarce resources between present and future uses.
13. Income for most people is determined by the market value of the productive resources they sell. What workers earn depends, primarily, on the market value of what they produce and how productive they are.
14. Entrepreneurs are people who take the risks of organizing productive resources to make goods and services. Profit is an important incentive that leads entrepreneurs to accept the risks of business failure.
15. Investment in factories, machinery, new technology, and in the health, education, and training of people can raise future standards of living.
16. There is an economic role for government in a market economy, whenever the benefits of a government policy outweigh its costs. Governments often provide for national defense, address environmental concerns, define and protect property rights, and attempt to make markets more competitive. Most government policies also redistribute income.
17. Costs of government policies sometimes exceed benefits. This may occur because of incentives facing voters, government officials, and government employees, because of actions by special interest groups that can impose costs on the general public, or because social goals other than economic efficiency are being pursued.
18. A nation's overall levels of income, employment, and prices are determined by the interaction of spending and production decisions made by all households, firms, government agencies, and others in the economy.
19. Unemployment imposes costs on individuals and nations. Unexpected inflation imposes costs on many people and benefits some others because it arbitrarily redistributes purchasing power. Inflation can reduce the rate of growth of national living standards because individuals and organizations use resources to protect themselves against the uncertainty of future prices.
20. Federal government budgetary policy and the Federal Reserve System's monetary policy influence the overall levels of employment, output, and prices.

*The VNCSE principles, given here, are stated in lay language. Economists seeking a quick translation into the terminology of the discipline may find it in Siegfried and Meszaros, *Op. Cit.* As stated in the text, each VNCSE standard also includes a one-sentence general statement of skill expectations, a few paragraphs of rationale, and about two pages of more detailed benchmarks.

Notes

[1] The 1989 National Education Goals, set by President Bush and the nation's governors, specified five subjects: English, mathematics, science, history, and geography. The arts, civics, and foreign languages were added to the list by 1991–92, when the Education Department made awards to national groups for the

establishment of standards. By including economics, the 1994 Federal Goals 2000 Act brought the number of academic subjects to nine. (See Diane Ravitch, *National Standards in American Education: A Citizen's Guide*, Brookings Institution, Washington, D.C., 1995.)

[2] National Council on Economic Education, *Voluntary National Content Standards in Economics*, 1998, New York: National Council on Economic Education (http://www.economicsamerica.org/standards/).

[3] Of course, the national history standards also drew much fire from outside the discipline, including the U.S. Senate. (As discussed below, I also criticized the history standards, over its economic content.) But the controversy would likely not have been sustained had there not been substantial disagreement among historians, e.g. Arthur Schlesinger, Jr.'s critique of the 1994 *National Standards for U.S. History.*

[4] The one significant, albeit minority view is from those economics educators who de-emphasize economic analysis in favor of a more business-oriented stress on marketing, accounting, and the like.

[5] Survey data analyzed by William Walstad led him to conclude, "What is especially disturbing is that people who have no basic knowledge about an economic issue are quite willing to state an opinion on that issue." ("Why It's Important to Understand Economics," *The Region* 12 (4), December 1998, Federal Reserve Bank of Minneapolis, pp. 23–26. This special issue, on economic literacy, contains a number of articles referred to below. It can be found at http://woodrow.mpls.frb.fed.us/pubs/region/98–12)

[6] Full disclosure: I was an open critic of the Massachusetts economics standards at the time, as detailed below.

[7] This section draws mainly on the VNCSE itself and John J. Siegfried and Bonnie T. Meszaros, "Voluntary Economics Content Standards for America's Schools: Rationale and Development," *Journal of Economic Education* 29 (2), Spring 1998, pp. 139–149.

[8] The other partners in this project were the National Association of Economic Educators, the Foundation for Teaching Economics, and the American Economic Association's Committee on Economic Education.

[9] By contrast, the national standards documents in history, social studies, civics, and geography average over 200 pages. One of the VNCSE's key objectives was parsimony. The document's relative brevity reflects the principles-based approach that defines economics, as opposed to the more expansive topics-based and necessarily factually substantive approach characteristic of history, geography and civics.

[10] See Siegfried and Meszaros for a fuller description.

[11] William B. Walstad provides relevant historical background in "Economics Instruction in High Schools," *Journal of Economic Literature* 20 (December 1992), pp. 2019–2051. Efforts to upgrade K–12 economics from the descriptive non-analytical approach of an earlier era date to 1960, when the American Economic Association and the Committee on Economic Development created the National Task Force on Economic Education. The Task Force recommended economics be taught with "central emphasis on the rational way of thinking." Its 1961 report

Discipline-Based Economics Standards 201

included a list of 45 concepts and institutions. In 1977, the Task Force report was replaced by the Joint Council on Economic Education (NCEE's previous name) *Framework for Teaching Economics: Basic Concepts.* The *Framework* streamlined the content to a shorter list, with better organization, again stressing the analytical and rational approach. It was revised in 1984, resulting in 22 basic economic concepts, under four categories: fundamental, microeconomic, macroeconomic, and international. According to Walstad, this document "significantly influenced economics instruction" through curriculum guides, textbooks, and other teaching materials. The VNCSE is the successor to these documents.

[12] See, for example, "The puzzling failure of economics," *The Economist,* August 23, 1997, p.11.

[13] Richard P. Feynman, *Six Easy Pieces: Essentials of Physics Explained by Its Most Brilliant Teacher,* Addison-Wesley, Reading, MA, 1995, p.3.

[14] This latter issue, that teachers or potential teachers are often intimidated by the perceived difficulty of economics, is perennially raised in discussions of teacher preparation, e.g. Walstad (1992), *Op. Cit.* This issue was directly raised in Massachusetts, as discussed in Note 55 below. Sometimes education policy makers and standard setters also seem to be intimidated by the subject.

[15] *The Region, op.cit.,* p.48.

[16] The 20 standards themselves eschew the discipline's terminology. Terms such as opportunity costs, equilibrium and externalities are relegated to the benchmarks.

[17] The VNCSE also refrains from using such technical concepts found in college courses as elasticity and diminishing marginal returns. Indeed, there has been at least one complaint that the VNCSE demands too little (K. Pennar, "Economics Made Too Simple," *Business Week,* January 20, 1997, p.32), a charge rejected by the VNCSE authors, and, I think, rightly so. The VNCSE authors aimed for standards "to be challenging but attainable" by 95 percent of high school graduates "exerting a sustained effort," and in seeking that level, the authors chose "to err in the direction of too challenging rather than insufficiently challenging" (Siegfried and Meszaros, *Op. Cit.,* p. 144). By the incremental logic of standard #2, we should first try to implement the rather substantial improvement represented by the VNSCE, before ratcheting up the demands any further, as Pennar suggests. A good candidate for the first omission to be rectified is the concept of present discounted value, which is central not only to matters of personal finance (such as mortgages), but also to understanding the future of Social Security.

[18] Standards #12, 17, and 20 have no fourth or eighth grade benchmarks; #18 has no fourth grade benchmark.

[19] The same thing can be said about calculus. College students can readily learn the rules to find a derivative, but are often unable to interpret a derivative in the context of actual variables; they are unable to translate the result into plain English. To the extent that these problems can be ameliorated by applying mathematical techniques to concrete problems in math class, economics provides a ready set of examples, both at the college and pre-college level. For example, the techniques for solving a pair of simultaneous linear equations can be readily illustrated for middle school students with supply and demand equations, yielding equilibrium (market-clearing) price and quantity.

20   W. Lee Hansen, "Principles-Based Standards: On the *Voluntary National Content Standards in Economics,*" *Journal of Economic Education* 29 (2), Spring 1998, pp. 150–156.

21   In times past, the external critique of economics standards was rather different. In 1961–1962, the *Wall Street Journal* ran four lengthy editorials tagging the Task Force report (VNCSE's predecessor) as "Statism for Sophomores" (Walstad (1992), *Op. Cit.,* p. 2034).

22   Instances where economists may have transgressed our strictures against mixing normative and positive economics have been pointed out by Jonathan Marshall ("On Economics: Council Setting Standards for Stamping Out Economic Illiteracy," *San Francisco Chronicle,* January 6, 1997) and by Julie A. Nelson and Steven M. Sheffrin ("Economic Literacy or Economic Ideology?" *Journal of Economic Perspectives* 5(3), Summer 1991, pp. 157–65), although William B. Walstad ("A Flawed Ideological Critique", *Journal of Economic Perspectives* 5 (3), Summer 1991, pp. 167–73) rejects Nelson's and Sheffrin's charge.

23   Warren E. Nord, "God and the National Economics Standards," *Education Week,* October 21, 1998. At the risk of over-emphasizing the importance of this piece, I shall use Nord as a convenient example of a number of shibboleths about economics. His innocence of the field is illustrated by his discussion of the environment, which seems oblivious to the well-developed economic analysis of environmental problems, and the practical policy prescriptions which have helped so much to clean up the nation's air and water in recent decades. Nord's empirical grasp is indicated by his assertion that "we find ourselves engulfed in a catastrophic environmental crisis."

24   The moral philosopher John Silber provides an insightful analysis of the minimum wage as an application of moral choice in the public arena *(Straight Shooting,* Harper-Collins, New York, 1990, pp. 191–2). He specifically cites the contribution of economics to the moral calculus: "The law of supply and demand is inflexible in this regard; there is no economic incentive to hire artificially overpriced labor."

25   The second sentence of standard #13 is unfortunately worded, a casualty of the tension between VNCSE's goals of accuracy, parsimony, and accessibility of language. In attempting to avoid the jargon of marginal productivity theory, the standard misrepresents that theory by stating that wages depend on "how productive" workers are. Without such qualifying phrases as "on the margin" or "how much the last worker adds to output," the statement is incorrect and seriously misleading since no meaning can be attached to the "productivity" of any given worker without reference to the other inputs, including other workers, capital, etc. Unfortunately, this type of inaccurate statement is partly to blame for the facile charge that economic theory provides an apology or justification for the distribution of income. Critics of marginal productivity theory wrongly ascribe to it the implication that wages are determined "fairly" because each worker supposedly gets his or her "contribution to output." But marginal productivity theory, properly understood, makes no such claim since it does not turn on any ill-defined "contribution to output." Indeed, it is perfectly consistent with marginal productivity theory for each worker's wage to *fall* when all workers exert, say, twice the effort. (This result obtains under certain conditions, when the adverse effect on wages of

expanding the effective amount of labor outweighs the fact that each worker is rewarded for more units of effective labor, i.e. for more effort.) Such a result clearly contradicts any reasonable meaning of "fair". Thus, marginal productivity theory simply does not say that wages are "fair." The wording of standard #13, unfortunately, contributes to this misunderstanding.

26 The term may seem uncharitable, but one hardly knows how else to characterize such statements as Nord's pointed use of the 1986 American Catholic bishops' statement on the economy: "economists, like all of us, must realize that 'human dignity, realized in community with others and with the whole of God's creation, is the norm against which every social institution is measured.'"

27 Of course it is true that, like non-economists, *some* economists may well be morally indifferent to the fortunes of the poor, in their personal or professional capacities, or both. Some economists certainly devote their considerable talents to helping investors get richer, while others devote their careers to studying income inequality. This no more defines the moral content of the economics profession than does the fact that the construction industry builds low-rent housing and luxury condominiums.

28 Textbook writer Paul Heyne, who came to economics as a divinity student, also argues against the normative/positive distinction on the grounds that market principles advance moral purposes ("Moral Misunderstanding and the Justification of Markets," *The Region, Op. Cit.* pp.29–32). His view is rooted in the consequences of markets for material well-being by virtue of the price system's superior informational properties. This is also a Hayekian theme, albeit a different one from the primacy of liberty.

29 Nord provides yet another convenient example of this confused line of attack. He argues that in contrast to economics' analysis of "self-interested utility-maximizers... no religious tradition allows self-interest to be accepted as normative... [VNCSE] show[s] no interest whatever in altruism or compassion."

30 As in the case of "justice," there is quite a bit of advanced work in the study of altruism and its opposite, envy. Should this be brought down to the elementary level? Perhaps, since many important phenomena, such as bequests and charity, cannot be understood without it. But many other insights can be obtained without such a generalization, and there are large benefits to simplification.

31 As Kenneth Arrow ("Methodological Individualism and Social Knowledge," *American Economic Review* 84 (2), May 1994, pp. 1–9) points out, methodological individualism is most rigorously followed in game theory, which is increasingly important in economic analysis although absent from VNCSE.

32 He might also have noted the exclusion of Austrian economics, i.e., Hayek, von Mises, et. al. Indeed, in 1963, Chicago economist (and later Nobel Laureate) George Stigler objected to the National Task Force report for exclusion of similar non-mainstream views (Walstad (1992), p. 2033).

33 Paul A. Samuelson, "How Economics Has Changed," *Journal of Economic Education,* 18(2), Spring 1987, pp. 107–110.

34 William Baumol's wry appropriation of the old saw has become standard. "I am here to report that there is absolutely nothing wrong with the current state of economics and that, besides, the discipline's fundamental problems are being

remedied as quickly as can reasonably be expected." As he aptly states, "Our political goals differ; our social goals differ. It is only our analyses that have a great deal in common. The last of these facts, incidentally, is one of the basic misunderstandings of the general public." With regard to the well-known criticisms of mainstream economics, he finds "no working alternatives to the mainstream approaches, with all their warts and blemishes." ("Economic Education and the Critics of Mainstream Economics," *Journal of Economic Education,* 19(4), Fall 1998, pp. 323–330).

[35] Robert J. Highsmith and Hirschel Kasper, "Rethinking the Scope of Economics," *Journal of Economic Education,* 18 (2), Spring 1987, pp. 101–105.

[36] Siegfried and Meszaros, *Op. Cit.*, p. 143.

[37] In making this comparison, I do not mean to suggest that the weight of scientific evidence in support of mainstream economics is as strong as that supporting evolution. I mean only to compare the confidence with which those outside these two professions substitute their judgment of the evidence for those within.

[38] Steven Arons makes this case on First Amendment grounds (*Short Route to Chaos: Conscience, Community, and the Re-constitution of American Schooling,* 1997, University of Massachusetts Press: Amherst).

[39] They confine themselves to the revised history standards, referred to below as UCLA-II. The original standards, UCLA-I, were considerably worse and, as discussed below, are still unfortunately influential. (Stephen Buckles and Michael Watts, "National Standards in Economics, History, Social Studies, Civics and Geography: Complementarities, Competition, or Peaceful Coexistence?" *Journal of Economic Education* 29 (2), Spring 1998, pp. 157–166).

[40] In fairness to UCLA-I, one of the teaching examples does pose the question, "Was slavery profitable?" to which much of Fogel's work was addressed. However, it is unclear whether the contributions of economic historians would be included, since both UCLA-I and UCLA-II call for students to "evaluate major debates among historians" on economic aspects of slavery.

[41] National Center for History in the Schools, *National Standards for United States History: Expanded Edition,* 1994, UCLA; National Center for History in the Schools, *National Standards for History: Basic Edition,* 1996, UCLA.

[42] Gary B. Nash, Charlotte Crabtree, and Ross E. Dunn, *History on Trial,* 1997, Albert A. Knopf: New York, p. 254. Nash and Crabtree co-directed the history standards project. As the authors explain, the standards were revised subject to the independent review of a Council on Basic Education committee that included such critics of UCLA-I as Diane Ravitch. "The NCHS assured the CBE commission that it would not reprint the first edition because the new book superseded it. But Nash and his associates rejected the 'defective Corvair' theory that the first editions… should be 'recalled' or withheld from teachers, libraries, or any citizens who wanted them."

[43] See my letter in the *New York Times,* February 2, 1995 or the *Chronicle of Higher Education,* February 17, 1995. Nash, Crabtree, and Dunn never mention this criticism in their account of the controversy. The failure of history textbooks to reflect the economic analysis of the Great Depression is an old story (Steven L. Miller and Stephen A. Rose, "The Great Depression: A Textbook Case of Problems

Discipline-Based Economics Standards 205

with American History Textbooks," *Theory and Research in Social Education*, 11 (1), Spring 1983, pp. 25–39).

[44] For a good summary of the current state of the debate, see Peter Temin, "The Great Depression," November 1994, National Bureau of Economic Research, Historical Paper No. 62; forthcoming in *The Cambridge Economic History of the United States*.

[45] The teaching examples do mention the collapse of the banks. But instead of mentioning the Federal Reserve's failure in this regard, UCLA-I seems to lead students to the opposite conclusion by asking them to consider the view that while Hoover "provided relief for banks, he refused it to people."

[46] The standards also seem to imply that the stock market crash contributed significantly to the Great Depression, a view that "time has not been kind to" (Temin, p.6), especially since the rather similar 1987 crash had no adverse effect on the economy. In addition, the teaching examples cite the Smoot-Hawley tariff, an argument that "fails on both theoretical and historical grounds," according to Temin, if for no other reason than the export sector of the U.S. economy was too small for any retaliatory tariffs to have much effect. Finally, the teaching examples for the causes of the Great Depression mention "the increased productivity of business in the 1920s" and note that "mechanization displace[d] workers." The point here is not clear, but some curriculum writers or state standard-setters might take this to refer to the archaic notion of "overproduction," a concept that is "not useful... in the investigation of the Great Depression" (Temin p. 5).

Two years after the national history standards controversy, the story was replayed in Massachusetts, and the example of the Great Depression's causes arose again. A November 1996 draft of the Massachusetts History and Social Science Frameworks asks students to consider the roles played "by industrial over-production or underconsumption, by income disparities, by unregulated stock market speculation," among others. As I explained to the Massachusetts Board of Education (January 15, 1997), such theories are "economically illiterate... If over-production caused 25% unemployment in 1933, then by the same logic, we should have 100% unemployment in the vastly more productive economy of 1997." The final standards, issued in September 1997, excise "over-production," and add the Fed, but still head the list of causes with the stock market crash and the idea that "low incomes of farmers and industrial workers... limit mass purchasing power." Some "imagined causes" die hard. It seems that some redistributionist critics of market economics have so little confidence in a direct appeal to equity considerations that they must also argue that income disparities depress aggregate demand. It may be a convenient argument but as an explanation of the Great Depression is not support by the evidence. After all, our own era's rise in income inequality since the 1970s is a matter of concern in its own right, even though it did not lead to any Great Depression or even to the lesser downturns we have experienced.

[47] There are other shortcomings in UCLA-I's treatment of postwar economics: (i) The "unprecedented economic growth" in the postwar period is attributed to increased defense spending and international prominence, compared to war-devastated Europe and Asia. This demand-side view is not much credited among economists, since defense and exports constitute relatively small portions of GDP, and in any case, is

irrelevant to what made the period's growth so "unprecedented," namely the high rate of productivity growth. (ii) Similarly, the growth in service sector employment is discussed in demand-side terms, without any reference to long-term supply-side trends. Ever since the enunciation of "Baumol's Law," it has been well understood that the main force driving up the service sector's share of employment has been the relatively rapid growth in manufacturing productivity. (iii) The standards ignore the role of monetary policy in both the inflationary period of the 1970s, and in ending that inflation, through the recessions of 1980–1982. But of course even if monetary policy were included, students would have little or no basis for understanding it, without a grounding in the principles of macroeconomics.

[48] Massachusetts Department of Education, *History and Social Science Curriculum Framework,* Malden, MA, September 1997 (http://www.doe.mass.edu/doedocs/frameworks/).

[49] He later resigned his position with a very public blast against the "Western" tilt taken by a subsequent drafting team. (Dan French, "Reform is undercut in favor of ideology," *Boston Globe,* January 14, 1997.)

[50] Sheldon Stern has commented on *Roots'* historical inaccuracy elsewhere in this volume. The slave trade is presented as the sole example of "how trade influences and/or transforms societies."

[51] For example, the draft asked students to "describe the renewed debates of the late 20th century over the degree, and aims, of government intervention in the American economy and government regulation of private economic power, and explain the rival interests involved." Note that the terms of the debate are limited to "rival interests" and power, with no reference at all to costs and benefits in terms of efficiency.

[52] This team used the Virginia standards as the basis for its work. Virginia's standards were rated top in the nation for history by the Fordham Foundation, but were thin on economics.

[53] Board member Roberta Schaefer took special note of the questionable economics in the history sections. For example, noting the somewhat tendentious standard that asks students to "assess the complicity of government and private institutions in perpetuation of economic injustice," Schaefer wrote "just what is meant by 'economic injustice': that some people are richer than others?"

[54] Richard Bennett, who had helped write earlier drafts, found that in the June draft "the economics strand grossly oversimplifies the field of economics, reducing it to studies in history and ethics... The economics strand is decidedly underwhelming." Marc Landy, chairman of the political science department at Boston College, also found that the economics strand "misses the essential... It doesn't explain free market principles... how the political economy of the United States works at the core. Supply, demand, price, marginal utility: these are not matters that can be left to college students." Finally, Stephan Thernstrom, the Winthrop Professor of History at Harvard University, noted the "woefully inadequate treatment of economics in general here that shows up in history."

[55] A related reason given was that the subject is too difficult for teachers. Silber wrote that discipline-based standards "would require teachers who are economics majors." Delattre told the Board that there was "no greater source of concern in the field

56 [apparently referring to the state's teachers] than the status of economics in the framework."

This view was reiterated by Delattre at the Board's June 16, 1997, meeting: "It has seemed to me clear that economics cannot be taught in schools fully to the standards of professional economists, who present economics in terms of mathematical models, especially those which turn on the calculus." Boston University's Professor Laurence Kotlikoff tried, to no avail, to correct this misperception about college economics, writing to the Board, "With the exception of certain advanced courses, we do not use anything beyond high school algebra in any of our undergraduate courses." In any case, as Peyser pointed out in the Board meeting, his April draft did not anticipate the use of calculus, differential equations or any other higher mathematics for the instruction of K–12 economics. The tools required, he pointed out, were no more demanding or abstract than required for K–12 mathematics and science: simple algebra and graphs.

57 This was the version approved by the Board at its June 16, 1997, meeting. The final published version replaced the phrase "...typical of a college-preparatory..." with "...required in a sound..."

58 Indeed, the introduction to the economics strand implies that it is unnecessary to teach marginal analysis: "We teach economics not to train children to be economic actors. They will become economizers regardless of how they are educated, because that is part of human nature." The point is false in important respects. Those uneducated in economics often confuse average and marginal benefits and costs, resulting in wrong-headed personal and policy decisions, including environmental policy.

59 As Peyser wrote, "this is hardly a central concept, unless you want to slam corporations for 'planned obsolescence.'"

60 Among historians of economic thought, there is some debate regarding what Aquinas and other medieval thinkers meant by "just price." According to Raymond DeRoover, Aquinas' concept corresponded to what economists now refer to as the long-run equilibrium price. John Duns Scotus' view was perhaps closer to the value-laden version associated with the term today.

61 In a similar vein, Delattre's remarks continued by defending the June draft's standard on the distinction between "needs and wants." This is a common feature of non-discipline-based economics standards, despite the fact that it has nothing to do with economics. The analysis of supply and demand applies in the same way to those goods commonly (if imprecisely) referred to as "needs" as they do to "wants." Delattre defended this standard by stating "we would scarcely be willing to encourage students to believe that not wanting to do something is the same as not needing to do it, whether in economic or other contexts." What seems to motivate this idea is that schools and parents can and should try to shape their children's priorities (or "preferences," to use the language of economics)—a perfectly defensible normative function of moral education. The function of economics is quite different, to provide a positive analysis of how preferences—of whatever type and origin—play themselves out in the market.

62 The student member of the Board was among those voting for the April draft, evidently rejecting the argument that discipline-based economics was too difficult for students.

63 Brookline is one district that reproduced the flawed state economics standards in its curriculum frameworks while excluding all of the "examples".

64 Laurence Kotlikoff wrote the Board urging it to have some "first-rate economist not just kibitz, but sit down and formulate the standard. The resulting product will not be above or beyond the teachers. What it will be is economics, not some non-economist's misconceptions of the field."

65 Board members Abigail Thernstrom and Roberta Schaefer strongly urged this step in response to my suggestion at the June 1997 Board meeting.

66 Interestingly enough, the content guide to the economics section of the Massachusetts teacher tests is much better than the curriculum frameworks.

67 See, for example, the contributions of William Walstad, Bonnie Meszaros, Mary Suiter, and Michael Watts (among others) in *The Region, Op. Cit.* Also, the VNCSE itself contains a separate rationale for asking students to understand each of the twenty standards. Of course, the fact that economic literacy is so low (as indicated in periodic surveys of the general public by the NCEE) in the world's most prosperous economy suggests that some modesty may be in order: if economic education does not take off, perhaps we shall continue to muddle through reasonably well anyway. Indeed, not all economics professors favor K–12 instruction if they think it will be so poorly done that students will have to be re-taught at college. As Paul Samuelson put it, in attributing this view to his teacher, "Jesuits like to work with virginal material" (Samuelson, *Op. Cit.*, p.107).

68 Board member Schaefer suggested a vote on this basic question but was overruled.

69 Writing in 1992, as the standard-setting movement was picking up steam but before economics was added to the national goals, Walstad, *Op. Cit.,* anticipated that the national standards movement might squeeze out economics in favor of other subjects.

70 For example, the economics standards in Delaware's Social Studies Framework is four pages long (vs. 46 for the VNCSE). It predates VNCSE (1995 vs. 1997) but is similar in spirit, perhaps because the University of Delaware's Centre for Economic Education and Entrepreneurship played a role in both undertakings. Delaware sets out many of the same VNCSE principles in a total of 18 benchmarks under four standards: microeconomics, macroeconomics, economic systems, and international trade.

71 See Walstad (1992) and (1998), *Op. Cit.* Also, AP economics courses were introduced in 1989. The number of AP examinations in economics has grown to about 1% of high school graduates. The significance of this development may exceed its numbers, by improving the content of the economics curriculum as well as teacher training, with possible spillovers to the non-AP curriculum.

72 This statement is based on a phone conversation with John Clow, who is preparing a report on these trends for the National Council on Economic Education.

73 For a different perspective on this dilemma, see Cecilia A. Conrad, "National Standards or Economic Imperialism?" *Journal of Economic Education* 29 (2), Spring 1998, pp. 167–169.

74 See, for example, Walstad (1992), *Op. Cit.*, Section V, Meszaros and Suiter, *Op. Cit.*, and Michael K. Salemi, "How Economists Can Improve Economic Education," also in the December 1998 issue of *The Region*, pp. 35–37. A 1985 transcript study found that social studies teachers candidates averaged 4.0 credit hours in economics, compared to 21.9 in history, 9.0 in political science, 8.0 in psychology, and 5.8 in sociology. Among elementary school teachers, fewer than half had any college courses in economics, as of the mid-1980s.

75 Professional development seminars may be able to improve K–12 economics *pedagogy* to those who already have a college-level background in this discipline.

76 See Walstad (1992), *Op. Cit.*, Section III.

77 Massachusetts may have another chance to get it right. Even as I write, in early 1999, James Peyser has become chairman of the Board of Education after John Silber stepped down and recommended Peyser as his replacement.

78 The Massachusetts *History and Social Science Curriculum Framework* provides an example of slanted coverage of education reform issues. In discussing the inner cities in the 1980s and 1990s, the framework states that "unequal school funding raise[d] new racial tensions" (p.38). It is curious that the Massachusetts Board of Education would put such a statement in the curriculum when many urban school districts, in Massachusetts and elsewhere, spend more than the state average per pupil.

79 Another example may be found in some of the transition economies, where, according to the NCEE, it is proving difficult to upgrade the low level of economic literacy after decades of Communist rule, even though the benefits to be gained might well be quite large. Some of these countries are apparently more interested in upgrading business training—marketing, management, etc.—than economics *per se,* according to Patricia Elder, "The Challenge of Economic Literacy in Post-Soviet Countries," *The Region, Op. Cit.*, pp. 51–53. Paul Heyne, however, reports that his students in Hungary understand market economy principles better than his American students because of their eagerness to transform a dysfunctional economy (Ronald Wirtz, "Econ 101: Is this the Best Way to Teach Economics?" *The Region, Op. Cit.,* p.57).

Chapter 9

The English Language Arts in American Schools
Problems and Proposals

Thomas Carnicelli
University of New Hampshire

The state of language arts instruction in American schools is not as good as it should be. As E.D. Hirsch demonstrated in his book *Cultural Literacy*, American students need to read and write better than they do, and they need to know more about their common intellectual heritage.[1] I don't know any college English teacher, from the most traditional to the most radical, who would not agree that incoming college students are lacking in traditional literacy. As to the cause of this general decline in literacy, I place most of the blame on the ideas of progressive educators, who dominate a large and powerful professional group that is commonly, and accurately, called the educational establishment. Thus, as I see it, we have in English language arts the same situation that exists in many other areas of American education today: students aren't performing well, and the educationists are a large part of the problem.

The obvious solution in some areas is to call in the subject-area faculty from the colleges and universities to rectify the situation. That solution won't work for language arts, however, because the situation in college and university English departments is just as bad or even worse. The teaching of English at the college level is more incoherent and lacking in common purpose than it has ever been in my thirty-five years of college teaching. In fact, with regard to the teaching of literature, the ideas and practices of literary theorists from higher education have contributed to the problems in the schools.

The most likely solution I see is for concerned citizens, led by scholarly critics like Hirsch and John Silber of Boston University, and legislators in every state to require necessary changes in our school curricula. That, of course, is what the standards movement is all about. In this reform effort, policy makers from outside education will find plenty of practicing English teachers to help them. Although the dominant ideologies of current educational and literary theorists are not helpful, there are still many good, sensible teachers, in the schools and in the colleges and universities, who know what needs to be done and are already doing it.

In this essay, I identify and critique the educational theories and professional forces that are influencing how the English language arts are currently being taught in America's schools. After a general overview, I go through the English language arts curriculum in detail, pointing out good things and bad. The picture is certainly not entirely bleak; there are many good things going on. I then collect all the good things into a specific list of what I myself regard as an ideal set of standards for the English language arts, ending the essay with some practical suggestions for policy makers that might lead to the adoption of sound standards in this real world.

Because this is a personal essay, based mostly on my own experience, I first need to explain what that experience has been. In my academic life, I divide my time equally between English and English education. I have been a full-time member of a college English department since 1962, teaching a variety of English literature courses, including courses in my speciality, medieval literature. Improbably enough, in 1979 I took on the added role of Director of the English Teaching Major at the University of New Hampshire (UNH). In this role, I teach courses in the teaching of grammar, composition, and literature, and I have been directly responsible for the training of hundreds of practicing English teachers, many of whom I regard now as my colleagues. Hence, from my professional responsibilities, I feel that I know what is going on in the teaching of English language arts at just about every level. I also have first-hand knowledge of public education more directly: I took a sabbatical from UNH a number of years ago to teach high school English, and I have been a member of a local school board for fifteen years.

The Current Scene: Progressives and Multiculturists

The group I have called the educational establishment is not a monolith, but it often acts and thinks like one. As I define it, it includes the faculty of college and university schools and colleges of education, the members of state and federal educational agencies, the leaders of professional organizations (in the case of language arts, the National Council of Teachers of English or NCTE), and the editorial boards of influential educational journals (such as NCTE's journals *Language Arts, English Journal,* and *College English*). Some would include the largest teachers' union, the National Education Association (NEA), in this group as well. Please note that I have not included practicing teachers. The educational establishment is not actually in the classrooms; its members are educational philosophers and theorists, public officials and staff members in educational agencies, and politically active members of teacher unions. This group already exerts enormous power over the training and professional certification of teachers, and over the whole national debate about the reform of public education. Needless to say, it is seeking to control the standards movement, which was developed in large part to counteract its power. That must not be allowed to happen.

The best critique of this group of people and ideas is offered by E.D. Hirsch in his recent *The Schools We Need and Why We Don't Have Them*, an indispensable book for any citizen interested in school reform.[2] Hirsch lays the blame for the failures of America's schools squarely on the progressive movement, which he sees as dominating American schools of education since the 1930s. Hirsch offers a brilliant critique of the "thoughtworld" of the current educational establishment, which he describes as "an impregnable fortress," intolerant of any ideas but its own progressive theories. He demonstrates how the progressive ideal of "child-centered education" has been taken much too far in American schools. In trying to "teach the child, not the subject," our schools have become "anti-knowledge" and "anti-subject-matter"; they are not helping students learn essential content knowledge, essential words, concepts, and facts. In trying to "teach skills, not mere facts," our schools are giving students neither facts nor skills, since skills are dependent on some degree of content knowledge. Finally, in trying to match the curriculum to the supposed "natural development" of children, our schools are holding students back from intellectual challenges they could readily meet. Hirsch's powerful critique clearly exposes the ideas and forces I have been bumping up against ever since I became a teacher of teachers. While I do not see American education in as dire straits as Hirsch does, I agree with his major premise: an excessive, dogmatic adherence to a student-centered philosophy by the nation's educational establishment is the main source of our educational failings.

Hirsch focuses mostly on the elementary grades, but the student-centered philosophy he describes has spread to American secondary schools as well, where it takes the form of a prevailing softness and lack of rigor, often accompanied by a particularly nasty political animus towards traditional academic goals and towards American society at large. Whether expressed in an NCTE periodical or a textbook on secondary English teaching, the progressive mindset consists of the same set of attitudes. The focus is on the individual student, who has the choice of what to read or write. There may be general curriculum goals, but there are no specific books that every student must read. The role of the teacher is that of a facilitator; explicit directions or direct assertions of authority by the teacher are highly suspect. Whole-class instruction is discouraged because it is dominated by the teacher; small peer groups, in which students can teach one another through "collaborative learning," are the preferred format. Competitive grading is dismissed as inherently arbitrary and destructive of a student's self-esteem. The better, "more authentic" way is for the teacher to focus on individual progress, not on common standards. Basic to this progressive mindset is a suspicion of all authority; the teacher is a potential oppressor, but, on the other hand, the poor teacher is also the potential victim of an oppressive, materialistic society. Society is bad. The student is innocent and good. Teachers may go either way: facilitators are good; lecturers are very, very bad. This complex of attitudes can be found in much of the professional literature in the field of English language arts. And it's not funny, although I have had a little fun with it here. In fact, when I finish reading a typical issue of the *English Journal*, I am usually so angry that I feel like going back to medieval literature on a full-time basis.

I actually recommend many of the practices I have just described, but not to the exclusion of other, more traditional methods. Student choice of what to read and write, small peer groups, alternative forms of assessment, all have their merits. Teachers need to know how to teach indirectly, as facilitators, just as they need to know how to take a more active and directive role. There are, however, two aspects of this extreme progressive approach that are very disturbing. One is the anti-social attitude, the refusal to make any connection between the individual and the society at large, the tacit assumption that good teaching must be a subversive activity. As I argue later, the implications of this attitude are dangerously undemocratic. The other is the assumption that the teacher has no legitimate authority to direct or judge student learning. When my prospective teachers read this kind of material, they begin to question whether teachers have a moral right to do anything at all. I have to argue that teachers have a perfect right, by virtue of their far-greater knowledge and experience, to give specific assignments, to conduct classes, and to assess student work. And then I have to point out what should be obvious: students need teachers in order to learn. It may seem bizarre that a university professor would have to convince prospective teachers that they have the moral right to teach, but that is what the progressive movement has led to. Fortunately, the pendulum is beginning to turn. When Nancie Atwell, the most accomplished and influential proponent of the facilitator approach, recently announced that she had "become a teacher with a capital T," it became respectable for teachers to take a more active and directive role in their own classrooms.[3]

While the progressive focus on student-centered learning is the major cause of the failures of America's schools, it is not the only cause of these failings. A second cause is the movement towards "diversity," a term which ranks right next to "student-centered" in the rhetoric of the educational establishment. I see merit in this idea, just as I do in many aspects of student-centered learning. I have no doubt whatsoever that our students and our society will benefit if more "diversity" is introduced into the school curriculum. I use the term very broadly, to refer both to minority groups and to women, since Anglo-American literary culture has certainly stressed male authors and perspectives throughout its history. Female and minority students need to have more chances to read books by and about people of their own gender and/or ethnic group. White male students need to become familiar with perspectives other than their own. Teachers need to be alert to differences in learning styles that *may* result from ethnic or gender differences. I stress these things in my own methods courses.

While I support, somewhat, this new emphasis on diversity, I also see two potential problems with it. As it is discussed by its strongest advocates, respect for diversity is often accompanied by a vicious, contemptuous mockery of traditional Anglo-American culture: to dismiss the classic literary works of this culture as the products of "dead white males" is not funny; it's barbarous. I can only hope that American school teachers are not expressing such an irresponsible attitude in their classrooms. My second, much more fundamental problem with this stress on cultural diversity is that it tends toward social disunity or social fragmentation. American society has traditionally been both diverse and unified: *E pluribus unum*. With the "student-centered" advocates stressing the individual and the multiculturalists stressing separate ethnic groups and traditions, how will our students acquire the common knowledge and understanding necessary for an effective democracy? Properly conceived, the English language arts can be a strong force for unity in this country; they can foster wider communication and common cultural knowledge, connecting individuals and groups to the larger society for the benefit of all parties. That unifying force must be strengthened. Both progressive individualism and today's version of multiculturalism serve to weaken it.

The English Language Arts Curriculum in American Schools

After this general philosophical prologue, I now look more closely at three specific areas of the English language arts curriculum in American schools: language, composition, and literature. I identify and assess the specific ideas which dominate the pedagogical literature, give my impressions of current practice, and speculate about future prospects. As I see it, the picture is mixed. In the teaching of language and composition, most of the dominant ideas are sound, and practice would be improved if those ideas were more widely followed. In the teaching of literature, the situation is quite the reverse: current practice is much sounder than the dominant ideas. If those ideas are more widely followed, the future will be very bleak indeed.

Language

I am satisfied with the general approach to language. There was so much agitation against the movement to make English the official language of the country that I was afraid that NCTE itself, the national body of teachers of English, might issue a political statement *against* the teaching of English! That didn't happen. Instead, in 1988, a unit of NCTE called the Conference on College Composition and Communication (CCCC) adopted a National Language Policy with three parts:[4]

1. To provide resources to enable native and non-native speakers to achieve literate competence in English, the language of wider communication.

2. To support programs that assert the legitimacy of native languages and dialects and ensure that proficiency in one's mother tongue will not be lost.

3. To foster the teaching of languages other than English so that native speakers of English can rediscover the language of their heritage or learn a second language.

Part one is an important statement. In it, a prominent group within NCTE is endorsing the traditional goal of English language arts instruction in American schools. Although the CCCC is a college group, one of its leaders, Geneva Smitherman, published an article about the new language policy in the January, 1995, issue of *English Journal,* NCTE's journal aimed at secondary English teachers; Smitherman argues that the policy should apply to "all levels of education," not just to colleges.[5] The term "the language of wider communication" can be very useful to teachers and writers; it fills a need for those educators for whom "standard English" is not acceptable. Constance Weaver uses this new term in her recent grammar text,[6] and I use it with the prospective teachers in my own courses.

The sponsors of this language policy stated that the three parts should be considered inseparable, but I doubt that parts two and three will have much impact. As the Ebonics fiasco in Oakland made clear, our society will not support efforts to improve proficiency in dialects of English in American public schools, and it should not. Still, all English teachers need to understand that dialects such as Black English are "legitimate" linguistic systems in their own right, not careless or ignorant approximations of mainstream English, a useful point made in part two. As for part three, one can object to the phrase "their heritage," inasmuch as native speakers of English have a whole Anglo-American heritage embodied in the language they speak, but the issue of teaching foreign languages will be perceived as irrelevant by English teachers in any case.

Several other language issues need comment. I am concerned about the rather casual inclusion of "viewing" (and its companion "representing") as a fifth language art in textbooks, curricula, and newly designed standards. There are only four language processes: reading, writing, speaking, and listening. Viewing is not a language process because it does not involve the use of language. Although interpreting a film may involve many of the same analytical strategies used in interpreting a story, viewing a film is not reading. I am more than willing to encourage the use of films, pictures, music, and dance as aids to the teaching and learning of the language arts. In fact, in today's society, creative teachers often have to rely on the more popular related arts to get recalcitrant students to learn to read and write. Still, the role of the related arts must remain supplementary. What I worry about—and it is happening all the time—is allowing work in the related arts to be substituted for work in the language arts: if a student is expected to write an essay, the teacher should not accept a drawing or computer graphic as a substitute for it.

Of the four true language arts, reading and writing should receive the most attention in our schools, as they certainly do in all the schools I know. Those two skills—which constitute traditional literacy—are the ones students will need the most help with, the ones students will need in order to become informed, contributing citizens. Speaking and listening are important, too, and probably should receive somewhat more instruction in schools than they generally do, even though students can learn them outside of school. Like viewing and creating visual images, speaking and listening activities can be useful ways to help students learn to read and write, and many creative teachers use them for that purpose.

The language issue about which most people have strong feelings is the teaching of grammar. On this issue the education people are right, and the general public, including most faculty members in colleges and universities, are uninformed and wrong. There is a strong record of empirical research showing that formal courses in grammar do not improve the writing performance of students. That record has been remarkably consistent over a half-century of studies. A statement by George Hillocks summarizing more recent studies can serve as an accurate summary of the entire research record:

> None of the studies reviewed for the present report provides any support for teaching grammar as a means of improving composition skills. If schools insist upon the identification of parts of speech, the parsing of diagramming of sentences, or other concepts of traditional school grammar (as many still do), they cannot defend it as a means of improving the quality of writing.[7]

It is important to clarify what this conclusion really means. It does not mean that teachers should ignore grammar when teaching students to write. Nobody denies that students need to use correct and effective grammar in their writing. What the research record indicates is that whole courses in grammar, courses in which grammar is studied as a body of knowledge, do not help students write better. The record also indicates that teaching specific aspects of grammar in the context of a student's actual writing is a much more effective and efficient approach. Formal courses in grammar do not work because they offer theoretical knowledge of grammar (such as the ability to identify parts of speech or diagram sentences), but students do not need this kind of knowledge in order to write well. What they need is functional knowledge, knowledge of how to use grammar, and they can best acquire that knowledge through actual writing and through receiving specific feedback from teachers and peers.

While I am strongly opposed to formal grammar courses in our public schools, I am strongly in favor of such courses for prospective language arts teachers. This is the consensus view: state and national standards for the programs in English education all require that such programs devote significant attention to the study of grammar. I would maintain that English teachers need both types of grammatical knowledge. They need functional knowledge so that they can write well themselves; an English teacher who cannot write well needs to choose another profession. They need theoretical knowledge of grammar so that they can explain grammatical issues accurately and clearly to their students; to explain, for instance, the problem with a dangling participle, a teacher needs to be able to identify a participle and understand how it works.

Composition

When I went to high school, I was taught to make a formal outline before I began to write; I did, of course, what most students did: I wrote the paper first and the outline afterward. The field of composition has come a long way since the days of the formal outline and the five-paragraph theme. The major difference I see is that composition theorists have tried to understand what writers actually do—few writers make formal outlines (although most good expository writers make informal outlines) —and to base instruction on the writing processes of practicing writers. This new approach, universally called the process approach, has been widely advocated in the pedagogical literature. It has been introduced quite widely into American public schools, and its basic assumptions appear in most of the state writing standards I have seen. I believe in this approach, and do so not only because two of its leading proponents,

Donald Murray and Donald Graves, were colleagues of mine at UNH until they retired recently. I believe in it because I have seen it work.

A number of ideas and practices are associated with the process approach. The most basic idea is that a piece of writing will usually evolve through several drafts; rewriting, or substantial revision, is the essence of the process. Typically, there are no assigned topics. The students are expected to find their own writing topics and their own forms. The teacher's role is to provide feedback in the midst of the process, usually through a conference with the student writer. In conferring with students, teachers have a clear set of priorities: they focus on larger issues like the basic idea, the overall organization, or the stance of the writer towards the audience when the piece is in its early stages; they focus on smaller points of style or grammar only when the piece is in the later stages of revision. In a typical writing process classroom, there is no whole-class activity: individual students are writing at their desks or conferring with their peers or with the teacher.

Clearly, this is a "student-centered" activity: the individual student has the choice of topic and form, and receives individualized instruction from the teacher. Although the lack of formal structure and the amount of student choice can be disconcerting, both for students and for teachers, the process approach can generate intense interest in writing among students; and it is certainly far superior to the mechanical approaches it was aimed at replacing. The major drawback of this approach is a product of the very freedom that makes it so appealing. Because students can choose their own topic and form, they tend to gravitate towards stories or narratives of their personal experiences. If they spend too much time on personal narratives, they may not get enough experience in non-chronological forms. Experienced teachers like Nancie Atwell nudge their students to write in a variety of forms, but too many teachers allow their students to write nothing but narratives, with the result that those students struggle to write analytical or argumentative essays when they get to college.

Another promising development in the teaching of composition is the use of "creative" writing assignments in response to literature. Writing a critical-analytical essay is still the most common way in which students respond to the literature they are reading, and it should be. But there are benefits from encouraging students to use other forms as well. Innovative teachers are encouraging their students to create monologues or dialogues involving characters in the book being read, to write alternative endings for stories or alternative stanzas for poems, or to write imitations of an author's style or form. These are "creative writing" activities, but they are done in response to literary works being read. The effect is to give students greater insights as readers by putting them inside the minds of the authors or characters. Such writing tasks serve to integrate the teaching of writing and reading and to enhance both skills at the same time.

Literature

It is difficult to summarize what is happening in the teaching of literature. There are many good practices but no clear curricular priorities, and the dominant theoretical ideas are seriously inadequate.

Curriculum

The traditional year-long surveys of British and Amer-ican literature can still be found in American high schools, but they have few defenders in the journals and textbooks. In the pedagogical literature, the emphasis is squarely on change: more books by and about women and members of ethnic minorities; more attention to world literature, usually defined as literature written in non-English languages or not by a British or American author.

The first of these changes has merit, I think. More works by and about women and members of American ethnic minorities should be read in American schools, if only to make literature more appealing to all types of students. Surveys of the literature curricula in American high schools show a certain amount of inertia: sturdy old chestnuts survive simply because the books have not fallen apart. Why not replace *Silas Marner* with *The Color Purple*? As for world literature, which usually means a new novel from Africa rather than *The Iliad*, I don't find the case for inclusion so compelling. To me, the primary goal of the literature curriculum should be to make American students well-versed in their own national culture. That national culture includes three bodies of literature: American literature, including works by American women and members of American ethnic minorities; literature from England, especially classic works that have influenced generations of American authors; and certain classics of world literature which educated British and American readers know. I am in favor of slightly more attention to contemporary world literature, but not at the expense of works that are more essential to the understanding of American culture.

When new things are added to the literature curriculum, old things get squeezed out. At the present time, British literature is receiving far less attention in American schools than it used to. This is not a positive trend, for two reasons. First of all, British and American literature are very closely related, by shared literary traditions and by a common language, and students cannot fully appreciate American literature without some knowledge of its British antecedents and counterparts. Secondly, British literature is a major world literature, with authors whose works are read in translation throughout the world. American students can read these works directly. Why should American students not read great literature written in their own language?

Another type of literature needs to be mentioned. A body of literature written especially for adolescents, once called Adolescent Literature but now called Young Adult Literature. Much of this literature is of surprisingly good quality, and students read it avidly, mostly in grades 5 through 8 or 9. Many teachers encourage their students to read it individually; some teachers read especially powerful works like Mildred Taylor's *Roll of Thunder, Hear My Cry* or Robert Cormier's *The Chocolate War* with their entire class. Traditional critics of schools tend to condemn Young Adult Literature, urging teachers to move students into adult classics at what some regard as too early an age. After studying the stages that adolescents go through as they develop their reading interests and tastes, G. Robert Carlsen concluded in *Books and the Teenage Reader* that requiring teen-agers to read adult classics too soon may have the effect of turning many of them away from literature entirely.[8] Carlsen takes a balanced view, urging teachers to use both good Young Adult Literature and adult classics, but to start with classics that adolescents are able to relate to and understand. I learned from my own bitter experience that the young lovers of *Romeo and Juliet* appeal to teenagers much more than do the middle-aged politicians in *Julius Caesar*. Likewise, many adolescent readers respond more fully to the stormy passions of *Wuthering Heights* than to the social complexities of *Pride and Prejudice.* No one is advocating using Young Adult Literature in the upper years of high school, where students should be reading adult works exclusively. The best current practice is to use Young Adult books as a way to encourage literary reading in the earlier grades and to use specific Young Adult books as "bridges" to thematically related adult books. Young Adult Literature can play an important transitional role in the literature curriculum of American schools, and that role should be recognized in standards for the English language arts.

Methods

How should literature be taught in the schools, especially in an age when reading does not seem to be highly valued by the general American public? Educational theorists and practicing teachers have come up with a variety of answers, some good, some not so good. On the plus side, I see a general effort to work harder to get the student to experience literature as literature, not to regard it as a body of knowledge to be "learned" like a list of facts. Some teachers still focus too exclusively on background information or definitions of literary terms. But most treat literature as an exploration of human experience, something students can relate to and learn from. In this case, student-centered learning coincides nicely with traditional views of the function of literature.

As for specific methods, in a world where the quiet pleasures of reading have to compete with all sorts of more active forms of stimulation, creative teachers are using those other forms as ways to get students into the reading of literature: films, pictures, videos, music, dramatic readings of literary texts, dramatizations of literary texts, all of the arts and humanities are being brought into the service of literary study. As I have warned earlier, although there are dangers in allowing some non-language activities like viewing and creating visual images to be substituted for reading or writing tasks, teachers do need to expand their repertoires in order to reach today's adolescents. That is the general pedagogical consensus, and I agree with it.

While getting reluctant or indifferent students to read literature is a real problem, the effort to solve it has led to a problem which is just as bad: the widespread acceptance of a literary theory that can undermine the value of reading literature in the first place. That theory, called reader response theory, dominates every new textbook on the teaching of literature. To explain what that theory is and why it is so pernicious, I must first describe the theory and practice it is seeking to replace.

Until quite recently, the teaching of literature, in the schools and in the colleges and universities, was dominated by something loosely called New Criticism. In this approach, the focus was on the text itself as the source of meaning; the reader was expected, through close, careful reading, to derive meaning from the text. The reader was not supposed to read meanings into the text, to bring in ideas or feelings that could not be supported by evidence within the text. Regarding the author's intentions, students were told to beware of "the intentional fallacy," which meant trusting what an author might say outside the poem (sly old Robert Frost was regarded as especially untrustworthy), and to let the words of the text be their only guides. In practice, though, since the author chose the words of the text, the meanings students found in those words were tacitly assumed to be intended by the author. New Critics strove to be as objective as possible, but they rarely agreed on single "correct" readings. Even though readers differed passionately, however, they were all playing by the same rules; they tried to base their claims on the words of the text, not on any external evidence or on their own personal experiences. In teaching literature, the teacher was expected to take an active role, to guide the students through the text, making sure all details were considered, sometimes to model fruitful ways of reading for the students. The teacher's authority was derived from a superior ability to read the text, which was the ultimate authority for all concerned. The goal of the whole operation was for students to learn how to read and appreciate literature, and to learn something useful from it. This method of teaching, which might be called simply "close-reading" or a "a text-centered approach," worked well for many teachers for many years, and it still does. But it is now universally condemned in the pedagogical literature.

In contrast to New Criticism, reader response theory sees the autonomous individual reader as a major determiner of meaning, and it greatly diminishes the roles of the text, the author, and the teacher. In this theory, the text is no longer regarded as an objective source of meaning. As Alan Purves, Theresa Roberts, and Anna Soter state in their popular textbook, *How Porcupines Make Love II: Teaching a Response-Centered Literature Curriculum*, "It used to be that the text was seen as the norm by which a reading and a response could be judged. Now it is no longer the norm—even theoretically."[9] According to reader response theory, readers do not "derive" a meaning that is already in the text; readers "create" meaning from their own experience, using the text simply as a stimulus. In another widely adopted textbook, *Response and Analysis: Teaching Literature in Junior and Senior High School*, Robert Probst describes the process of reading literature as follows: "The poem is, in a sense, something that we create as we read. We bring to the text our understanding of the words, our expectations of the behavior of people, our ingrained biases and predilections, and from them create the experience that becomes for us the poem."[10] Probst, like many of the reader response advocates, has been influenced by the theories of Louise Rosenblatt, a literary scholar whose first writings on response to literature came out in the 1930s.[11] Rosenblatt sees meaning as created through the "transaction" between the reader and the author's words. This view would seem to be a moderate, compromise position, allowing for the contributions of both the reader and the author. In practice, however, reader response theory has tended to minimize the role of the author's text and to overemphasize the value of the reader's personal experiences and opinions.

Let me demonstrate how reader response theory looks in practice with examples from two popular language arts textbooks for prospective teachers. In the opening chapter of their *Teaching Literature in the Secondary School*, Robert Beach and James Marshall present a vignette of a typically heavy-handed New Critical teacher trying to force "her own reading" of Hemingway's "The Undefeated" on a class of students who do not like the story because they don't like the bullfighting.[12] Beach and Marshall acknowledge that the teacher's reading of the story is "right," but they claim that the response of the students is also a "reading" of "the text." That, however, is where the words *reading* and *text* get twisted. The text is Hemingway's words, the way he is presenting the subject, and reading the text means interpreting those words. The students are ignoring Hemingway's text, not reading it. They are responding not to Hemingway's treatment of bullfighting but to the mere subject of bullfighting. Their personal opinions about this subject prevent them from even seeing the author's point of view.

Another example is from the first chapter of Probst's highly influential textbook mentioned above. Probst gives an example of a poem in which the author, or the author's speaker, clearly blames a social worker for causing the death of an ignorant widow. Probst readily admits that the words of the poem express sympathy for the widow, not the cruel social worker, yet he goes on to say this: "It is important that students who sympathize with the social worker have enough perspective not to confuse response to the poem with interpretation of the writer's intention. That is not to say they should repress their response; they should simply not assume the writer shares it." Defining a reaction which directly contradicts the intended meaning of the text (as Probst determines by his own close analysis) as a "response to the poem" simply does not make sense. The student who sympathizes with the social worker is not responding to the author's poem, the author's artistic portrayal of the character. The student is simply ignoring the author's words in order to hold onto a previously formed opinion. Again, it is hard to see that this student is even reading the text, let alone learning anything from it.

Although they do make some slight allowance for error, reader response theorists come very close to pure relativism, the position that any one reading is as valid as the next. In this position, the author's text becomes irrelevant, and the individual reader becomes the sole determiner of meaning. Beach and Marshall list the assumption that "Some Interpretations Are Better than Other Interpretations" as one of the old, out-moded New Critical beliefs that need to be replaced. Purves, Rogers, and Soter offer the following as one of the guiding objectives of their response-centered curriculum: "An individual will respect the responses of others as being as valid for them as his is for him." Probst argues that the teacher's readings are no better than those of any other reader: according to Probst, if teachers "keep in mind that the poem they create as they read is one of many possibilities shaped by their experiences and attitudes as well as by the words on the page, they will recognize that their readings have no special claim to authority."

Reader response theory is not a viable basis for teaching literature in a useful and responsible way. It provides no clear standard of validity for either teachers or students. It gives the teacher no clear basis of authority: how is the teacher to direct a class discussion or grade a paper if all responses are equal? Finally, it undermines the whole purpose of having students read literature in the first place: to learn new perspectives on human experience. How can students learn anything new from literary texts if they do not pay careful attention to what the authors have to say?

The widespread acceptance of this questionable theory is an ominous trend. Reader response theory utterly dominates the journals and textbooks devoted to the teaching of literature in American schools. It is the consensus view that most prospective language arts teachers get, and its acceptance is reinforced by the student-centered philosophy that dominates teacher education generally. It is not, however, the consensus view of veteran secondary teachers who were trained in the New Critical tradition and who continue to teach literature in a text-centered way. As these veterans retire, however, I can only wonder what their successors will do. I have had teaching interns who marched off to the schools full of reader-response zeal and got killed in action; they returned from the dead as text-centered teachers. Will reality get the better of reader response theory in the end? I can only hope so.

Although one might also hope that prospective English teachers would develop more useful ideas about teaching literature from their college and literature courses, I am not too sanguine. In many ways, literature teaching in colleges and universities seems to be in even worse shape than it is in the schools. English in higher education is a field without a common mission. Its members have rejected any responsibility for assuring that all students have a common literary heritage; there is little agreement on what books students should read. College and university faculty can't agree on what to read or even on how to read. The traditional notion that students should read books to find out what the authors have to say is regarded as hopelessly naive by current literary theorists. Every aspect of the writing and reading of literature has been "problematized" in current literary theory. Some theorists even deny that there is any such thing as an autonomous author; they see the author simply as a "space" where various cultural forces operate. As for reading and interpretation, most current theorists see the quest for "the author's meaning" as quixotic at best; they see literary texts as ultimately "indeterminate." It is this line of thinking that led to the development of reader response theory, which was passed to the education theorists from literary theorists in colleges and universities. Many popular current theorists are aggressively ideological in focus; they look at all texts in terms of social and political issues. Ideological critics might grant that "the author's meaning" can be determined, but they dismiss it as irrelevant anyway; they claim the right to read every text in terms of the issues of gender, race, and class, no matter what concerns the author of the text might have. In courses dominated by ideas like these, I do not see a prospective teacher picking up much that would be useful in teaching literature in the schools. Quite the contrary!

Still, in the colleges and universities, as in the schools, there is often a large gap between the dominant theories and actual practice. While New Criticism is no longer widely accepted as an adequate literary theory, it can still survive in practice, as I discovered recently in my own department. The English department at UNH is chock-full of all the latest trends. The scholarly writings of some of the newer professors are so dense and theoretical that most of the other professors cannot read them: in promotion and tenure cases, we tend to defer to the few colleagues who can decipher these writings and evaluate them for the rest of us. As a department, we have very few common requirements for the literature major, and there is no chance whatsoever that we could ever agree to add any more. Still, when it comes to actual teaching, we have a lot more in common than our very diverse critical and theoretical orientations might suggest. Recently, we were able to revise our one prerequisite course, called "Writing about Literature," to make it focus more on "close reading" and on writing "analytical essays" based on "textual evidence." We did so because the course was becoming an introduction to various critical approaches, and we did not want that. We wanted our students to learn close reading and analytical writing first: the various critical approaches were left for later. Hence, even in a very diverse, very up-to-date literature department, there was still common agreement that a form of New Criticism should be the common starting point for all students. Prospective teachers can certainly get a good understanding of basic critical reading and writing in the literature program offered in my department. I would not be surprised if the same situation still exists in many other college and university English departments as well.

Suggestions for Policy Makers

In summarizing the current state of the language arts curriculum in American schools, I want to identify good ideas as well as bad. Let me summarize the best ideas and practices in a list of suggested policies or principles. Some of these apply to teachers; some apply to students. Some could be used in composing standards for teacher education programs. Others could be used in composing standards for language arts curricula in the schools.

Language

1. **All students should develop facility in using English.** Language arts can be practiced in any language, but there is a firm consensus that, in American public schools, every student should learn English because it is, in the words of a recent CCCC policy statement, "the language of wider communication."

    All teachers should understand that dialects are coherent linguistic systems, not careless or ignorant approx-

imations of some more widely used language. Since many students come into the schools from homes where a dialect of English, such as Black English Vernacular, is spoken, teachers must be aware that insensitive "corrections" of a student's language may be taken as insults to that student's family and culture. Teachers must be able to teach mainstream English without portraying other dialects as somehow inferior to it.

2. **All English teachers should be able to identify and understand the major grammatical structures of English.** Teachers need detailed, theoretical knowledge of English grammar so that they can explain grammatical problems and options clearly to students.

   All students should be able to write English with correct and effective grammar. The goal for students should be operational or functional knowledge of English grammar. Students can meet this goal without acquiring the detailed, theoretical knowledge of English grammar that teachers must have. Students should not be required to take full, formal courses in English grammar. Research has shown conclusively that such courses do not lead to improved writing performance.

3. **Reading and writing, or traditional literacy, should be the primary focus of language arts instruction in American schools.** These are the skills which students need the most help with, the skills students will need to be informed, contributing citizens. The other language arts, speaking and listening, are also important, but they do not need as much instructional emphasis since students can learn them outside of school.

   Activities which are not language-based should not be allowed to replace work in the language arts. Despite its casual acceptance as the fifth language art, viewing is not a language art since it does not involve the use of language. Making or interpreting visual images should not be substituted for reading and writing activities. Visual arts, multimedia projects, music, and even dance can have great value in the language arts classroom, but their role must remain supplementary.

Composition

1. **All teachers should base their teaching of writing on the ways writers actually write.** Practicing writers do not produce a perfect piece of writing on the first try; they revise their work, often through several drafts. Teachers need to allow and encourage students to revise their writing before turning it in.

   In responding to student writing, a teacher should focus on the larger issues first: on content, organization, and rhetorical stance. These are the big issues for any writer, the problems that must be solved before a piece can take shape. A teacher needs to help a student writer solve these problems before directing attention to smaller points. Grammatical errors need to be dealt with, but only later in the development of a piece, after the larger issues have been worked out.

2. **In writing nonfiction prose, students must be expected to perform a variety of tasks: they need experience in narrating, describing, explaining, analyzing, and arguing.** When encouraged to write about their personal experiences, as they are in "writing process" classrooms, students quite naturally turn to narration, to telling stories. While personal narratives are certainly valuable, an over-emphasis on them does not prepare students to write essays that are not based on chronology. Far too many students come to their Freshmen English course unable to write an analytical or argumentative essay. Secondary English teachers need to make sure that their students write more than just personal narratives.

3. **In writing in response to literature, students should be expected to write in a variety of forms besides the critical essay.** The traditional critical essay should continue to be emphasized, but it need not be the only way in which students write in response to literature. Students should also be encouraged to write in creative or imaginative forms: to create monologues and dialogues involving the

authors and/or characters in literary works they are reading, to write alternative endings or additional stanzas, to write imitations of the literary styles and forms they encounter in their reading. In this way, the teaching of writing and reading will be integrated, and the student's writing and reading skills will be enhanced at the same time.

Literature

1. **The primary focus of the literature curriculum should be on American and British literature.** American students need to read the significant political and literary writings of American authors in order to understand the culture they live in. Since America and England share a common language and, to a considerable degree, a common literary heritage, the literature curriculum in American schools should include a substantial portion of British literature as well.

   > **The "canon" of specific American and English works studied needs to include significant works by and about women and members of ethnic minorities.** This standard can be met without sacrificing either historical accuracy or literary quality; meeting it can, in fact, improve the curriculum in both regards. Curriculum surveys have identified a certain amount of "dead wood" in the typical secondary school curriculum, while literary scholars have shown that a number of significant works by and about women and members of ethnic minorities have been neglected or ignored.

2. **Literature should be taught as a source of human experience, not as a body of information.** Teachers should focus their attention on helping students experience the works they are reading. Focus on historical or biographical information, or on literary terms and techniques, can be useful means to this end, but they should not become ends in themselves.

3. **Students should be expected to analyze and interpret literary texts in writing.** While students should certainly be encouraged to

read for personal pleasure, they also need to become critical, discriminating readers. The acts of analysis and interpretation can increase their appreciation of a writer's artistry and their understanding of a work's meaning. Because it is a useful way for students to develop their skills in analysis and interpretation, the writing of critical essays should be a significant part of the literature curriculum.

4. **Teachers should be widely familiar with significant works of Young Adult Literature.** There are many fine literary works written expressively for young adults. These works have great appeal to young adult readers, and they are an effective means of interesting students in literature and in reading generally.

5. **Teachers should be familiar with works of world literature that are part of Anglo-American literary culture.** Certain classic works written in non-English languages have influenced American and British authors and are known to most educated readers. American students need to read some of these books, both to understand their own culture better and to gain an awareness of other cultural traditions.

Political Considerations

Decisions about the teaching of English language arts are necessarily matters of choice; there are not many objective facts to draw upon. There is a broad political consensus that the language arts are important and should be taught, but just about every other issue is hotly contested in this contentious time. The principles I have just listed could generate a host of angry questions: Why should reading and writing be given special preference? Isn't our society relying more and more on oral and visual communication? What about computer "literacy"? Isn't that as important as, or more important than, traditional literacy? Why should British literature be given special attention in American schools? What about the literature of other countries, non-Western countries? Why shouldn't those literatures receive as much, or more, attention than British literature has traditionally had? Why is literature so important, anyway? Why not just teach students how to read practical things? There's no "right" or "wrong" way to resolve such questions; they have to be decided through a political process. Some of the policy suggestions I have listed can be supported by empirical research, but most of them simply reflect my personal and professional beliefs. Since many of my suggestions are quite traditional, I am sure they would be greeted with scorn and derision by people in the progressive camp. I am equally certain that some of my more progressive suggestions would be scorned by people with more traditional views. I offer these suggestions because I believe in all of them, and because the whole package might be balanced enough to appeal politically to both sides. Reaching some kind of balance among diverse views is what policy-making is all about.

Policy makers who want to draw up standards in the field of English language arts need to realize just how political that process will have to be. It's not a matter of getting "experts" from Education and English departments together and coming up with something "objective." If a committee of typical Education and College English faculty were charged to come up with standards, they would come up with a document based on their personal and professional beliefs, and those beliefs would undoubtedly be very different from mine. They would focus more on isolated individuals and diverse groups. I focus more on what Americans have in common or on what they could have in common. I believe that the teaching of the English language arts, by fostering better communication and an understanding of a common cultural heritage, can be a powerful force for unity in American society. Such unity would be the ultimate social benefit of a new set of language arts standards.

My best advice to policy makers seeking to set up a standard-setting committee is to choose the members with great care, being sure to get some sense of their educational and professional views. I recommend that people interested in serving on such a committee be interviewed or at least asked to submit personal statements. I would recruit at least half of the committee members from the educational establishment and from college English faculty. It is certainly possible to find good, reasonable people within these two groups; not all the members are zealots and ideologues. Once a suitable number of committee members have been selected from these two groups, I recommend filling out the rest of the committee with experienced secondary English teachers; their practical experience would keep the committee grounded in reality.

A group like this can be very productive. I know that from experience, since I have just finished serving on one. There were twelve of us. We met four times last fall and developed new standards for certifying teacher education programs in the state of New Hampshire. We all contributed, and we produced a strong, well-balanced set of standards that represent a good balance of current and traditional thinking. They are realistic and reasonable enough that competent people can live with them, learn from them, and do a better job by following them. And that, of course, is just what standards should do.

As to the ultimate prospects for positive reform of American schools, I see many hopeful signs. The strong public response to E.D. Hirsch's proposals for a more traditional, knowledge-centered curriculum has been most encouraging. As Hirsch reported in his 1996 book, more than 200 schools in 37 states were already using the model K-8 curricula developed by his non-profit Core Knowledge Foundation. Today, over 700 are, according to the Foundation's recent newsletters.

There are positive signs even within the educational establishment. In 1995, Albert Shanker, then president of the American Federation of Teachers (AFT), launched a national campaign focused on "standards of conduct and standards for achievement."[13] Under Shanker's leadership, the AFT became far more supportive of strong academic ideas than the NEA. However, the current climate is such that even Bob Chase, current president of the NEA, is beginning to sound more like a responsible educator rather than a self-serving defender of the educational status quo.

The standards movement itself is a hopeful sign, but, as recent critics like Sandra Stotsky have shown, there are good standards and bad ones.[14] The standards movement has the potential to become the most positive force of all, but it is a direct threat to the dominant ideas of the educational establishment and of the English profession generally. The standards movement can succeed only if wary public policy makers can keep its opponents from co-opting it.

Notes

[1] Hirsch, E.D., Jr. (1987). *Cultural Literacy: What Every American Needs to Know.* Boston: Houghton Mifflin.

[2] Hirsch, E.D., Jr. (1996). *The Schools We Need and Why We Don't Have Them.* New York: Doubleday.

[3] Atwell, Nancie. (1998). *In the Middle: New Understandings about Writing, Reading and Learning.* 2nd ed. Portsmouth, NH: Heinemann, p.21.

4. Conference on College Composition and Communication (1998). *The National Language Policy* (position statement). Urbana, IL: National Council of Teachers of English.
5. Smitherman, Geneva. (1995). Students' Right to Their Own Language: A Retrospective. *English Journal,* 81 (1).
6. Weaver, Constance. (1996). *Teaching Grammar in Context.* Portsmouth, NH: Heinemann.
7. Hillocks, George, Jr. (1986). *Research on Written Composition: New Directions for Teaching.* Urbana, IL: ERIC Clearinghouse on Reading and Composition Skills and the National Conference on Research in English. Distributed by the NCTE, p. 138.
8. Carlsen, G. Robert (1980). *Books and the Teenage Reader.* 2nd rev. ed. New York: Harper & Row.
9. Purves, Alan, Theresa Rogers, & Anna Soter. (1990). *How Porcupines Make Love II:Teaching a Response-Centered Literature Curriculum.* New York: Longman. The quotations from this text are on pp. 43 and 47, respectively.
10. Probst, Robert. (1988). *Response and Analysis: Teaching Literature in Junior and Senior High School.* Portsmouth, NH: Heinemann. The quotations from this text are on pp. 15, 19, and 23, respectively.
11. Rosenblatt, Louise. (1978). *The Reader, the Text, the Poem: The Transactional Theory of the Literary Work.* Carbondale, IL: Southern Illinois University Press.
12. Beach, Robert & James Marshall. (1991). *Teaching Literature in the Secondary School.* New York: Harcourt Brace Jovanovich.
13. Shanker, Albert. (1995). Why Schools Need Standards and Innovation. *Education Week.* December 6.
14. Stotsky, Sandra. (1997). *State English Standards: An Appraisal of English Language Arts/Reading Standards in 28 States.* Washington, D.C.: Thomas B. Fordham Foundation.

Chapter 10

The State of Literary Study in National and State English Language Arts Standards
Why It Matters, and What Can Be Done about It

Sandra Stotsky
Harvard Graduate School of Education

As most citizens would readily acknowledge, the English language arts play the central role in the K–12 curriculum. Implementation of strong English language arts standards could clearly improve academic achievement in every subject area. For this reason, we must be concerned that only eight states have relatively good standards for the English language arts, a judgment I make based on my analysis of 28 state documents in a Thomas B. Fordham Foundation monograph and on a subsequent critique of a number of others.[1] As good as they are, however, even these documents have limitations, chiefly because their standards lack specifics on literary content and fail to specify the level of reading difficulty expected of their students at the grade levels they assess.

In addition, many standards documents seem to be guided by an animus against literary study. Literary study, especially in high school, appears to be suffering the same fate that has befallen the study of history in many state documents—exclusion from the curriculum on the grounds of irrelevance. As one social studies educator put it in a 1996 *Handbook on Teaching Social Issues* for the National Council for the Social Studies, "Unlike in any other period in human history, the study of the past is of limited relevance and questionable usefulness to today's youth in helping them to prepare for their futures."[2] Conveying a similar anti-intellectual spirit, the national standards developed by the National Council of Teachers of English (NCTE) and the International Reading Association (IRA) want literary works for K–12 chosen first for "relevance to students' interests" and their "roles in society and the workplace." Because NCTE and IRA are the two major organizations for teachers of English and reading in this country, what their document says has considerable influence on educational policy. There are no other national professional voices for English and reading teachers.

The anti-intellectualism now driving efforts to proletarianize the entire school curriculum has been a characteristic of our educational establishment for most of this century, as such commentators on curricular trends in our public schools as Richard Hofstadter, Arthur Bestor, and E.D. Hirsch, Jr. have noted. But it has not appreciably affected the contents of school literature programs until recent decades. The quality of our K–12 school literature programs is a far more important concern than most public officials realize; works embodying our civic and literary heritage are the major source of the quality of the language of public life in this country. A significant diminishing of the quality of the literature programs that students are provided in our public schools will have serious effects on the quality of our public life itself. It will have the most negative effects on students whose homes cannot compensate for their lack of exposure to the language of literature in their schools.

The chief purpose of this essay is to show more precisely how the current manifestation of this anti-liberal spirit has affected standards documents for the English language arts and reading. In the first section, I set forth the major limitations I found across the 28 standards documents I analyzed in the Fordham monograph. In the second section, I trace the specific sources of these limitations. I then show how these limitations influenced a state's assessments even when the state had relatively good standards. I also show how these limitations were effectively overcome in a state test based on state standards. I conclude by suggesting several ways in which public officials responsible for educational policy can address the decline of authentic literary content in their state standards and assessments and help arrest the deterioration of the language of our public life.

Major Limitations in English Standards across States

In order to judge the quality and rigor of a state's standards for the English language arts and reading, I developed 34 criteria (shown in the Appendix) and applied them to the 28 state documents in the English language arts judged acceptable in an earlier rating of all 50 state documents by the American Federation of Teachers. If I had rated all 50, undoubtedly the problems I found across the 28 documents would have been even more pronounced. The problems discussed below emerged as the chief limitations in their content. As will be seen, all tend to weaken the quality of literary study in our schools and the use of English as our public language.

The failure to build in general literary requirements in the standards
In only eleven documents is American literature specified by name, whether in introductory material or in the standards themselves. In five others, the word "American" is used in other ways to hint at the existence of an American literature without actually naming it (e.g., "American cultural heritage"). In twelve documents it is not mentioned anywhere, in either the introductory material or the standards. Worse yet, literary study as a whole is given short shrift in many documents. In Minnesota's, for example, it seems to be almost an afterthought in the secondary school, to judge from the attention it gets. In addition, most documents fail to build in general literary requirements in their standards; Virginia is among the very few exceptions to this general failing, with such standards as: "contrast periods in American literature," "differentiate among archetypal characters in American literature," "describe the major themes in American literature," "describe contributions of different cultures to the development of American literature," and "compare and contrast the works of contemporary and past American poets." In most documents, a visitor from Mars wouldn't find a clue about the specific country in which the literary standards are to be met if all the visitor could read were the standards.

A visitor from Mars might also be puzzled about what the language of the typical American classroom is. In only about one-half of the documents may a reader assume that English will be the language of the English language arts class. That is only because there is nothing to suggest otherwise. In a few others, it is not clear whether other languages may be used. In many others, it seems that other languages will be used. For example, Kansas wants students to show "in their speaking and writing that they value their own language and dialect." Indiana includes as a "supporting component" of its document a position statement on classroom practices by NCTE declaring that students should have "guidance and frequent opportunities... to bring their own cultural values, languages, and knowledge to their classroom reading and writing." This position statement is repeated in Ohio's document. Several states do not use the word "English" at all in the title of their standards document, leaving the language of reading and writing unspecified, or using "Communication Arts" as the euphemism. Fewer than half of the 28 documents make it clear that all students are expected to demonstrate competence in using standard English orally and in writing. Only four of the 28 documents require knowledge of the history of the English language itself, a topic that was once common in all school curricula.

The failure to build rigor into the reading standards
Many standards look good on paper, but, in the final analysis, the only way that a document can indicate the rigor of its English language arts standards is by specifying the level of reading difficulty it expects students to achieve at the grade levels it assesses. It can do so by (1) requiring the reading of some recognized titles in its standards; (2) suggesting some recognized titles as examples of the reading level expected; (3) requiring exposure to some specific authors (not titles) in its standards; (4) suggesting examples of the authors that students should be familiar with by these grade levels; or (5) offering samples of literary and non-literary passages showing the reading level expected at these grade levels. Nevertheless, not one document builds any required literary titles or authors *into its standard*s to make clear what level of reading difficulty is expected at each educational level to be assessed. Not one offers sample passages at the grade levels to be assessed. Only eight of the 28 states even offer *examples* of specific titles of literary or academic works to suggest the level of reading difficulty they would like students to achieve by a particular educational level. Nebraska, whose standards document was completed and approved in February 1998, is the only state to indicate in its examples the specific reading level it expects students to attain for the grade levels it will assess.

The failure to identify vocabulary development as a crucial reading skill
Most of the 28 documents lack clear and precise expectations for development of a reading vocabulary. Some states (e.g., Arizona, Michigan, and New York) do not mention the development of a reading vocabulary at all. Others mention the topic in a very general way (e.g., "develop a reading vocabulary"). Yet others provide some detail, but their statements on the topic seem to prescribe extremely limited ways in

which teachers can approach development of a reading vocabulary. The omission of vocabulary development as a reading skill, or the mandating of a narrow or inadequate approach to it, is a serious matter; in one hundred years of research in education, vocabulary knowledge has consistently turned up as the major component of reading ability.

Anti-literary or anti-intellectual requirements or expectations
Many documents exhibit what I have termed anti-literary or anti-intellectual requirements or expectations. Unfortunately, the concept of "representation" has been misappropriated from the field of political science and misapplied to literary works (and by literary works, I mean both nonfiction as well as imaginative works). Some states want students to read literary works that "represent" a culture, as if any literary work can be said to "represent" a complex culture; they imply that what is in any one literary work is an accurate and comprehensive portrait of the author's culture, rather than a part of a complex whole that might well include other works with very different views of the culture. What is worse in some documents is the grandiose but totally unrealistic expectation that K–12 students learn the essential characteristics of *all* cultures in the world from their literature programs. If they learn a great deal about just our own, most parents would be content.

About two-thirds of the documents require or want students to relate the literature they read to their lives, or to interpret what they read from within the framework of their personal experiences. Some go beyond expecting students to make a connection between their personal lives and the literature they read and want them to apply what they read in a literary work to their own and others' lives. Indeed, Michigan has an entire category of standards for which students are to "apply knowledge, ideas, and issues drawn from texts to their lives and the lives of others." But to compel students to reduce the experiences within a work to those with which they are already familiar is to violate what the literary experience should be; the purpose of a literary work is to expand, not reduce, the reader's horizons. Moreover, requiring personal application of literary understandings is also fraught with hazard. Students may bring misunderstood ideas as well as bad ideas in what they read to their own or others' lives. Such standards or expectations encourage an irresponsible and potentially dangerous pedagogy.

Over one-third of the documents emphasize using literature to study contemporary social issues. This is a gross misuse of the time allotted for literary study, as well as an abuse of literature itself. To expect or encourage teachers to choose works for classroom study for this purpose is to militate against literary quality as well as the construction of a civically balanced literature program for K–12.

Finally, over one-third of the documents expect students to learn, to varying extents, that literary works are susceptible of a variety of interpretations. That some texts may be open to more than one interpretation is an unarguable generalization to teach students if they learn at the same time that the quality or weight of the evidence for an interpretation must be taken into account. However, these documents do not point out that different interpretations of a text may not necessarily be of equal validity. Several even imply that an infinite number of interpretations are possible for other kinds of texts as well, leaving teachers with the erroneous and damaging idea that a medicine label may be as open in meaning as a poem.

Sources of these Limitations

One major reason for the limitations in many state documents is the abysmal failure of NCTE and IRA to provide a model of what good English language arts and reading standards might look like. Although the two organizations were given almost $2,000,000 in 1991 by the U.S. Department of Education to develop national standards, the Department of Education decided against further funding of their joint project in 1994 on the grounds that their interim report contained nothing resembling standards. NCTE and IRA went ahead to complete a set of national standards with money from a private foundation as well as their own resources. But their final document, released in March 1996, was no better. It was criticized by a senior adviser to Secretary of Education Richard Riley, by Albert Shanker, then president of the American Federation of Teachers, and by a *New York Times* editorial, a range of sources suggesting the validity of the criticism.

If anything, the twelve "content standards" in the NCTE/IRA document provide precisely the wrong models for academic standards. As one example, it suggests the use of mainly invisible processes or strategies as the heart of its standard for composition: "Students employ a wide range of strategies as they write and use different writing process elements appropriately to communicate with different audiences for a variety of purposes." It is doubtful that any reader of a communication cares how many strategies or process elements the writer used. Or that any were used at all. All that a normal reader is apt to care about is whether the writer has communicated in a way that is appropriate for the particular piece of writing the reader is asked to read. But NCTE/IRA's standards do not tell us what sorts of things make a communication appropriate. In essence, the real question has been begged by this so-called standard. Moreover, there is no evidence from studies conducted by the National Assessment of Educational Progress over the past two decades to suggest that the use of the writing process in our schools *has* led to better writing.

A second major reason for the abundance of content-empty standards in many state documents is intention. Many both inside and outside of education do not want state standards and state testing. Indeed, a prominent English educator on the NCTE/IRA standards development committee said openly at a session at the 1993 NCTE conference that "the committee didn't want standards which some students might fail."[3] With that kind of philosophy guiding the development of national English language arts standards, it is not surprising that no real standards were developed. (One must wonder why these organizations accepted $2,000,000 from the federal government for the presumed purpose of developing standards.) Vague standards, in literary study especially, serve a variety of interests, and the banner of local control is frequently waved to justify such vagueness. Some local control advocates want only a very traditional literature curriculum and will not accept much broadening of it. Others seek to tailor the local literature curriculum to what they see as the needs of particular "cultural" groups and do not want uniform standards or a common literary core for all. On the other hand, most secondary school English teachers have traditionally opposed state or federal mandates; they value their professional autonomy in selecting literature for their students to read.

Why so few literary indicators, including mention of American literature?
At least three forces are responsible for the lack of general literary indicators in the standards documents. One is the attitude of NCTE's leadership toward literary study in the English curriculum and toward the role of the English language in this country's public life. Another is the attempt by many multicultural educators to use the literature curriculum to cultivate subgroup identity across national boundaries; a core list would interfere with their goal. A third is simply the nature of committee

deliberations among any group of English teachers for such a task; it is not easy to work out a small core of required or suggested literary titles.

Despite the fact that literary study has been the major focus of the high school English class and the major interest of high school English teachers, the relative absence of attention to literary study in the NCTE/IRA standards document was deliberate. Even though they are not ideological enemies, NCTE's leadership chose to exclude members of the Modern Language Association (MLA) from its standards development committee, I was told by an MLA staff member, because NCTE's leadership did not want its standards to embed the extent or quality of literary study that MLA members—mainly college faculty—would have sought. And so far as I can tell from the lists of names of committee members in the state documents themselves, few literary scholars participated as members of their standards development committees. Reduced attention to literary study is also apparent in the English language arts standards put out by the New Standards Project, a joint venture of the Learning Research and Development Center at the University of Pittsburgh and the National Center on Education and the Economy. Their joint project on literacy drew on the services of NCTE members who were selected by NCTE's leadership.

The NCTE/IRA document abdicates its professional responsibility for providing an intellectual framework for literary learning in K–12 and diminishes the central role of literary study in the English class in several ways. The utter vacuity of the one "content standard" it offers for literary learning reveals its conceptual bankruptcy. Standard Two proposes that "students read a wide range of literature from many periods in many genres to build an understanding of the many dimensions (e.g., philosophical, ethical, aesthetic) of human experience." Although the document goes on to suggest that literary reading should encompass both "classic and contemporary" works, it chose to illustrate this polarizing and invalid distinction with an example of a "classic literary text" that is a piece of adolescent literature written in 1967 (S.L. Hinton's *The Outsiders*). Nothing could better symbolize the corruption of NCTE's professional role than its choice of a piece of adolescent literature written in 1967 as an example of a classic literary text. And that is the extent of the intellectual framework it offers teachers.

It further diminishes literature by classifying it simply as one of many kinds of "text." To be sure, the document takes care to point out that "texts that we call 'literary' have a special function in our culture and in

The State of Literary Study in English Language Arts 245

student learning." But the very first "standard" makes it clear that literary texts will have to compete in the English class with a "wide range of print and nonprint texts" if students are "to build an understanding of texts, of themselves, and of the cultures of the United States and the world." These "print texts" range from novels and poems to popular journals, letters, family and "community" documents, and the writing of peers. The document expressly wants students to read each other's writing as a way "to build self-confidence" and mutual "respect." In addition, students' reading experiences are to include an equally vast range of "spoken texts" such as "playful talk" and something NCTE calls "visual texts." This peculiar concept is intended to designate illustrations, television, advertisements, multimedia resources, and an infinite host of other kinds of "graphic and visual messages." This egalitarian textual mandate is unlikely to leave English teachers much time to engage their students in serious literary study. And when they do get their students to focus on the work itself, it is quite clear how small a role the work itself is to have in influencing their understanding of it. That is because the NCTE document wants students to discover that "any given text can be understood in a variety of ways, depending on the context."

Although the document admits that literary works are "valuable not just as informative or communicative vehicles, but as artistic creations and representations of human culture at particular times and in particular places," it nevertheless suggests that works for classroom study should be chosen first for "relevance to students' interests" and their "roles in society and the workplace" before literary quality is considered. As the document makes clear in a discussion of its first standard, the purpose of students' experiences with "text" is to enable them "to view and critique American and world history and contemporary social life." No longer is its goal to develop their literary taste or literary knowledge.

The antipathy of many NCTE members to English as the language of this country is also playing a role in the downgrading of literary study. After all, the literature that students must read is in English. This antipathy shows up in the attempt to remove the word "English" from the very title of the National Council of Teachers of English. Its title has been characterized by the "NCTE Name Change Committee" as "too narrow to convey who we really are in terms of our profession's comprehensive role in guiding the development of students' reading, writing, speaking, listening, and thinking skills."[3] This committee is concerned that the title conveys a misleading notion about "our national identity." At NCTE's annual conference in November 1995, at a session held to discuss name-changing, several members objected to the word "English" as non-inclusive.[4] One delegate stated that "if we are to offer diversity, there can be a conversation about language arts, but not about English," adding that the word "English" excludes bilingual teachers. Nothing was decided at this conference. Although there may well be other reasons for the ambivalence in many standards documents about the language to be used in the English language arts class, the thinking verbalized by NCTE's Name Change Committee suggests why educators writing standards documents have been inhibited from "privileging" English as the language of the English language arts class.

Prominent scholars, educators, and bilingual education advocates are also attempting to convince teachers that it is beneficial to let immigrant students use their home language in the English language arts class. Although they claim this practice aids in learning English and other academic subjects, there is no consistent body of evidence from the research on bilingual education to back this up at all. The report titled "Improving Schooling for Language Minority Children," issued by the National Research Council in 1997, notes that "there is not really a strong consensus about what is best for the education of English-language learners." Nonetheless, NCTE/IRA's standards also want our schools to expect "students whose first language is not English [to] make use of their first language to develop competency in the English language arts and to develop understanding of content across the curriculum."

Even if the creation of this document did not cost $2,000,000 of the taxpayers' money, we would have reason to be appalled at its intellectual emptiness, anti-literature stance, and political pretensions. NCTE's standards document is much more than an example of professional irresponsibility; it is a prime example of the widespread intellectual and moral confusion now affecting those to whom citizens would normally turn for leadership in a desperate effort to raise academic expectations for all our children but especially those whose homes are limited in the resources available to them.

Standards perceived to support the development of common literary knowledge (and, hence, a common civic culture) are particularly anathema to educators and groups consumed by identity politics. As the very first "content standard" in the NCTE/IRA document subtly implies in its phrase, "the cultures of the United States and the world," the United States of America is viewed as an entity consisting of many cultures; students are to see themselves as citizens of the world, with primary loyalties to their ethnic or racial group. The attempt to cultivate group identity through the school curriculum invariably affects the choice of literary works assigned to minority students. As a Santa Monica high school English teacher remarked to me, minority students in her school system have been given little else to read in recent years but literature about their own group, most of them poor autobiographies in her judgment.

Even if educators do not support the goals of identity politics, many view almost all British and American literature as the expression of white male, Protestant, and Eurocentric sensibilities only and convey their views openly to their colleagues or subordinates. A staff member of the Oregon Department of Education states in a video program it produced for teacher training that teachers need to look at copyrights when they choose literary works for their students to see if they were written in "culturally insensitive" times. This is a new and interesting form of McCarthyism; it is now books that may be guilty of association with the wrong times. There is even a date for these "culturally insensitive" times. A member of an English language arts assessment committee in Massachusetts in 1996 offered us her opinion that anything written before 1970 is inherently racist or sexist. I was told elsewhere that test publishers have been told the same thing. This is clearly a strategy designed to inhibit both English teachers and test publishers from exposing students to any older literary works at all. A more subtle inhibiting strategy is to claim that offering selections by well-known authors of the past would favor students who had already read some of their works (in school or at home), and that only works by contemporary authors (or by totally unknown authors) would be fair.

The practical problem militating against the construction of core reading lists for standards documents is the unwillingness of standards committee members to thrash them out. Most teachers don't want to spend their time on standards committees arguing about titles, authors, or literary periods. So they avoid the task altogether. And state boards of education are just as reluctant, it seems. In states where I have served as a consultant for their standards document, I've had no success so far in getting either a standards development committee or a state board of education to build into their standards just a few, presumably non-controversial, titles, such as Lincoln's Gettysburg Address and the Declaration of Independence. At a NCTE conference several years ago, an active NCTE member remarked that our seminal political documents are also a "canon" question. One wonders if our state boards of education think likewise.

Why no suggested reading levels?
Standards development committees could have included sample passages from a variety of literary and academic works to indicate the range of difficulty desired for achievement at a particular grade level. It is not clear why most did not. One reason may be the fact that there is no consensus anywhere on the level of reading achievement desired for a high school diploma. However difficult a decision that is to make, state boards of education are going to have to bite the bullet on this very difficult educational issue someday. If there is no indication of what a high school diploma should mean with regard to level of reading ability attained, how then do academic expectations get upgraded for all students in the comprehensive American high school? Are differentiated high school diplomas a solution? Most other countries have differentiated high schools and high school programs to address differences in talent, motivation, and goals in its adolescent population. This question begs for widespread public discussion.

Why so little attention to vocabulary development?
The lack of attention to vocabulary development reflects the influence of those who have claimed that only an organic approach to reading and writing (i.e., the reading and writing of "whole texts") will do—and who have successfully discredited skill work or discrete learning of any kind. For the past two decades or more, they have inhibited teachers from doing anything much about vocabulary development in a systematic way. Documents that promote "whole language" teaching in the primary grades are usually among those that do not expect students to acquire knowledge of word meanings through systematic, noncontextual study of words. But, in the case of vocabulary teaching, the weight of the research evidence is abundantly clear; the need for some explicit attention to vocabulary development has been a consistent implication of the results of educational research for almost one hundred years.

Why anti-literary or anti-intellectual recommendations or standards?
There are at least two major reasons for most of the anti-literary or anti-intellectual pedagogical recommendations or requirements in the docu-

ments I examined. They are seen by faculty in schools of education as strategies for addressing the problem of the unmotivated or poor reader, and they make it easier for poorly trained teachers to teach literature. Grounding literary interpretation in students' experiences is thought to make literary study more relevant to and understandable by all students, especially unmotivated ones. Further, the notion that any work is susceptible to multiple interpretations and that differences in interpretation reflect a student's race, ethnicity, and gender tends to remove the need for a close reading of a work to determine what its author seems to have said and for judgments about the quality of the evidence supporting an interpretation. The use of issue-oriented selections to raise students' political consciousness and to encourage them to think in particular ways on specific issues further obviates the need for a close reading of a text or analytical thinking. Interestingly, the notion that a "cultural" group has only one perspective helps address the background limitations of English teachers who are not apt to be trained in the literature, culture, and history of any of the dozens of social groups around the globe that they are now expected to portray through the literary selections they choose. Encouraging teachers to think that one work may "represent" a culture makes it easier for them to use one work as the source of all knowledge about a particular group and to forgo in-depth graduate coursework in its language or literature.

Why Specific Literary or Reading Standards Matter

A state assessment is the tail that wags the curricular dog. Ultimately, state assessments are far more important than the standards on which they are based. Because of local control of school curricula in this country, state standards are in theory voluntary. State assessments, on the other hand, must be given to all students in all public schools in a state. (The criteria used for exempting "special needs" or English-as-a-second-language students from state assessments are highly controversial in many states and are inconsistent across states. Their application can also be inconsistent from one school district to another even within a state, depending on how school administrators interpret the criteria.) The penalties or rewards attached to student achievement on state assessments are the only real leverage a state has on the content of local curricula. Scores on the high school assessments can be related to the granting of a high school diploma or admission to the state system of colleges and universities. As a result, there may be pressure from a variety of sources to design state assessments in such a way that they may achieve the opposite of what the public and the state legislature funding them believe they are doing—increasing academic expectations for all students. That is why the failure of an English language arts/reading document to specify the reading levels it expects students to achieve by certain grade levels or the kinds of literature it expects students to read in K–12 can be so serious. The reading tests used in Texas from 1995 to 1998 for assessing reading achievement in grades 4, 8, and 10 are a case in point.

Texas's English language arts/reading standards, like almost all other states' standards, do not specify the level of reading difficulty expected on a state assessment (i.e., no sample passages or suggested grade levels). As a result, the overall level of difficulty for the reading selections on each grade level assessed is determined by its department of education, the testing company hired to construct the assessments, and the particular teachers or school administrators chosen to review the selections and the questions the company provides. Most Texas educators and politicians were very pleased with the results of the tests from 1995 to 1998; student scores in general rose from year to year, and the gap between the scores of minority students and the others decreased regularly. This showed the value of having high state standards, so most Texans thought.

But some Texans were suspicious of this regular rise in scores; students were not showing higher scores on other, independent indices of academic achievement, and so I was asked by an independent agency to analyze the contents of Texas's reading tests (and three mathematicians were asked to analyze the math tests for those years). Using a well-known readability formula as the most objective and reliable measure possible, I found an almost regular decline from year to year in the overall difficulty level of the reading tests at each grade level assessed, such that all the 1998 tests were easier (and shorter) than all the 1995 tests.[5] Indeed, the 1998 tests in grades 4 and 8 were *much* easier than those given in 1995. What this meant in effect was that there might have been no real improvement in students' reading skills, and no closing of the gap between the scores of minority students and those of other students. Indeed, there could even have been a decline in students' reading skills. We simply don't know.

If grade levels had been specified in the standards, the company constructing the tests, Texas's department of education, and the committee reviewing the tests would have had to check on difficulty level each year and maintain that level from year to year, regardless of the other criteria they were using in selecting or approving reading passages for each test. Better yet, if a core list of known titles or authors had been specified in the standards, English teachers around the state reviewing the tests before they were given would have been able to determine immediately if they were suitably challenging at the grade levels assessed because they would have known from their knowledge of these works or authors and from their own teaching experience if the selections were appropriate for those grade levels. When state assessments in the English language arts consist of selections constructed by a test contractor or of unknown pieces of literature (even if they are "authentic" because they have been published somewhere), it is not easy for teachers as well as parents to determine whether the tests are of equal difficulty from year to year without using a readability formula or, just as important, whether they are suitably difficult for the grade level being assessed.

The Massachusetts experience, on the other hand, shows the benefits of offering specific guidelines on literary content in its standards document, even though its suggestions for a K–12 literature curriculum were not built into its standards *per se*. Its document contains two appendices: one lists key authors (and a few works) that may be considered to comprise the literary and cultural heritage of English-speaking people; the other lists authors of contemporary American literature as well as of world literature past and present. The document advises teachers to draw from both lists in constructing a balanced literature program. Massachusetts also chose to have its English language arts tests developed by a committee consisting chiefly of teachers. Not only were its English language arts/reading standards good, but the members of its assessment development committee were directed to draw equally from the authors listed in the two appendices for their choice of literary selections for the tests. And as highly experienced English teachers or supervisors, they tried to make sure that the passages they selected were at a suitable level of difficulty and covered a range of literary periods, genres, and authors, the questions suitably challenging at the different levels of the test, and the writing prompts worded in such a way that students would have to draw on the content of the selections for their written responses.

Even before the tests were given in May 1998, an article in the *Boston Globe* suggested that the right pedagogical message had come through to English teachers around the state about how to prepare students for the tests for grade 8 and grade 10. When the head of the Weston Public School's English department was asked how his teachers were preparing students for the tests, he replied that they were "reading and discussing poetry in class as usual—but also lately have been asking more questions about vocabulary and the poet's intentions." The contents of the grade 10 test, released to the public after the tests were given, assured the public that its contents were appropriately challenging because the authors of the test selections, Faulkner, Flannery O'Connor, Shakespeare, Thomas Wolfe, and Richard Rodriguez among others, are all recognizable names and no one could say that it is unreasonable to expect students at the end of grade 10 to be able to read their work. Since release of the contents of the grade 10 test, there have been no public complaints about the difficulty level of the test, even though only 40% of Massachusetts high school students were judged proficient or advanced in their total scores on this test. Before the test was given, writers of letters to the editor of the *Boston Globe* regularly complained that the tests were going to be beyond what we could legitimately expect of high school students and were intended to destroy the public schools. According to the feedback the Massachusetts Department of Education received from teachers in the schools, there were only two criticisms of the content of the test—that the Flannery O'Connor excerpt was too hard, and that basic skills students shouldn't have to read Shakespeare.

How Literary Content Can Be Strengthened

There are several ways that the literary content of literature-starved state standards and assessments can be increased. These suggestions can be initiated or promoted by state boards of education, which are responsible either to the governor of the state, to the state legislature, or to the electorate directly.

First, a state board of education can take steps to make sure that the English teachers chosen to be members of standards or assessment development committees are highly experienced English teachers with reputations for high academic expectations; they need not be active in their major professional organizations. A board can do so in large measure simply by asking them to submit a copy of their course syllabi or classroom curriculum and then noting the quality of the literature they have expected their students to read at whatever grade levels they teach.

To strengthen its English language arts/reading standards, a board of education can direct its standards committee to do any or all of the five things mentioned earlier in order to build rigor into its standards. If it seeks to have a list of recommended authors or titles in an appendix (state boards of education cannot mandate specific curricula), two lists of authors, as constructed in the Massachusetts document, are much more effective than one if it requires use of both lists for the construction of each test; it guarantees that some of the literary selections on the test will reflect the literary heritage of English-speaking people.

The composition of the assessment development committee, if there is one, is more crucial. That is because this committee decides how difficult the literary passages should be, what the literary passages should be, what questions should be asked, how academic in thrust they will be, and what constitutes the range of performance on each item (that is, the rubrics or criteria that raters will use in judging the levels of performance in the written responses to open-ended questions). A committee driven by compassion or without high standards can dumb down a test no matter how good the standards on which it is based are, although it is easier to do so if they are vague. Such a committee can provide sophisticated questions for passages with a low level of reading difficulty. Or it can provide easy questions for hard passages. Or it can accompany the right answers on the multiple choice part of test with distractors that are so far off that they are easy for students to eliminate.

Most effective of all, a board of education can mandate custom-made tests for the English language arts and reading that use selections by well-known literary authors. Custom-made tests using passages by well-known authors are far superior to tests with mock "literary" passages constructed by a test contractor and to tests containing selections from published material by unknown authors. Tests with literary passages constructed by a test contractor or selected from published material by unknown authors cannot give teachers or the public the assurance they deserve that students are being asked to read appropriately challenging works for the tests—and by extension in their school curriculum. It is not reasonable to expect the ordinary citizen to use a readability formula to determine if the reading selections on a test are on grade level, and for many literary works, especially poems, a readability formula is inappropriate to use. Teachers and the public at large should be able to recognize the names of some of the authors of the literary selections on the assessments, especially for grade 8 and above.

State boards of higher education can play a role in enriching literature-deprived high school programs. They can cooperate with boards of education responsible for K–12 by requesting college faculty in their public colleges and universities to devise reading lists for students who seek admission to them. These lists could serve as part of their entrance requirements, with different readings required for admission to a public university or a state college. Just as expecting students to have studied at least one foreign language for two to three years made high schools offer foreign language courses and made students take one, so too could such reading lists (broadly conceived) have a salutary effect on high school English programs and, hence, on freshmen reading ability and literary knowledge. State boards of higher education can request the creation of these lists in conjunction with members of the Association of Literary Scholars and Critics and The History Society, two relatively new professional organizations for college faculty.

State boards of education can also ask college faculty in literature departments to develop standards for honors or advanced English courses in the high school. Unless honors or advanced classes are preserved, with meaningful standards for staying in them, acceptable college-preparatory work is unlikely to be demanded of those capable of it in many high schools, widening the gap between those who have demanding, sophisticated parents and those whose parents do not realize that their children are being patronized or how.

Appendix: Criteria for Judging English Language Arts and Reading Standards

A. Purpose, audience, expectations, and assumptions of the standards document(s):
  1. The document is written in clear English prose, for the general public as well as for educators.
  2. It assumes that English is the language to be used in English language arts classes, and the only language to be used.
  3. It expects all students to demonstrate use of standard English, orally and in writing.
  4. It acknowledges the existence of a corpus of literary works called American literature, however diverse its origins and the social groups it portrays.

The State of Literary Study in English Language Arts

5. It expects students to become literate American citizens.
6. It expects explicit and systematic instruction in decoding skills in the primary grades as well as the use of meaningful reading materials.
7. It expects students to do regular independent reading through the grades, suggesting how much reading students should do per year as a minimum, with some guidance about its quality.
8. It expects the standards to serve as the basis for clear and reliable statewide assessments.

B. Organization of the standards:
1. They are presented grade by grade or in clusters of no more than 3 to 4 grade levels.
2. They are grouped in categories reflecting coherent bodies of scholarship or research in the English language arts.
3. They distinguish higher order knowledge and skills from lower order skills, if lower level skills are mentioned.

C. Disciplinary coverage of the standards:
1. The standards clearly address listening and speaking. They include use of various discussion purposes and roles, how to participate in discussion, desirable qualities in formal speaking, and use of established as well as peer-generated or personal criteria for evaluating formal and informal speech.
2. The standards clearly address reading (and viewing) to understand and use information through the grades. They include progressive development of reading skills and a reading vocabulary, and knowledge and use of a variety of textual features, genres, and reading strategies for academic, occupational, and civic purposes.
3. The standards clearly address the reading (or viewing), interpretation, and critical evaluation of literature. They include knowledge of diverse literary elements and genres, different kinds of literary responses, and use of a variety of interpretive and critical lenses. They also specify those key authors, works, and literary traditions in American literature and in the literary and civic heritage of English-speaking people that all students should study because of their literary quality and cultural significance.
4. The standards clearly address writing for communication and personal expression. They include use of writing processes, established as well as peer-generated or personal evaluation criteria, and various rhetorical elements, strategies, genres, and modes of organization.
5. The standards clearly address oral and written language conventions. They include standard English conventions for sentence structure, spelling, usage, penmanship, capitalization, and punctuation.
6. The standards clearly address the nature, dynamics, and history of the English language. They include the nature of its vocabulary, its structure (grammar), the evolution of its oral and written forms, and the distinction between the variability of its oral forms and the relative permanence of its written form today.

7. The standards clearly address research processes, including developing questions and locating, understanding, evaluating, synthesizing, and using various sources of information for reading, writing, and speaking assignments. These sources include dictionaries, thesauruses, other reference materials, observations of empirical phenomena, interviews with informants, and computer databases.

D. Quality of the standards:
1. They are clear.
2. They are specific.
3. They are measurable (i.e., they can lead to clear, comparable results across students and schools).
4. They are comprehensive.
5. They are demanding.
   a. They are of increasing intellectual difficulty at each higher educational level and cover all-important aspects of learning in the area they address.
   b. They index or illustrate the nature of growth through the grades for reading by referring to specific reading levels or to titles of specific literary or academic works as examples of a reading level.
   c. They illustrate the nature of growth expected through the grades for writing with writing samples.
   d. For other subdisciplines, they provide examples of specific reading, writing, or oral language features, activities, or assignments that clarify what is expected for each standard or benchmark.
6. Their overall contents are sufficiently specific, comprehensive, and demanding to lead to a common core of high academic expectations for all students in the state, no matter what school they attend.

E. Anti-Literary or Anti-Academic Requirements or Expectations: Negative Criteria
1. The document implies that the literary or popular culture of our or any other country is monolithic in nature.
2. The reading/literature standards require students to relate what they read to their lived experiences.
3. The reading/literature standards want reading materials to address contemporary social issues.
4. The document implies that all literary and non-literary texts are susceptible to an infinite number of interpretations and that all points of view or interpretations are equally valid regardless of the logic, accuracy, and adequacy of the supporting evidence.
5. The examples of classroom activities or student writing offered are politically slanted or reflect an attempt to manipulate students' feelings, thinking, or behavior.
6. The standards teach moral or social dogma.
7. The document explicitly or implicitly recommends one instructional approach for all teachers to follow.

Notes

[1] Stotsky. S. *State English Standards: An Appraisal of English Language Arts/Reading Standards in 28 States.* Washington D.C.: Thomas B. Fordham Foundation, 1997.

[2] Longstreet, W. S. (1996). *Handbook on Teaching Social Issues.* Washington, D.C., Council on National Standards.

[3] "A Message from the NCTE Name Change Committee," a clip-out questionnaire in the June 1995 issue of *The Council Chronicle*, the newsletter of NCTE.

[4] K.L. Billingsley, "Teachers of English bash it." *The Washington Times*, November 19, 1995. Reprinted in *Network News & Views*, January/February 1996, p. 134.

[5] Copies of the report are available from the Tax Research Association of Houston and Harris County, Texas. To judge by the results of the New Dale-Chall Readability Formula, the tests used in 1995 at all grade levels were appropriate grade-level tests. In grade 10, there were as many selections below grade 9–10 as above 9–10, but most were at grade 9–10. On the other hand, in 1998, for grade 10, only two selections were above grade level, while four were below it, suggesting that this test is not as demanding as it should be for grade 10. In grade 8, the 1995 test had two selections above grade 7–8, three selections below grade 7–8, and three selections right at grade level. This test is also right on target. But by 1998, there were three selections below grade level (two considerably below), and only one selection on grade level. Even though there were still two selections above grade 7–8, the pitch of the test is clearly below grade level. In grade 4, the 1995 test had two selections above grade level, two below, and three right at grade level. By 1998, there were only two selections at grade level; four were below grade level. This test is much too easy for grade 4 students.

Chapter 11

Toward Improved English Language Arts Standards for K–12
What a College Professor Wishes Her Students Had Read

Jeanne J. Smoot
North Carolina State University

Most college professors today have modest but profoundly felt expectations of their incoming students. We would like them simply to be able to read and write. But even these modest expectations may no longer be realizable unless state boards of education and others charged with setting state standards for K–12 and for teacher certification insist upon standards that have more specific expectations for what K–12 students read than do professional educational organizations, such as the National Council of Teachers of English (NCTE) and the International Reading Association (IRA). One solution might be for state boards of education to ask the English faculty in their public colleges and universities, perhaps in conjunction with faculty in other fields, to come up with lists of works or authors that students ought to have read prior to college. If this kind of reading took place, those of us at the college level could again teach reasonably demanding works of literature to first-year college students rather than spend our time, and taxpayers' money, in remedial work or in teaching the most elementary introduction to literary discourse—what many of us must do at present.

In the past there were widely accepted works—both British and American, classical Greek, and Roman as well as other offerings—that constituted a liberal arts education. Generally these works were on required reading lists for potential master's and Ph.D. degree candidates in literary fields. Very able students in the secondary school were sometimes also given these lists by their teachers. In more recent years, these lists, which in effect constitute a canon—those works that are recognized as more culturally and aesthetically important to society than others—have come under attack. The irony in all this is that the canon has always been fluid, and the works that comprise it almost without exception have had to fight their way onto it. Shakespeare was once an upstart dramatist. Cervantes was the failed Spanish soldier who wrote that Moors and Christians should respect one another. Neither one pleased contemporary critics, just as newly emerging canonical writers are sometimes viewed in our own time as usurpers.

Conflicts over the canon, then, are nothing new; in fact, they are quite normal. The problem is that many teachers and professors of English—not by nature confrontational beings—are intimidated by this most natural process. Rather than forging ahead with a new and more vital canon, they fear presenting any list at all because it might be culturally offensive to a particular group. Even worse, sometimes, in the attempt to please everyone, they draw up a list that includes everybody's name, and the list becomes so unwieldy that it is useless. Who, then, are the losers? The students themselves, who are left with little guidance as to what to read. And society itself, which is greatly diminished.

In this essay, I discuss where the attack on the canon is coming from and then offer my own guidelines for setting literary standards as well as the standards themselves. I want to show, as best as I can, why standards like these would make a difference to college professors like me.

From Where is the Attack on the Canon Coming?

The canon is now under attack in the very place where it ought to be nurtured—on college campuses throughout the country. And literature, which used to be the core of the language arts, has been increasingly marginalized. Literature is increasingly studied for its political rather than aesthetic or literary content. Lesser works that are more "politically correct" are nudging out the great works of the past. For example, at my own university, essays like Michael Moore's "Why Doesn't GM Sell Crack?" are replacing those like Jonathan Swift's "A Modest Proposal" as examples of literary irony. A relatively unknown writer like E. Fuller Torrey, author of "Who Goes Homeless?" now replaces Mark Twain, whose *Huckleberry Finn* treats the same subject in a much more profound and aesthetically pleasing manner.

The major professional organization of college professors of English and other modern languages, the Modern Language Association of

America (MLA), has increasingly supported these changes, often contradicting its own rhetoric. In response, new professional organizations have emerged. The Association of Literary Scholars and Critics (ALSC) and the Association for Core Texts and Courses are major examples. Though they have somewhat different goals and constituencies, they uphold the primacy of literature and standards for reading. Similar groups are forming among historians equally disenchanted with approaches to the study of history that serve blatantly political goals.

John Ellis, historian and literary critic, and one of the founders of the ALSC, has studied the marginalization of literature and the concomitant loss of intellectual objectivity on college campuses. In *Literature Lost: Social Agendas and the Corruption of the Humanities*, he sees the assault on literature deriving primarily and, ironically, from a very positive and distinctly Western impulse: the utopic desire.[1] Always seeking the ideal, Western culture has tended to be self-analytic and, by extension, self-critical. When this impulse becomes exaggerated, however, or blinded to the positive things Western culture has produced, chaos is likely to result. This is what Ellis thinks has happened on college campuses today.

Ellis sees what he calls the race-gender-class critics as falling into the trap of utopia-or-nothing criticism. These academicians tend to see literature as the struggle among races, genders, and classes. They prefer to call themselves by more specific names, such as feminists, or African-Americanists, or Marxists, or multiculturalists; and they will, in fact, specialize in, or select, works for reading in their classes based on how prominently these works depict oppression of a particular group or class. What makes this confusing is that there are other critics who also refer to themselves by these names but who do not adopt the more radical approaches of the race-gender-class critics. I myself have written some articles that would be termed "feminist criticism," studies of literary works by or about women, although I have never suggested that all men are engaged in a conspiracy against all women. The race-gender-class critics, however, tend to see literature as a validation of their particular political view of the world. For these critics, who were often forged in the social-protest era of the 1960s, literary works once seen as portraying the commonality of human emotions and the human experience have become tools used by a conniving establishment to maintain its "power." That even great writers can hold certain biases is simply a testament to our frailty as human beings. But to suggest eliminating them from the curriculum on these grounds claws at the very fabric of a free society.

And to imply that the authors in our own literary heritage are little more than callous manipulators of their readers' emotions or that all readers are so blindly led is insulting.

An outrageous example of this wrongheaded utopianism involves an Arizona State University professor, Jared Sakren, who was, in effect, fired for teaching canonical works. As recorded in a November 4, 1998, *Wall Street Journal* story titled "The Bard, Barred," Shakespeare was singled out as one of the authors whom "the feminists" on campus found most objectionable. Sakren had taught at Yale University and the Julliard School of Performing Arts before he was hired by Arizona State "to establish a nationally respected actor training program." And he had many contemporary successes to his credit, having trained movie actors Annette Bening, Kelly McGillis, and Val Kilmer among others. Sakren was accused of a "conservatory approach" for focusing on such dramatists as Shakespeare, Congreve, and Ibsen. According to a letter from his department head, Lin Wright, "The feminists are offended by the selection of works from a sexist European canon that is approached traditionally." In another memo she charged, "there is a tension between the use of a European-American canon of dramatic literature and production vs. post-modern feminist/ethnic canons and production styles."

Unfortunately, no amount of support from students past and present, male and female, or even from Annette Bening herself and another student who described herself as a feminist, could halt the ax that fell on him. In her memo to Sakren, Wright warned, "No one in this political climate is a free agent." Sakren is now fighting fire with fire, suing the university and claiming racial discrimination against those of European background and the selection of European works. In the meantime, the Bard, William Shakespeare—if he is taught at all—is truly barred unless he is viewed through the filters of the race-gender-class critics.

Lack of Leadership in Maintaining Standards

How can public officials and educational administrators help strengthen the backbones of those of us in the classroom when under assault, whether on the university or the K–12 level? And strengthen our backbones someone must, because we are not walking upright on our own too well.

Consider, for example, the joint attempt by NCTE and IRA to develop standards for the English language arts. Their project, initially funded by

Toward Improved English Language Arts Standards for K–12

the U.S. Department of Education, was begun in 1991. After they spent close to $2 million of a federal grant over a three-year period, the Department of Education refused to continue funding it on the grounds that the interim draft report failed to address the important issues it was expected to address.[2] The document was eventually completed with money from members and a private foundation. But almost as soon as it was released, it was heavily criticized by many sources, including the ALSC. The ALSC charged that the NCTE/IRA standards "drastically diminish" the role of literature. In its Fall 1996 *Newsletter*, quoting the document, the ALSC Committee on Curriculum noted that:

> Literature is the subject of only ONE of the twelve standards.
>
> Literature is reduced to merely one kind of "text" among a vaguely defined "wide range of print and nonprint texts," such as peer writing, "family" and "community" documents, "spoken" and even "visual" texts.
>
> Artistic quality is firmly subordinated to political and social objectives: the purpose of literature is now to enable students to "view and critique American and world history and contemporary social life."
>
> The standards offer no recommended list of literary works, authors, or periods.
>
> The unique character and significance of literature are obscured by the evasive and often mischievous doctrine that "any given text can be understood in a variety of ways, depending on the context."
>
> Literary criteria are subverted by a relentless and misguided intellectual egalitarianism.[3]

Those who wrote the *Standards for the English Language Arts* either lost or forgot the love of literature that presumably led them to teaching in the first place. But perhaps they also feared the disapprobation of colleagues who might have objected to their choice of works to read, and so they came up with no real lists and no real standards whatsoever. In short, they abandoned their role as educators. The *ALSC Newsletter* chided them also for writing that classroom texts should be chosen first "for relevance to students' interests."

The ALSC urged its members to find out what was happening in their individual states and report back to the editor of the *Newsletter*. Many did, and the Fall 1997 issue noted as one example the "strong influence" of the NCTE/IRA standards in the manual put out by the Texas State Board of Education to prepare teachers for certification.[4] According to this member, the manual says teachers can use "a variety of expressive and expository discourse (e.g., magazines, novels, autobiographies, movies, radio programs)." Although there is nothing wrong with learning from the media that the manual mentioned, where is poetry, satire, and stage drama? And why is a novel mentioned after a magazine?

The *Newsletter* further noted the influence of the race-gender-class specialists on the Texas certification standards. "Among the few authors mentioned, much space is devoted to Toni Morrison, Gwendolyn Brooks, Langston Hughes, and N. Scott Momaday, but none to, for example, Shakespeare, Milton, Chaucer, Dickens, or Twain." Perhaps the drafters of the Texas manual felt the authors that they were highlighting had been underrepresented in the past, or would be, in the future. But public documents have a way of becoming standards, especially if they are written as guidance for certification; and the privileging of writers like Morrison, Hughes, and Momaday has the net effect of diminishing or perhaps even eliminating such literary giants as Shakespeare and Mark Twain. Instead of incorporating more recent canonical authors, such as Langston Hughes and Gwendolyn Brooks, into its curriculum in the natural way actual canon formation occurs, the Texas document insinuates antagonisms. As the *Newsletter* noted, the Texas manual contains "[a] long passage from Momaday [that] praises the distinctive 'vision' of native Americans—their 'unifying perception of the interconnectedness of all things'—and contrasts this with the 'cultural nearsightedness' of American society." "Here the respect demanded for all cultures seems absent," the *Newsletter* continued. In contrast, it observed, California's English language arts standards draft upholds the primacy of literature and refers to the "universal themes in significant works of American, British and world literature."

Suggested Guidelines for Setting State Standards

All educational standards need not be the same to be equally good. Standards could vary from state to state and still be worthwhile and meet the needs of the students in each state. And, yes, they should be written in a joint effort by state and local educators and others to ensure that all students receive a genuinely liberal and rigorous education. Such standards would help assure us at the college level that we might be able to teach literature in earnest, rather than struggle with poorly prepared, culturally adrift students who do not have the literary, historical, or contemporary knowledge to fathom what they read.

To meet these goals, I want to suggest guidelines for creating such standards and follow them up with a list of works or authors that would fulfill them. Many of these guidelines will sound familiar or commonsensical, and are, I believe, self-explanatory.

- K–12 reading lists should vary over time as new writers emerge or others gain more prominence, but literary quality should be the paramount consideration.

- Works should be drawn from a variety of literary periods and genres.

- Students should be exposed to those writers who seem to have a quickening effect in stimulating student reading. Certain novelists—Dickens, in my experience—seem to have this effect and should be stressed for this life-shaping value.

- Students should read some works that are just plain fun. One of the strongest criticisms of the current race-gender-class specialists comes from the students themselves. Their literary choices and criticism are often depressing because they dwell so exclusively on victimization.

- K–12 reading lists should recognize the extraordinary literary-shaping power of the Bible, especially the King James Version. The literary study of Biblical selections in K–12 does not violate the separation of church and state, as Marie Wachlin points out in a review of the legal decisions on the use of the Bible in K–12.[5] Indeed, such study is necessary for several reasons. First, about half of all literary allusions in works written in English prior to 1940 are to the New or Old Testament.[6] Students with no knowledge of this material cannot understand much of what they read, in the general media as well as in literary works. Second, an understanding of the Judaeo-Christian tradition is essential in understanding our culture in general and our system of ethics in particular. I am not exaggerating the extent of this ignorance on the part of students. At present, many colleges, including my own, must make up for this deficiency by offering such courses as "Classical Backgrounds in English Literature," which surveys the major stories and themes of the Bible, as well as similar material from Greek and Roman Antiquity, so that students can begin to read their own national literature. I regularly have students to whom the phrase "he is a Judas," or "I'm going to wash my hands of this matter," or "he has clay feet" means absolutely nothing. And this in the Bible Belt of North Carolina! On the other hand, these "well-schooled," often very "politically correct" students regularly capitalize words like Zeus, Athena, Allah, or Buddha, but lowercase God even when the term refers clearly to the Judaeo-Christian God. That's not even good capitalization. These students have been taught about other regions and religions and their cultural and literary significance, but not the predominant one in their own country, and probably their own.

- Standards should be truthful. A list of British authors should contain only British authors, for example. Under the category of World Literature we should place authors from other countries whose works have been translated or who write in English. The Nigerian Chinua Achebe, for example, is often placed in lists of British literature.

Suggested Standards for American Literature

- Students should have an awareness of the Puritan heritage. That may come in the form of the journals of William Bradford, the governor of the Plymouth Bay Colony, the poetry of Anne Bradstreet, the first published American poet, or the verse of Phillis Wheatley, the first major African-American poet published; or in the idealized reconstructions of the later romantic Henry Wadsworth Longfellow.

- Students should have some sense of who Benjamin Franklin was and what he did—if for no other reason than that they would know not to tell me that he was our first president. Selections from Franklin's *Autobiography*, or his satirical "The Speech of Polly Baker," constitute a good sampling of his work.

- Students should read several of the essays of Thomas Jefferson or Thomas Paine and, above all, the Declaration of Independence. Parts of the Declaration of Independence should even be committed to memory.

- I would like my students to have read Washington Irving because he was the first major American author to make his living as a writer and because his "The Legend of Sleepy Hollow" and "Rip Van Winkle" are now part of American folklore.

- While the nature and civic poetry of the Romantic Period is not particularly popular with literary critics today, the poetry of William Cullen Bryant, Longfellow's "The Song of Hiawatha" and his powerful "Thou, too, sail on, O Ship of State! Sail on O UNION, strong and great!" from his *The Building of the Ship,* written during the troubled years before the Civil War when the nation still hoped for reconciliation, are still stirring to read and give students an understanding of that period.

- I want freshmen to have read John Greenleaf Whittier's "Barbara Frietchie"—about a brave old woman, who, when the Confederate invaders were marching through Maryland, refused to stop waving Old Glory and suffered a bullet wound for her patriotism—in order to call attention to the fact that Chief Justice William Rehnquist had cited this poem when he wrote a dissenting opinion, maintaining that the American flag is such a unique symbol of our national heritage that it ought not to be desecrated.

- From the Romantic Period, I want my students to have read selections by James Fenimore Cooper, who created America's first mythic hero in the figure of *The Deerslayer*; short stories by Hawthorne and Melville; and selections from Thoreau's *Walden.* Then I would be better able to teach them one of America's greatest novels, *Moby Dick.*

- I would like all my students to have read major portions of the *Narrative of the Life of Frederick Douglass,* the story of one man's journey out of slavery.

- Familiarity with the poetry of Edgar Allan Poe, Emily Dickinson, and Walt Whitman are musts for college freshmen in my courses. I can then concentrate on the revolutions in verse form which they introduced and move rapidly into the study of modern poetry and the pervasive influence of these authors beyond America's shores.

- Of the regionalists and realists, I would want my students to have read something by Mark Twain. *A Connecticut Yankee in King Arthur's Court* is a good choice because it helps them learn the techniques of satire in an enjoyable manner. Short stories by William Dean Howells, Bret Harte, Sarah Horne Jewett, Charles Chesnutt, Kate Chopin, Jack London, and Edith Wharton are often easy to read and quite short, yet teach a great deal about narrative styles and the milieus in which they are set. The more sophisticated novels of a demanding novelist such as Wharton could then be taught at the college level. Stephen Crane's *The Open Boat* or *The Red Badge of Courage* would be read in secondary school so that it could be read again in college with a greater degree of profundity. These works also help students to understand that today's short-story writers and novelists are writing in a tradition. I could then teach about the evolution of a literary genre more effectively, giving students benchmarks against which to evaluate recent authors to whom they are drawn because of their contemporaneity, as well as a better sense of the traditions today's authors are often writing against. As we know, some of the very best break new ground. But their accomplishments cannot be fully appreciated without an awareness of those who have blazed the trail beforehand, a situation that holds for all literary genres.

- For twentieth century American writing, short stories by Willa Cather, Sherwood Anderson, F. Scott Fitzgerald, William Faulkner, Ernest Hemingway, Eudora Welty, Richard Wright, Ralph Ellison, Bernard Malamud, Saul Bellow, James Baldwin, Flannery O'Connor, Toni Morrison, John Updike, Anne Tyler, Alice Walker, and Amy Tan would introduce students to a range of the very best American short-story writers. Poems by Edwin Arlington Robinson, Robert Frost, Carl Sandburg, e. e. cummings, Wallace Stevens, William Carlos Williams, John Crowe Ransom, Allen Tate, Langston Hughes, Theodore Roethke, Gwendolyn Brooks, Robert Lowell, and A.R. Ammons would do the same for American poetry. If students could become familiar with these authors, college professors would be able to build a more authentic understanding of the twentieth century writing of authors from other countries and cultures. This is true for dramatists as well.

- Eugene O'Neill may be too difficult and morose for most high schoolers to grasp, but they can respond to Tennessee Williams's *The Glass Menagerie*, for example. In recent years, I find students either weary of Arthur Miller's *Death of a Salesman* or without the ability to empathize with the hapless Willy Loman. *All My Sons*, Miller's play about fraud in the arms industry, might resonate more with today's high schoolers. Edward Albee, though not as popular today with critics as he was in the 1960s when he achieved almost instant success, is sadly accessible to today's youth who see frightening mirror images of the breakdown of the family in the constant quarreling and insane self-destructive behavior of characters like George and Martha in *Who's Afraid of Virginia Woolf*. A familiarity with Williams, Miller, and Albee would enable college professors to move more easily to more recent playwrights, such as August Wilson, who deals with the dissolution of the African-American family, or the postmodernist Irish author Brian Friel, whose *Dancing at Lughnasa* has been made into a motion picture. The works of Friel and other postmodernists are daunting to students unless they can see common threads—the concern for family that runs throughout virtually all great drama from the very beginnings of the theater, or the desire for innovation and freedom of expression. Friel, like the earlier Miller and Williams, is a rebel against a literary tradition that both nourishes and crystallizes his expression.

Suggested Standards for Classical Literature

- Although ancient myths and legends can be found in all cultures, primacy should be given to Greco-Roman myths and works from the Judaeo-Christian tradition because they have been central in shaping Western literature. In the early grades, students can read adapted stories about the Trojan Horse or the slaying of the valiant Hector by Achilles. This would help students understand many common allusions like "Achilles heel" that a teacher like me now has to take time to explain. At the very least, students should be aware of such fundamental Greek precepts as "Nothing in Excess" and "Know Thyself." High school students should read passages from Homer's

Iliad and *Odyssey*. I prefer Sophocles's *Antigone* to his better known *Oedipus Rex* because high school students can more readily identify with a young girl who defies the State in the name of a higher good or the gods than they can identify with a tyrant whom they often naively see as unknowingly committing incest. For an introduction to Roman material, selections from Virgil's *Aeneid* are desirable. Students should be aware of such Roman ideals as the respect for law and the State, which Virgil elevated even above respect for the individual.

- Bible stories should be taught from an early age on. Much of the great art of the Medieval Period and the Renaissance demands a knowledge of biblical themes and characters. Indeed, much American literature cannot be fully understood unless students see the influence of the Bible, even on modern authors like Faulkner. The Bible also had a strong influence on early African-American authors, often as they adapted biblical stories to African folktales. And a clear picture of the evolution of the short story form requires a look at the apocryphal story of "Susanna," considered one of the oldest tales in Western culture, or at some of the parables of Jesus, "The Prodigal Son," often cited in college texts as one of the most economic short stories ever told. The poetry of St. Paul's epistle on the nature of love that begins, "Though I speak with the tongues of men and of angels, and have not love I am become as sounding brass or a tinkling cymbal" (I Corinthians 13), ought not to be discounted because it is found in a sacred book any more than we would discredit great works of the Hindu or Buddhist tradition simply because they were found in the holy writings of the Vedas or the Tripitaka. High school students should know the Creation Story from the Old Testament and the stories of Joseph, Ruth, and the suffering Job. They should know some psalms. "What is man that thou art mindful of him?" (Psalm 8) is a profoundly felt and eternal question, regardless of the religion of its singer. Students should have some familiarity with the historic Jesus and His significance. His Sermon on the Mount created a revolution in ethical behavior and enters into the modern psychological realm of the relationship between intention and action, which students should recognize as such.

- Students should be familiar with the Eddas, which relate the stories of Northern mythology, and the Vedas, which form the Hindu Scriptures.

Suggested Standards for British Literature

Students should be familiar with the complete sweep of British literature because so much of American literature—and virtually all of it prior to 1825—is based on it. Accomplishing that would enable students not only to read any literature more effectively but would also allow those who are college-bound to move with ease into more specialized university courses in specific literary periods or genres, which still form the bulk of most college offerings, despite the trend among the race-gender-class specialists to such themes as "Women in Literature" and "Gender in Literature."

The study of British material could begin in the elementary grades, depending on the selections chosen, with more formal study of British literature reserved for the twelfth grade year. Though it could be argued that if students got a classical or mythic background in the tenth grade, British study might more appropriately come in the eleventh grade, with the senior year reserved for American literature study, which would represent the culmination and/or response to all these various influences.

- Students need familiarity with some work from the Middle Ages. This is vital for college-level study in almost any European literature or history course. I would be delighted if my students knew the story of *Beowulf* and some of the stories in *The Canterbury Tales*.

- From the Renaissance, I would want my students to know Edmund Spenser but not to have their love of literature killed by an overzealous teacher who insisted on dragging them all the way through the *Faerie Queene* if they weren't up to it. There are sonnets by Spenser that are accessible to high school students and give the flavor of his elegance and love of language.

- The Great Bard would not be barred from my standards list but would be highlighted. Teachers need to resist the temptation to teach a lesser known play because they have taught *Hamlet* or another major play so often they sometimes can recite whole passages in their sleep. It is for this very reason that we should continue to teach the best known plays by Shakespeare. So many common sayings, even our philosophic attitudes and rhetorical styles, come from plays like *Hamlet* and *Macbeth*. At the college level, more problematic plays like *Othello* and *King Lear* can then be studied because of the background students gain from reading the better known plays at the high school level.

- I would want some exposure to Shakespeare's sonnets as well. Shakespeare is our greatest poet, and it is always a great sadness to me to find that some students—for whatever reason—have not been exposed to his verse until I do expose them to it at the college level. Shakespeare's sonnets can be a window to the whole world of figurative language and the literary beauty of the Renaissance.

- John Donne should not be ignored. Students should have some acquaintance with the metaphysical poets in general, and I would want them to have read Andrew Marvell as well.

- Selections from the work of John Milton should also be on the reading list for students interested in going to college—the seduction of Adam by Eve, for instance, in *Paradise Lost*. That would give students in my classes who are weary of everything being blamed on men some grist for their mill. In addition, Milton's fiery descriptions of Lucifer become important in later Western depictions of the devil. A familiarity with *Paradise Lost* can give students a window on both the old world and the new if their teachers point to Milton's borrowings from Dante, who borrowed from Virgil, who borrowed from Homer. Or it can help them look ahead to Romantic treatments and glorifications of the Rebel/Devil figure in Byron and others. Because censorship has become an issue at the college level in so many subtle ways, I would also like students to have read Milton's *Areopagitica*, one of the seminal works on censorship. It never hurts to show the enduring relevance of great literature.

- From the Restoration and the eighteenth century, I would want my students to be familiar with John Dryden, even if they had only read a selection from one of his longer poems. Jonathan Swift's *Gulliver's Travels* or "A Modest Proposal" can introduce high school students to the world of satire equally as well. They should also have heard of

James Boswell and his mentor, Dr. Samuel Johnson, and have some sense of the importance of Johnson's wonderful dictionary, his *The Lives of the Poets,* and "The Preface of Shakespeare" in shaping public taste and reading habits. Finally, exposure to Alexander Pope's saucily witty "The Rape of the Lock" and his "Essay on Criticism" would be desirable, if no other reason than to help students realize that poetry is "[w]hat oft was thought, but ne'er so well expressed."

- To enable college teachers to go deeper into the Romantic and Victorian Periods, I would like school students to have read some poems by William Blake, Robert Burns, William Wordsworth, Samuel Taylor Coleridge, George Byron, William Keats, and Percy Bysshe Shelley. Fortunately, some of their works, such as the ballads of Burns or the nature poems of Wordsworth, can be introduced early. Even when middle school students can't understand the full implications of some of the works they might read or hear, such as Blake's "The Tyger," they can still respond to the rhythm and power of the language. From the Victorian Period I would want students to have at least read the two Brownings, Elizabeth Barrett and Robert, as well as some poems by Tennyson and the two Rossettis, Dante Gabriel and Christina.

- From the twentieth century, I would want students to have read some poetry by Thomas Hardy, perhaps the play *Pygmalion* by George Bernard Shaw or one of the dramas by Samuel Beckett, and selections from Joseph Conrad, who is appropriately seen as a British author. Poems by William Butler Yeats, D. H. Lawrence, Dylan Thomas, and T. S. Eliot, the American expatriate turned British citizen; selections from novels or short stories by Virginia Woolf and James Joyce; and short stories by Katherine Mansfield would round out works that would give any high school graduate excellent preparation for college work.

Suggested Standards for World Literature

Under the world literature category, my ambitions would be far more modest. Realizing how difficult it is for young people to acquire an awareness of American culture, much less other cultures, and that most K–12 teachers are not trained in world literature but graduate from our colleges and universities with concentrations in American or British literature, I would not want students overwhelmed by much culturally alien material. A good course on British or American literature is better preparation for college for them than a poorly taught course on world literature covering dozens of different cultures. However, much of the mythic background necessary for the understanding of our own national literary heritage is world literature—the Greco-Roman tradition and the mythologies of all the great religions of the world. Native American stories and poems also form part of this great mythic tradition. In addition, I would like students to have read selections from the following authors because of their importance in literary history and their enduring influence: Dante; Cervantes, father of the novel; Goethe, master of the great Faust myth; Flaubert, one of the greatest writers of the so-called modern novel; and one of the nineteenth century Russian novelists, such as Tolstoy, Dostoevsky, or Turgenev.

Concluding Remarks

Educators and others charged with preparing lists of core authors or works to be read in K–12 might wish to look at the lists of (chiefly) authors appearing in the English language arts standards document approved by the Massachusetts State Board of Education in January 1997, in order to see the pitfalls of lists prepared by committees. While that document is an outstanding piece of work and a commendable attempt to offer teachers at the K–12 level some guidance in what to teach, it is literally (pardon the pun) overwhelming. I have been teaching or administering at the college level for more than thirty years, and even if I had had that list at the start of my career and followed it religiously with the very best students available, I doubt that I could have covered all those authors. Hence, I have tried to keep my own suggestions brief in order to give teachers room for creativity in their teaching based on their own particular talents and the needs and heritages of their students.

Teachers need to make connections from the core that I have offered to good ethnic literature in order to provide what is today called an "inclusive" literature program. Rightly used, an awareness of one's own heritage or the heritage of one's region does not result in cultural antagonisms but rather in a deeper sense of self and an awareness that all of our various peoples, whether native or immigrants to our shores, have enriched our national life. For example, students from school districts

Toward Improved English Language Arts Standards for K–12 275

with large numbers of Native Americans might delight in studying some of *The Tales of Manabozho* or the speeches of Native American chiefs like Logan (c. 1725–1780), whose rhetoric Thomas Jefferson compared with that of Demosthenes and Cicero.

K–12 reading lists should vary from community to community as well as from state to state. An Asheville, North Carolina, school district, for example, might logically foreground its native son Thomas Wolfe, and the entire state could emphasize Charles Frazier's *Cold Mountain*, which won the National Book Award in 1997. *Cold Mountain* could then lead to the study of Homer's *Odyssey*, on which much of the novel is based, or to the study of the Civil War and its impact on the lives of men and women who lived in that era, the ostensible subject of this novel about a man who yearns for his home. A Lake Charles, Louisiana, school district might proudly present *A Good Scent from a Strange Mountain*, a collection of short stories by 1993 Pulitzer Prize-winner Robert Olen Butler, who writes about the region and the Vietnamese refugees who settled there. Or a Louisiana teacher might wish to use works from turn-of-the-century author Kate Chopin, who depicts the Creole traditions of the region in often scathing detail.

I have tried to shy away from the syndrome that has seized most of the editors of world anthologies, who continue to produce textbooks that would take a lifetime to master. So intent are these editors on producing something that is all things to all people or that won't offend any interest group that the anthologies are ridiculously long. *The Norton Anthology of World Masterpieces: Expanded Edition in One Volume* runs 3052 pages. Most Bibles, Old and New Testaments combined, don't run even half that long. Somehow we've got to stop worrying so much about offending others and think in terms of what is pedagogically possible for the teacher and financially manageable for the student!

We also need to recognize that good standards alone cannot assure the public of freshmen prepared for authentic college-level courses, especially if partisan race-gender-class theorists or others with political rather than literary agendas seek to circumvent them. Sadly, good standards can be circumvented in many ways. In some cases, the principle of local control has been invoked in an effort to thwart the development of any standards at all. In other cases, arguments have been manufactured to undermine those that already exist. In some states, committees are already at work to determine if the literature now read in the schools meets affirmative action criteria.

At the 1998 annual meeting of the National Council of Teachers of English, for example, I served on a panel where representatives of the Oakland, California, school system spoke of reviewing literary works to see if they met such criteria as diversity, ethnicity, sexual orientation, or disability.[7] While on the surface these nonliterary, nonaesthetic criteria seem innocuous enough, what exactly do they mean? Would a novelist like Cervantes fulfill one of the categories because he had a maimed hand and hence was disabled? Would Melville, in contrast, be excluded because he was a healthy heterosexual white male? And would much of pre-1970 literature be excluded because depictions of women, African-Americans, and others might show them in roles that were no longer considered acceptable or might not show them in the wide range of roles such individuals can enjoy and assume today? Already there are those who say *Huckleberry Finn* should not be taught because this realistic novel uses the word "nigger," a standard term in the pre-Civil War Period. Even a love story like the story of Ruth in the Bible is reduced to a tale of pimping and female degradation in the hands of some feminist critics. The past is not the present, and, as John Ellis has said, "Instead of learning from the past, [some critics] denounce it for not being the present."[8]

If we are to educate our young people for adult life as well as college (if they seek further education), we must rid ourselves of the immature desire for utter perfection that drives us to despise our own culture rather than to recognize it not only for its faults but also for its excellences and to build upon those. One way to do that is through the design and implementation of strong and specific reading standards by the local or state community.

Notes

[1] Ellis, J. *Literature Lost: Social Agendas and the Corruption of the Humanities*. New Haven, CT: *Yale University Press,* 1997.

[2] Stotsky, S. *State English Standards: An Appraisal of English Language-Arts/ Reading Standards in 28 States* (Washington, D.C.: Thomas B. Fordham Foundation, July 1997), p.1.

[3] ALSC Newsletter, Vol. 2, No. 4. (Fall 1996), p.6.

[4] Vol. 3, No. 4.

[5] Wachlin. M.G. The Place of Bible Literature in Public High School Classes. *Research in the Teaching of English,* Vol. 31, No. 1, February 1997, 7–50.

[6] James Squire, Harvard Graduate School of Education, is quoted as saying this in a personal communication to Sandra Stotsky, December 1996, in endnote 20 of *The Commonwealth of Massachusetts Department of Education English Language Arts Curriculum Framework,* 1997 (http://info. doe.mass.edu).

[7] The panel, "Literature, The Heart of a Language Arts Curriculum: Is There a Place for a National Canon?," was held on November 20, 1998, in Nashville, Tennessee.

[8] Ellis, p. 207.

II.

The Influence of Federal Purse Strings

Chapter 12

Lessons from the Sputnik-Era Curriculum Reform Movement
The Institutions We Need for Educational Reform

Mary Campbell Gallagher
New York City

In scattered universities at the middle of this century, in the gloom of the Cold War, a few of America's leading scientists, mathematicians, scholars, and educators began what was to become a brilliant national movement to reform American science and mathematics education. The curriculum projects they founded prospered and multiplied, ultimately receiving millions of dollars in federal and foundation support, producing scores of textbooks, films, and teaching aids, spreading across the curriculum to English and other subjects, and in time reaching hundreds of thousands of students, in the majority of America's schools. And then, having blazed into glory, just as abruptly, Curriculum Reform fell from sight. Curriculum Reform lives principally now in the memories of the surviving Curriculum Reformers, and I am one.

Glowing embers of the movement do nonetheless survive. Of the dozens of high school science and mathematics textbooks that the projects published in the 1950s and 1960s, three in fact remain in print. One is the physics textbook from the Physical Sciences Study Committee (PSSC), and two are biology textbooks from the Biological Sciences Curriculum Study (BSCS). Supplementary books, films, and other teacher aids also survive.[1] The Biological Sciences Curriculum Study, one of the many groups of scientists, writers, and teachers developing curricula in the 1950s and 1960s, operates with a growing staff today, in Colorado.[2]

Some say it was the naiveté of the Curriculum Reformers themselves, some that it was the perfidy of the educational establishment, and others, that America's untrained classroom teachers brought the movement down. I believe that we Curriculum Reformers were so certain of our scientific and pedagogical theories, and so confident of continuing support from the government, that we failed to correct our politically untenable situation. Our certainty was all the more dangerous because we lacked a way into the heart of American educational politics. That heart is not in Congress or the national research universities, but in the states and towns of this country. Events were to prove that it was not enough for brilliant men to be theoretically right.[3] Curriculum Reform teaches us that to transform America's schools, a revolution needs to hold onto its gains by erecting permanent institutions in the core and sinew of American education. Most important, it must establish new teacher training schools.

Remarkably little has even been written about Curriculum Reform over these past twenty-five years. Many of the founders of Curriculum Reform in the 1940s, 1950s, and 1960s have scattered or have passed away, and almost all of the seventy-some textbook publishers in existence in 1960 have merged into oblivion. When I speak here of Curriculum Reform, accordingly, I speak of the principles of the movement, of the projects I knew first-hand, and of those projects in mathematics and the sciences that I can best document. Ralph Raimi, professor of mathematics emeritus at the University of Rochester, is now tracing the history of the Curriculum Reform mathematics programs, sometimes called the New Math. Jamey Cohen-Cole, a doctoral student at Princeton, is studying the political causes of Curriculum Reform's loss of support in Congress in the 1970s. These histories will perform a great service. In the meantime, for a historical treatment of the era that includes Curriculum Reform, one may consult Jack S. Goldstein's excellent biography of the physicist Jerrold R. Zacharias, a prime mover of Curriculum Reform, *A Different Sort of Time: The Life of Jerrold R. Zacharias, Scientist, Engineer, Educator*.[4] A good short critical account of the rise and fall of Curriculum Reform appears in Diane Ravitch's history of postwar education, *The Troubled Crusade: American Education 1945–1980*.[5] I interpret both the eclipse of Curriculum Reform and its present status somewhat differently from Dr. Ravitch, as will appear below.

I am interested here less in history for the sake of history, however, than in suggesting some of the lessons that those in the state standards movement can learn about the politics of American education from the

Lessons from the Sputnik-Era Curriculum Reform Movement

experience of the scientists and scholars who led Curriculum Reform. I have been most fortunate in interviewing some of the surviving leaders of Curriculum Reform for this essay.

Origins of the Curriculum Reform Movement

The Curriculum Reform movement began in the 1940s and 1950s. Disgusted with the dull and inaccurate lessons in commercial school textbooks in science and mathematics, a handful of scientists, mathematicians, and educators in scattered universities from Oregon to Massachusetts undertook a kind of writing that university faculty rarely attempt: writing new precollege curricula. These earliest pioneers, whether educators or scientists, were men of extraordinary energy and enterprise. They wanted to give precollege students the opportunity to experience real science. Students would learn science and mathematics through experiment and discovery, just as working scientists do.

Possibly the first of all of the Curriculum Reformers was David Page, founder of the University of Illinois Arithmetic Project at the College of Education of the University of Illinois in Urbana. "The University of Illinois Arithmetic Project was sort of the first step, it pre-dated everything," Arthur Singer told me. Singer, who spoke with me very generously and at length, is now a consultant to the Sloan Foundation. He worked at MIT, became President of the non-profit organization spun out of MIT to handle PSCC in the 1960s, and then served as Vice President of the Sloan Foundation. He speaks from personal knowledge of every one of the founders of the movement. Page, he said, was "a genius," a man whose classroom teaching of small children could not be duplicated.[6] Max Beberman, whom I knew myself, was an ebullient educator who founded the University of Illinois Committee on School Mathematics (UICSM), in Urbana. As early as 1952–53, with a grant from the University of Illinois and support from the Carnegie Corporation, Beberman and his staff were testing their first mathematics textbook in University High School.[7]

Some of the founders of the Curriculum Reform movement were scientists. Preeminent among them was Jerrold Zacharias of MIT, who had worked on the Manhattan Project at Los Alamos and had designed the first atomic clock and who, along with James R. Killian, Jr., spearheaded the effort for federal support for science education.[8] With Francis Friedman of MIT and other colleagues, and with initial support from MIT, Zacharias founded the Physical Sciences Study Committee (PSSC) in 1956. Almost immediately, PSSC received a grant from the National Science Foundation, which was supplemented by funds from the Sloan and Ford Foundations.[9] Friedman, according to Martin Mayer's 1961 study of American education *The Schools*, was largely responsible for the organization of the PSSC course and "worked miracles in forcing the use of Socratic techniques to teach the material."[10]

I spoke with MIT professor of physics emeritus Philip Morrison, one of the PSSC founders, in a high-spirited joint interview with his wife Phylis Morrison, a teacher who moved from New Jersey to Cambridge to author supplementary books for PSSC.[11] Singer had told me that Philip Morrison had also been "the father of Elementary Science Study," a science program for grade school students, with "ingenious" materials. "What Zach had done was think of all his friends who had some energy," said Philip Morrison, who was brought into the project by a colleague at Cornell, and who then spent so much time working on PSSC at Cornell and MIT that eventually he simply moved to Cambridge.[12] PSSC began to develop materials rapidly.

Then, in an event that shook the nation's faith in American science and technology, on October 4, 1957, the Russians launched the first artificial earth satellite, dubbed Sputnik. Sputnik beeped its way across the sky, a plain symbol to Americans of losing the Cold War. Suddenly, mathematical and scientific education became not just objects of public criticism, but subjects of an urgent national crusade. In a special address to Congress on January 27, 1958, President Eisenhower argued for extraordinary legislation to support a five-fold increase in the education activities of the National Science Foundation (NSF), as well as expanded programs through the Department of Health, Education, and Welfare.[13] Scientists and defense experts also urged immediate action, and within a few months Congress passed the largest grant of federal aid to education, including precollege education, in American history, called the National Defense Education Act (NDEA). The NDEA addressed public concern about federal funding frontally, declaring by its terms that there would be no federal control of education.[14]

The NDEA provided student loans; allotments to the states for matching grants for the purchase of school equipment; graduate fellowships; grants to the states for testing, guidance, and counseling to encourage students to attend college; language centers in colleges and universities; language institutes for teachers; and research and development of audiovisual techniques for teaching. Two years of my own study toward a Ph.D. in linguistics were funded by the NDEA. Congress continued to fund the NDEA until 1975.

How had supporters of federal funding for science programs won the President and Congress over? From *Brainpower for the Cold War: The Sputnik Crisis and National Defense Education Act of 1958*, Barbara Clowse's detailed legislative history of the NDEA, it is clear, first, that supporters had one overwhelming argument in favor of urgency, namely, the Cold War; and second, that they effectively marshaled the support of such respected national authorities as Admiral Hyman Rickover, who had long been speaking out for higher educational standards.[15] The National Defense Education Act was thus in every sense national legislation.

A flood of federal support spurted in the millions of dollars through NSF and other agencies, and flowed into increasing numbers of curriculum development projects around the United States. Founded in 1950, NSF was by then already underwriting both the fledgling PSSC at MIT and summer institutes for high school science teachers. Now came numbers of projects, designed by men at the highest levels of the sciences. NSF appropriations for education went from $19.5 million in 1958 to $62.0 million in 1959.[16] In 1968, the year of its highest expenditures, the NSF spent $12,242,921 on curriculum development.[17]

The early years of Curriculum Reform sizzled with small national meetings, as here leading physicists, there leading chemists, debated with excitement how they might best teach high school students the sciences and mathematics. The most important meeting by far was that at Woods Hole, Massachusetts, in September of 1959, at a time when there were still only a few curriculum projects scattered over the university landscape. This extraordinary conclave of thirty-three men and one woman, the psychologist Bärbel Inhelder, included scientists, mathematicians, historians, educators, psychologists, and filmmakers. They assembled for ten days in a little Cape Cod town otherwise best known for a national oceanographic institute and for the terminus of the ferry to Martha's Vineyard.

The conference was called by the National Academy of Sciences, with support from the National Science Foundation, the U.S. Office of Education, the Air Force, and the Rand Corporation, in consultation with the American Academy for the Advancement of Science and the Carnegie Corporation.[18] The participants included the leader or his deputy from many of the pioneering curriculum projects, and it began with reports on those projects. Each project head was a scientific and educational entrepreneur and founder in his own right, including David Page, founder of the University of Illinois Arithmetic Project in Urbana, Edward Begle of Yale, founder of the School Mathematics Study Group, which was to become the dominant mathematics program for the secondary schools, and Jerrold Zacharias, founder of PSSC. Herbert E. Vaughn of Urbana was there representing the group that Max Beberman had founded, the University of Illinois Committee on School Mathematics.[19] These and other leaders of Curriculum Reform had come to Woods Hole to hammer out a unified shape for their movement.

I must emphasize that while the Curriculum Reform movement benefited from national interest in keeping up with Russia's scientists, the Reformers themselves believed so passionately in their subjects that they wanted to teach *all* students, not just aspiring scientists and mathematicians. Phylis Morrison told me, "A thing that we saw again and again, not only in the Elementary Science Study work and in Africa, where we worked, is that if you treat science as an open-ended exploration, *all* the students" learn science.[20]

We can find no better starting point for studying Curriculum Reform than the account of the Woods Hole conference written by its chairman, Jerome S. Bruner, a cognitive psychologist from Harvard University. Based on the reports of the conference's five work groups, as refined through subsequent comment and criticism from the conferees and others, *The Process of Education* explodes with the excitement of the Woods Hole conference.[21]

The Process of Education stated three principles of Curriculum Reform. First, school programs should teach the intellectual *structure* of each field. Second, they should do so in accordance with the guidance of the most gifted scientists. Third, classroom lessons should provide for students to make *discoveries*, just the way scientists do. Most Curriculum Reformers had little patience with the old teaching methods in the sciences in which the teacher states a rule, explains it, and illustrates it with an experiment. They believed that students should form and test their own hypotheses. The fundamental principle of Curriculum Reform, however, was the primacy of the intellectual structure of each discipline. Accordingly, Bruner wrote, "We begin with the hypothesis that any subject can be taught effectively in some intellectually honest form to any child at any stage of development."[22] With its clear-eyed faith that every basic field has an intelligible structure, its confidence in children's intellectual abilities, and its clarion call for educational excellence, *The Process of Education* stirred the American public and opened before the reformers an ambitious high road to a great and historic national achievement. The book is still in print today.

Since the Curriculum Reformers' second principle was that the most gifted scientists should lead curriculum projects, it was all but mandatory that Nobel laureates should direct curricula for high school students, and indeed at least one did so. *The Process of Education* said that the "best minds in any particular discipline must be put to work on the task" of designing a curriculum that is true to the underlying structure of its subject matter. Thus, the School Mathematics Study Group (SMSG), the University of Illinois mathematics projects, the Physical Science Study Committee (PSSC), and the Biological Sciences Curriculum Study (BSCS) had already been "enlisting the aid of eminent men in their various fields," by means of summer projects, "supplemented in part by year-long leaves of absence for certain key people involved."[23] Further, to "decide that the elementary ideas of algebra depend upon the fundamentals of the commutative, distributive and associative laws, one must be a mathematician in a position to appreciate and understand the fundamentals of mathematics..." In general, only "by the use of our best minds in devising curricula will we bring the fruits of scholarship and wisdom to the student just beginning his studies."[24] "It was the *best* people in the universities," emphasized Singer. That was the key to success.[25] Bruner has told me, too, that the most eminent scholars were positively eager to help with Curriculum Reform, and that often all they wanted in return was one of his wife's home-cooked meals.[26]

The history of the CHEM Study Program, which began in a June 1957 conference sponsored by the American Chemical Society (ACS) and the Crown-Zellerbach Foundation, illustrates the Curriculum Reformers' principle that the best scientists should head curriculum projects. By the fall of 1959, a preliminary committee of college and high school chemistry teachers had attained NSF support and was looking for the leadership of a person of Nobel laureate stature in chemistry. It follows from the second Curriculum Reform principle stated in *The Process of Education* that ACS and NSF sought out Glenn T. Seaborg, a Nobel laureate at the University of California at Berkeley. The Curriculum Reformers' vision of education was so great that Professor Seaborg agreed to head CHEM study.[27]

Finally, according to the third principle supported by many if not all Curriculum Reformers, students should learn by *discovery*, by asking questions, not just by being told the rules. For chemistry that meant helping the high school student to *discover* the structure of chemistry, the way a scientist does.[28] Bruner reported that the "central conviction" of the Woods Hole meeting was that "intellectual activity anywhere is the same, whether at the frontier of knowledge" or in a grade school classroom:

> What a scientist does at his desk or in his laboratory, what a literary critic does in reading a poem, are of the same order as what anybody else does when he is engaged in like activities—if he is to achieve understanding. The difference is in degree, not in kind. The schoolboy learning physics *is* a physicist, and it is easier for him to learn physics behaving like a physicist than doing something else...[29]

I must emphasize that such discovery teaching occurred within the rigorous structure of the scientific or mathematical discipline. Many pioneers of Curriculum Reform believed in students' making discoveries, yet their theories had little else in common with the theories of John Dewey, at least in "progressive" schools. For Curriculum Reformers students' discoveries had to arise out of and occur within the framework of scientific knowledge. Thus, *The Process of Education* stated that the effectiveness of a "good intuiter" must rest upon "a solid knowledge of the subject," which "gives intuition something to work with."[30]

Because the Curriculum Reformers aimed to teach students that science is an *activity,* not a body of facts, discovery teaching was a hallmark of many of the curricula within the movement. In his preface to the first edition of PSSC *Physics*, James R. Killian, Jr., said, "The textbook is the heart of the PSSC course, in which physics is presented *not as a mere body of facts* but basically as a *continuing process by which men seek to understand the nature of the physical world...*" (emphasis added).[31] This was a departure from traditional practice. Speaking of UICSM mathematics, Max Beberman said in his 1958 Inglis Lecture at Harvard that the key was a discovery process.[32] Teachers were to lecture very little. Precollege students were to learn mathematics and science largely from formulating hypotheses and doing experiments, like researchers. Philip Morrison said, "The most remarkable thing in science and mathematics is that the good students don't come to the end of what they can learn."[33]

While many Curriculum Reform projects emphasized students' doing experiments and making their own discoveries, there were nonetheless differences in method. Typically, it seems to me, the UICSM mathematics materials and the other projects that came out of Illinois asked students to figure out puzzles, and *then* to verbalize the mathematical theory that their solutions brought out. Virtually every lesson plan was a discovery lesson plan. Discovery was almost a talisman. Others may take issue with me, but the PSSC *Physics* text, by contrast, seems to me to provide students with a great deal of physics theory first, and only then to suggest experiments and questions for further thought.[34] In any event, I think that both approaches teach the student that science is an *activity,* not a set of facts. Neither approach is the traditional method in which the teacher first states a rule and then illustrates it with experimental demonstrations.

Following the example of the sciences and mathematics, in the early 1960s, English, too, became the New English. The Curriculum Reform principles enunciated in *The Process of Education* were now applied to English. First, curricula in English must teach the *structure* of each field. Second, they should do so in accordance with the guidance of the most gifted leaders. Third, classroom lessons should be set up so that students would make *discoveries.* Particularly under the federally-funded Project English, numerous projects arose under the leadership of university scholars, and many published their own series of textbooks, which were offered to commercial publishers. Some of of those projects included linguistics, the scientific study of language.[35] There was one group at Indiana University, whose textbooks were commercially published,[36] one at Carnegie Mellon,[37] another at the University of Oregon,[38] one at Hunter College,[39] and one at the University of Nebraska.[40]

The Oregon project was directed by Albert Kitzhaber, and it included work in linguistics led by Wayne A. O'Neil, now the chairman of the Department of Linguistics and Philosophy at MIT. O'Neil proposed a language curriculum featuring transformational grammar and "not only developed the theoretical framework underlying the original version but trained the first pilot teachers in transformational grammar..." He was co-author of the original seventh and eighth grade textbooks from the Oregon project.[41] O'Neil, who kindly sent me his impressions by e-mail, has written a good deal about scientific study of language in the schools, and he spoke at the Linguistic Society of America annual meeting in Los Angeles, in January of 1999, about the Oregon project.[42] Other projects with foundation, state, or university funding, such as the English project at the University of Illinois, where I worked, also produced textbooks.[43] Let me note that, having worked in an English project with excellent lessons in literature, a number of which I wrote myself, I still do not entirely understand the differences between the Curriculum Reform methods suited to literature and those suited to the sciences, including linguistics. That issue is beyond the scope of this paper.

I arrived at the University of Illinois in Urbana to work as a curriculum writer in the English project in the summer of 1963, with three years of public school English teaching behind me, the master's in education that I had needed to qualify for a New York State teaching credential, a Barnard degree in philosophy, and graduate work in English. The English project was headquartered in a small grey house next to the academic Gothic bulk of University High School, the principal laboratory for UICSM and the other University of Illinois high school projects. As director of the English project, a project for gifted students, the state had chosen Professor James M. McCrimmon, author of the widely-used *Writing with a Purpose*. McCrimmon was an extraordinary teacher, and a man wise in the politics of both the university and the National Council of Teachers of English, headquartered in Urbana's twin city, Champaign.

Urbana was not only the birthplace of Curriculum Reform but was at that time the home, to name only a few of the energetic people involved in the movement there, of four of the Woods Hole conferees, David Page, founder of the University of Illinois Arithmetic Project, which had been the first Curriculum Reform project; Herbert G. Vaughn, professor of mathematics in the university and chief mathematician in Beberman's group, the University of Illinois Committee on School Mathematics; the psychologist Lee Cronbach; and, finally, the physicist Gilbert Finlay, who was head of the team assessing feedback from teachers who used the PSSC physics materials.[44] The Woods Hole conference had also been shown a demonstration film by Richard Suchman of the Illinois Studies in Inquiry Training, "dealing with how children may be educated to the formulation of searching questions."[45] The faculty of the College of Education also included Carl Bereiter and his colleague Siegfried Engelmann, that perennial iconoclast, who has since gone on to bedevil the education establishment on the West Coast, opposing "whole math."[46] The times were full of hope and energy, and we had a lot of fun.

Here is an example of discovery pedagogy in English, in a classroom lesson in rhetoric that McCrimmon devised for the University of Illinois Curriculum Laboratory series *Rhetoric in Thought and Writing*.[47] The object of these lessons is to persuade students that they must use specific facts and examples when they write. In one lesson, one student stands at the rear of the room, with his back to the class. He describes a diagram that he is holding in his hand, so that another student standing at the blackboard, and the rest of the class at their seats, can reproduce it from his description. Each day for several days, as different students take turns at the back of the room, the diagram becomes progressively more complicated. The next lesson in the same series asks students to read an adventure story, to decide where there are insufficient details, and to re-write those passages, adding the needed detail.

Exceptional as McCrimmon was, nonetheless, by every standard, from creativity to force of personality to grantsmanship, Beberman, his project, UICSM, and UICSM's highly developed theories about discovery pedagogy, dominated University High. Beberman was not only a leader but a critic of Curriculum Reform, and the personification of the high spirits of the movement. I can still see him leaning back in his desk chair in his shirtsleeves, gesturing broadly and pontificating with the greatest good-humor on the seemingly ineradicable follies of the schools.

According to Beberman, to take a brief example of his discovery-oriented discussion of the teaching of mathematics, the UICSM contention is that the algorithms for manipulation and simplification of algebraic expressions should be invented by students. They are "merely short cuts in applying basic principles":

> Consider, as an example, the expression "$3x + 5x$". After just a very few replacements of the "x's" by numerals, the student is ready to conjecture that "$8x$" is equivalent to the given expression... So he demonstrates the equivalence of the two expressions by deriving the simpler one from the given one as follows:

> By the commutative principle for multiplication, for every x, $3x + 5x = x3 + x5$. And, by the distributive principle, for every x, $x3 + x5 = x(3 + 5)$. Again, by the commutative principle, for every x, $x(3 + 5) = (3 + 5)x$, or $8x$. So, for every x, $3x + 5x = 8x$.

> Our students are urged to invent whatever procedures they can to arrive at simpler expressions as efficiently as possible... [However, the] close ties maintained between the manipulation of expressions and the basic principles do not enable us to eliminate drill in manipulation...[48]

Similarly, all three BSCS biology curricula emphasized that science is an *activity*. Each student text stresses asking questions. As with the PSSC materials in physics, the BSSC teacher's materials suggest classroom activities that will show students the importance of solving these puzzles, as puzzles, not as facts. Each curriculum also includes laboratory activities: students learn by experience the importance of observation and measurement as they perform experiments to test and confirm hypotheses.

In the first edition of the BSCS "Blue Version," called *Molecules to Man*, the opening chapter, "Science as Inquiry," starts by asking "What is science?" It continues:

> Is it a body of factual information? Is it a set of theories? Is it an activity or set of procedures for finding facts and developing theories?

It goes on to say that "science is really a combination of all three of these." This book, however, "will emphasize the activity of science."[49]

This opening chapter describes coral atolls, providing abundant photographic illustrations, and asks how best to account for them. Coral atolls are usually ring-shaped. Each one contains a lagoon. As the student text and the *Teacher's Guide* explain, Darwin's hypothesis was that (1) a volcanic mountain emerged from the surface of the ocean, (2) coral animals became attached to the sides of the mountain at the ocean's surface and coral rock began to accumulate; and (3) the mountain then sank, while the coral went on accumulating. Darwin's hypothesis takes into account the fact that living coral exists only near the surface of the ocean. To account for that fact, Darwin had to add to his original hypothesis the idea that the mountain had been above the ocean's surface and had then gradually sunk beneath the surface.[50] Darwin's hypothesis enabled him to predict that these islands rested on a base of volcanic rock. Later testing confirmed this prediction, which provided support for his hypothesis. However, the confirming experiment revealed new facts that had to be incorporated into the thinking about the coral atolls.[51] The student text also presents, and provides illustrations for, the competing hypotheses to account for coral atolls, the glacier hypothesis, the crater hypothesis, and the coral pile hypothsis, each hypothesis accounting for a different set of facts, and each one making different predictions. Students thus see how scientists make predictions, how they test hypotheses by experiments, and how scientists must adjust their hypotheses to account for new facts. The laboratory exercises that accompany this part of the course teach careful measurement and observation.

Pilot Schools and Program Evaluation

The Curriculum Reform projects typically produced curriculum materials that were then tested in pilot schools, revised by project staff, and re-tested. It was necessary to test out Curriculum Reform lessons in the classroom to make sure they worked. Most Curriculum Reform projects not only cooperated with teachers in the schools who wanted to try the curricula, they also hired teams of teachers and technicians to write curriculum materials, to revise the materials, and to supplement the materials with apparatus and films. Classroom teachers reported back on their success using the draft materials. Beberman wrote of how UICSM used the responses from the teachers who taught from UICSM materials:

> We are continually apprised of the success of our efforts as a result of our close communication with the classes in our pilot schools. The weekly reports from participating teachers, the regional training conferences, the results of our testing program, and the detailed reports made by our teacher coordinators, who visit the pilot schools, all serve as sources of information on which to base revisions.[52]

The accounts that Paul E. Marsh gives of the development of PSSC are examples of first-class educational scholarship. Not only was this sequence of trying out and revising the lessons scientific but, as Marsh notes, it was also key to demonstrating the educational feasibility of the project materials to the funding sources.[53]

A large Curriculum Reform project might employ dozens of scientists, teachers, filmmakers, and writers, work with hundreds of classroom teachers in several states, and bring fifty or more writers and scholars together in the summer to revise teaching materials in the light of feedback from the classroom teachers who had used the materials during the school year. More than a hundred high school and university teachers took part in writing the experimental forms of the ecology version of the Biological Sciences Curriculum Study course in 1960 and 1961. A team of six scholars and teachers then produced the book.[54] According to the BSCS, over a thousand teachers and 150,000 students in 35 states and the District of Columbia had worked with the experimental materials to determine if their emphasis was relevant and if they could be "comprehended by the average American tenth grade student."[55]

While the lessons were being tested, many projects made great efforts to help teachers teach the discovery lesson plans. Even as they were revising the lessons, the projects continued to give participating teachers assistance. Some, most prominently PSSC, had been actively involved in the work of retraining teachers from the beginning.[56] In fact, the spread of PSSC was related to, although not identical with, teacher participation in NSF-sponsored summer institutes in physics.[57] Similarly, almost half of the nation's high school teachers of mathematics attended at least one mathematics institute during the 12-year life of SMSG...[58] Some projects also offered demonstration classes in designated demonstration centers.

All of the projects prepared heavily-annotated teacher's editions of their textbooks. At the English project in Urbana, we writers wrote many hundreds of pages of teacher scripts, showing the teacher what questions to ask about a poem or play or novel, and what the students might say in response. We knew that most teachers would have trouble adjusting to discovery teaching, particularly as few teachers had good preparation in the subjects they taught. For example, according to a 1964 report by NCTE, only half of the teachers of English in 1960 had majored in English.[59]

We had other activities that I think are typical of what the various projects did to assist teachers. We gave demonstration classes for teachers at University High in Urbana, and we ran demonstration centers around the state. We spoke at NCTE's annual meetings. We wrote articles. I made a demonstration movie, sponsored by the Department of Health, Education, and Welfare, showing our teaching techniques. The NDEA eventually sponsored summer institutes for English teachers modeled on NSF-sponsored science and mathematics institutes. These English institutes trained 18,000 teachers over the course of four years.[60] As part of one such institute at the University of Illinois, I taught a demonstration class of eighth graders in front of the assembled teachers. I also obtained funding from the university and produced a series of demonstration classroom videotapes, at the request of the instructor in the first course for prospective English teachers in the College of Education. This was unusual. I wish that we had been able to focus more of our efforts on teacher training.

By all of these devices, the Curriculum Reform projects reached hundreds of thousands of students. In the five years between 1960 and 1965, the PSSC Physics course was taught by 6,000 teachers, to 640,000 students.[61] In May of 1970, 47 percent of the students who took the College Board Achievement Test in Biology had taken a course of the Biological Sciences Curriculum Study (BSCS).[62] In the 1976–77 school year, almost 60 percent of all school districts were using one or more of the federally-funded science programs in grades 7 through 12, 40 percent were using more than one, and even in the elementary grades about 30 percent of the districts reported using at least one of the NSF science curricula.[63] David Ridgeway, one of the founders of Chem Study, told me that Chem Study materials were translated into thirty-three different languages.[64] The nation ultimately invested more than a billion federal dollars, and millions more from foundations and universities, in curriculum reform and in training institutes for K–12 teachers.[65]

Thus, the Curriculum Reform projects tested and corrected their teaching materials and reached ever increasing numbers of teachers and students. Other than among those classroom teachers across the country who embraced these new curricula, however, the movement's support was almost exclusively in the universities and the national government.

Curriculum Reform and the Political Structure of Education

Before reflecting on the Curriculum Reform movement's decline, I think it appropriate to pause for a moment, to show respect for that movement, and to attempt to learn from its spectacular successes, both political and educational. It is a great tribute to the national leaders of the movement, including especially Jerrold Zacharias, that the nation was ever moved to invest so heavily in precollege education and that Congress was moved to enact the National Defense Education Act in 1958, in view of the longstanding American adherence to local control of education, and longstanding American concern about federal control. It is a great tribute to the university community that so many talented scholars eagerly took leaves from their own research careers in order to help shape precollege curricula.

How did the projects actually get the word out to the teachers and the schools? How were the projects related to the political structure of American education? The answer is not that these projects attached themselves to some sort of hierarchical structure, for example, one through which they could direct state superintendents of education to impose Curriculum Reform materials on the schools. Instead, NSF got the word out. The Curriculum Reform projects worked mainly through scholarly and scientific channels, and only worked with local school districts when invited, however they may themselves have provoked the invitations.[66] This was for two reasons. First, the federally-funded projects were expressly forbidden to try to control education in the states. Second, as anyone who has taught in a public secondary school knows, local teachers generally have a great deal to say about shaping their own curricula, within the constraints of local custom and the available textbooks. What other school districts in the area are doing is usually more influential than what the state says. Except in New York, where the Regents examinations do determine certain public school curricula, teachers are not usually tightly constrained by state departments of education.

How do the Curriculum Reform projects fit with the political structure of American education? I think that in fact every project fit in a slightly different way. For the sake of providing a general scheme, however, as well as disabusing the reader of any lingering sense that Curriculum Reform must have employed the power of the state bureaucracy, I offer the flowchart in Figure 1, prepared by researchers at the Rand Corporation in 1975.[67] Although this flowchart is imperfect, it does illustrate key facts about the Curriculum Reform materials: that they were created by projects that worked with the schools with constant testing, and that the preliminary versions of the texts went straight from the universities into schools. They did not first pass through the teachers colleges or publishers or, in most cases, the state boards of education.

Let me list here two of the criticisms of Curriculum Reform in its prime years. Each criticism strikes at the attachment of the Curriculum Reform movement to some particular part of the political structure of American education. First, even within the movement, some critics argued that these programs failed to teach basic skills. This criticism weakened the attraction of Curriculum Reform among parents, in particular. Insofar as this was correct, this criticism is pointed to the theoretical, not practical, bias in curriculum reform.

Lessons from the Sputnik-Era Curriculum Reform Movement

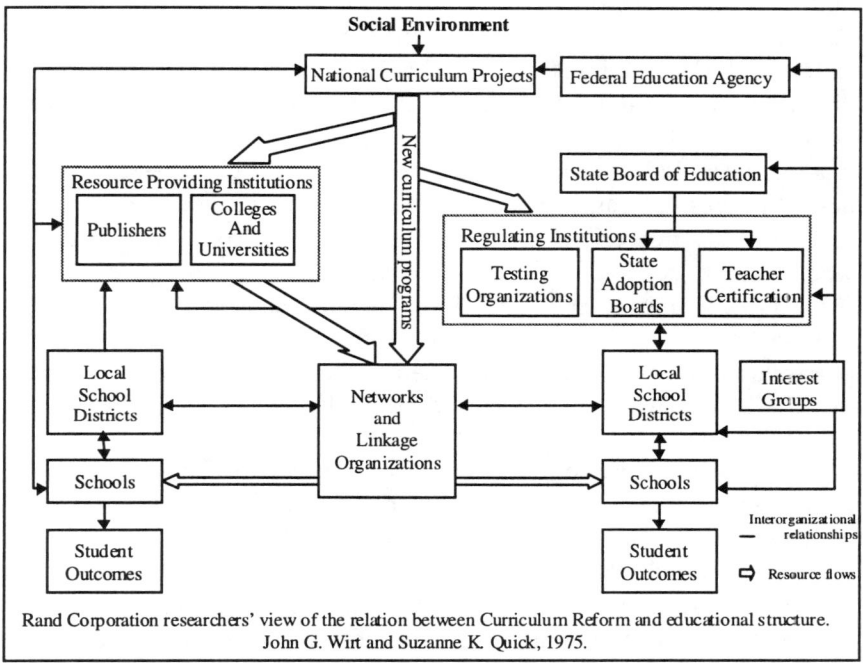

Rand Corporation researchers' view of the relation between Curriculum Reform and educational structure.
John G. Wirt and Suzanne K. Quick, 1975.

Figure 1

Critics of the New Math complained that students knew set theory but they no longer knew how to add and subtract.[68] Beberman himself made this criticism, saying that experimental materials had been introduced into schools too quickly, and that this was unfair to children who would need simple arithmetical skills. To illustrate this point he told a story about an experiment he had conducted in a second-grade class in Urbana. The story was so typical of Beberman that *The New York Times* included it in his obituary in 1971. About 200 children, in their first day in the second grade, were asked to add 19 and 3. Not one had the answer. Many answered "112," using the New Math concept of "9 plus 3 is 12, carry 1, and bring down 1." Then each was asked how many cookies he would have if he had 19 and was given 3 more. Nearly all replied: "22."[69]

The "back to basics" movement seized on this weakness in criticizing the Curriculum Reform programs. According to Ralph Raimi, Tom Lehrer's 1965 song titled "New Math," which lampooned "the pretentious language used to justify an inability to calculate," had the mathematical community itself laughing at the new mathematics education.[70] My University High School colleague Charlene Tibbets told me that parents started complaining that the English programs were not giving their children enough facts.[71] Beberman once said, "We're treating these kids as though they were little researchers—and they're not."[72] Enthusiastic as Bruner continued to be about discovery teaching, in a 1965 paper describing discovery lessons in the social studies project whose grade school units he directed, "Man, a Course of Study" (MACOS), Bruner said he had doubts about discovery as the *principal* vehicle of education. It is, he said, "the most inefficient technique possible for regaining what has been gathered over a long period of time."[73] In this he echoed what the UICSM representatives had said at the Woods Hole Conference in 1959.[74]

Thus, where Curriculum Reform projects made discovery teaching their linchpin, teachers' criticisms of discovery teaching weakened the already fragile links between Curriculum Reform and classroom teachers. Second, the key obstacle for Curriculum Reform was the weakness of American teacher training. Curriculum Reform came out of the most rigorous and demanding of scientific and mathematical disciplines. When Curriculum Reformers talked about discovery teaching, it was discovery within those rigorous disciplines, discovery that employed the knowledge and techniques appropriate to those disciplines, in a sophisticated way. While some public school teachers were outstanding, however, most teachers knew little about the subjects they taught.

The teacher training institutes sponsored by NSF and other government agencies did give teachers a better grip on the subject matter and improved their chances of teaching the materials well. This was in part because many institutes walked the teachers through the project materials, giving them exactly the science they would need in order to teach the precollege lessons in the project materials. I can testify both from my own experience and from observation that such training is completely different from what passes for teacher training in the schools of education. "Conventional teacher training in the United States," as Martin Mayer observed in 1963, "has virtually no point of contact with this procedure." Unlike NSF summer institutes in physics, for example, which taught teachers physics, courses in schools of education are usually highly generalized and abstract. They are seldom if ever based on the specific textbooks, materials, and experiments that teachers will teach. Nor do they teach exactly the science or other subject matter that the teachers will need to know in order to teach their high school or grade school courses.

Nor, despite wide adoption of the Curriculum Reform programs in the schools, did professors of education ever teach their students to conduct discovery lessons. Diane Ravitch asserts that "the lack of involvement of teacher educators undoubtedly slowed the absorption of the new materials by those who trained new teachers..."[75] This is undoubtedly true, and we Curriculum Reformers should have done more to involve professors of education from other universities in our Curriculum Reform projects. I do not know how effective it could have been. I note from my own experience, however, that many excellent teacher educators at the University of Illinois in the early 1960s were interested in the Curriculum Reform projects there, kept abreast of our publications, occasionally sat in the back of our demonstration classrooms, and even taught discovery methods. Whoever should have taken the initiative, in any event, as Mayer noted, 1960's graduates from the teacher-training institutions "are about as ill equipped to teach the new math and science material as their predecessors [in 1950]—everybody still has to be retrained at a summer program."[76] The same remains true today. According to Michael Dougherty, until recently Associate Director of BSCS, teachers are insufficiently secure with the science they must teach for them to benefit from generalized instruction in "teaching methods." They cannot implement a generic approach to discovery teaching because they don't have the knowledge of science that discovery teaching requires. "They say, 'Give us content first, and then we'll listen to the message about not lecturing.'"[77]

If lack of subject matter knowledge fully accounted for teachers' resistance to the projects' discovery teaching methods, surely all of the training programs and manuals we wrote ought to have helped. Beberman told me, however, that the teachers often failed to use the UICSM teacher manuals and the guides that explained the mathematics. When members of our English project went out into the schools in Illinois, we sometimes discovered teachers not using discovery teaching at all, but lecturing from our textbooks. One of my colleagues found a teacher who had painstakingly *rehearsed* his students for the lesson—which proceeded flawlessly! Ignorance of subject matter does not explain this.

There were at least two other causes of the teachers' resistance to discovery pedagogy, I think. First, discovery teaching requires superior skill in classroom management and superior intellectual stamina. A teacher who asks questions instead of lecturing risks unleashing irrelevant or impertinent shouting, and risks having students ask questions he can't answer. As Jon Greenberg, now Curriculum Project Manager at BSCS, said to me, inductive teaching is intellectually much more strenuous than lecturing. "You constantly have to be intellectually engaged, trying to get the students to come along."[78]

In all, discovery teaching requires a strong teacher who is deeply knowledgeable in the discipline he is teaching, one able to follow and lead an intellectual discussion and maintain control. This almost always requires a strong principal. And a strong principal usually requires a community of supportive parents. These conditions do not always prevail. Second, given the popularity of "tell 'em and test 'em," as Beberman called it, how many teachers believed that their students should make discoveries? As Phylis Morrison said, schools are usually invested in answers, and "suggesting that questions are more important is not comfortable."[79]

Martin Mayer presented, I think, not only a fair but an insightful portrait of American education in the late 1950s in his book *The Schools*, published in 1961. Mayer generously praised the work of David Page, Jerrold Zacharias, Francis Friedman, and the other founders of Curriculum Reform projects. Of PSSC, he said, however, that the course was "less successful than many commentators seem to believe," largely because the planning of the text, the lab, and the films had taken precedence over thinking about the training of teachers. "Anyone who has visited several dozen PSSC classes across the nation," said Mayer, "knows that many of the teachers do not understand how to help their students master the course, and that some of the teachers are unconsciously sabotaging the program by comments which destroy the approach."[80]

Even without such resistance to Curriculum Reform, the Curriculum Reform movement might still have collapsed after the political ground underneath it suddenly shifted in the 1960s. Curriculum Reform was a national movement, strongest at the federal level, not in the states. The interests of the federal government turned sharply away from the Cold War and towards not only the Vietnam war but school integration and the large government programs of President Johnson's Great Society. "The

Vietnam war made a big disaffection between the campus and the Congress," Philip Morrison said.[81] When the sense of national urgency for science and mathematics teaching disappeared under the force of seemingly more urgent national concerns, and funding for education became subject to other political agendas, in any event, with it went the dominance of the National Science Foundation and the authority of even Nobel laureates to tell the nation what high school students should learn.[82] Academic excellence and intellectual rigor were no longer the rallying cries in education. Thus began the slide towards the eventual end of federal funding for the NDEA in the 1970s, a story I shall leave for others to tell.[83]

In debating adopting the NDEA in 1958, Congress had had to find a way to satisfy the American pressure for equality. Some proponents of educational reform had supported their arguments with a theory of equality under which, in the terms in which such matters were debated in the 1950s, the "brightest" students had the same right to have their talents developed as did students who were less bright.[84] Since those students had, by definition, superior academic talents, they would not enjoy *equality* unless their full talents were developed. Thus, if we were to have equality, we had to have highly demanding programs for gifted students.[85] It was also Jerome S. Bruner's argument in *The Process of Education*, the bible of Curriculum Reform, that excellence meant helping all students, including the better students, to achieve their optimal intellectual development.[86] Dr. Clowse notes dryly that this recasting of equality during the Sputnik crisis "caused many in the Congress a great deal of uneasiness" in debates about the NDEA.[87]

Jerrold Zacharias was himself among those at the highest levels of national influence during the Johnson presidency who were most concerned to improve the education of America's minorities.[88] The shift of national attention in the 1960s away from the training of mathematicians and scientists, however, weakened the public's tolerance for special attention to very able students, and for that special use of "equality" that had in part insulated the new curricula from pressures to level school curricula down. In the Curriculum Reform movement we had unashamedly written materials for gifted students: we assumed that if we set high standards, many students would rise to meet the standards. Bruner wrote in *The Process of Education*, "The top quarter of public school students, from which we must draw intellectual leadership in the next generation, is perhaps the group most neglected by our schools in the recent past..."[89] BSCS was "not for the whole market."[90] In fact, the PSSC physics text is nowadays usually used in Advanced Placement courses.[91]

At the same time that national attention was skidding away from training mathematicians and scientists, teachers who had trouble teaching their students with Curriculum Reform texts and discovery methods were deciding that their problems must arise either from the characteristics of their students or from defects in the Curriculum Reform materials. Teachers of English thus read with interest reports in professional journals, convention sessions, and books about ideas from the month-long 1966 Anglo-American Seminar on the Teaching of English, known as the Dartmouth Seminar, which was financed by the Carnegie Corporation and sponsored by NCTE, the Modern Language Association, and the National Association for the Teaching of English (United Kingdom).[92] The British participants, in particular, favored personal growth through unstructured learning, a return to a progressive, romantic, view of education.[93] "The serious English-language curriculum work of the sixties in the U.S. was eventually undone by the British and their North American sympathizers [at the] Dartmouth conference," Wayne O'Neil wrote to me in March of 1999. "The examination of language rationally, i.e., scientifically, for example, was put down by folks whose sympathies simply did not lie with rational inquiry, or worse, who did not even understand it," he said. "This was the beginning of, or return to, the idea that language study should be a developmental and not an intellectual endeavor."[94] This was also the era of "open education."[95]

In addition, the rhetorical relationship of the Curriculum Reform movement to the local schools and the parents was fragile from the start, and it weakened. Relying on a national emergency to persuade the public that educational reform is necessary suffices only so long as the emergency continues. Speaking mainly to scholars, scientists, legislatures, agencies, and experts suffices just so long as the ordinary citizen has not started asserting a new control over the local schools. Paul Marsh criticized the PSSC for not having communicated better in its early days with school principals and teachers, a failing that he says delayed or, in some places perhaps, defeated implementation of that physics program at the outset.[96] I see the defect in communication as having been more endemic, more damaging and, ultimately, as having forced the cause of more rigorous and demanding precollege schooling back into its present corner.

Perhaps our Curriculum Reform projects were particularly vulnerable because they were supported by short-term grants, and even the NDEA was originally proposed as a short-term program. Using demonstration centers, teacher manuals, and summer institutes, we kept trying and trying to retrain all teachers so that they would all understand the subject matter and be able to do discovery teaching. Perhaps we should have looked for additional ways to train teachers in the subject matter—or to recruit better-trained teachers. Perhaps in an ideal world with abundant long-term funding we should have shifted our primary focus to teacher training. Nor did we look for the social reasons for teachers' adopting or leaving Curriculum Reform programs. Paul Marsh reports that teachers succeeded with PSSC when they were in "clusters" of nearby schools using that curriculum, whether private or public.[97] The clustering of schools using the same materials in order to give teachers support may be one key to lasting curriculum reform.

Curriculum Reform was a flower of the great American universities in their post-war emergence into federally-supported national research institutions. It had national strength, but that strength was insecure because it was not balanced by strength in the states.

The Eclipse of Curriculum Reform

What, then, became of Curriculum Reform? We cannot simply shrug our shoulders and assert that somehow racial issues, the Vietnam war, political opposition to the social studies program called "Man, a Course of Study" (MACOS), and other accidents of American history determined that Curriculum Reform would disappear. That would be an evasion of responsibility. It would also be circular, albeit true, to say that Curriculum Reformers developed no adequate rhetoric with which to persuade the public that while school integration was proceeding, the education students received inside the schools ought not to suffer. Had we offered a persuasive justification for rigorous and demanding precollege education in the 1960s and 1970s, Curriculum Reform—or something equally rigorous and demanding—would not have disappeared. Obviously, we did not. In fact, although it goes beyond the scope of this paper, I think scholars still have no good way to talk to the public about demanding education in the liberal arts.

In 1980, Jerrold Zacharias castigated younger scientists for their unwillingness to continue the work of Curriculum Reform.[98] Ralph Raimi, following William Duren, blames the demise of the Curriculum Reform movement on the resurgence of the professional education bureaucracy. Of the Curriculum Reform pioneers, he writes that their "prestige was unchallenged, their genius without peer, and their pipeline of pure gold," but the "realities overwhelmed them." The "pipeline" was the funding from Washington. The "realities" were the limitations of the teachers and the limits of public patience, together with the education bureaucracy, in particular, which "was gathering its strength for the political battle that finally turned the pipeline back in their direction."[99]

I believe that however sophisticated we Curriculum Reformers were in other political spheres, for the realities of the institutional politics of American precollege education our projects were too optimistically conceived. First, we failed to create permanent institutions in the political structure of American education, particularly institutions for teacher training. Second, we made no effort to assure the future commercial viability of our books and projects. Third, we instituted no examination system or other structures that would make students accountable for learning the approaches and material in our courses.

We assumed that excellence would speak for itself, that it would be universally adopted, and, most important, that it would thereafter survive for the long term on its own merits. We were so confident of the rightness of our programs and our pedagogy that many of our Curriculum Reform projects were intentionally designed to have short institutional lifespans. The aim was not for the universities to administer precollege education, certainly not indefinitely. The aim of many projects was to direct the creation of excellent precollege curricula, with government support, so as to make them *available* to the commercial publishers and the schools, and then for the projects to fade into mere management of the materials. Those projects were, again, supported by short-term grants. The commitment of scholars, scientists, and writers was for the short term.

We Curriculum Reformers assumed either that the government would continue its support where it was needed, or that the evident merit of our materials would ultimately make government support unnecessary. Government support in the early days of Curriculum Reform not only funded the development of good materials, it also made sure that teachers heard about the materials. In today's commercial terms, that is, the original federal government support of PSSC and the other science and mathematics projects paid for both "project development" and "marketing." Today, however, as we Curriculum Reformers could never have predicted, the government does not even give special support to the Curriculum Reform textbooks that are still available.[100]

The observers I have talked with believe that the original Curriculum Reform textbooks influenced some aspects of later textbooks.[101] As was obvious from an early date, Curriculum Reform projects in science and mathematics had immediate and conspicuous effects on college teaching of those subjects. By 1970, there was a drive to alter and revise college instruction in chemistry as a result of "the requirements and pressures for change in the basic college chemistry course that CHEM Study and the Chemical Bond Approach (CBA)" had created. The other Curriculum Reform projects had similar effects on college instruction.[102]

If good curricula are to drive out bad, as we all hope, our experience in the Curriculum Reform movement shows that the contributions of scholars and scientists are necessary to make good curricula. However, scholars' intellectual authority alone does not suffice for the long term. We need excellent teacher training more than we need anything else. We need to train teachers in subject matter, and to teach them how to teach our lessons while they are still in training. We need to give inservice teachers both solid training in subject matter and the kinds of lessons they want to teach. We need to show them how to teach these lessons, and to give them day-to-day support.

We also need all of the institutional paraphernalia and permanent political structures that now support lesser programs: we need textbooks, tests, teacher certification, enthusiastic school boards and principals and parents and teachers. If my suggestions for education reform are correct, then we need to invigorate all of the agencies in the structure of American education, not only the state standards in the various subject areas, but the tests students take, the school boards running the schools, the testing boards, the training and certification of teachers, in sum, the entire political framework of American education.

Author's Note: The author gratefully acknowledges use of the Department of Special Collections, Milbank Memorial Library, Teachers College, Columbia University. Dr. William Wirt, now of the United States Department of Education and formerly lead investigator in the Rand Corporation, Santa Barbara, California, kindly gave permission to use Figure 1, which appeared originally in an unpublished manuscript prepared under his direction at the Rand Corporation in Santa Monica, California, 1975.

Very little has been written about the Curriculum Reform movement, so that the usual footnote-trail cannot be followed: few institutions of the Curriculum Reform movement remain; most of the seventy-some textbook publishers in existence in 1960 have merged into oblivion; and a number of the leaders of Curriculum Reform have passed away. My reward for following the trail even where it was faint, however, has been not only unhoped-for information and resonant evocations of the early days of Curriculum Reform, but delightful interviews with distinguished pioneers of the Curriculum Reform Movement. Their vigorous support of the Curriculum Reform objectives and their articulateness on its behalf are rebukes not only to the movement's eclipse but to the namby pamby "values" locutions of much educational palaver today. To the leaders of Curriculum Reform who kindly consented to be interviewed, I can only say that they have my gratitude, and that I know that they may disagree with me. I am particularly grateful for the assistance of Arthur Singer, now a consultant to the Sloan Foundation.

My former student Enealia S. Nau, who is both an attorney in private practice and a curriculum specialist in the New York City Board of Education, was extremely helpful while I was preparing for the presentation of an earlier version of this paper at the conference in Worcester, Massachusetts, in May 1998, and I thank her. I have benefited greatly from the discussion of some of the points in this essay with Ralph Raimi. Among the many readers of earlier versions, all of whom have my thanks, Richard Goodman and Bettina Drew made suggestions for which I am particularly grateful. The editor of this volume, Sandra Stotsky, has been a model of persistence. No one is responsible for my errors and oversights, except me.

Notes

[1] *BSCS Catalogue* (Colorado Springs, Colorado: BSCS, 1999).

[2] Michael Dougherty, Ph.D., then Associate Director, Biological Sciences Curriculum Study (BSCS), telephone interview by the author, April 13, 1999.

[3] The word "men" is used advisedly. Society has changed drastically over the last 40 and 50 years. The leaders of the Curriculum Reform movement were overwhelmingly men, rather than women. Accordingly, in the interest of accurate scholarship, the author uses the word "men," here and elsewhere in this essay when speaking of the leaders of Curriculum Reform. No slur is meant against the women who took part in Curriculum Reform, the author herself included.

[4] Jack S. Goldstein, *A Different Sort of Time: The Life of Jerrold R. Zacharias, Scientist, Engineer, Educator* (Cambridge, Mass.: MIT Press, 1992).

[5] Diane Ravitch, "Reformers, Radicals, and Romantics," in *The Troubled Crusade: American Education 1945–1980* (New York: Basic Books, 1983), 228–234, 261–266.

[6] Arthur Singer, telephone interview by author, February 25, 1999.

[7] Max Beberman, *An Emerging Program of Secondary School Mathematics* (Cambridge, Mass.: Harvard University Press, 1958)(Inglis Lecture in Secondary Education, Harvard Graduate School of Education), 39, 44.

8   *New York Times*, 18 July 1986, p. D17, col. 1. See Goldstein, *A Different Sort of Time*.
9   James R. Killian, Jr., preface to the first edition, Physical Science Study Committee ("PSSC"), *Physics*, quoted in preface, Uri Haber-Schaim, Judson B. Cross, John H. Dodge, and James A. Walter, authors, PSSC, *Physics*, third ed. (Lexington, Mass.: D.C. Heath and Company, 1971). The quotation from Dr. Killian goes on to say that the NSF has given the main financial support, and the "Ford Foundation and the Alfred P. Sloan Foundation have also contributed to the support of the program."
10 Martin Mayer, *The Schools* (New York: Harper & Brothers, 1961), 264.
11 Alan Holden and Phylis Singer, *Crystals and Crystal Growing* (New York: Doubleday & Company, 1960), reprinted as Alan Holden and Phylis S[inger] Morrison, *Crystals and Crystal Growing* (Cambridge, Mass.: M.I.T. Press, 1982).
12 Philip Morrison and Phylis Morrison, telephone interview by author, March 3, 1999.
13 Bess Furman, "President Sends Congress Billion Education-Aid Plan," *New York Times*, 28 January 1958, sec. 1, p. 1.
14 "Nothing contained in this Act shall be construed to authorize any department, agency, officer, or employee of the United States to exercise any direction, supervision, or control over the curriculum, program of instruction, administration, or personnel of any educational institution or school system." National Defense Education Act of 1958, Pub.L.No. 85–864, 72 Stat. 1580 (1958)(codified at 20 U.S.C. §421 (1976)(omitted for lack of funding since 1975 at 20 U.S.C. §421 (1994)), Title I, sec. 102.
15 Barbara Barksdale Clowse, *Brainpower for the Cold War: The Sputnik Crisis and National Defense Education Act of 1958* (Westport, Conn.: Greenwood Press, 1978). For criticism of American education immediately before Sputnik, see, for example, Hyman Rickover, *Education and Freedom* (New York: E.P. Dutton, 1959), which is a collection of Admiral Rickover's speeches on education.
16 Suzanne Kay Quick, "Secondary Impacts of the Curriculum Reform Movement: A Longitudinal Study of the Incorporation of Innovations of the Curriculum Reform Movement into Commercially Developed Curriculum Programs" (Ph.D. diss., Stanford University, 1978), 28–29, citing an internal National Science Foundation study.
17 Internal National Science Foundation Study, cited in Quick, "Secondary Impacts," 34, Table 2.
18 Jerome S. Bruner, preface to *The Process of Education* (Cambridge, Mass.: Harvard University Press, 1960), xix.
19 Jerome S. Bruner, preface to *The Process of Education* (Cambridge, Mass.: Harvard University Press, 1960), xix-xx; "Members of the Woods Hole Conference," front matter to *The Process of Education*.
20 Philip Morrison and Phylis Morrison, telephone interview by author, March 3, 1999.
21 Jerome S. Bruner, preface to *The Process of Education,* xxii-xxiii.
22 Ibid., 33.
23 Ibid., 19–20.
24 Ibid., 19.
25 Arthur Singer, telephone interview by author, February 25, 1999.
26 Jerome S. Bruner, telephone interview by author, April 30, 1998.

27 Quick, "Secondary Impacts," 36.
28 Bruner, *The Process of Education*, 21.
29 Ibid., 14 (italics in original).
30 Ibid., 56–57.
31 PSSC, preface to *Physics*, fifth ed.
32 Beberman, *Emerging Program*, 24–39.
33 Philip Morrison and Phylis Morrison, telephone interview by author, March 3, 1999.
34 To stimulate such learning by discovery, the projects used simple apparatus. Jerrold Zacharias used a combination of a flashlight and a water tank made of an old window frame, designed to illuminate basic concepts of wave motion in fluids and light. *New York Times*, 18 July 1986, p. D17, col. 1. Some science curricula, especially those designed for the elementary grades in the sixties, relied more on apparatus that students or teachers made than on textbooks. The elementary science programs were the Science Curriculum Improvement Study (SCIS), the Elementary Science Study (ESS), and Science—A Process Approach (SAPA). Peter C. Gega, "Building a Better Science Program," *The National Elementary Principal* (January 1980): 44. So far were the Curriculum Reform projects from dictating curriculum that the same project might offer several different courses on the same subject. The Biological Sciences Curriculum Study (BSCS), for example, established in 1958 by the Education Committee of the American Institute of Biological Sciences, originally published three separate full-length curricula, with three different publishers. Rand McNally & Co., in Chicago, published *Biological Science: An Ecological Approach* (Green Version); while Harcourt, Brace, Jovanovich, Inc., in New York, published *Biological Science: An Inquiry into Life*. Houghton Mifflin Co., in Boston, published a third version, called *Biological Science: Molecules to Man* (Blue Version). Yet other publishers published, respectively, the teachers guides, research problems, films, newsletters, topics in biological science and specialized books and pamphlets. For later editions of the BSCS Green and Blue versions currently in print, see note 1, above.
35 For a general treatment of the New English or Curriculum Reform approach to the teaching of precollege English, see Mary Gallagher, "The New English Approach to the Teaching of English," Section II, Chapters 6 through 12, of Thomas Brown, Mary Gallagher, and Rosemary Turner, *Teaching Secondary English: Alternative Approaches* (Columbus, Ohio: Charles E. Merrill Publishing Company, 1975), 147–338.
36 Edward B. Jenkinson and Philip B. Daghlian, *Teaching Literature in Grades Ten Through Twelve* (Bloomington, Ind.: University of Indiana Press, 1967).
37 Erwin Steinberg, gen. ed., *Insight* (New York: Noble and Noble, 1968)(a series of anthologies and guides for the ninth through twelfth grades).
38 Albert R. Kitzhaber, gen. ed., *The Oregon Curriculum: Literature I*, etc. (New York: Holt, Rinehart & Winston, Inc., 1968) (a series of anthologies and guides for the seventh through twelfth grades). The language series from the Oregon Curriculum Study Center is *Language/Rhetoric* (New York: Holt, Rinehart & Winston, Inc., 1968).
39 Marjorie B. Smiley, ed., *Macmillan Gateway English: A Literature and Language Arts Program* (New York: The Macmillan Company, 1964)(the Hunter College Gateway English Program).

40 Lincoln, Neb.: University of Nebraska Press, 1970.
41 Albert R. Kitzhaber, gen. ed., Acknowledgments, *The Oregon Curriculum: A Sequential Program in English* I (New York: Holt, Rinehart and Winston, 1968).
42 Wayne O'Neil, Chairman, Department of Linguistics and Philosophy, M.I.T., e-mail letter to the author, March 4, 1999. The title of the Linguistic Society of America session in which O'Neil took part on January 7, 1999, was "Linguists in Education: Positive Approaches to Collaborative Work." The title of his presentation was "Project English in Oregon."
43 The University of Illinois Curriculum Laboratory, *Rhetoric in Thought and Writing* (New York: Holt, Rinehart & Winston, 1972).
44 PSSC, Appendix 1, *Physics*, fifth ed. (Lexington, Mass.: D.C. Heath and Company, 1981), 568.
45 Bruner, preface to *The Process of Education*, xx; "Members of the Woods Hole Conference," front matter to *The Process of Education*.
46 See Siegfried Engelmann, *War Against the Schools' Academic Child Abuse* (Portland, Or.: Halcyon House, 1992).
47 The University of Illinois Curriculum Laboratory, *Rhetoric in Thought and Writing*, I: 12–15. The series consisted of four paperback textbooks, along with four teachers' manuals, with teaching aids and directions for lesson plans.
48 Beberman, *An Emerging Program*, 29–30. For an excellent explication of the New Math, see Stephen White, *Students, Scholars, and Parents: An Exploration of the Ideas Behind the New Math and Other Curriculum Reform* (Garden City, NY: Doubleday & Co., Inc., 1966.)
49 BSCS, *Biological Science: Molecules to Man* (Boston: Houghton Mifflin Company, 1963)(BSCS Blue Version), 3.
50 BSCS, *Teacher's Guide to Accompany Biological Science: Molecules to Man* (Boston: Houghton Mifflin Company, 1963)(BSCS Blue Version), 9.
51 BSCS, *Biological Science: Molecules to Man*, 9–10.
52 Beberman, *An Emerging Program*, 39.
53 Paul E. Marsh, "Wellsprings of Strategy: Considerations Affecting Innovations by the PSSC," Chapter 10 in *Innovation in Education*, Matthew B. Miles, ed. (New York: Teachers College, Columbia University, 1964), 258–260; Paul E. Marsh and Ross A. Gortner, *Federal Aid to Science Education: Two Programs*, The Economics and Politics of Public Education 6 (Syracuse, NY: Syracuse University Press, 1963). This extensive testing of materials in the public schools casts doubt on Diane Ravitch's assertion that "the paucity of representative teachers probably deprived the projects of persons familiar with the wide range of abilities represented in the average public school classroom." Ravitch, *The Troubled Crusade*, 265. The teachers who actually wrote materials for the curriculum projects, in addition, while not representative teachers, had enough teaching experience to be thoroughly familiar with the range of students' abilities.
54 BSCS, front matter, *Biological Science: An Ecological Approach*, third ed. (Chicago: Rand McNally & Company, 1973)(BSCS Green Version)(Teachers Edition).
55 Ibid., foreward.
56 Marsh, "Wellsprings of Strategy," 261–262.

57 Ibid., 262–263; Paul E. Marsh and Ross A. Gortner, *Federal Aid to Science Education: Two Programs*, 70–76.
58 Ralph Raimi, "Whatever Happened to the New Math?" *Chronicles* 20 (January 1996): 40.
59 Committee on the National Interest, *The National Interest and the Continuing Education of Teachers of English* (Champaign, Ill.: National Council of Teachers of English, 1964), 5.
60 J.N. Hook, *A Long Way Together: A Personal View of NCTE's First Sixty-Seven Years* (Urbana, Ill.: National Council of Teachers of English, 1979), 197.
61 PSSC, preface, *Physics*, third ed., quoting preface to the second edition. Unpaginated.
62 BSCS, foreward to *Biological Science: An Ecological Approach,* third ed. (Chicago: Rand McNally & Company, 1973)(BSCS Green Version)(Teachers Edition).
63 Quick, "Secondary Impacts," 36–37, cited in Ravitch, *The Troubled Crusade*, 261–62.
64 David Ridgeway, telephone interview by author, February 27, 1999.
65 Barbara Barksdale Clowse, *Brainpower for the Cold War: The Sputnik Crisis and National Defense Education Act of 1958* (Westport, Conn.: Greenwood Press, 1978), 155.
66 For an excellent description of these crucial facts of the political structure of American education, see Paul E. Marsh and Ross A. Gortner, *Federal Aid to Science Education: Two Programs*, The Economics and Politics of Public Education 6 (Syracuse, NY: Syracuse University Press, 1963), 1–14.
67 John G. Wirt and Suzanne K. Quick, "Research Plan and Final Outline for a Study of the Curriculum Reform Movement of the 1960's" (Santa Monica, Cal.: July 1975, mimeographed), 20. This unpublished material, written while Dr. Wirt was a lead investigator with the Rand Corporation, is used here by permission of Dr. Wirt. Computer re-drawing by Mary Campbell Gallagher.
68 See, for example, Diane Ravitch, *The Troubled Crusade: American Education 1945–1980* (New York: Basic Books, 1983), 263, and sources cited at n. 63.
69 The author recalls Max Beberman's having often complained in conversation at Uni High about deficient teaching of basic arithmetical skills. The anecdote quoted appears in *The New York Times*, 26 January 1971, p. 36, col. 1 (obituary).
70 Ralph Raimi, "Whatever Happened to the New Math?" *Chronicles* 20 (January 1996): 40–41.
71 Critics of the New English had other complaints, including the accusation that the literature programs were insufficiently "affective," this is, that they appealed more to students' intellects than their emotions. Louise M. Rosenblatt, "Patterns and Process—A Polemic," *English Journal* (October 1969): 1006; John J. DeBoer, "The 'New' English," *The Educational Forum* (May 1968): 393–402; J.N. Hook, "English Teachers in a World We Never Made," *English Journal* (February 1969): 185–92. See also, Brown, Gallagher, and Turner, *Teaching Secondary English,* 178.
72 Charlene Tibbetts, telephone interview by author, April 14, 1998.
73 Jerome S. Bruner, "Some Elements of Discovery," originally presented at a conference in 1965 of the Committee on Education and Development of the Social Science Research Council, published in L. Shulman and E. Keislar, *Learning by Discovery*

[74] (Chicago: Rand McNally, 1966), re-published in edited form as Chapter 4 of Jerome S. Bruner, *The Relevance of Education* (New York: W.W. Norton, 1973), 68.
[74] Bruner, *The Process of Education*, .
[75] Ravitch, *The Troubled Crusade*, 265.
[76] Martin Mayer, *Where, When, and Why: Social Studies in American Schools* (New York: Harper & Row, 1963), 179.
[77] Michael Dougherty, Ph.D., then Associate Director, BSCS, telephone interview by author, April 1, 1999.
[78] Jon Greenberg, Ph.D., Curriculum Project Manager and Staff Biologist, BSCS, telephone interview by author, March 1, 1999.
[79] Philip Morrison and Phylis Morrison, telephone interview by author, March 3, 1999.
[80] Martin Mayer, *The Schools* (New York: Harper & Brothers, 1961), 264.
[81] Philip Morrison and Phylis Morrison, telephone interview by author, March 3, 1999.
[82] For another and more detailed account of the historical causes of Curriculum Reform's decline and the rise of "open education," see Diane Ravitch, *The Troubled Crusade: American Education, 1945–1980* (New York: Basic Books, 1983), 233–266.
[83] A brief beginning on telling this story appears in Ravitch, *The Troubled Crusade*, 263–64.
[84] It is one of the Copernican changes that have occurred in American educational discourse that in the perennial conflict of Nurture and Nature, nowadays educationists choose words that give Nurture all the credit. They speak only of students who are "very able," for example, and not of students who are "bright"; they say students have "abilities," not that they have "talents." In the 1950s, by contrast, we spoke freely of "talented" students, "gifted" students, and "bright" students. Naturally, we also talked about the quite separate question of whether students had in fact developed their abilities from the gifts they possessed. We knew that natural gifts exist, and that nurtured abilities also develop out of natural gifts. President Eisenhower's special education message to Congress on January 27, 1958, devoted a full section to the topic "Reducing the Waste of Talent." The President said that many able high school graduates do not go to college, and "This represents a waste of needed talent." "Text of President's Education Message to Congress," *New York Times*, 28 January 1958, sec. 1, p. 18.
[85] Clowse, *Brainpower for the Cold War*, 38–39, citing Educational Policies Commission, *Manpower and Education* (Washington, D.C.: Educational Policies Commission, 1956), 99. The definition of "equality" discussed here appears in Arthur E. Bestor, Jr., *The Restoration of Learning: A Program for Redeeming the Unfulfilled Promise of American Education* (New York: Alfred A. Knopf, 1956), 364; Arthur E. Bestor, Jr., "We Are Less Educated than Fifty Years Ago," *U.S. News and World Report* (November 30, 1956), 69–71.
[86] Bruner, *The Process of Education*, 9–10.
[87] Clouse, *Brainpower for the Cold War*, 39.
[88] Jack S .Goldstein, *A Different Sort of Time*, 217–237.
[89] Bruner, *The Process of Education*, 10.
[90] Jon Greenberg, telephone interview by author, March 1, 1999. As Greenberg explained to me the goals of the current BSCS revisions, they include not only bringing the BSCS materials up to date with current research, but also writing the

materials in simpler language. Simpler language! "We will keep the same high conceptual level," he said, "but the reading level will not be as high." Now, according to Dr. Greenberg, "the attempt is being made not to dilute so much as to bring a larger number up to the level of honors."

[91] Joseph Haverland, operations Coordinator, Kendall-Hunt, telephone interview by author, April 1, 1999.

[92] John Dixon, *Growth through English: A Report Based on the Dartmouth Seminar 1966* (Reading, England: National Association for the Teaching of English, 1967); Herbert J. Miller, *The Uses of English: Guidelines for the Teaching of English from the Anglo-American Conference at Dartmouth College* (New York: Holt, Rinehart and Winston, Inc., 1967).

[93] J.N. Hook, *A Long Way Together: A Personal View of NCTE's First Sixty-Seven Years* (Urbana, Ill.: National Council of Teachers of English, 1979), 220–222.

[94] Wayne O'Neil, e-mail letter to the author, March 4, 1999.

[95] Ravitch, *The Troubled Crusade*, 223–261.

[96] Marsh, "Wellsprings of Strategy," 266–267.

[97] Paul E. Marsh and Ross A. Gortner, *Federal Aid to Science Education: Two Programs*, 71–76.

[98] Jerold R. Zacharias, "The Case of the Missing Scientists," *The National Elementary Principal* (January 1980): 14–17.

[99] Ralph Raimi, "Whatever Happened to the New Math?" *Chronicles* 20 (January 1996): 41.

[100] Joseph Haverland, Operations Coordinator, Kendall-Hunt, telephone interview by author, April 1, 1999.

[101] Wayne O'Neil, e-mail letter to the author, March 4, 1999.

[102] Phillip Morrison and Phylis Morrison, telephone interview by author, March 3, 1999.

Chapter 13

The National Science Foundation Systemic Initiatives
How a Small Amount of Federal Money Promotes Ill-Designed Mathematics and Science Programs in K–12 and Undermines Local Control of Education

Michael McKeown
Mathematically Correct

David Klein
California State University, Northridge

Chris Patterson
Education Connection of Texas

Since its inception in 1950, the National Science Foundation (NSF) has played a strong, positive role in making American scientific research and technological application the best in the world. Through its funding of peer-reviewed, investigator-initiated research proposals, it has supported basic research in a wide variety of scientific disciplines, such as mathematics, biology, physics, chemistry, geology, astronomy, and psychology. American science owes much to the support it has received, and continues to receive, from NSF. This chapter deals with a program in the Education and Human Resources Division called the NSF Systemic Initiatives Program, not with NSF programs related directly to the support of basic research. We are highly critical of this particular NSF program. Not only do the Systemic Initiatives undermine local control of education, but, as our analysis in this chapter suggests, they also seem to lower academic standards for mathematics education and weaken the educational base for American science.

This chapter is composed of three sections. The first section, an overview of NSF Systemic Initiatives, was written by Michael McKeown. The second section, an analysis of the development and features of the Los Angeles Systemic Initiative, was written by David Klein. The third section, an analysis of the development and features of the Texas Statewide Systemic Initiative, was written by Chris Patterson.

Problems Raised by the NSF Systemic Initiatives

A private individual comes to the principal of a school and offers to pay $5 per student to help students improve in mathematics and science. Although this is a minuscule amount ($100 to $150 per classroom), it sounds appealing. But there is a catch: The donor makes it clear that he will insist on a complete revamping of the way the school teaches mathematics and science, including the choice of textbooks, the school district's academic standards, and possibly even its graduation standards. Of course, he won't buy the textbooks or allow public discussion of the methods of instruction he thinks are appropriate. He will let his money be used only if the school district undertakes to implement everything he has spelled out. Should the school take the money (about 0.1% or less of the true cost of running the school)? Of course not.

Now substitute the federal government for a private donor, and a state education agency or an urban school district for a single school, but keep all the other conditions in place, including insistence on changes in key educational policies for a minuscule financial contribution. Should the state or school district take the money? In a hypothetical world, the answer should still be "No." But in the real world, the answer has been "Yes" for 24 states and 22 major urban school districts (see Table 1). Each of these states and school districts accepted an NSF Systemic Initiative grant to make "fundamental, comprehensive, and coordinated changes in science, mathematics, and technology education through attendant changes in policy, resource allocation, governance, management, content, and conduct."[1] NSF wants changes in all these areas in order for schools to achieve the kind of "systemic reform" it has in mind.

Table 1. State and Urban Systemic Initiatives

State Systemic Initiatives

Arkansas	California	Colorado	Connecticut	Delaware
Florida	Georgia	Kentucky	Louisiana	Maine
Massachusetts	Michigan	Montana	Nebraska	New Jersey
New Mexico	New York	North Carolina	Ohio	South Carolina
South Dakota	Texas	Vermont	Virginia	

Urban Systemic Initiatives

1994

Baltimore	Chicago	Cincinnati	Detroit
El Paso	Miami	New York	Phoenix

1995

Cleveland	Columbus	Dallas	Fresno
Los Angeles	Memphis	New Orleans	Philadelphia

1996

Milwaukee	San Antonio	San Diego	St. Louis

1998

Atlanta	Jacksonville

The nature and scope of the policy changes that the NSF Systemic Initiatives Program is enticing state and local educational systems to adopt raise two broad questions that need far more open discussion than they have so far received. The first concerns the federal government's unpublicized assumption of what have historically been local educational responsibilities and the way in which it is assuming them. The second concerns the value or effectiveness of the science and mathematics programs, policies, and curricular materials that this NSF program expects state and local school districts to adopt as the condition for securing its funds. In this chapter, we show how the NSF Systemic Initiatives Program enables employees of a federal agency to foreclose further state and local educational decision making on matters of curriculum and pedagogy, without broad public examination and discussion of their educational philosophy. We also describe the serious deficiencies in the instructional programs and materials this program is promoting.

Foreclosing State and Local Control of Curriculum and Instruction, and Redirecting Educational Resources

School districts throughout the country, especially urban districts, are strapped for funds. Growing student populations, increases in the proportion of at-risk students, increases in the services expected of schools, increasing salaries of aging teachers and administrators, and deteriorating facilities all put pressure on school budgets and on the money available for new classroom materials and continuing professional development of the teaching force. In such a situation, any money outside the usual sources of funds that may increase the available budget is highly valued. Eagerness by school administrators for additional outside money creates a great deal of leverage for those who can supply these highly coveted marginal dollars. An external funding agency seeking specific changes in a school district's educational policies, programs, and curricular materials may be able to make the granting of its funds contingent upon the district's meeting the agency's conditions.

Traditionally, education in the United States has been a responsibility of states and local school districts. The federal government played a relatively minor role in educational matters until Congress passed the National Defense Education Act in 1958 and other legislation in the 1960s as part of President Johnson's War on Poverty. Even today, it makes a small financial contribution relative to the funds raised locally to support the public schools. NSF itself has made no attempt until recently to change and redirect the entire network of educational policies in a state or school district; the mathematics and science programs that it helped develop before and after Sputnik in the 1950s were made available to the schools without strings attached.

The relationship between NSF and state and local school systems began to change in the late 1980s because the national government sought to bring about a series of changes in local school systems that it believed would improve mathematics and science education in this country. At the 1989 Education Summit attended by President Bush and all 50 governors, participants made a commitment to make U.S. students first in mathematics and science by the year 2000.[2] As its contribution to that goal, NSF launched its first Statewide Systemic Initiatives (SSIs) in 1991 to achieve systemic reform in a number of target states. In 1994 the first Urban Systemic Initiatives (USIs) appeared, followed by the Rural Systemic Initiatives (RSIs). Funding for the SSIs peaked in 1993, and the bulk of funding currently goes to the USIs. In 1999, the approximate funding levels are $21 million for the SSIs, $86 million for the USIs, and $10 million for the RSIs.[3]

In general, the SSIs contribute approximately $2 million per year to state education departments, while the USIs contribute $3 million per year to local districts. At first glance, a contribution of $3 million a year to an urban school district seems a major boon, but when the actual per student support is calculated, it becomes clear how small a fraction of actual costs is covered by NSF funds. For example, in San Diego, with 130,000 students, USI funding averages $23 per student, about one half of one percent or less of total costs. In the larger Los Angeles school district, per student support is less than $4. This is like a 4 cent saving on a $50 purchase. Yet, the amount seems to be large enough to seduce school districts into making substantial changes in programs and policies as the condition for receiving NSF funds. This small amount of money, in effect, enables the federal government to shape or reshape state and local educational policies and direct use of their resources even though local and state taxpayers are footing most of the bills.

The use of NSF money at the margin of the budget to leverage systemwide changes in educational policies and programs at the state or local level is not an inadvertent consequence of well intentioned programs; it is NSF's plan. Luther Williams, Assistant Director for Education and Human Resources and a microbiologist by training, made that clear in a July 1998 USI Summary Update.[4]

> The NSF investment that promotes systemic reform will never exceed a small percentage of a given site's overall budget. The 'converged' resources are not merely fiscal, but also strategic, in that they help induce a unitary... reform operation. The catalytic nature of the USI-led reform obligates systemwide policy and fiscal resources to embrace standards-based instruction and create conditions for helping assorted... expenditures to become organized and used in a single-purpose direction.

Williams goes on to spell out exactly how districts have redirected other resources to meet the conditions of the USI grant: "Cleveland devoted half of its available bond referendum funding" for USI-related instructional material. "Los Angeles... is one of several cities in the USI portfolio that places all Title II funding resources under the control of the USI." "In the Fresno Unified School System, $31 million of Title 1 funds have been realigned in support of USI activities." It is clear that Williams both seeks and approves of use of school district funds to support Systemic Initiative programs.

It is not unreasonable, and it is often desirable, for the federal government to attach guidelines for the use of the funds it makes available to states and local communities for many purposes. That this NSF program mandates a particular direction on matters for which the federal government does not have educational responsibility—matters of curriculum and pedagogy—becomes clear when there is deviation from, or opposition to, what this program sees as fundamental components of its notion of systemic reform. These components include the *particular* sets of K–12 science and mathematics standards that this program favors: those created by the National Council of Teachers of Mathematics (NCTM), the American Association for the Advancement of Science (AAAS), and the National Research Council (NRC). The problem is not that this program requires school districts across the country to use academic standards in the redesign of science and mathematics programs for K–12. The problem is that this NSF program implicitly if not explicitly mandates the use of certain sets of standards instead of others (including those developed by the states themselves), as well as certain curricular, instructional, and classroom management practices instead of others.

That this NSF program is attempting to impose its administrators' beliefs about what they think is best for the students in our public schools with respect to standards, pedagogy, and curriculum was clearly revealed in 1997 when the California Board of Education adopted a new set of statewide mathematics standards.[5] As we discuss below in the context of the Los Angeles Systemic Initiative, these grade-by-grade standards are clear, demanding, and free of pedagogical mandates. That is, they are open to a complete range of pedagogical strategies. They are also easily measured and enjoy widespread support from the public as well as from mathematicians and scientists. Nevertheless, in December 1997, Williams sent a sharply worded letter to the California Board of Education with an implicit threat to withdraw $50 million worth of NSF funding to districts in the state unless the Board rejected this set of mathematics standards (Appendix A). California's Board refused to yield to Williams' threat, and his superior, Neal Lane, Director of the National Science Foundation at the time, sent a letter in January 1998 reinterpreting and downplaying Williams' threats (Appendix B), possibly in response to questions raised about Williams' letter in the press and in Congress.

Although California's Board of Education stood firm against Williams' attempt to direct state policy on matters of pedagogy, curriculum, and standards, in other states NSF-funded programs are clearly in control of the development of educational components that have traditionally been state and local responsibilities. For example, in Texas, the SSI not only uses its $2 million per year to develop the state mathematics and science frameworks, it "assumed responsibility for the management and redesign of the state's discretionary K–12 Eisenhower Program," and it explicitly and specifically mirrors the NSF itself by creating "novel incentive programs to encourage (1) school districts to redeploy their Title 1 and Compensatory Education funds to support implementation of Standards-compatible integrated math, science, and literacy curricula; and (2) higher education faculty to link their educational activities more closely to the state's reform agenda." In Texas, NSF has empowered a new bureaucracy that is using the leverage of NSF money not only to take charge of state education programs and policies but also to steer the state, school districts, and the faculty at the state's universities in particular educational directions with respect to pedagogy and curriculum.[6] The third section of this chapter offers further details on the Texas SSI.

Thus, without public discussion and with little fanfare, NSF Systemic Initiatives have turned on its head the process by which state and local school policy decisions on matters of standards, curriculum, and pedagogy are made. Whereas decisions were previously made in states and local districts by local citizens subject to election and recall, they are now made by federal employees who are essentially anonymous and not accountable to the people who are most affected by their actions.

Promoting Educational Policies and Programs of Unproven Efficacy

The reforms "encouraged" by the NSF Systemic Initiatives program bear as close examination as does the way in which its state, urban, and rural initiatives use their funds to leverage control of decision making on what have traditionally been state and local educational matters. There are good reasons even for those favoring a larger role for the national government in the effort to improve mathematics and science education in this country to oppose the particular educational components promoted by the Systemic Intitiatives program.

Like most educational programs, the Systemic Initiatives began in response to real problems and serious problems, in this case the low academic performance of American students in mathematics and science, and the notable achievement gap between certain minority students (chiefly African American and Hispanic) and other students. Although the general educational philosophy underlying the Systemic Initiatives program had long been supported by NSF, the initial SSIs were given substantial freedom to develop their own strategies for reform. As the program evolved, the guidelines became more and more explicit, culminating in 1996 with the release of what NSF calls the "Six Drivers" of systemic reform:[7]

> Driver 1: Rigorous, standards-based instruction for all students, and the curriculum, professional development, and assessment systems to support that instruction.
> Driver 2: A unified set of policies that facilitate and enable Driver 1.
> Driver 3: A unified application of all resources to facilitate and enable Driver 1.
> Driver 4: Mobilization of the full community of stakeholders on behalf of facilitating and enabling Driver 1.
> Driver 5: Increased student attainment in science, mathematics, and technology.
> Driver 6: Reduction in attainment differences between those traditionally underserved and their peers.

Taken at face value, it is hard to disagree with these "drivers," especially Drivers 5 and 6, the long-range educational goals. Of the other four items, Driver 1 is the primary operational statement; all the rest support Driver 1. Thus it is critical to understand exactly what is meant by Driver 1 in order to understand the nature of the Systemic Initiatives program. Fortunately, this release elaborates what it means by "standards-based instruction," as well as what it views as effective instructional practice, allowing the public to judge if the NSF educational vision is what it wants. It contains the following pedagogical beliefs "based on an understanding that learning is an active process wherein the learner is the full participant, not a passive recipient":

- All children can learn by using and manipulating scientific and mathematical ideas that are meaningful and relate to real-world situations and to real problems.

- Mathematics and science are learned by doing rather than by passive methods of learning such as watching a teacher work at the chalkboard. Inquiry-based learning and hands-on learning more effectively engage students than lectures.

- The use and manipulation of scientific and mathematical ideas benefits from a variety of contributing perspectives and is, therefore, enhanced by cooperative problem solving.

- Technology can make learning easier, more comprehensive, and more lasting.

- This view of learning is reflected in the professional standards of the National Council of Teachers of Mathematics, the American Association for the Advancement of Science, and the National Research Council of the National Academy of Sciences.

As these statements make clear, NSF expects Systemic Initiative awardees to implement programs that emphasize group-based discovery learning, the use of "manipulatives" (items such as blocks, beads, and dice in mathematics class), and the use of technology, such as calculators. Although this list of pedagogical desiderata is devoid of reference to actual mathematical or scientific content, the final bulleted item makes clear that the NSF view of appropriate pedagogy comes from, or is supported by, the standards documents put out by NCTM, as well as AAAS and NRC. In order to judge the quality of this NSF program, therefore, we need to know more about both the instructional methodologies it endorses and the quality of the standards it uses to define academic content.

From NSF's willingness to mandate specific instructional practices, one might be tempted to conclude that there is a clear consensus among cognitive psychologists, supported by well-designed, large-scale studies, that these practices are head and shoulders above all others. This is not the case. Not only is there no research-based consensus to this effect, cognitive psychologists do not believe there are substitutes in mathematical learning for practice and for a well thought through sequence for instruction based on the structure of the discipline, not events in the outside world or students' idiosyncratic interests. As Steven

Pinker, a noted neuroscientist at MIT, discussed in his book, *How the Mind Works*:[8]

> The... way to get to mathematical competence is similar to the way to get to Carnegie Hall: practice. Mathematical concepts come from snapping together old concepts in a useful new arrangement. But those old concepts are assemblies of still older concepts. Each subassembly hangs together by the mental rivets called chunking and automaticity: with copious practice, concepts adhere into larger concepts, and sequences of steps are compiled into a single step. Just as bicycles are assembled out of frames and wheels, not tubes and spokes, and recipes say how to make sauces, not how to grasp spoons and open jars, mathematics is learned by fitting together overlearned routines. Calculus teachers lament that students find the subject difficult... because you can't do calculus unless algebraic operations are second nature, and most students enter the course without having learned the algebra properly and need to concentrate every drop of mental energy on that. Mathematics is ruthlessly cumulative, all the way back to counting to ten.
>
> The ascendant philosophy of mathematical education in the United States is constructivism, a mixture of Piaget's psychology with counterculture and postmodernist ideology. Children must actively construct mathematical knowledge for themselves in a social enterprise driven by disagreements about the meanings of concepts. The teacher provides the materials and the social milieu but does not lecture or guide the discussion. Drill and practice, the routes to automaticity, are called "mechanistic" and seen as detrimental to understanding.
>
> (Constructivism) ignores the difference between our factory-installed equipment and the accessories that civilization bolts on afterward. Setting our mental modules to work on material they were not designed for is *hard*. Children do not spontaneously see a string of beads as elements in a set, or points on a line as numbers... and without practice that compiles a halting sequence of steps into a mental reflex, a learner will always be building mathematical structures out of the tiniest nuts and bolts, like the watchmaker who never made subassemblies and had to start from scratch every time he put down a watch to answer the phone.

Not only does the NSF program directive explaining Driver 1 ignore, if not downgrade, all traditional forms of learning such as practice, it also ignores, if not downgrades, the benefits of teacher-directed whole class instruction. Nevertheless, reviews of mainstream research that include (1) studies comparing alternative teaching methods, (2) basic research in cognition, learning, and other areas of cognitive psychology, and (3) international comparisons suggest that methods other than those encouraged by NSF are more effective. These more effective methods include teacher-directed whole class instruction, clarity in the goals of each lesson and the key points of the lesson, clarity in presentation, review, repetition, rapid feedback, and practice.[9] Whether or not NSF-advocated methods are effective in some situations, there is no research-supported consensus establishing them as integral components of a de facto national curriculum in mathematics and science education, never mind as the sole components.

Just as the NSF Systemic Initiatives Program has chosen to endorse a particular set of instructional methods and effectively excluded all others, it has chosen to endorse particular sets of "standards" to address the content of science and mathematics. In mathematics, as we have seen, NSF puts the NCTM standards on a pedestal. This endorsement has led to a particularly confusing situation. Advocates of "systemic reform" in mathematics usually use the words "standards-based" to refer not just to the disciplinary content of the NCTM standards but also to the pedagogical principles recommended in this standards document. These pedagogical principles emphasize the value of guessing rather than getting right answers, favor learning based on student interest and inquiry instead of on direct instruction, and de-emphasize the learning of mathematical content in favor of empty reasoning processes. Thus, a phrase that once had a limited but clear meaning pointing mainly to disciplinary content in mathematics has come to refer to an educational philosophy encompassing particular pedagogical approaches and curricular configurations. This is what the "standards-based" learning promoted in Driver 1 now entails. This confusion can, intentionally or unintentionally, mislead educated people into supporting "standards-based" programs that they might not favor if they understood everything "standards-based" brings in its wake. As the standards wars in California have demonstrated, many people can support a K–12 curriculum in mathematics based on a set of clear and demanding content standards and at the same time reject a curriculum promoting only the specifics of Driver 1.

As the above discussion suggests, it is important to note some of the details of the NCTM standards because they define the content of NSF-advocated mathematics programs. The NCTM standards are striking in a number of ways.[10] First, they differ substantially from previously accepted ideas about needed mathematical content. This is most notable in the "less emphasis" lists. These are lists of mathematical content that NCTM feels should be given "less emphasis" in school mathematics. These de-emphasized items include the teaching of traditional algorithms for basic arithmetic operations, paper and pencil calculation, logical deduction and proof, and analytical methods in general. The actual content standards of the standards also contain few clear statements about what students should know, do, and understand at any level. They apply to gradespans, not individual grades, virtually guaranteeing curricular differences from school to school and from program to program. The content standards that are there tend to be loosely worded and speak in broad generalities rather than mathematical specifics. Finally, the NCTM standards are dedicated to inquiry-based learning and the constructivist philosophy described under Driver 1 and in Pinker's comments. Just as the classroom practices promoted by Driver 1 have been criticized, so too have the NCTM standards been criticized, by parents,[11] mathematicians,[12] and others knowledgeable about mathematics education.[13] In striking contrast, as we noted earlier, California's new Mathematics standards offer standards that are specific to each grade, clear as to mathematical content, and devoid of pedagogical imperatives.[14]

What the NSF vision for mathematics means in the classroom can be seen in the textbooks and instructional programs that it "encourages." Table 2 lists "NSF-approved" programs for the New York City USI,[15] as well as additional programs advocated by the Los Angeles USI. Nearly all of these programs are committed to an extreme version of discovery learning, a constructivist philosophy, and a radical interpretation of the NCTM standards, including constant availability of calculators starting at kindergarten, extreme de-emphasis of paper and pencil calculation, and de-emphasis of analytical and deductive methods. Although these programs are strongly supported by some teachers, they have also generated significant public outcry from parents, especially those who actually know mathematics and use it in the real world.[16]

For example, *MathLand*, an elementary school program, lacks student texts and does not present standard algorithms for multiplication and division in any of the elementary school grades. It relies heavily on calculators, and has a near total commitment to discovery learning, including "invented algorithms" for multiplication and division.[17] When it was implemented in the Department of Defense Overseas Schools, which serve approximately 81,000 students, there was an immediate and significant drop in student performance across all ethnic groups and an *increase* in the gap between the scores of white and Asian students and those of students of other ethnic groups.[18] A similar drop in test scores took place after the introduction of *MathLand* into the Santa Barbara,

California schools. *Investigations in Number, Data, and Space,* another elementary school program, also lacks student texts, is completely committed to discovery learning and invented algorithms, and does not teach second grade students how to do such critical mathematical operations as borrowing and carrying when adding and subtracting.[19]

Table 2. NSF-Approved Mathematics Curricula as Reported by the New York City USI

Elementary
Investigations in Number, Data, and Space (Dale Seymour Publications)
VOYAGER, A Mathematical Journey Using Science and Language Arts (Voyager Expanded Learning, Inc.)
Everyday Mathematics (Everyday Learning Corporation)
MathLand (Creative Publications)
Real World Mathematics (Addison Wesley Longman)

Middle School
Grade 7 Algebra
Connected Mathematics Program (Dale Seymour Publications)
Seeing and Thinking Mathematically, MathScape (Creative Publications)
Math in Context: A Connected Curriculum (Britannica Educational Corporation)
Six Through Eight Mathematics (STEM) Math Thematics (McDougal-Littell/Houghton Mifflin)
Middle-school Mathematics Through Applications Projects (IRL, MMAP Project)

High School
Applications/Reform in Secondary Education (ARISE) (Consortium for Mathematics and Applications)
Interactive Mathematics Program (IMP) (Key Curriculum Press)
Core-Plus Mathematics Project (Everyday Learning Corporation)
Math Connections (The Learning Team)

Additional High School Programs Approved for Use by the Los Angeles USI
College Preparatory Mathematics (CPM) (College Preparatory Math)
Integrated Math (McDougal-Littell/Houghton Mifflin)

At the middle school level, NSF-approved programs continue to be committed to discovery or project-based learning and give students insufficient or inadequate materials with which to acquire the skills and knowledge necessary for success in algebra 1, the key course in a high school mathematics program. *Connected Mathematics Program* is one such middle school program. Although some key topics that are prerequisites for algebra receive some coverage, the amount of time spent on irrelevancies (such as writing in journals about imaginary bicycle trips) is so high that the depth and practice of what is important is limited. The program's worth is further eroded by the constant availability of calculators, which eliminates the need for students to understand key concepts and manipulations.[20] The threat of introducing this program contributed to a parent uprising in at least one school district.[21]

At the high school level, there is a continuing emphasis on discovery learning and a significant de-emphasis of algebraic skills and logic. Indeed, one program, *Interactive Mathematics Program*, has candidly noted that all items listed for "less emphasis" in the NCTM standards, such as manual calculation and proof, were completely eliminated.[22] Many key topics are presented in ways that are unlikely to lead to a high level of mastery, while introduction of the quadratic formula, a topic fundamental to high school algebra, is delayed until the twelfth grade.[23] *Integrated Math 1, 2, and 3* has been criticized as being seriously lacking in key content areas, ill-designed for mastery learning, full of contrived problems, and unlikely to prepare students for mathematics-based science courses or college mathematics.[24] The *Core-Plus Mathematics Project* generated massive resentment among the students who were the experimental subjects during early implementation. Many students found themselves ill-prepared for college, even though they came from highly educated homes and had a high likelihood of success.[25]

What Accounts for the Support of Unproven Educational Ideas?

The emphasis on constructivist pedagogical methods by NSF and NCTM, as well as by the authors of Systemic Initiative-approved instructional programs, raises the question why so many people in so many groups can support them in the absence of both a large body of consistent evidence from high quality research *and* a national consensus on what is educationally effective. If, as we suggest, these methods are flawed, why do they receive so much support from so many educators? An analogy with the attitudes of many educators toward the constructivist counterpart in reading instruction—Whole Language— may be useful. An approach to beginning reading that encourages context-based guesswork, Whole Language was strongly supported by reading educators in the schools and teachers colleges in the 1980s and became the favored approach to beginning reading in schools of education by the 1990s, to judge by the conference proceedings, professional publications, and public pronouncements of the International Reading Association and the National Council of Teachers of English, the two major organizations for reading teachers. Whole Language came to be seen as an ill-advised approach to beginning reading only after a whole generation of children fell short in reading skills and a large number of mainstream reading researchers and linguists showed not only that its theoretical base was flawed but also that there was little methodologically sound research to support it. Even so, many educators continue to stress a Whole Language approach and downplay the usefulness of systematic phonics instruction in beginning reading.[26] Thus, we note that many educators have been advocating and implementing constructivist pedagogical methods in other subject areas as well as in mathematics and science education without a body of sound research evidence to support them.

Although one cannot read the minds of others, there are reasons why constructivist ideas about learning are promoted so regularly and enthusiastically in this country. As E.D. Hirsch notes, romantic ideas about how children learn have a century-long history in our education schools.[27] America is particularly partial to constructivist ideas in education because the image of the creative and even iconoclastic individual is very much a part of our national identity. What could be more American and more liberating than discovering for oneself, in one's own way, the great ideas of mathematics and science? That this philosophy fails in the classroom and leaves students unprepared for truly creative problem solving at high levels does not seem to reduce its appeal.

A second reason for the strength of constructivist methods in education is more disturbing. A current strain of thought suggests that non-Asian minorities and women need to be taught in ways involving less emphasis on deductive and analytical methods and more emphasis on inductive, intuitive, constructivist methods because of gender and racial/ethnic differences in learning. As one example, in a radio discussion associated with NCTM's 1996 annual meeting, Jack Price speaking in his role as NCTM President commented that "women, for example, and minority groups do not learn the same way" as "Anglo male(s)." "They learn differently." In clarification of his remarks, Price went on to reinforce stereotypic views of men, women, and minorities: "males, for example, learn better deductively in a competitive environment... the kind of thing that we have done in the past... We have found with gender differences, for example, that women have a tendency to learn better in a collaborative effort when they are doing inductive reasoning."[28]

Price is not alone in his stereotypic views, disguised as they may be in academic jargon. For example, educational researchers have also come up with broad stereotypes of African Americans, as suggested by a report on "African American students' mathematical problem solving" by two researchers in mathematics education. As they note: "Studies of learning preferences suggest that the African American students' approaches to learning may be characterized by factors of social and affective emphasis, harmony with their communities, holistic perspectives, field dependence, expressive creativity, and nonverbal communication... Research indicates that African American students are flexible and open-minded rather than structured in their perceptions of ideas."[29] These characteristics imply that African Americans cannot engage in rigorous analytical thinking and articulate their ideas in academic prose. Similarly, a writer on American Indian education asserts that Native Americans are "right brained" and implies that they cannot engage in structured forms of learning because the "functions of the left brain are characterized by sequence and order while the functions of the right brain are holistic and diffused."[30]

The author of an article in a March 1999 issue of *The New Republic* suggests that at least some African American educators themselves reject constructivist methods and assumptions.[31]

> Many pipeline programs are driven by untested ideological premises, such as the idea that black students can learn only from black teachers or that their "learning style" is somehow fundamentally different from that of other kids. It doesn't help that most of the efforts are poorly evaluated, if at all.

> Still, a few things are known. The programs that are most successful at producing black scientists are at historically black colleges and universities. Though they enroll only 25 percent of black college students, these schools grant 40 percent of black science and engineering degrees, and they account for six of the ten undergraduate schools that send the largest number of blacks on to earn science doctorates. Private and public, small and large, these colleges vary enormously—making it difficult to generalize. Yet, if Xavier University of Louisiana is any guide, the key is an emphasis on basics—both the basics of science and the basics of how to get through college.

A small school with a modest endowment and entering freshmen who are relatively poorly prepared, Xavier combines support services with rigorous academic standards. Introductory chemistry and biology courses set the tone. The faculty members have created their own textbooks, which walk students step by step through subjects, introducing basic vocabulary, emphasizing and reemphasizing key concepts, even dictating exactly how to work problems. "These kids need to learn some basic things before branching out," pre-med adviser J.W. Carmichael explains. "I don't leave anything out. I take them through every single detail... People say we're hand-holding. Yeah, we are, particularly in the early years."

Summing Up

NSF's Systemic Initiatives seem to be designed to enable the federal government to foreclose further local decision making on policies, programs, and materials for mathematics and science education. In order for state and local education agencies to secure NSF funds for improving mathematics and science education, they must be willing (at least implicitly) to adopt particular academic standards, instructional methods, textbooks, curricular configurations, and classroom management practices that are, at best, controversial and unsupported by a national consensus on their efficacy. At worst, these specific program components, like the use of Whole Language as a beginning reading methodology, exclude the use of other, effective methods for meeting children's educational needs.

In order to provide a national perspective on NSF's Systemic Initiatives Program, we turn first to a description of the development and consequences of the Los Angeles Systemic Initiative, an example of a systemic initiative at the local level.

The Los Angeles Systemic Initiative

Instituted in 1995, the second year of the National Science Foundation Urban Systemic Initiative Program, the Los Angeles Systemic Initiative (LASI) exerts a powerful influence on a district whose 1997–1998 budget exceeded $5.8 billion. At $3 million per year, NSF contributes, through funds for its Urban Systemic Initiative (USI), only about one twentieth of one percent of the school district's budget. Yet, for a mere $3.79 per student, NSF has been able to make fundamental and, as we will show, damaging changes in the nation's second largest school district. The ambitious scope of the Los Angeles Systemic Initiative is described in its Project Summary:

> The Los Angeles Unified School District, in partnership with Los Angeles professional, business, scientific, and education communities and through the vehicle of the Los Angeles Systemic Initiative, has reformed the content, delivery, and learning of mathematics, science, and technology in its 722 schools, affecting more than 792,000 students.[32]

In order to lay the foundation for deep systemic changes within the Los Angeles Unified School District (LAUSD), LASI solicited the support of powerful local and national organizations at its inception. Los Angeles Mayor Richard Riordan's office agreed to act as one of its public relations arms. Mike Roos, chief executive officer of LEARN (the Los Angeles Educational Alliance for Restructuring Now), was enlisted as an advisory board member, along with representatives from many other organizations, including several universities in the Los Angeles area. In concert with Bruce Alberts, president of the National Academy of Sciences, and educators from two other California cities, LASI planned the creation of a "California Coalition" to implement a total reform of science education in the state. LASI also gained access to resources within LAUSD, including ten science and technology centers for professional development of teachers, as well as to KLCS Channel 58 television.

Gaining Control

The first task for LASI was to institutionalize academic standards in LAUSD that facilitated NSF's goals for its systemic initiatives. LASI was singularly successful. LAUSD's official adoption of academic standards reflecting NSF's educational philosophy in 1996 was a watershed event in the LASI strategem. A 1998 NSF report boasted that "in Los Angeles, USI accountability became the framework for a major policy initiative establishing benchmarks and standards in all subject areas for the entire school system."[33]

With its mathematics standards adopted in Los Angeles, the next step for LASI was to implement NSF-approved curricula. One clear reason for LASI to insist on NCTM-based mathematics standards is that they comport with the weak mathematics curricula advanced by the LASI project. But even with LASI-supported standards in place, further systemic changes were necessary in LAUSD in order to implement all the components of NSF's educational philosophy. The 1997 LASI annual report makes this clear:

> LAUSD's urban systemic initiative is well under way with its efforts to renew and unify districtwide instruction using standards-based curricula. These curricula are characterized by hands-on, inquiry based, problem solving, integrated/coordinated, student-teacher interactive instruction in math, science, technology for grades K–12. These efforts are supported and strengthened by needs-based staff development, increased communication among teachers and staff, changes in administrative policies that are essential for student access to the systemic benefits, and checks on progress and process at preselected gates in the system's superstructure.[34]

LASI and NSF versus California

While NSF was institutionalizing NCTM-based mathematics standards in Los Angeles, flanked by stratospheric proclamations, the State of California was moving resolutely in the opposite direction. In December 1997, the California Board of Education adopted the Mathematics Academic Content Standards, developed with the assistance of four Stanford mathematics professors, Gunnar Carlsson, Ralph Cohen, Stephen Kerckhoff, and James Milgram.[35] The California state mathematics standards were broadly supported by the California mathematics community. An open letter directed to the chancellor of the California State University system, circulated by David Klein, was endorsed by one hundred California college and university mathematics professors, including the chairs of mathematics departments at leading universities and several world-renowned mathematicians. Jaime Escalante, of "Stand and Deliver" fame also added his personal endorsement to this open letter calling on California State University Chancellor Reed "to recognize the important and positive role California's recently adopted mathematics standards can play in the education of future teachers of mathematics in the state of California."[36]

In addition, in March 1998, the Thomas B. Fordham Foundation published an independent review of the mathematics standards from 46 states and the District of Columbia as well as Japan. California's mathematics standards received the highest score, outranking even those of Japan.[37] The American Federation of Teachers (AFT) also conducted a study of K–12 academic standards for all states, the District of Columbia, and Puerto Rico. California was the only state in its November 1998 report to receive a perfect score of check marks under the statements, "clear, specific, and grounded in content" for standards in the four content areas: mathematics, science, English, and social studies.[38]

Immediately after the California Board of Education adopted its new mathematics standards in December 1997, leaders of NSF's Systemic Initiative in Los Angeles counterattacked. They recognized that their ideological house of cards could be toppled by California's evolving content-focused educational policies. LAUSD Superintendent Ruben Zacarias, with assistance from LASI in "framing... the issues," released an Informative to LAUSD board members, dated December 8, 1997, asserting that "the LAUSD standards include and go beyond the State Board standards" (see Appendix C). The Informative further explained that:

> The high expectations for student achievement set forth by the [LAUSD] school board and the Superintendent will be met by implementing the standards-based curriculum recommended by the Los Angeles Systemic Initiative.

and

> If textbooks are written to meet, but not surpass, the expectations in the State Board standards, then LAUSD teachers will be forced to supplement the programs to deliver the rigorous, challenging mathematics program our students deserve.

As we can see from this response, the NCTM-based LAUSD standards were defended as more demanding than the content standards approved by the California Board of Education. NSF's Assistant Director for Education and Human Resources, Luther Williams, also joined in the counterattack against California's K–12 academic standards. Serving also as head of the Systemic Reform office, Williams wrote a letter, dated December 11, 1997, to the California Board of Education excoriating the new California mathematics standards (see Appendix A). Williams explained that the Board's decision to adopt the mathematics standards "vacates any serious commitment to elevating problem solving and critical thinking skills..." He charged that: "The Board action is, charitably, shortsighted and detrimental to the long-term mathematical literacy of children in California." Citing NSF support in excess of $50 million for systemic initiatives in California, including the one in Los Angeles, Williams warned that the NSF might terminate its support, and, speaking for the National Science Foundation, he chastised, "We view the Board action in California with grave disappointment and as a lost opportunity for the cities we support—indeed, for the entire state."

In the year following the state adoption of the new California mathematics standards, members of Mathematically Correct and others tried unsuccessfully to persuade the LAUSD Board of Education to replace its inferior mathematics standards with the new California standards.[39] The state's standards are voluntary for school districts, although yearly STAR (Standardized Testing and Reporting) examinations and state-approved textbooks are to be based upon them. Transcripts of the relevant board meetings are available on the Mathematically Correct website and they record unbending support for the LAUSD mathematics standards by the LASI advisors to the LAUSD Board. At the request of one board member, David Tokofsky, two of the authors of this chapter, together with other mathematicians, developed a detailed comparison of the LAUSD mathematics standards with the California standards. The comparison established beyond any possible doubt the superiority of the California standards and the almost comical shortcomings of its LASI-supported rival.[40]

Dumbing Down the Standards and the Curriculum

What are the weaknesses of the LAUSD mathematics standards? Beyond the canonical rhetoric, they have little mathematical content. In addition, they are redundant between grade levels and vague.[41] For example, with no elaboration whatsoever, one typical LAUSD benchmark requires students to "make connections among related mathematical concepts and apply these concepts to other content areas and the world of work." The LAUSD mathematics standards stipulate the use of calculators and other "appropriate technology" before the end of third grade, thus undermining mastery of arithmetic. The word "triangle" does not appear at all in the document, only one of many key terms that are missing. By design, trigonometry and all other algebra II topics do not appear in any grade level benchmarks. The intentional omission of these topics from the LAUSD mathematics standards was eventually acknowledged in an Informative dated June 4, 1998 from LAUSD Superintendent Ruben Zacarias to the LAUSD School Board, and it demonstrates the vacuity of LASI platitudes.[42] The low level of LASI standards belies NSF's superlatives about critical thinking, real-world applications, "standards-based" education, and "world-class" standards. The original LASI grant proposal even gushed, "We further believe that the conceptual understanding of algebra and physics can and must begin with the entry of that student in kindergarten."

The high intensity verbiage surrounding NSF's educational philosophy can be disarming to an unsuspecting public. But parents and mathematical scientists in Los Angeles found common cause in pointing out the importance of basic skills—missing in the LAUSD mathematics standards—for laying the foundation for deeper scientific understanding. Glamorless necessities like elementary addition and subtraction facts find little support in an NSF-supported education program which, without a trace of irony, can advocate "conceptual understanding of algebra and physics" for entering kindergarten students.

The mathematics curricula supported explicitly by LASI are as deficient as its standards. Indeed, the "standards-based curriculum recommended by the Los Angeles Systemic Initiative" explicitly includes some of the worst mathematics programs in existence. In a letter critical of California's new mathematics standards, dated January 21, 1998, Superintendent Ruben Zacarias wrote: "*MathLand,* which was highly recommended by the California Instructional Resources Evaluation Panel, is one of the LASI recommended curricular programs" (see Appendix D).

The 1997 LASI annual report also affirmed LASI's support of *MathLand* and the *Connected Mathematics Program,* described in the first section of this chapter, for elementary and middle school programs. LASI explicitly endorses shallow curricula at the high school level as well. The goal is to purge LAUSD of algebra I, geometry, and algebra II/trigonometry, referred to as "traditional math," and replace it by a mish-mash known as "integrated math." At a June 15, 1998 meeting held at Nobel Middle School in LAUSD, LASI unveiled its plans to an audience of approximately 100 skeptical parents and a few journalists.[43] Using overhead projectors, LASI personnel explained that within five years all middle and high schools in LAUSD would be teaching integrated mathematics only, using one of the following series: *Core-Plus Mathematics Project, Interactive Mathematics Project, College Preparatory Math,* or *Integrated Math.* The plan is not to allow the more logically organized "traditional math" at all. According to Robert Hamada, mathematics coordinator for the district's Los Angeles Systemic Initiative, integrated mathematics had already been instituted in the majority of LAUSD schools by the summer of 1998. Objections to "integrated math" by parents in attendance on the grounds that the top performing schools in LAUSD—including national Academic Decathalon champions—teach only traditional mathematics were brushed aside by LASI personnel.

The incompatibility of traditional mathematics curricula with the NSF-sponsored variety was acknowledged in the 1997 LASI report:

> Math teachers want credit for both absolute and comparative growth. They have analyzed their staff development model and revised it to include coaching for the 3-year integrated, comprehensive math program that bumps heads with the algebra-geometry tradition. They anticipate that test scores may fall a bit before they rise and stay up because it takes 3–5 years to see real effects of curricular reform that builds from lower grades to higher.

The last sentence of this quotation from the LASI report is a tactical finesse designed to fight off evidence-based criticisms. Test scores might fall, we are told, in advance of the "real effects of the curricular reform." But how is anyone to know whether student performance is getting worse in ways that will lay the groundwork for later improvement, or whether student performance is getting worse because the programs are worse and it will never get better? The near absence of mathematical content in the NSF-sponsored curricula weighs heavily in favor of the latter contingency.

Protecting Mediocrity

LASI also created evaluation strategies to curb teacher resistance. According to its grant proposal:

> Teacher performance will be evaluated by pre- and post-program surveys designed to identify changes in the following: instructional strategies and the amount of classroom time spent in direct lecture, student activities, investigations, demonstrations, cooperative learning, and direct textbook work. In addition, teachers are encouraged to develop their own systems for self-monitoring, using portfolios and journals to record their professional growth.

With the immanent STAR exam tied to the demanding California mathematics standards, classroom teachers have felt pressure to improve test scores, and some worry that the LASI program won't do it. This was acknowledged in a grant proposal to the California State University

Chancellor's office from the Northridge campus, undertaken with LASI collaboration. The funded grant proposal to retrain middle school mathematics teachers warned: "There is general panic about the SAT 9 [STAR exam], and teachers are reverting to traditional methods of teaching rather than uncovering the mathematics in the curriculum they currently have." "Uncovering the mathematics" in the NSF-sponsored "curriculum they currently have" would be more easily carried out by magicians than mathematicians, as it is nearly invisible.

LASI's influence on education extends to the state level in other ways. The selection process for district representatives to the California State Science Curriculum Framework Committee is a case in point. This committee is charged with writing a state guide for the implementation of the science standards; the guide deals with pedagogical issues and serves as a blueprint for textbooks. The committee consists of K–12 teachers and members of other public constituencies.

Douglas Lasken, an LAUSD elementary school teacher and union chapter chair for his school, sought permission from the district to apply for a position on the Science Curriculum Framework Committee based on his understanding and strong support of the new California Science Standards and his experience giving inservice science lessons for other teachers. He needed a district administrator's signature on his application indicating that LAUSD would pay for a substitute teacher when he attended required meetings in Sacramento. The signature would have been perfunctory if Lasken had embraced the teaching philosophies of LASI. But LASI personnel had testified against the state science standards before they were approved, and Lasken had supported those standards.

As it happened, the district administrator, who was associated with LASI, refused to give Lasken the signature until dozens of Lasken's supporters requested help from LAUSD Board member David Tokofsky. The district administrator then signed Lasken's application, which was submitted to the appropriate state agency. It was only later that Lasken learned that this administrator had secretly rescinded the signature, signaling the state agency that no substitute teachers were available. Meanwhile, other LAUSD candidates sympathetic to LASI's educational philosophy proceeded with their applications unimpeded. Lasken was prevented from participating on the Framework Committee. Other teachers who supported the new science standards and who applied to the Framework Committee had experiences similar to Lasken's.

Thus, a single Urban Systemic Initiative Program, like LASI, not only has the power to impose the NSF agenda on a local school district, including weak standards and curricula, it can even influence educational policies at the state level. As the next section of this chapter demonstrates, influence in the reverse direction can be of greater consequence. The Texas Statewide Systemic Initiative is the prototypical example. It imposed its leadership on the entire state education apparatus, affecting every school district in the state.

The Texas Statewide Systemic Initiative

In 1994, the National Science Foundation (NSF) awarded Texas a four-year grant of $2,000,000 annually to implement a Statewide Systemic Initiative (SSI). For the matching funds required by NSF, the Texas Legislature approved an Appropriations Bill designating $1,000,000 annually to the SSI. The legislation clearly defined the parameters intended for the SSI. Funding was to be provided for discrete mathematics and science programs in the schools contingent on evaluations by the Commissioner of Education demonstrating their success.[44] Legislators did not suspect that they were funding a federally directed program that would replace the state's authority in education, supersede community control of schools, and construct a system wielding the most centralized control over educational policy ever established in the state.[45]

Over the past four years, the SSI has come to direct a variety of state programs, provides leadership for a vast array of agency partnerships, and influences all aspects of education in Texas. Curricula, instructional practices, textbooks, assessment, professional development of teachers, teacher evaluation, teacher certification, and preservice teacher education all now fall under the purview of the Texas SSI. The Texas SSI also claims to exert influence over the largest and most important sources of money for education in the state "in ways that reflect our mission."[46] It does not exaggerate when describing itself as "wearing the mantle of leadership in Texas" and playing a "central role in the reform of education" in its Program Effectiveness Reviews of 1997 and 1998.

The changes in classroom instruction, state policy, and educational governance now being implemented in Texas by the SSI reflect the design for the nationwide system of educational policies and programs created by the federal legislation passed in 1994: Improving America's

Schools, Goals 2000, and School-to-Work.[47] This legislation promotes comprehensive change in state educational systems based on the constructivist standards created by national professional and educational organizations in the late 1980s and early 1990s. To encourage states to adopt uniform educational policies and programs based on these standards, NSF was charged to assist the U.S. Department of Education.[48] When the federal legislation was passed in 1994, NSF had a ready-made vehicle—its Statewide Systemic Initiatives Program—for conveying specific policies and programs to the states. Originally created in 1991 to help states improve mathematics and science education, the Statewide Systemic Initiatives Program was redesigned to deliver the Department of Education's particular vision of standards-based educational reform to the states.

The changes in classroom instruction, state policy, and educational governance introduced by the Texas SSI define the form and content of what federal agencies, schools of education, and others refer to as "standards-based systemic reform." The means used by the SSI to acquire authority over educational policy and programs in Texas, and the outcome of these efforts so far, reflect a vision of education and government that is very different from the one we have traditionally enjoyed.

Acquiring the Three R's: Respectability, Relationships, and Resources

In 1994, the Texas SSI was established in the Charles A. Dana Center, a research facility of the College of Natural Sciences at the University of Texas at Austin. The director of the Dana Center became and remains the SSI's Principal Investigator and Executive Director. The executive director of the Texas Business and Education Coalition agreed to serve as vice chairman of the SSI's board. For over ten years, the Coalition has been recognized as the most powerful non-governmental force in state education. Because the University of Texas at Austin is highly respected as a center for educational research, these initial associations assured public reception of the Texas SSI and created an image for this initiative as a legitimate leader in the state, serving education with academic independence and scholarly objectivity.

The SSI was initiated into state educational policy through contracts with the Governor's Office and the Texas Education Agency (TEA). The SSI forged an intimate relationship with the TEA by naming the state commissioner of education as Co-Principal Investigator of the SSI.[49] In 1995, the TEA awarded the SSI the contract to develop new state curriculum standards for mathematics and science.[50] Later, the TEA contracted with the SSI to develop services and products to support the new curriculum standards and, in 1998, the TEA designated the SSI as the Center for Educator Development in Mathematics and Science.[51]

Since 1995, the SSI has brokered formal working relationships with the Texas Higher Education Coordinating Board, the State Board for Educator Certification, the Texas Legislature, the Texas Ed Flex Committee, the College Board in Texas, the Texas Education Network, the Texas Business and Education Coalition, the 20 Education Region Centers, the Texas Engineering Foundation, the Southwest Educational Development Laboratory, regional School-to-Work Partnerships, the Texas Educational Productivity Council, the Alliance School Network (Texas's 22 largest school districts), various citizen groups, and professional associations of mathematics and science teachers, school boards, principals, and superintendents. According to the Texas SSI's Annual Reports for 1997 and 1998, it has established partnerships with almost every state agency and organization focusing on education in Texas. These relationships enable the SSI to coordinate its work across the various components of state education. Today, the Texas SSI is:[52]

- Directing the state-sponsored professional development of all primary and secondary teachers in mathematics and science.

- Developing guidelines for state teachers colleges preservice programs for teachers of mathematics and science, funding teachers colleges to implement the guidelines, and conducting preservice mathematics and science programs.

- Assisting the TEA in the development of state assessments (TAAS and end-of-course exams) for primary and secondary education.

- Creating services and products for schools to support mathematics and science reform.

- Managing the state's K–12 Eisenhower Program funds for TEXTEAM, which trains teachers to be catalysts for reform in their schools.

- Working in cooperation with the State Board for Educator Certification to revise rules governing new teacher evaluation and certification.

- Managing the state's Comprehensive Assistance Center for Elementary and Secondary Education Act Programs (STAR) in directing the expenditure of state and federal compensatory education funds.

In addition, according to its 1998 Program Effectiveness Review, the SSI is coordinating its activities across the myriad of state initiatives managed by the Dana Center and mobilizing the resources of all initiatives in support of SSI objectives. Initiatives managed by the Center include: Texas Head Start, the TERC School-to-Career Program, the Texas Education Network, the Center for Community Engagement and Volunteerism, Title I School Improvement Project, Homeless Education, AmeriCorps, and the Accelerated Schools Program. Coordination between the SSI and the Dana Center has blurred operational boundaries and confounded public perception of organizational distinctions. This ambiguity has been meticulously cultivated by the SSI. Publications, such as its 1998 Program Effectiveness Review, advise the public to view the SSI within the broad context of the Dana Center. Many publications identify various functions of the SSI and Dana Center as the combined organization, Dana Center/SSI. Integrated with a state agency and surrounded by a variety of state programs, the SSI has successfully masked its federal identity and the source of its particular objectives.

Since a core purpose of the NSF programs is providing minority and economically disadvantaged students what NSF believes is educational equity,[53] gaining acceptance by minority communities is fundamental to success. For the Texas SSI, securing this support has been especially important because Hispanics and African-Americans compose 55% of the student population. The 1997 Annual Report published by the SSI declared its commitment to access and equity, promising to reduce the achievement gap between student populations. One of the SSI's primary means for conveying "standards-based reform" to minority students has been the Title 1 Schools Improvement Program, which has furnished grants to over 100 schools in the state with high concentrations of disadvantaged students. Through other initiatives described as public service, the SSI has garnered even more minority support and involvement for programs based on constructivist standards. An illustrative program, Emerging Scholars, was featured in a nationally syndicated column in the *Washington Post*, in which William Raspberry compared the SSI's executive director with Jaime Escalante (given fame as a hero for minority education by the movie *Stand and Deliver*). A relationship with the Intercultural Development and Research Association, a statewide organization devoted to the educational advancement of Hispanic and economically disadvantaged students, has furnished the SSI with direct access to minority policy makers and the opportunity to engage them in a reform of mathematics and science education based on the constructivist standards NSF is promoting. Publishing articles in the Association's monthly newsletter, the SSI has widely disseminated the message that instruction based on constructivist standards is specifically designed to meet the special educational needs of minority students.[54]

While developing the strategic relationships and programs required to influence state-level changes, the Texas SSI simultaneously works as a self-described "catalyst for change" in all local school districts. As noted in the SSI's 1997 Annual Report, "the implementation of a standards-based curriculum in every classroom, for every child" is its driving objective. Various strategies to accomplish this goal are described by the report. A cadre of trainers is deployed by the SSI to serve as intermediaries with schools in the development and maintenance of changes based on constructivist standards, introducing programs, influencing policy, and training teachers. The 800 member cadre (recruited from regional centers, the largest school districts, Urban Systemic Initiatives, Rural Systemic Initiatives, and teachers associated with *Connected Mathematics Project*) has trained almost 4,000 teachers across Texas to use instruction based on constructivist standards. The SSI also introduces mathematics and science programs developed by NSF. Offering incentive grants, the Texas SSI has implemented NSF-developed curricula in 609 schools in the state. The SSI is working to introduce all NSF-developed curricula throughout the state, but it is presently concentrating on scaling up the *Connected Mathematics Project* in Texas as the prototype of a middle school curriculum based on constructivist standards.[55]

The SSI has assembled a network of almost 100,000 individuals in Texas (trainers, activists, action team members, associates, and subcontractors) to work in all of the 1044 school districts.[56] Nearly one-third of Texas's 3,700,000 students use instructional materials sponsored by the NSF.[57] The SSI anticipates that efforts to introduce NSF-endorsed programs into every classroom in Texas will be increasingly successful because "as the newly designated Center for Educator Development for both mathematics and science, we are in an ideal position to promote and prepare districts for adoption of curricula."[58]

The SSI provides direction and support for other NSF and federal Initiatives in Texas. The NSF's Urban Systemic Initiatives in Dallas, San Antonio, and El Paso, as well as the new Rural Systemic Initiative, coordinate activities and resources with the Texas SSI. Funding from the Pew Charitable Foundation enabled the SSI to develop the Working-to-Learn Summer Institutes that train teachers in the methodology required by the federal School-to-Work law, a methodology also based on constructivist standards.[59] Contracting with TERC, a Massachusetts-based research and development organization, the SSI has created a School-to-Work Team to assist School-to-Work Partnerships in developing constructivist-oriented curricula.[50] The SSI is also working with the Capital Area Workforce Development Board to introduce *Connected Mathematics Project* as a model curriculum for School-to-Work initiatives in Austin area schools.[61] Helping school districts to implement the new federal Comprehensive School Reform Development Project, an initiative that specifically funds NSF-developed mathematics and science programs,[62] enables the Texas SSI to significantly expand instruction based on constructivist standards.

How the Texas SSI Promotes and Funds Systemic Reform

The vast array of programs directed or coordinated by the Texas SSI, the innumerable programs directly influenced through partnerships or cooperative efforts, and the complex network of organizational relationships just described all contribute to systemic change. In the past four years, the Texas SSI has worked to coordinate all policies, programs, agencies, organizations, funding, personnel, and materials into a coherent framework promoting a constructivist approach to learning. The coordination or alignment of all the components of the educational system creates a tight infrastructure, one component reinforcing another.

Textbook adoptions by the schools in the next few years will serve to measure the influence of the systemic reform introduced by the SSI. In 1998, its influence became evident with the SSI's effort to constrict the adoption of mathematics textbooks to an NSF-developed program. In Texas, the purchase of textbooks by school districts is underwritten by the state if the textbook selected meets the expectations for learning established by the state curriculum standards. The TEA reviews textbooks and publishes a list of textbooks meeting the instructional objectives established by the state mathematics curriculum standards. In the fall of 1998, immediately prior to the State Board of Education adoption of the textbook list, the Texas SSI published a list of mathematics textbooks for schools listing only NSF-sponsored textbooks and developed a state conference to showcase these textbooks, most of which were not included on the state textbook list.[63] The SSI also issued a newsletter to schools that identified the SSI as the state's Center for Educator Development (CED) with responsibility for helping schools implement the state curriculum standards, and emphasized the necessity of selecting the appropriate textbooks.[64] This newsletter advises schools that selecting textbooks on the state's list might not be the best choice, offers the assistance of SSI-trained staff at Education Region Centers, and encourages schools to use the SSI guideline in selecting textbooks.[65] The SSI's *Instructional Materials Analysis and Selection* guideline opens with advice for schools to select textbooks based on NCTM standards and provides a checklist that includes criteria based on these standards that textbooks should contain to qualify for selection.[66]

While the direct influence over textbook selection is enormous, the indirect influence is far more extensive. Every education policy in the state has been shaped by the SSI to reinforce the selection of textbooks based on NSF-endorsed standards. Assessment of student learning, school ratings based on student assessment, instructional approaches taught in professional development programs for teachers, instructional methods used for evaluating teachers, instructional approaches used to train prospective teachers, and teaching demonstrations required for teacher certification—all are now based on constructivist standards. The selection of a knowledge-oriented textbook would conflict with all aspects of educational policy. To help make sure that schools would make the correct choice, the SSI's 1998 Annual Report noted: "We trained more than 60 mathematics leaders from around the state to use the SSI-developed Instruction Materials Evaluation and Selection Process Manual in district textbook adoption processes so that the new textbooks adopted for the next decade will be standards-based." It remains to be seen how many schools select NSF-endorsed mathematics textbooks.

Systemic reform of education is clearly incomplete without the alignment of fiscal resources. The Texas SSI has accomplished this by influencing the largest and most important sources of state and federal money for education "in ways that reflect our mission," according to its 1997 Annual Report. The report claims the SSI influences the expenditure of approximately $2 billion dollars annually of federal and state monies (designated for programs such as Head Start, Title I, Compensatory Education Program, and the Technology Infrastructure Fund). As well as aligning state and federal education monies to serve the objectives of the SSI, direct funding of almost $18,000,000 is acquired annually by the SSI from a variety of sources, including the University of Austin, NSF, local school districts, and private or corporate donations, according to the 1997 Program Effectiveness Review. Of the $18,000,000 acquired by the SSI in 1998, more than $4,000,000 was provided by local school districts as matching funds for SSI programs, contributed from their Title I monies for improving the education of disadvantaged students.

How the Texas Statewide Systemic Initiative Promotes Constructivist Instructional Methods

Policies, guidelines, and reports published by the SSI and partner organizations in Texas provide a clear definition of education based on constructivist standards in its application to teaching and expectations for learning. The details in the following documents identify the primary role that instruction, not curricular content, plays in systemic reform and reveal the extent to which systemic reform rigidly scripts instructional methods.

The *Mathematics TEKS Toolkit, Clarifying Activities,* published by the Texas SSI on the Texas Education Network Web Site,[67] offers teachers methods to translate the state curriculum standards for mathematics into classroom instruction. Sample lessons illustrate the activities teachers should use to introduce specific state standards for grade-level instructional expectations. For example, the first state standard for kindergarten mathematics (K.1) requires students to use numbers to name quantities. The lesson furnished for this standard has students holding a handful of small objects, naming the number of each

National Science Foundation Systemic Initiatives 345

object, and recording the process of counting by adding the objects on a calculator. This lesson incorporates several principles of systemic reform. Calculators are introduced as the first and primary method of recording and computing numbers. Numbers and counting are introduced in the context of a complex problem (for kindergartners). Students are expected to construct for themselves the meaning of numerical symbols on the calculator, as well as the algorithm of addition by counting, as the first lesson in mathematics presented in elementary school.

The *Mathematics Center for Educator Development, Mathematics and Instruction,* published by the Texas SSI on the Texas Education Network Web Site,[68] provides instructional methods for implementing the state mathematics standards. Position papers advocate constructivism, noting that students learn best when constructing their own learning instead of receiving direction or information from teachers. Ability grouping of students is identified as harmful to student learning. Cooperative grouping (where students teach one another), as well as group grading, is recommended. Teachers are advised to encourage students to use calculators (because technology removes the necessity for students to learn supposedly low-level skills). The use of concrete manipulatives is encouraged to augment the use of mathematical symbols in every grade level. Teachers are discouraged from providing students with correct answers or asking them to seek correct answers. And teachers are exhorted to avoid presenting mathematics as any sequence of mathematical knowledge or skills. As a resource for curriculum, only the specific mathematics programs developed by NSF are listed.

The *Mathematics Center for Educator Development, Mathematics Assessment,* published by the Texas SSI on the Texas Education Network Web Site, dispenses any notion that assessments are to be conducted primarily for teachers to use for evaluating student achievement. This section clarifies that assessments should be used as an instructional strategy to provide students with an opportunity to evaluate themselves. An open-ended problem (with no right answer), an investigation, or a product or products are identified as the different forms assessment should assume.

The *Guidelines for Mathematical Preparation of Prospective Elementary Teachers,* published by the Texas SSI on the Texas Education Network Web Site,[69] identifies the mathematical content that preservice teachers are required to master for both classroom instruction based on the state curriculum standards and the examination for teacher certification. It also identifies the instructional methods teachers should use. The instructional section begins with an admonition against rote memorization, mathematical rules, mathematical definitions, and mathematical formulas, and a commendation for constructivist learning. Calculators are praised for removing computational burdens. Cooperative groups and investigative projects are identified as important classroom strategies. The section concludes with a warning against teaching mathematics as a linear progression of topics and skills, thereby dismissing centuries of carefully constructed systems of mathematics developed by the best minds of every culture.

The *Mathematics Center for Educator Development, Professional Development and Appraisal System for Texas Teachers,* published by the TEA on the Texas Education Network Web Site, provides schools with a recommended plan for teacher evaluation, incorporating the criteria required by state law. This plan identifies the instructional methods that teachers must demonstrate in the classroom, including promoting students toward self-directed learning, introducing facts and skills through complex problem solving, and connecting mathematics with other subjects and work. The degree to which teachers comply with national and state policies is also an evaluation criterion.

Equity in the Reform of Mathematics and Science Education, published in 1994 by the Southwest Educational Development Laboratory of Austin, Texas, describes the instructional methods introduced by "systemic reform" and NSF's various Statewide Systemic Initiatives. This report begins by claiming that traditional instructional methods erect a barrier to the education of minority students, and it describes the special educational needs of minorities. The instructional strategies that supposedly hurt minorities are identified, including standardized tests, ability grouping, curricula that emphasize right answers, competitive activities, teacher-centered classrooms, and remedial instruction. And it defines the instructional methods that minorities supposedly require for educational success, including mixed ability classroom grouping, constructivist curricula, cooperative learning groups, project-based instruction, and authentic assessment. The report admits that education programs based on constructivist methods lack a substantial empirical research base to support them, but it does not suggest that this failing should logically restrict the use of these experimental methods on minority students.

The *Texas Essential Knowledge and Skills for Mathematics,* published by the TEA, lists the standards of learning for students in kindergarten through grade 12. Instructional objectives are expressed as performances that students are expected to demonstrate at each grade (although almost one-quarter of the expectations are repeated year after year). As recommended by NCTM's standards, instructional objectives focus not on correct answers or specific facts but on process (called "higher order skills" to make thinking processes sound preferable to knowledge and as something not necessarily requiring knowledge). For example, fifth grade students are expected to "use multiplication to solve problems involving whole numbers (no more than three digits times two digits without technology)." The dominant operative verb is "use," not "solve," so students can fully comply with this instructional objective by using multiplication to solve a problem whether or not they solve it correctly. This example also demonstrates the reliance on calculators for more complex, although arduous, computations. There is not one single state standard for mathematics, from kindergarten through grade 12, that explicitly requires students to produce a correct answer. Only in three instances are students required to memorize or acquire mental automaticity of facts or skills. In kindergarten, students are required to count to 100 (although students may meet this expectation by counting incorrectly or using a calculator); in grade 2, students are required to recall basic addition facts (sums to 18); and, in grade 4, students are required to recall multiplication facts through 12 x 12.

In addition, every instructional objective is expressed as an application of learning that relates to everyday experience. For example, eighth grade students are expected to "use the Pythagorean Theorem to solve real-life problems" and "use geometric concepts to solve problems in fields such as art and architecture" (although the standards do not offer any clues as to what this could mean). Approximately one-fourth of each grade-level expectation requires students to demonstrate mathematical competencies that are separate and distinct from mathematical academic content, such as these examples from grade 8: "identity and apply mathematics to everyday experience"; "validate his or her conclusions"; "select tools such as real objects, manipulatives, paper/pencil, and technology or techniques such as mental math, estimation, and number sense to solve problems"; and "use a problem solving model that incorporates understanding the problem, making a plan, carrying out the plan, and evaluating the solution for reasonableness."

Evaluation of Systemic Reform and Constructivist Instructional Methods

The instructional methods associated with "systemic reform" represent an educational approach known as "progressivism." Despite the inference that these methods are new, they have been used in American classrooms throughout the 20th century under a variety of names. These instructional methods were, and continue to be, introduced as social reforms, intended to make education more equitable. A teaching guide, *Moving into the Mainstream,* published on the Texas SSI state curriculum web site, explains that they have vital importance because equal opportunity and equal access have proven inadequate in furnishing educational equity to minorities.[70] This guide claims that discovery learning (constructivism), cooperative learning, learner-focused (student-directed) classrooms, contextual (problem solving) instruction, everyday applications (applied learning), project-based (thematic) instruction, connections (interdisciplinary learning), and authentic (performance-based) assessment have proven to be effective strategies in "leveling the playing field" to derive equal academic outcomes. To the contrary, empirical research has produced substantial evidence attesting to the harm that "progressive" instructional methods inflict on all students' academic achievement.[71] And these instructional methods most harm minority students, according to *Project Follow Through*, a 25-year study conducted by the U.S. Department of Education to determine the most effective instructional strategies for disadvantaged students.[72]

The immediate impact of systemic reform on mathematics instruction in Texas is difficult to evaluate. Assessments of state standards conducted recently by national organizations identify Texas's new standards as average (or mediocre, depending on the perspective). The 1999 *Education Week Quality Counts* rated Texas's standards as B+ (although it gave an F to Iowa, the state producing the highest SAT scores in the nation). The Fordham Foundation's 1998 *State Mathematics Standards* rated Texas's mathematics standards as B (giving 12 states higher ratings). The Council for Basic Education's 1998 *Great Expectations? Defining and Assessing Rigor for Mathematics and English Language Arts* rated Texas's mathematics standards also as B (giving 15 other states a higher rating).

Because the new curriculum framework was not officially implemented until January 1999, and the first selection of textbooks aligned with constructivist standards has yet to be completed, the effect of the new curriculum framework on student achievement cannot be evaluated at this time. It is possible, however, to review the impact of the instructional policies embedded in the NSF programs introduced to Texas over the past four years by the SSI.

Annual reports published by the Texas SSI proclaim success for the NSF programs, contending that these programs have increased student achievement in Texas. This claim should be closely examined for several reasons. Most of the individual schools employing NSF curricula use authentic assessment—non-standardized, subjective evaluations of student achievement. SSI reports rely on scores from the state academic proficiency test, TAAS (Texas Assessment of Academic Skills). With few exceptions, TAAS scores have climbed annually for every school in the state. The SSI has yet to publish data that indicates a statistically significant difference in TAAS scores between students in the 609 schools engaged in SSI programs and non-participating students. No study of Texas SSI programs has been conducted by any independent and disinterested researcher. In short, no valid and reliable data have been generated to date in Texas to support SSI's claims for academic success. The absence of quantitative data for SSI programs in Texas replicates the situation in other states. A five-year analysis of SSIs sponsored by NSF itself could not find enough test score data to support claims that NSF-endorsed mathematics and science programs raise academic achievement or reduce the achievement gap between student populations.[73]

Student scores on national tests provide mixed news about the mathematical achievement of primary and secondary school students in Texas. Although a 1998 study of NAEP data indicates significant mathematical gains for Texas fourth and eighth grade students from 1992–1996, with a significant narrowing of the achievement gap between minority and white students,[74] only 25% of fourth grade students and 21% of eighth grade students score at or above the proficiency level. Although the TEA also reports regular improvements in TAAS scores across the grades, and a significant shrinking of the achievement gap since 1995, two research studies conducted independently in 1998 revealed serious flaws in the TAAS grade 8 mathematics test; it assesses content and difficulty about two grades below grade 8 and in effect does not assess performance in the top half of the achievement curve.[75] A third study published in 1999 confirmed that the standards for mathematical learning in Texas are one to two years lower than most states in grade equivalence.[76] Although both NAEP and TAAS scores show a closing of the achievement gap between student populations, the combined SAT score for Texas remains unchanged at 995 since 1996, and the achievement gap slowly widens. Since 1996, mean SAT scores for Hispanics and African Americans in Texas have declined two points, and combined SAT scores in 1998 place Texas as the seventh lowest state in the nation. The disparity between the scores on the SAT, a college preparatory exam, and the scores on TAAS, a minimum proficiency exam, strongly suggests that educational practices in Texas constrain high-level achievement, especially in the higher grades and most especially for minorities.

How the Texas Statewide Systemic Initiative Is Challenging Communities and the State for Control of Education

The curricula and methods of instruction for mathematics and science being implemented as part of systemic reform in Texas are supported by a new infrastructure of policy and governance created by the SSI.[77] Operating as the axis of this infrastructure, the SSI prescribes specific educational practices, specific uses for educational dollars, and specific educational policies in the state. As a result, systemic reform has compromised the ability of parents, teachers, and elected public officials to shape day-to-day classroom instruction or develop alternative educational policies and programs. The following examples illustrate how the Texas SSI constrains informed or independent local and state educational decision-making. The first deals with its behind-the-scenes influence on Texas's standards.

In late 1996, the state released drafts of the revised standards for K–12, allowing Texans 30 days for review prior to State Board of Education adoption. The public was not officially notified of the review until several weeks into the scheduled time period, and then only because of a letter to Texas newspapers written by a teacher on one of the state writing teams. Public outcry ensued. Criticisms were levied against both the abbreviated time for review and the extreme vagueness of the proposed standards, especially in mathematics. Several members of the State Board requested public review be extended and experts consulted. The Governor subsequently described the proposed standards as "mush" and extended time for public review. In the months following, and continuing until the standards were adopted in late 1997, the State Board of Education was deluged with citizen testimony criticizing the influence of national standards documents on the new Texas expectations for learning. Much public concern was voiced that national organizations, such as the National Center for Education and the Economy, worked with writing teams assembled by the TEA to shape state standards according to the standards developed by NCTM and other national professional organizations. Much public concern was voiced that Goals 2000 funding had influenced the new state standards for learning. The TEA denied that the proposed standards were based on national standards and denied any influence on the proposed standards by the state's Goals 2000 Plan, any national organization, or any federal agency. The TEA repeatedly stressed that the new standards were written by Texans for Texas.

Representing concerns of their constituents, several members of the State Board of Education continued to press the TEA for information about these influences and their adverse impact on state expectations for learning. Newspapers throughout the state published the TEA's description of these inquiries as a reflection of paranoia about a federal conspiracy. High profile legislators threatened to draft bills replacing the elected board with an appointed board if these board members persisted in what was described as obstructing education reform.

In the meantime, attribution of the Texas SSI as contract writer for the state standards in mathematics and science (listed on the first public draft) was removed from subsequent drafts. Then, in response to a request by the State Board of Education for a list of the writers responsible for the standards, a list was provided that identified the SSI only indirectly; it designated specific members of the Dana Center as contributing writers working with a selected group of Texas teachers. Not until late 1998 were facts available to the public; the SSI, funded by Goals 2000 for the express purpose of developing the mathematics and science components of the state's Goals 2000 Plan,[78] had indeed designed the state's standards, based on guidelines developed by NCTM and the National Research Council.[79] Misrepresentation of the origin of the standards had caused members of the board to give false reassurance to the public and prevented some members from representing constituent interests effectively. Full disclosure might well have prevented approval of these standards as well as legislation filed in the 76th Texas Legislature to replace the elected state board of education with an appointed board (a vote is pending at this time).

Systemic reform is also disenfranchising teachers from decision making on classroom instruction in Texas. Historically, teachers have served on school textbook selection committees and furnished local school boards with recommendations best suited to student needs. In 1999, school districts either discontinued the custom or limited the authority of teachers on textbook selection committees. After distributing a review of mathematics textbooks to school district textbook selection committees throughout Texas, I received dozens of calls. Teachers across the state relayed concerns that textbook selection had been predetermined to select NSF-endorsed textbooks and described a variety of strategies used to "skew" selection: The textbook selection guideline published by the SSI ruled out any instructional materials other than NSF-endorsed textbooks; SSI-trained teachers directed school textbook selection committees; school administrators distributed an NSF-sponsored textbook analysis and advised teachers that those with the highest ratings met Statewide and Urban Systemic Initiative goals; school administrators advised teachers that the Urban Systemic Initiative would withdraw funding if the NSF-endorsed textbooks were not selected; and one school board provided teachers with a notice from an Urban Systemic Initiative identifying the two acceptable choices for adoption. These teachers also reported little or no support for these NSF-endorsed textbooks.

Systemic reform is eroding the ability of parents to participate in informed ways in local school decisions as well. In early 1998, a group of parents in Plano asked their local school board for permission to withdraw their children from the *Connected Mathematics Program*, an NSF-endorsed middle school mathematics program, because the children were failing to learn basic mathematic skills. The parents asked the district board to provide a traditional instructional alternative. When the district board refused, parents began an extensive investigation of the *Connected Mathematics Program*. They uncovered a report issued by the TEA indicating that the *Connected Mathematics Program* satisfies only slightly more than half of the state requirements for grade level instruction. They also discovered that its teacher's manual warns that students may score lower on standardized tests of computational skills than students in traditional classes. The parents requested data from the SSI that would support the academic claims of the *Connected Mathematics Program* and were given only the 1998 scores from TAAS for schools using the program even though the program had been used by several schools for several years. The parents then obtained records documenting the solicitation of schools in their district by the Dana Center/SSI to implement the *Connected Mathematics Program* as an experimental program and determined that their local school board had never reviewed or voted on the program.[80] The parents also discovered that statutory protections of parental rights in education would not apply when children participate in programs sponsored by the Texas SSI. Federal law exempts NSF from any obligation to obtain parental consent when children take part in educational experiments.[81] And as an authorized agent of the Secretary of Education, the SSI is also exempt from any obligation to obtain parental consent for collecting and releasing personally identifiable information about children.[82]

Refused the ability to withdraw their children from the SSI program by the district board and exempted from an appeal to parental rights by federal legislation, the Plano parents hired legal counsel and appealed to the State Board of Education in January 1999. The parents argued that the State Board should share responsibility for resolving their problem because the SSI is authorized by the TEA to provide educational services to school districts and to implement mathematics programs that are to be evaluated by the Commissioner of Education. They appealed to the Commissioner to conduct an evaluation of the *Connected Mathematics Program* as charged by law. In response, the State Board advised the parents to resolve the problem with their school district and described the problem as one of local, not state, control, subject to the authority of the local community. No response was furnished by the Commissioner of Education, and to date, the parents have yet to be notified of any state evaluation of the *Connected Mathematics Program*.[83] An editorial by a Plano parent in the *Plano Star Courier* raised questions about the accuracy of the director's claim that the Dana Center does not endorse adoption of any instructional programs and noted the State Board's responsibility to ensure that schools offer a curriculum based on the state's standards.[84] Nonetheless, the Plano parents must rely on the SSI's Co-Investigator, the Commissioner of Education, to review SSI programs with objectivity. The difficulty these parents encountered in obtaining full information from the SSI or about the programs it supports suggests how the SSI views accountability to the public.

Finally, systemic reform may curtail the development of maverick educational programs that defy the constructivist approach to curricula and instruction prescribed by the Texas SSI. Arguing against replacing content-based pedagogy with experimental programs based on lower academic standards for minority students, Manuel Berriozabal, a mathematician at the University of Texas at San Antonio, developed TexPREP in 1979. His goal was to open the door to higher education for minority students by disproving the stereotype that minority students cannot succeed in content-oriented courses. Since 1979, TexPREP has provided middle and high school students with substantive programs in mathematics and science that offer direct instruction in a structured classroom environment. In Texas today, TexPREP is offered in 23 schools and engages 3,000 students. Over the past 20 years, almost 16,000 students have enrolled in TexPREP. The high school graduation rate for TexPREP students is 99%, 93% of TexPREP students are admitted to college, and 87% graduate from college.[85] Although TexPREP has proven the most successful educational program for minority students in Texas, and eight other states have replicated the program, TexPREP is now struggling to secure fiscal resources. Its state funding has regularly decreased in recent years, and its future is uncertain in Texas.

The common threads in the experiences of these parents, teachers, and elected officials in the examples above indicate that the Texas SSI has little or no responsibility to the public. The SSI, in fact, has no statutory obligation to provide full and factual disclosure of information, to implement programs that reflect public interest, and to engage constituents in decision-making. Without statutory accountability, the SSI can bypass established processes of educational governance and effectively diminish the authorities of individuals statutorily (or customarily) invested with educational decision-making, described in Texas as "local control."

In Texas, local control means decisions are made by locally elected officials with knowledge needed to represent the unique interest of their communities. Over the past decade, legislators in Texas have reduced the authority of state officials and agencies in order to locate primary control of education in communities. Legislation pared regulations from the Texas Education Code, trimmed both staff and responsibilities from the TEA, and sheared authorities from the State Board of Education. Having established new K–12 standards and graduation requirements, the principal state authority for public education is now limited to enforcing school accountability for academic results, while school districts wield authority for classrooms and day-to-day learning.

Reduction of state authority in Texas was intended to augment and strengthen the authority of local communities for educational decision-making. The Texas SSI, however, found that deregulation had created a political environment "ideally suited for systemic reform," as noted in its 1998 *Annual Report and Strategic Plan*. The SSI's 1997 Annual Report boasts, "We have built, in a state known for its spirited resistance to centralized leadership and central control, a powerful structure" and explains how the transition of power from state to community left Texas vulnerable. "Rapid and dislocating changes in the system's loci of power and authority have created unprecedented opportunities to shape and reshape instructional practice, to influence allocation of resources, and to develop new... policy at the state and local levels." The new role of parents, teachers, and elected officials on school boards is to support NSF's vision of systemic reform, according to *A Report on the Evaluation of the National Science Foundation's Statewide Systemic Initiatives*. It frankly admits that "systemic reform calls for districts and schools to jettison their traditional role as regulators of local practice and assume the new role of technical assisters."

Transferring authority from a locally elected board to a federal initiative is not a choice that people in Texas or any other state would probably make consciously. A 1997 national opinion poll conducted by the Center for Education Research in Washington found that over 70% of Americans supported little or no involvement of the federal government in public education.[86] And a national poll conducted in 1998 by Public Agenda, a non-profit, non-partisan research organization, indicated that only 22% of Americans think decisions about curricula and instruction should be made by the federal government, while only 14% think officials in Washington make good educational decisions.[87]

Public opinion research also indicates that the vast majority of Americans oppose the curricula and instructional practices endorsed by the SSI and systemic reform. A series of national polls conducted from 1996 to the present by Public Agenda has documented overwhelming public support (exceeding 85%) for schools to devote more time for mathematics instruction and to increase the emphasis on mathematical facts and calculation by hand. It has also documented corresponding opposition to the supposedly new teaching methods endorsed by the SSI programs, especially in mathematics where 90% of the public rejects the use of calculators and believes that teaching should focus more on mathematical facts.[88] NSF has acknowledged that the efforts of SSIs to gain public support for its vision of systemic reform has enjoyed limited success, and increased public awareness has, in fact, provoked considerable public opposition, such as in California.[89]

Concluding Remarks

In this chapter we have examined the National Science Foundation Systemic Initiatives Program and the role it is now playing in K–12 mathematics and science education in this country. In the first section, we examined this program's goals and educational philosophy, quoting directly from documents written or authorized by Luther Williams, Assistant Director of the Education and Human Resources Division of NSF and head of the Office for Systemic Reform. We also pointed out the limitations in the mathematics standards and textbooks it endorses, as well as the sudden declines in student achievement in instructional programs using these textbooks. In the second section, we described the development and components of a prominent Urban Systemic Initiative, documenting weaknesses in the policies, standards, programs, and materials it has implemented in this large school district. In the third section, we examined the components of a Statewide Systemic Initiative, documenting its ongoing efforts to consolidate educational authority and policy in the state, to promote its educational philosophy in every aspect of education in the state, and to limit informed and meaningful participation by teachers, parents, and elected officials in decision making on matters of curriculum and instruction. These three sections demonstrate the many flaws in the design of this NSF program and how these flaws are efficiently carried to the states and local school districts that participate in the program.

Our analysis of the NSF Systemic Initiatives Program raises two issues that require scrutiny by governors, Congressional and state legislators, state boards of education, local school boards, and parents, as well as by others seeking to improve the quality of mathematics and science education in this country. The first is the desirability of this program's purposes and goals, the second is the warrant for the educational philosophy it is promoting.

NSF has clearly spelled out its plan to reshape and control the total network of state and local educational policies that determine a school district's academic standards, assessment mechanisms, classroom management practices, curriculum configurations, instructional methods, textbook choices, preservice and inservice teacher training programs, and teacher certification requirements through the conditions it applies to the granting of modest amounts of money to school districts and states and through the ensuing infrastructure it sets up. Yet, there have been no local, state, or national discussions on how this NSF program is affecting the principle of local and state control of education. Is the small amount of money it offers worth the significant loss in autonomy and educational flexibility it seems to entail? NSF's educational policies seem to have been decided upon by only a very small number of appointed officials in the U.S. Department of Education and the National Science Foundation.

In addition to its attempt to direct the use of local educational resources and local decision making without informed discussion in the local community, NSF has promoted standards and programs in science and mathematics that are not supported by a broad-based consensus among professional experts or knowledgeable members of the public. They are in fact not supported by any body of research evidence, are contrary to the findings of mainstream research, and may lower, not improve, student achievement in science and mathematics.

We urge a discontinuation of the Systemic Initiatives Program and the use of its funds for other programs in mathematics and science education. We particularly urge that NSF drop its unwarranted reliance on a dogmatic and exclusionary educational philosophy and encourage—and evaluate—a multitude of approaches to mathematics and science education.

Appendix A

NATIONAL SCIENCE FOUNDATION
4201 Wilson Boulevard
Arlington, Virginia 22230

December 11, 1997

Mrs. Yvonne W. Larson
President, California State Board of Education
721 Capitol Mall, Room 532
Sacramento, CA 95814

Dear Mrs. Larson:

California appeared poised to make an important contribution to the national discussion regarding the appropriate balance of mathematical problem solving, procedural skills, and critical thinking with the September, 1997 proposal of the Commission for the Establishment of Academic Performance and Content Standards. Instead, the decision last week by the California State Board of Education, with little or no public input, to adopt alternative standards vacates any serious commitment to elevating problem solving and critical thinking skills to K-7 mathematics standards. The Board action is, charitably, shortsighted and detrimental to the long-term mathematical literacy of children in California.

The wistful or nostalgic "back-to-basic" approach that characterizes the Board standards overlooks the fact that the approach has chronically and dismally failed. It has excluded youngsters from engaging in genuine mathematical thinking and therefore true mathematical learning, and has proposed a disproportionate mathematically illiterate citizenry.

The National Science Foundation currently maintains a portfolio exceeding $50 million in awards to six public school systems in California (East Side Union, Fresno, Los Angeles, Oakland, Paramount, and San Diego). These districts are undertaking systemic initiatives to offer their students much greater opportunities to learn and achieve in high-quality, rigorous mathematics and science. These awards, though only moving into their second and third years of implementation, are beginning to stimulate significant gains in mathematics and science achievements. A growing body of research also shows significant learning gains elsewhere. You must surely understand that the Foundation cannot support individual school systems that embark on a course that substitutes computational proficiencies for a commitment to deep, balanced mathematical learning.

We view the Board actions in California with grave disappointment and as a lost opportunity for the cities we support—indeed, for the entire state. We have followed the debate closely. We obviously share your stated interest in improving the rigor of the mathematics instruction in the state. We disagree, decisively, with the Board's decision to systematically remove components from the standards that focus on problem solving and other elements of the rigorous and powerful use and learning of mathematics.

Sincerely,
(signed)
Luther S. Williams
Assistant Director

Cc: DeLaine Eastin
    Superintendent for Public Instruction

Appendix B

Office of the Director
National Science Foundation
4201 Wilson Boulevard
Arlington, Virginia 22230

January 8, 1998

Mrs. Yvonne W. Larsen
President, California State Board of Education
721 Capitol Mall, Room 532
Sacramento, CA 95814

Dear Mrs. Larsen:

Because science, mathematics, engineering, and technology education at all levels is an agency wide priority for the National Science Foundation, I follow media coverage of these issues on a regular basis. As you must be aware, the deliberations of the California State Board of Education on mathematics standards have received a great deal of attention. In some of the articles since the middle of December, reference was made to end quotes taken from a letter sent to you in the course of those deliberations by my colleague Luther Williams, NSF's Assistant Director for Education and Human Resources. I was concerned about some of the interpretations of this letter in the press. At my request, Dr. Williams recently shared his letter with me. I believe it can easily be and in some instances has been misconstrued. I want to be sure that there is no misunderstanding in your mind about NSF's position on two very important matters.

(1) It is NSF policy not to prescribe particular standards for mathematics and science education to NSF proposers and grantees or to the states in which they reside. NSF's K–12 mathematics and science education activities are funded through competitive programs to which interested organizations apply. The proposals made to us by states, districts, schools, and other educational organizations are evaluated based on established criteria, which usually include reference to high-quality, rigorous standards to be designed and implemented by the participating entities. NSF believes that it is the responsibility of states and local school districts to establish and implement the standards to which they hold themselves.

(2) NSF does not regard the State Board's action with respect to statewide standards as grounds for terminating funding to what we believe are critically important projects in California school districts. Dr. Williams' letter expressed his personal concern that the statewide standards you were considering could have a negative impact on the ability of the school systems listed to live up to the objectives of the cooperative agreements negotiated in the award process. Unfortunately, his letter has been interpreted as a threat to terminate the awards, if the State Board enacted the standards under consideration. Neither he nor I would countenance such an action.

Finally, my reading of the media articles surrounding the California standards for K–12 mathematics is that, while the standards have been adopted, the underlying issues remain controversial in your state, as they are in other parts of the Nation. I hope California will take the lead in initiating a broad public discussion of what is important in mathematics education that avoids the polarization of issues that has characterized much of the debate thus far. This could be vitally important to other states involved in establishing standards and in the periodic revision of standards that is expected to occur.

While the California standards are described as placing their focus on basic computational skills, I see also clear recognition on your part that the needs for mathematics education do not stop there. All students must be able to use basic skills effectively in developing means of solving more complex problems. We need to find a way to demonstrate that basic skills and the contextual framework of real-world problems or more advanced mathematics in which they can be used reinforce one another, accomplishing what we all want—a set of varied approaches that in combination provide what is best for the students.

Please feel free to contact me if I can provide any additional clarification on these matters.

Sincerely,
(signed)
Neal Lane
Director

Appendix C

INFORMATIVE
TO: Members, Board of Education
DATE: December 8, 1997
FROM: Ruben Zacarias, Superintendent
SUBJECT: Standards-Based Mathematics Curriculum

The following information is provided to inform members of the Board as to the progress towards implementation of the LAUSD Mathematics Standards, in light of the recent California Board of Education acceptance of its K-7 mathematics standards. The Division of Instructional Services' Standards and Assessment Office and Los Angeles Systemic Initiative have assisted in framing the following issues for the Board's consideration.

*Does the District need to adjust its Mathematics standards in response to the State Board standards?
 No. The high expectations for student achievement set forth by the school board and the Superintendent will be met by implementing the standards-based curriculum recommended by the Los Angeles Systemic Initiative.

*Given the State Board standards, will the District continue to use its own Standards?
 Yes. The LAUSD Standards include and go beyond the State Board standards.

*How will LAUSD students be affected by the State Board standards?
 When teachers continue to provide student centered instruction, students will have the balanced program called for in the Mathematics

Advisory to the State Board of Education. Such a balanced program will enhance student achievement, not only on assessments such as the State assessments which are aligned to the State Board standards but also with the District assessment program (Stanford 9, performance-based assessment, and teacher judgment component).

*How will District standards-based curriculum be impacted by the State Board standards?

Basic skills are incorporated in the all of the LA-SI recommended curricula. Instructional delivery in the implementation of these curricular tools will deliver a balance of problem solving, basic skills, and conceptual understanding.

*How will classroom instruction be impacted by the State Board standards?

LAUSD classroom teachers will continue to provide instruction which best ensures the success of all of our students. A variety of instructional strategies will be used in these classrooms.

*Specifically, what is the appropriate role of calculators in the classroom?

All teachers support the mastery of basic skills. Calculators provide students opportunities to apply and extend their mathematical skills appropriate for the "Information Age" in which they will live and work.

*Would textbooks that are aligned to the new State Board standards meet the LAUSD standards?

If textbooks are written to meet, but not surpass, the expectations in the State Board standards, then LAUSD teachers will be forced to supplement the programs to deliver a rigorous, challenging mathematics program our students deserve.

Appendix D

January 21, 1998

David Klein
Professor of Mathematics
California State University, Northridge

Northridge, CA 91330

Dear Dr. Klein:

This letter is in response to your comments to Julie Korenstein criticizing the Los Angeles Unified School District's reaction to the new math standards adopted by the State of California. The common goal that we believe is expressed in both your letter and the LAUSD mathematics standards is for students to have facility with basic skills as well as the conceptual underpinnings of mathematics that make it possible for them to extend and apply these skills in many contexts, academic as well as real-world. We urge the professors whose names are attached to this letter to heed the words of Secretary of Education Richard W. Riley, as reported in the Los Angeles Times on January 21, 1998. Secretary Riley stresses the positive advances in mathematics results during the current decade. More important to this response is his urging us to move beyond the "shortsighted, politicized, and harmful bickering over the teaching and learning of mathematics." Certainly we all want students graduating from LAUSD to succeed at the university level as well as in the workplace.

My comments in an informative to the LAUSD Board of Education implying a deficiency in the state board mathematics standards are consistent with statements made by well-respected mathematicians and scientists from California and other states. For example, mathematics professors Dr. Scott Farrand, California University, Sacramento and Dr. Calvin Moore, University of California, Berkeley, have stated: "The imbalance in the direction of skills that these (state board) Standards would create is an affront to the stated Board policy of balance." The mathematics education community has gone on record in support of the California Educational Roundtable standards for graduating seniors. This consensus document, created by a coalition of Community College, California State University, and University of California mathematicians, among others, was strongly endorsed by teachers and administrators in the LAUSD. Dr. Luther Williams, Assistant Director of Education and Human Resources for the National Science Foundation, stated in a letter to Yvonne Larson, President of the State Board of Education: "The wistful or nostalgic "back-to-basics" approach that characterizes the Board standards overlooks the fact that the approach has chronically and dismally failed. It has excluded youngsters from engaging in genuine mathematical thinking and therefore true mathematical learning."

There is an unstated assumption present in this letter which expresses one view of school mathematics: if students have mastered (memorized) the "basics" at a lower level, then they will be able to perform better in the higher level classes taught by mathematics experts. Mathematics is not free of different philosophies and approaches. The two Stanford mathematics professors who wrote the state standards (assisted by a professor emeritus of UC Davis) certainly are entitled to their perspective of mathematics as a fixed set of facts and procedures to be learned.

However, another reknown mathematician from Stanford, the late George Polya, promoted a view of mathematics as problem solving. Polya's seminal work in this area and with classroom teachers, was very influential on the development of mathematical curricula during the 80's to the present. The LAUSD Standards maintain a balanced approach, honoring both perspectives of mathematics, as we feel most educators do.

Mathland, which was highly recommended by the California Instructional Resources Evaluation Panel, is one of the LASI recommended curricular programs. The Mathland program is not the LAUSD math standards as stated in your letter, but one of several math programs selected by school staffs. Teachers who use this program as intended, supported by District professional development, continue to stress basic skills while preparing students for the 21st century by providing them with opportunities to analyze and question data and statistics in order to fully participate in our democracy as informed citizens.

Thank you for expressing your concerns.

Sincerely,
(signed)
Ruben Zacarias
Superintendent of Schools

Cc: Julie Korenstein [LAUSD Board Member]

Notes

[1] National Science Foundation. "The National Science Foundation's Systemic Initiatives" (http://www.ehrz.nsf.gov/EHR/ESR/index.htm).

2. Mervis, J. "Mixed Grades for NSF's Bold Reform of Statewide Education." *Science*, *282* (Dec. 4, 1998) pp. 1800–1805.
3. Ibid.
4. Williams, L. "The Urban Systemic Initiatives (USI) Program of the National Science Foundation: Summary Update," July 1998 (http://www.ehr.nsf.gov/EHR/ESR/reports/963014M.pdf).
5. *The California Mathematics Academic Content Standards*, 1998 (http://www.cde.ca.gov/board/k12math_standards.html).
6. Texas Statewide Systemic Initiative "Mission" (http://macdns.cc.utexas.edu/ssi/mission/default.html).
7. National Science Foundation. "The National Science Foundation's Systemic Initiatives" (http://www.ehr.nsf.gov/EHR/ESR/index.htm).
8. Pinker, S. *How the Mind Works*. 1997. W.W. Norton & Company, pp. 341–343.
9. Hirsch, E.D., Jr. *The Schools We Need and Why We Don't Have Them*. 1996. New York, Doubleday, pp 127–175.
10. National Council of Teachers of Mathematics. *Curriculum and Evaluation Standards for School Mathematics*. Reston, VA: National Council of Teachers of Mathematics, 1989 (http://www.enc.org/reform/journals/ENC2280/nf_280dtoc1.htm).
11. Evers, B., Hoffman, H., Plume, M.A., Polyak, M., Wurman, Z., Steering Committee, Honest Open Logical Debate (HOLD) on math reform. "Suggestions and recommendations for improvement of 1989 NCTM Standards." Submitted to the Commisssion on the Future of the Standards, National Council of Teachers of Mathematics, January 15, 1996 (http://mathematicallycorrect.com/holdnctm.html). Also, Quirk, W.G. "The Truth About The NCTM Standards" (http://www.wgquirk.com/TruthK12.html).
12. Allen, F. "A Critical View of NCTM Policies with Special Reference to the Standards Reports" (http://mathematicallycorrect.com/allen1.htm); AMS Association Resource Group (ARG) for Revision of NCTM Standards in Mathematics. "Reports of the AMS Association Resource Group on NCTM2000." *Notices of the AMS*, February, 1998 (http://www.ams.org/notices/199802/comm-amsarg.pdf); Haimo, D.T. "Are the NCTM Standards Suitable for Systemic Adoption?" *Teachers College Record of Teachers College, Columbia University 100*, (1) Fall 1998, pp.45–64; Howe, R. "The AMS and Mathematics Education: The Revision of the NCTM Standards," *Notices of the AMS*, February, 1998. (http://www.ams.org/notices/199802/howe.pdf); Ross, K. Report from the Task Force on the NCTM Standards, *MAA Online*, January 27, 1997 (http://www.maa.org/past/maanctm2.html); Ross, K. Second Report from the Task Force *MAA Online*, June 17, 1997 (http://www.maa.org/past/maanctm3.html); and Wu, H.H. "The Mathematician and the Mathematics Education Reform." *Notices of the AMS*, December 1996 (http://www.ams.org/notices/199612/forum-wu.html).
13. Stevenson, H.W. "Professor Harold W. Stevenson on the NCTM Standards" (http://mathematicallycorrect.com/hwsnctm.htm).
14. *The California Mathematics Academic Content Standards*, 1998 (http://www.cde.ca.gov/board/k12math_standards.html).
15. New York Systemic Intitiative, "Curriculum"

(http://nycusi.org/Curriculum/curriculum.htm).

[16] Antonucci, M. "'New, new math' has parents crying 'back to basics'" *World Net Daily*, July 18, 1997 (http://www.worldnetdaily.com/exclusiv/97071); and "Do you live in a new-new math city?" (http://www.mathematicallycorrect.com/citylist.htm).

[17] Open Letter by Martin Scharlemann, Chair of the Mathematics Department, University of California, Santa Barbara, October, 1996 (http://mathematicallycorrect.com/ml1.htm); Herriot, R. "Palo Alto Parent Compares Three Reform Texts" (http://www.mathematicallycorrect.com/pausd.htm); McArther, D. "An Example of the Low Expectations and Lack of Progression from Third Grade to Eighth Grade" (http://206.86.183.194/math/McArthurAppendixD.htm); and McArther, D. "Mathematics Reform in Theory and Practice, and its Implications for DoD Students" (http://206.86.183.194/math/McArthurText.htm).

[18] McArther, D. "Mathematics Reform in Theory and Practice, and its Implications for DoD Students" (http://206.86.183.194/math/McArthurText.htm); "MathLand and Glencoe Interactive Mathematics Programs in Department of Defense Dependents Schools (DoDDS)" (http://mathematicallycorrect.com/dodds1.htm).

[19] Herriot, R. "Palo Alto Parent Compares Three Reform Texts" (http://www.mathematicallycorrect.com/pausd.htm); and Clopton, P, et al. "Mathematics Program Reviews for Grades 2, 5, and 7" (http://www.mathematicallycorrect.com/books.htm).

[20] Tsang, B. "CMP at Okemos Middle Schools" (http://www.nscl.msu.edu/~tsang/CMP.html); Clopton, P., et al. "Mathematics Program Reviews for Grades 2, 5, and 7" (http://www.mathematicallycorrect.com/books7a.htm).

[21] "Unofficial Plano Independent School District School Page" (http://www.pisd.org/cmp/index.html).

[22] Mackey, K. "An overview of IMP years 1 and 2" (http://www.mathematicallycorrect.com/imp.htm).

[23] Mackey, K. "IMP: A student's view with comments" (http://www.mathematicallycorrect.com/impkm.htm); Mackey, K. "IMP: A Teacher's Review for Parents" (http://www.mathematicallycorrect.com/kmimp.htm); and Datta, S. "IMP: Manifesto on an Experimental Concept Gone Awry" (http://www.mathematicallycorrect.com/impsf.htm).

[24] Fogler, D. "A Review of an Integrated High School Mathematics Program" (http://www.mathematicallycorrect.com/integrat/htm).

[25] Milgram, R.J. "Outcomes Analysis for Core Plus Students at Andover High School: One Year Later" (ftp://math.stanford.edu/pub/papers/milgram/andover-report.htm).

[26] Helfand, D. "Some Professors Resist State's Reform Formula; Education: Many aspiring teachers are instructed in using whole-language method. Law mandates phonics." *Los Angeles Times* October 25, 1998; and Helfand, D., Smith, D. "Zacarias orders overhaul of new phonics materials; Education: Superintendent acts after 2,500 L.A. teachers have already been trained with program that draws on discarded methods." *Los Angeles Times*, March 12, 1999.

[27] Hirsch, E.D., Jr. *The Schools We Need,* pp. 69–126.

28. "Math radio: The debate in San Diego." Excerpts from the Roger Hedgecock show of April 24, 1996 (http://mathematicallycorrect.com/roger.htm).
29. Malloy, C. and Jones, G.M. "An Investigation of African American Students' Mathematical Problem Solving," *Journal for Research in Mathematics Education*, 29, no. 2, March 1998, pp. 143–163.
30. Ross, A.C. *Journal of American Indian Education*, Special Issue, August 1989.
31. Jacoby, T. "Color Blind: The African American absence in high tech," *The New Republic* March 29, 1999 (http://www.thenewrepublic.com/magazines/tnr/current/jacoby032999.html).
32. Site Description, Los Angeles Urban Systemic Initiative (http://www.ehr.nsf.gov/EHR/ESR/sysinit/angeles.htm).
33. Williams, Luther, The Urban Systemic Initiatives (USI) Program of the National Science Foundation: Summary Update, July 1998 (http://www.ehr.nsf.gov/EHR/ESR/reports/963014M.pdf).
34. National Science Foundation Program Effectiveness Review for Los Angeles Urban Systemic Initiative in Mathematics, Science, and Technology, December 9, 1997. Prepared under the auspices of the Los Angeles Unified School District for the Los Angeles Systemic Initiative Office, Division of Instructional Services, Los Angeles Unified School District, by staff in Program Evaluation and Research Branch, Los Angeles Unified School District, and in Vital Research, LLC, an external research group.
35. Available at (http://www.cde.ca.gov/board/k12math_standards.html).
36. "Open Letter to CSU Chancellor" (http://www.mathematicallycorrect.com/reed.htm).
37. Raimi, Ralph A. and Braden, Lawrence S. *State Mathematics Standards*. Volume 2, Number 3. (March 1998) Washington, D.C.: Thomas B. Fordham (http://www.edexcellence.net/standards/math.html).
38. American Federation of Teachers. Making Standards Matter 1998. Washington, D.C.: American Federation of Teachers (http://www.aft.org/edissues/standards98/index.htm).
39. Mathematically Correct (http://www.mathematicallycorrect.com/).
40. Mathematically Correct. "A Comparison of the LAUSD Math Standards and the California Math Standards" (http://mathematicallycorrect.com/lausdstd.html).
41. Los Angeles Unified School District Student Learning Standards, 1996 (http://www.lausd.k12.ca.us/lausd/offices/instruct/standards/).
42. Klein, David. "LAUSD's Refusal to Adopt the California Mathematics Standards" (http://www.mathematicallycorrect.com/laagain.htm).
43. Mejia, Victor. "Fuzzy Fracas." *New Times Los Angeles*, July 31, 1998. See also David Klein. "The Freedom to Agree." *California Political Review*, July/August 1998.
44. *Appropriations Bill of the 75th Texas Legislature*, Austin, TX, 1997.
45. *A Report on the Evaluation of the National Science Foundation's Statewide Systemic Initiatives Program*, SRI International, 1998, p.53. It is contended in Texas that the SSI is not a federal initiative; this document confirms that it is an SSI. An article on this report, entitled "Mixed Grades for NSF's Bold Reforms of Statewide Education," by Jeffrey Mervis, appears in the December 4, 1998 issue of *Science*.

46 *Annual Report,* Texas Statewide Systemic Initiative, Austin, TX, 1997, p.6.
47 *Preparing Students for the Twenty-first Century,* National Governors' Association Issue Brief, Education Policy Studies Division, April 13, 1998, p.1 (http://www.nga.org/Pubs/IssueBriefs/default.asp).
48 *Public Law 103-227. Goals 2000: Educate America Act,* Title 2. National Education Reform Leadership, Standards, and Assessments, Sec. 232. Federal Leadership. The testimony of Richard Riley, Secretary of Education, to the Committee on Science, U.S. House of Representatives, July 23, 1997 describes the collaboration between the U.S. Department of Education and the National Science Foundation (Federal Document Clearing House,1997 WL 11235230).
49 Ibid, p.1.
50 *Texas, State Profiles,* Education and Human Resources, National Science Foundation (http://www.ehr.nsf.gov.EHR/ESR/state/profiles/tx.htm).
51 *Program Effectiveness Review,* Texas Statewide Systemic Initiative, Austin, TX, 1998, p. 3.
52 *Annual Report,* Texas Statewide Systemic Initiative, Austin, TX, 1998, pp.5, 6, 9, 10, and 19; and *Annual Report,* 1997, pp.5-9.
53 *A Report on the Evaluation of the National Science Foundation's Statewide Systemic Initiatives,* p.37.
54 *Math and Science,* IDRA Newsletter, Intercultural Development Research Association, San Antonio, March 1998.
55 *Annual Report,* Texas Statewide Systemic Initiative, 1997, p.9. The SSI testified that it does not promote any specific program of instruction to school districts, State Board of Education Meeting, November 13-15, 1998.
56 Ibid, p.7.
57 *Program Effectiveness Review,* 1998, p.13.
58 *Annual Report,* Texas Statewide Systemic Initiative, 1997, p.9.
59 *Substate Application for Projects Funded under the School-to-Work Opportunities Act* submitted by the Capital Area School-to-Career Partnership to the Texas Workforce Commission School-to-Careers Office, Austin, TX, June 30, 1998, p.48.
60 *Annual Report and Strategic Plan,* 1998, p.21.
61 *Capital Area School-to-Work Partnership, Substate Application for Funds, 1997*
62 *Guidance on the Comprehensive School Reform Demonstration Program,* U.S. Department of Education, 1998 (http://www.ed/gov/offices/oese/compreform).
63 *NSF Curriculum Showcase Conference Registration Form,* Texas Statewide Systemic Initiative, Sheraton Austin Hotel, Austin, TX, November 11-13, 1998.
64 Recognizing the conflict of interest posed by the SSI's administration of the CED while promoting NSF-developed textbooks, the Commissioner of Education warned the Dana Center/SSI that these activities should be clearly separated. Correspondence of November 11, 1998.
65 *What It Means to Implement the TEKS,* Issue Brief, Texas Statewide Systemic Initiative, Vol.1, No.1, Fall, 1998.
66 *Instructional Materials Analysis and Selection for K-5 and 6-8 Mathematics,* Texas Statewide Systemic Initiative, Austin, TX, 1998.
67 (http://www-tenet.edu/teks/math).
68 (http://www-tenet.edu/teks/math).

69 (http://www-tnet.cc.utexas.edu/ssi).
70 By P.B. Campbell and N. Kreinberg.
71 Hirsch, E.D., Jr. *The Schools We Need*, pp 127–175.
72 Becker, Wesley and Engelmann, Siegfried, "Sponsor Findings from Project Follow Through," *Effective School Practices*, Vol. 15, No. 1, Winter, 1996, p.35.
73 *A Report on the Evaluation of the National Science Foundation's Statewide Systemic Initiatives Program*. SRI International, 1998 (http://www.sfi.com/policy/cehs/edpolicy.html).
74 Grissmer, David, and Flanagan, Ann. *Exploring Rapid Achievement Gains in North Carolina and Texas*. Washington, D.C.: National Education Goals Panel, November, 1998.
75 *Setting Higher Sights*. American Federation of Teachers, Washington, D.C., 1998; Wayne Bishop, David Klein and Paul Clopton, *Statewide Mathematics Assessment in Texas*, Tax Research Association, Houston, TX, 1998.
76 Clopton, Paul., McKeown, Erica, et al. *Mathematics Program Reviews for Grades 2, 5, and 7*. Mathematically Correct (http://www.mathematicallycorrect.com).
77 *Program Effectiveness Review,* 1998, p.19.
78 *Texas, State Profiles.*
79 *Program Effectiveness Review*, the Statewide Systemic Initiative, Austin, TX, 1997, p.2.
80 Letter to Susan Modisette, Principal, Haggard Middle School from Darlene Yanez, Research and Evaluation Specialist, Texas Statewide Systemic Initiative, January 29, 1998; and Testimony to the Plano Independent School District Board Hearing of the Level 1 Complaint related to the *Connected Mathematics Program* by Don Mills, January 14, 1999.
81 Code of Federal Regulations, Title 45 Public Welfare, Volume 3, Chapter VI National Science Foundation, Part 690.101 (a) and (b).
82 Code of Federal Regulations, Title 34 Family Educational Rights and Privacy Act, Subpart D, Section 99.31 (a) 93) (ii).
83 Testimony to the Texas State Board of Education by Kenneth Johnson, Plano, TX, January 8, 1999; and Letter to Chris Patterson, Education Connection of Texas, from Kenneth Johnson, Plano, TX, February 1, 1999.
84 Johnson, Kenneth, "Connected Math curriculum should be reviewed impartially," *Plano Star Courier,* January 22, 1999; and "New Instructional Materials Approved," *Texas Education News,* Vol.15, Issue 37, November 23, 1998.
85 Berriozabal, Manuel, "Why Hasn't Mathematics Worked for Minorities?" *UME Trends*, San Antonio, Vol. 1, No. 2, May 1989; and *1999 Legislative Agenda*, Texas Prefreshman Engineering Program, University of Texas at San Antonio, January 1999.
86 *National Survey of Americans' Attitudes toward Education and School Reform.*
87 *Public Agenda Online 1998.*
88 *Different Drummers: How Teachers of Teachers View Public Education,* Public Agenda, New York, 1997; *Given the Circumstances: Teachers Talk about Public Education Today,* Public Agenda, New York, 1996.
89 *A Report on the Evaluation of the National Science Foundation's Statewide Systemic Initiatives Program.*